BOLLINGEN SERIES LXXIV

ERICH AUERBACH

Literary Language & Its Public

IN

LATE LATIN ANTIQUITY

AND IN

THE MIDDLE AGES

Translated from the German by
RALPH MANHEIM

BOLLINGEN SERIES LXXIV

PANTHEON BOOKS

THIS IS THE SEVENTY-FOURTH
IN A SERIES OF BOOKS SPONSORED AND PUBLISHED BY
BOLLINGEN FOUNDATION

Translated from *Literatursprache und Publikum in der lateinischen Spätantike und im Mittelalter*, Bern: Francke Verlag, 1958.

Library of Congress Catalogue Card No. 65-10141
Manufactured in the United States of America
DESIGNED BY ANDOR BRAUN

For Marie and Clemens

CONTENTS

NOTE OF ACKNOWLEDGMENT

FOR THIS edition in English, translations of quotations have been supplied in all but the most obvious cases, with special attention to the author's German versions wherever they occur. Grateful acknowledgment is made to Professor Stanislaus Akielaszek, Mr. A. S. B. Glover, and Professor Daniel J. Sullivan for their help with many of these translations, and to the following publishers for permission to quote as indicated: J. M. Dent & Sons and E. P. Dutton & Co., for a passage translated by Mrs. Theodore Beck in E. Underhill's *Jacopone da Todi;* Harvard University Press, for passages from J. C. Rolfe's translation of Suetonius and F. A. Wright's of Jerome, in the Loeb Classical Library; The Hogarth Press and The Harold Matson Company, Inc., for a passage from C. Day Lewis's translation of Virgil's *Aeneid* (copyright 1952); and Sheed and Ward, for passages from F. J. Sheed's translation of Augustine (copyright 1943).

A list of works cited, compiled by Mr. Glover and Professor Akielaszek, has been added to this edition, and references have accordingly been abbreviated in the text and footnotes. The index is the work of Mr. Glover.

The publishers are grateful to Mrs. Auerbach and Mrs. June Guicharnaud for preparing the bibliography of Erich Auerbach's publications printed at the end of this volume.

PREFACE

I wish to thank Bollingen Foundation of New York City for its generous support of my undertaking and Henri Peyre for his friendly solicitude, which did much to lighten my task.

Mention is made, in the introduction, of influences on my thinking and of its relationship to that of others. But I take this opportunity to thank several of my colleagues at Yale University whom I asked for advice and information, from time to time, in connection with the matters treated in this book. They are Thomas G. Bergin, Sumner McK. Crosby, Erich Dinkler (now at Bonn), E. Talbot Donaldson, G. Lincoln Hendrickson, Helge Kökeritz, Bernard M. W. Knox, Robert S. Lopez, John C. Pope, F. Stephen Reckert, Konstantin Reichardt, Henry B. Richardson, and René Wellek.

E. A.

New Haven, Connecticut
Late February 1957

Literary Language and Its Public
IN
LATE LATIN ANTIQUITY
AND IN
THE MIDDLE AGES

INTRODUCTION

Purpose and Method

THE SITUATION of Romance philology in Germany has always been unique. Inaugurated by Uhland and Diez, this branch of scholarship is rooted in German historicism, a movement whose successive proponents, from Herder to the Schlegels and Jacob Grimm, were committed to the idea of an historical development manifested in the individual *Volksgeist*. They made this idea into the guiding theme of philology. Romantic historicism created a dialectical conception of man, dialectical because it was based on a diversity of national individualities; it was profounder and more realistic than the concept of man put forward by the pure Enlightenment with its unhistorical and undialectical approach. Nowhere else—nowhere in Europe, at least—have historical concepts been so naturally favored as in German Romance scholarship. The German scholars working in this field were not dealing with the spirit of their own nation; thus there was little danger that they would be carried away by a patriotic involvement with their own national character. Despite a common Latin background, the peoples under investigation differ greatly among themselves and still more from the German people; yet all, including the Germans, are related through a common substrate of classical and Christian civilization. Thus from the very first the approach of German scholars to the Romance languages and literatures has disclosed an historical perspective embracing Europe as a whole, though it is true that in the latter half of the nineteenth century this European consciousness was seldom clearly and explicitly expressed,

5

partly because there was no urgent need or motive for it at the time, and partly because of increased specialization and the sheer bulk of the work being done.

Since the beginning of our century many different intellectual currents have combined with the inward and outward crises of Europe to give German Romance scholars an historical consciousness and make them aware of the historical and cultural reality of Europe. Scholars made their appearance who, to my way of thinking, were without equal in any other field of philology or in any other country (except for Benedetto Croce, who had close ties with German thought); their breadth of vision justifies us in calling these men *European* philologists. I am thinking, first and foremost, of Karl Vossler, Ernst Robert Curtius, and Leo Spitzer.

The ensuing fragments—like my work as a whole—spring from the same presuppositions as theirs. My work, however, shows a much clearer awareness of the European crisis. At an early date, and from then on with increasing urgency, I ceased to look upon the European possibilities of Romance philology as mere possibilities and came to regard them as a task specific to our time—a task which could not have been envisaged yesterday and will no longer be conceivable tomorrow. European civilization is approaching the term of its existence; its history as a distinct entity would seem to be at an end, for already it is beginning to be engulfed in another, more comprehensive unity. Today, however, European civilization is still a living reality within the range of our perception. Consequently—so it seemed to me when I wrote these articles and so I still believe—we must today attempt to form a lucid and coherent picture of this civilization and its unity. I have always tried, more and more resolutely as time went on, to work in this direction, at least in my approach to the subject matter of philology, namely literary expression. The task may seem to be too enormous to allow of any serious attempt at accomplishing it, and yet I believe there may be a relatively simple way of approaching the problem. This method, which will be discussed in greater detail below, is to select, develop, and correlate strictly limited and readily accessible problems in such a way that they will operate as keys to the whole. Thus disclosed, the whole takes on a character of dialectical unity, of a drama or, as Vico once said, of a serious poem.

The name of Vico brings me to the general considerations underlying this method. Early in my studies I became acquainted with Vico's conception of philology and of the "world of the nations"; in a very specific way this conception has complemented and molded, in my thinking and in my work, the ideas deriving from German historicism. I should like to enumerate those of Vico's ideas that have influenced me and discuss them in relation to the inferences I have drawn from them for my present purpose.

First there is Vico's theory of historical knowledge. It developed out of his polemic against Descartes' geometrical method and is grounded in the principle that we can only know what we ourselves have made. The history of mankind, or the "world of the nations" (in contrast to the world of nature, which God created), was made by men themselves; accordingly, men themselves can know it. Even the earliest and most remote forms of human thought and action must be present in the potentialities (Vico's term is *modificazioni*) of our own human mind, and this is what enables us to understand those early forms. With his theory Vico tried to provide an epistemological foundation for his vision of the beginnings of culture, of the genesis of the first social forms, and of the poetic, ritualistic origins of human thought and expression. Vico's was probably the first systematic attempt at a theory of historical knowledge, and it offers a clear statement, if not a logical justification, of an important and inescapable fact, namely, that we judge historical phenomena and all human affairs, whether of a private, economic, or political nature, according to our own experience, that we try, in other words, "to find their principles within the modification of our own human mind." Since Vico's time, it is true, far more rigorous methods of observing and recording human behavior have been devised; but they have neither shaken nor supplanted our empirical confidence in our spontaneous faculty for understanding others on the basis of our own experience (actually this faculty has been very much enriched by the findings of modern science). Indeed, strict scientific methods are not applicable to historical phenomena or to any other phenomena that cannot be subjected to the special conditions required by scientific experimentation. Thus the investigation of historical processes in the broadest sense (we shall presently discuss the scope of the term "historical" as used in the present context) still depends very largely on the investigator's judgment, that is, on his faculty for "rediscovering" them in his own mind. Historical research, indeed, has an exact side, which perhaps should be termed learned rather than scientific, namely the techniques of finding, transmitting, interpreting (in the more elementary sense), and comparing documents. But where selection, interpretation (in the higher, more general sense), and classification enter into the picture, the historian's activity is far more comparable to an art than to a modern science. It is an art that works with scholarly material.

Another aspect of Vico's theory of knowledge is his equation of the historical with the human. For him the world of the nations, *il mondo delle nazioni*, embraces not only political history but also the history of thought, of expression (language, literature, the fine arts), religion, law, and economics. Because all these follow from the cultural state of human society in a given period and consequently must be understood in relation to one another or else cannot be understood at all, an insight into one of these facets of human creativity at a given stage of development must provide a key to all the others at the same stage. Vico goes still further; for him there is an "ideal, eternal history" enacted in three stages, a basic, cyclically recurring pattern, no part of which can be understood except in relation to the whole. But in his view, the early stage of development is the most important object of historical understanding because it is the most difficult. The early forms of civilization, he believed, were wholly governed by instinct and fantasy, and an extreme effort is required to rediscover them in our minds that have reached the stage of fully developed reason. It is in describing the unity of the early cultures that Vico sets forth his incomparably grandiose conception of what modern criticism calls style, that is, the unity of all the products of an historical epoch. It has recently been asserted that Vico had little significance for esthetics, that he should be regarded more as a philosopher of history or a sociologist; this is to belittle him for failing to establish a system of esthetics and for creating, instead, a world in which esthetics has its place. But in any case his whole thinking begins with a critique of the human forms of expression, of language, myth, and literature (*una nuova arte critica*).

It is only a short step from Vico's theory of knowledge to his justification of historicism. He wrote his book in a period which did not take kindly to the idea of historical development. Holding that history had produced all manner of irrational and mutually incompatible institutions, many of the leading thinkers of the age repudiated the products of historical development in favor of an original, authentic, and rational human nature, which they sought to restore. In response to this argument Vico insisted that man has no nature other than his history. *Natura di cose*, he wrote (*Scienza nuova* 147), *altro non è che nascimento di esse in certi tempi e con certe guise, le quali sempre che sono tali, indi tali e non altre nascon le cose.* The first part of this proposition—the nature of things (human institutions) signifies only that they came into being at certain times and under certain circumstances—is a formulation and justification of historical relativism or perspectivism; the second—when the times and circumstances are thus and so, "things" come into being thus and so and not otherwise—is a statement that historical nature is subject to law. In many passages of the *Scienza nuova* the word *natura* means quite simply "historical development" or a stage in it; the "nature" of the nations, what they have in common, is simply the lawful course of their history; this is their common nature, *la natura comune delle nazioni*, and this is the subject of the *New Science*.

According to Vico, this lawful or natural course of history is the work of Divine Providence. Although the means with which Providence operates are purely historical, its work is a complete and perfect whole; accordingly, each stage of development is necessary, complete in itself, and good. Vico attaches great importance to showing that the plan of development he imputes to Providence is simple and well ordered; despite perpetual change, history as a whole is "an eternal Platonic Republic." Thus Vico's form of historical relativism is concerned chiefly with the law as disclosed in each successive historical stage and far less with its variants, that is, its development in the particular nations. Consequently Vico's form of historicism did not lend itself nearly as well to practical application in philology as did that of Herder and his successors, which took as its starting point the individual spirit of the peoples. Vico did not deny the variants in the overall development, but they were not what interested him. He was concerned with the universal law that is manifested in the development of all nations; the historian's aim, he held, must be to understand the stages of this development, each on the basis of its own presuppositions, each perfect in its own way, as a temporal manifestation of eternal Providence.

In any event, this was the beginning of historicism and of the concept of style that is its companion piece; it is, I believe, the Copernican discovery in the cultural sciences. The influence of this discovery, since the Romantics made it generally accessible, has been enormous. It put an end to the dogmatic judgments based on rigid canons whose authority, while no longer absolute even in the neoclassical period, had been relaxed only by considerations of "good taste." This historical approach opened vast new horizons and provided the foundation for the investigation of archaic and foreign cultures carried on since the beginning of the nineteenth century. Our historicism in esthetic questions has become so self-evident to us that we are scarcely aware of it. We bring equal readiness for understanding to the art, literature, and music of the most divergent peoples and epochs. The cultures which we call primitive and which it cost Vico so much effort to understand (to most of his contemporaries they were not intelligible or even interesting) have long possessed a very special charm for us. Not only the scholars and critics among us, but also a large and steadily growing section of the general public, have ceased to be frightened by the diversity of peoples and epochs. This willingness to see things in their proper perspective, it is true, ceases as soon as politics becomes involved; but in the esthetic field our power of adaptation to diverse cultural forms or epochs is constantly brought into play, often in the course of a single visit to a museum or a single concert, and it may even prove indispensable to our understanding of a film, an illustrated magazine, or a travel poster. That is historicism, in the same sense as, in Molière's *Le Bourgeois Gentilhomme*, Monsieur Jourdain's everyday speech turns out, to his vast astonishment, to be prose. Most of us are no more aware of our historicism than Monsieur Jourdain was of his prose.

In the last few decades influential critics have once again been propounding descriptive or dogmatic categories of judgment for which they claim absolute validity. Of course, no one hopes any longer to equal the clarity and richness of certain of the great "prehistorical" critics who within their own fields classified the existing genres, defined their structure and purpose, and authoritatively pointed out the supreme achievements in each. Nevertheless there is a widespread tendency to reject historical perspectivism tacitly or explicitly; particularly in the field of literary criticism, this tendency is related to a distaste for philology of the nineteenth-century type, which is looked upon as the embodiment par excellence of historicism. Historicism, many believe, results in antiquarian pedantry, in overestimation of biographical detail, in failure to appreciate a work of art as such, and, by doing away with all categories on which one might base value judgments, in eclecticism. These critics forget, first of all, that the historicism of Vico, of Herder and the Romantics, or of Hegel, though underlying philological specialization, is not identical with it. It is true that many scholars, including some to whom we owe a great deal, became so absorbed in specialization that they forgot the purpose of their efforts; but this cannot be taken as an argument against a philosophical outlook which unfortunately they have lost. It is true, too, that preoccupation with biographical details, and above all the endeavor to interpret all literary productions as biographical in the most literal sense, are exceedingly naïve and often absurd. But it seems to me that this brand of scholarship has been sufficiently attacked and ridiculed. The simple fact that a man's work stems from his existence and that consequently everything we can find out about his life serves to interpret the work loses none of its relevance because inexperienced scholars have drawn ridiculous inferences from it. The notion, often met with nowadays, that a work should be considered independently of its author is justified only in so far as the work often gives a truer, more integrated picture of its creator than do the sometimes fortuitous and misleading bits of information that we possess concerning his life. In order to discern the proper relation between an artist's life and his work, a critic requires experience of his own, discretion, and an open-mindedness based on a thorough knowledge of the material. In any event, what we understand and love in a work is a human existence, a possibility of "modifications" within ourselves.

It is a grave mistake to suppose that historical relativism results in an eclectic incapacity for judgment, and that judgment must be based on extrahistorical standards. Historicism has nothing to do with eclecticism. To grasp the special nature of an epoch or a work, to perceive the nature of the relations between works of art and the time in which they were created, is an endless problem which each of us, exerting the utmost concentration, must endeavor to solve for himself and from his own point of view. For historical relativism is relative in two respects—of the material and of those who are striving to understand it. It is a radical relativism, but that is no reason to fear it. The area in which we move in this effort at understanding is the world of men, to which we ourselves belong. This gives us every reason to believe that our problem is open to solution, for *dentro le modificazioni della medesima nostra mente umana* it must be possible to find all forms of human life. But the problem itself involves us so closely with the common human factor, with human potentialities which may have escaped our attention and perhaps lie latent within us, that there can be no question of the arbitrary, irresponsible selection that is ordinarily identified with eclecticism. In such activity we do not lose the faculty of judgment; on the contrary, we acquire it. We cease, it is true, to judge on the basis of extrahistorical and absolute categories, and we cease to look for such categories, precisely because the universally human or poetic factor, which is common to the most perfect works of all times and which should consequently provide us with our categories of judgment, can only be apprehended in its particular historical forms, and there is no intelligible way of expressing its absolute essence. In the historical forms themselves we gradually learn to find the flexible, always provisional, categories we need. Little by little we learn what the various works meant in their own epochs and what they mean in the perspective of the three millennia concerning the literary activity of which we have some knowledge. Lastly, we learn what they mean to us personally, here and now. All this is a sufficient basis on which to judge a work, that is, to view it in relation to the conditions under which it came into being and to assign a rank to it. It is also a sufficient ground for reflection on what elements in common the most significant works have. In my opinion, however, the result of such reflection can never be expressed in abstract or extrahistorical terms, but only as a dialectic, dramatic process. This is precisely what Vico tried to do. He did not fully succeed, but his work remains an irreplaceable prototype.

By this dialectical method Vico succeeded in defining the essence of poetry, which he viewed as the predominant if not the exclusive form of thought and expression in early periods of history; in these early periods, he believed, the faculties of reason were undeveloped, while the fantasy knew no bounds. In this view, which was then revolutionary, Vico was a precursor of Herder,

Rousseau, and the early Romantics. But while the latter looked upon the poetic fantasy of the early periods as undisciplined, unpolitical, and alien to all constituted order, Vico regarded it as politically constructive, an element in the plan of Providence, leading, by way of mythical conceptions which men invented but at the same time believed in (*fingunt simul creduntque*), to a constituted order and the establishment of society. Vico held that though this early activity of the poetic fantasy was based on the passions, it led not to an emotional lack of order but to the crystallization of clearly defined myths which he terms *universali fantastici*. These are universal ideas originating in fantasy, that is to say, concretely visualized, hypostasized syntheses by which a ritualistic imagination seeks to ward off chaos. They in turn give rise to the first social institutions, which were governed by magic ritual and which for Vico were likewise "poetic." He did not, like the Romantics, develop his ideas in opposition to neoclassical rhetoric; rather, he derived them from it. He himself was a professor of rhetoric for the greater part of his life. In the rhetorical figures of the schools he saw vestiges of the original, concrete, and sensuous thinking of men who believed that in employing words and concepts they were seizing hold of things themselves. He held that in rational, unpoetic times these true symbols, which contained the object itself, had degenerated into mere ornaments. Recent critics have gone back to the language of rhetoric in their attempts to define the essence of poetry. They have suggested various terms, particularly the word "metaphor," as a means of expressing the ineffable essence of poetry, that something which is at once concrete and universal. Vico called it the *universale fantastico*. This too is a mere cipher, but it strikes me as more comprehensive, more specific, and more meaningful than "metaphor."

With his conception Vico freed poetic theory from all the dogmatic, purely technical criteria based solely on external form. He recognized poetry to be an autonomous mode of human perception and self-orientation. Poets, it is true, always strive, and particularly in early periods, for a rhythmical discourse rich in phonetic symbolism; for Vico, however, what is decisive is not the external criteria but immediate intuition unguided by systematic reason. In his view true poetry is limited to the early periods, to so-called "primordial times"—a prejudice which he shared with Herder and his successors. Like many prejudices, it was to prove extremely fruitful. It was the source of Storm and Stress and the Romantic Movement, of historicism and of the idea that each nation had its characteristic genius; through Vico's notion of the poetic symbol, it was the source of the first reasoned insight into the difference between the language of poetic evocation and that of rational communication. But a prejudice it remains. The relation between imagination and reason is not one of pure temporal succession; imagination and reason are not mutually exclusive; the two can work together, and reason can serve to enrich the imagination. Vico himself recognized that his classification of epochs did not have universal validity; the vestiges of early cultural states, he wrote, linger on in much later periods, "much as great and rapid rivers continue far into the sea, keeping sweet the waters borne on by the force of their flow" (*Scienza nuova* 412, tr. Bergin-Fisch). But he held that late periods are overwhelmingly dominated by an unpoetic rationalism and, like the Romantics after him, believed that poetry was limited to the early periods of culture, which he termed the age of gods and heroes.

The unity of Vico's vision is evident in his treatment of each of the periods of human development, but particularly so in connection with the early period. Among these early men all thought and action was poetic. Their metaphysics, their logic, their ethics, politics, economics, and so on—all were poetic. The science which seeks, by interpreting documents, to determine what they held to be true is called philology. Thus philology is enlarged to mean what in Germany is called *Geistesgeschichte*, to include all historical disciplines, including the history of law and economic history. But the full force of Vico's idea of philology is understood only if we employ his own terms. He contrasts philology with philosophy: philology investigated what the various peoples regarded as true at each cultural stage (although this truth was a product of their limited perspective) and what accordingly formed the basis of their actions and institutions. Vico calls this the *certum* (the certain or established); the *certum* is subject to historical change. Philosophy, on the other hand, is concerned with the immutable and absolute truth, the *verum*. For Vico this truth is never manifested, at least not in history. Even in the age of fully developed reason, the third age of history, it is present only as a potentiality; for Vico this third age is only a stage, doomed to degenerate and relapse into barbarism. One aspect or another of the Platonic *verum* is actualized in every stage of history; no historical period embodies the whole of it. It is fully contained only in the plan of Providence or in the total course of history; and it can be known only through a knowledge of history as a whole. Thus the truth sought by philosophy is inseparable from philology, which investigates the *certa* both singly and in their systematic context. The systematic context of all human history, the *comune natura delle nazioni*, is Vico's subject, which, in line with Vico's own terminology, we may equally well call philology or philosophy. This philological philosophy or philosophical philology is concerned with only one thing—mankind.

Such is the conception of philology that I have learned from Vico. It can readily be seen how well it falls in with the European "mission" of which I spoke at the beginning of this introduction. But how, in practice, can this task of synthesis be performed? Vico succeeded none too well. The strictly learned and technical part of his book, his demonstrations and interpretations, are often mistaken and sometimes absurd; and his errors cannot be explained entirely by the limited knowledge of his day but must be attributed in part to his one-sidedness and unconscious bias. Possessed by his vision, at a loss for material with which to support it (for he knew next to nothing of ethnology, the Orient, or the Middle Ages, fields which were not systematically studied until after his time), he often put forced interpretations on the ancient material that was available to him—myths, poetry, historical and juridical texts. He made particularly free with etymologies. Sometimes he forgot or overlooked the excellent work done by his own contemporaries. This is no longer of concern to us; what remains significant is his idea of the structure of history. Also his method—induction from documents—remains important regardless of the mistakes Vico made in putting it into practice, for today in any case such an undertaking would have to be based on research of an entirely different kind. Indeed, we cannot but admire the force of the idea which produced a work of such stature from such inadequate material. We are deeply moved by Vico's struggle to give shape to his thoughts; he derived the strength to do so from his determination—which did not exclude prejudice and partial blindness—to interpret facts and to find their underlying design.

Since Vico wrote the *Scienza nuova*, the difficulties in the way of a synthetic historical philology aspiring to encompass the cultural destinies of Europe have greatly increased. Enormous amounts of material have been made available, resulting in hundreds of specialized disciplines, most of them quite unheard of in Vico's time, each concerned with some very partial aspect of the European problem. No one can possibly master all these branches of study. Their bibliographies have become so enormous that only a few specialists can keep abreast of them. Productive as it may be, such specialization is becoming more and more unsatisfactory, because all these matters are interrelated, and it is impossible to interpret the particular without a living awareness of the whole. But how is such an awareness to be gained?

Furthermore, superabundance of material is not the only difficulty in the way of a philologist striving for synthesis. Viewpoints and methods have multiplied in the same way, deriving not only from the various branches of historical philology but also from other disciplines such as sociology and psychology. They must be appraised and, to some extent at least, taken into account. A philologist who is not satisfied with strict specialization must find his way amid a welter of assertions and impressions of which it is seemingly impossible to form a considered judgment. No one can hope, in a single life span, to accumulate all the available knowledge on a given subject and reduce it to a synthesis. By unflagging effort a scholar receptive to new ideas can, to be sure, broaden his horizon and mature his judgment on the basis of wide learning. But this can only be done unsystematically, as inclination and opportunity dictate; any method whatsoever would result in exhaustion or specialization. Yet, though unsystematic, open-minded effort is no doubt a necessary prerequisite for synthesis, it is not the synthesis itself.

It is patently impossible to establish a synthesis by assembling all the particulars. Perhaps, however, we shall be able to do so by selecting characteristic particulars and following up their implications. This method consists in finding unusually fertile areas or key problems on which it is rewarding to concentrate, because they open up a knowledge of a broader context and cast a light on entire historical landscapes. I first made deliberate use of this method in 1930 in my work on French classicism. It seemed to me at the time that the section of society which in the seventeenth century constituted the literary public was something new, markedly original, fraught with consequence for the future, and radically different from anything existing in earlier times. My knowledge, to be sure, was enriched by modern works on the political structure, economic life, and society of the day, but they provided no specific approach to my problem, because the arrangement of the material in them was not what my task required. I was enabled to come to grips with the problem when my attention was attracted to the phrase *la cour et la ville*, by which contemporaries referred to the social stratum in question. By collecting passages containing this term or similar terms and by interpreting each example in its context, I easily established what *la cour* and what *la ville* meant, how the two groups had arisen, and how they had become associated to form a unity. It was a natural step to follow the subsequent transformations of this social complex and to compare it with similar groupings and developments in other countries.

Thus I had found a simple, purely philological starting point or impulse that led far beyond the original subject under investigation—"the French public in the seventeenth century."

Since then I have in similar fashion often made use of characteristic words or phrases as starting points for investigations aiming at historical synthesis. But there are many other possible points of departure—grammatical, rhetorical, stylistic phenomena, or even events. Anything that is characteristic can serve the purpose. Only one condition must be met: whatever is taken as a starting point must be strictly applicable to the historical material under investigation. A loose analogy will not suffice, and the relationship must be of a suggestive kind. Modern or abstract categories of classification such as "baroque" or "Romantic," or "the idea of destiny," "mythos," "the concept of time," are not suitable. Such words, to be sure, may occur in the exposition itself when the context makes it clear what they mean, but as points of departure they are too ambiguous and do not follow directly from the material. The starting point should not be a category which we ourselves impose on the material, to which the material must be fitted, but a characteristic found in the subject itself, essential to its history, which, when stressed and developed, clarifies the subject matter in its particularity and other topics in relation to it.

An almost ideal starting point is provided by the interpretation of textual passages. If we assume with Vico that every age has its characteristic unity, every text must provide a partial view on the basis of which a synthesis is possible. I have often applied this method, particularly in *Mimesis*. It forms a tie between me and the group of philologists who have interpreted style, above all with Leo Spitzer, whose work has long influenced my own. And yet there is a great difference between his use of the method and mine. First of all, of course, because no one—and particularly no one who is not fundamentally a linguist—can hope to equal him in subtlety of discernment, in flair, or in vastness of erudition. But the purpose, too, is different. Spitzer's interpretations are always concerned primarily with an exact understanding of the individual linguistic form, the particular work or author. Quite in accord with the Romantic tradition and its impressionist and individualist developments, he is concerned primarily with an exact understanding of the individual forms. I, on the contrary, am concerned with something more general, which I shall have occasion to describe later on. My purpose is always to write history. Consequently I never approach a text as an isolated phenomenon; I address a question to it, and my question, not the text, is my primary point of departure. In *Mimesis* I started with the ancient conception of the three levels of style and asked all the selected texts in what way they were related to it. This was tantamount to asking what their authors regarded as sublime and significant and what means they employed to represent them. In this way I was able, however inadequately, to disclose something of the influence of Christianity on the development of literary expression, and even to throw light on an aspect of the development of European culture since antiquity. These themes are of the utmost importance for us, but far too vast and varied to be treated as a whole; one can hope to throw light on them only by tracing them back to specialized points of departure. Of course a single starting point cannot suffice for such enormous subjects; at most it can perform a function of guidance and integration; each part of the investigation raises problems of its own and demands its own points of departure.

The universal element that I am concerned with does not reside in laws or categories of classification. Vico thought he had discovered laws; they were and remain very fruitful. Fertility and influence on others are the most that can be achieved by this kind of intellectual activity. But his laws, as it happens, are not sound; they are too simple to cover the sum of developments. History does not necessarily unfold as he represents it, but with far greater variability; the conclusions which he drew from his study of the history of the Mediterranean countries and of Europe cannot be accepted as universal laws. His theory of cycles, the idea of the eternal recurrence of the same development, has been rendered extremely improbable by the progressive leveling of world civilization. The barbarians who, according to his system, destroy the civilizations that have passed their prime and initiate a fresh cycle would have to come from another planet. Today it is no longer possible to represent the history of our life style, that is, the history of the last three thousand years, as a process governed by laws. It may become possible much later, in another perspective and a larger context; and by then no doubt the particularities that our history has taken on in the course of these three thousand years will have lost their significance and sunk into oblivion. Today, only certain partial phenomena—those accessible to the statistical methods of the natural sciences—can be classified according to laws; for the whole this is not possible. The most inspired and influential attempt to apprehend modern history as a whole in terms of laws is dialectical materialism; it grew from the situation in a particular moment of history, and the limits of its validity have now, after a century, become clearly discernible. Other attempts have been made in the past century to base an understanding of history on extrahistorical, ethical, or psychological factors; they can be interesting when they originate with ingenious and well-informed persons. But there is always something arbitrary about them. One might find many such factors and groups of factors, all of them applicable with a certain amount of good will, but no one of them fully convincing.

The general conception that can be set forth is, I believe, that of an historical process, a kind of drama, which advances no theory but only sketches a certain pattern of human destiny. The subject of this drama is Europe; I have tried to approach this subject in a number of partial investigations. What can thus be achieved under the most favorable circumstances is an insight into the diverse implications of a process from which we stem and in which we participate, a definition of our present situation and also perhaps of the possibilities for the immediate future. In any event, such a method compels us to look within ourselves and to set forth our consciousness of ourselves here and now, in all its wealth and limitations.

Has such an approach scientific validity? It matters little. My own experience, and by that I mean not merely my scientific experience, is responsible for the choice of problems, the starting points, the reasoning and the intention expressed in my writings. No other approval is sought but the consent (which is bound to be variable and never complete) of those who have arrived at similar experience by other paths, so that my experience may serve to clarify, to complement, and perhaps to stimulate theirs. Of course I have aimed at precision in my quotations from documents and my linguistic interpretations, and in the use I have made of earlier research. But this precision applies only to the material.

The four fragments here submitted may be regarded as a supplement to *Mimesis*. Of course *Mimesis* presents a number of obvious gaps which are not filled in. But such gaps struck me as less important than my neglect of the early Middle Ages. Between the section on the fifth century ("The Arrest of Peter Valvomeres") and the chapter on the *Song of Roland*, there is only the analysis of a single text by Gregory of Tours; the long epoch from 600 to 1100, which, though it is the poorest of all the periods in the time span under consideration, is the one most in need of interpretation, is almost entirely neglected. In Istanbul it was impossible to deal with this period, if only because of the lack of a satisfactory library for research in the Western Middle Ages. On my arrival in the United States, I therefore began as soon as possible to investigate in greater detail the theme, already broached, of the *sermo humilis*, the Christian form of the sublime, and to follow it into the early Middle Ages; my starting point was a passage from Augustine (*De doctrina christiana*, 4.18) taken in conjunction with an investigation of the meaning of the word *humilis*. This investigation resulted in the first two chapters of the present book;[1] the second chapter, which extends to the tenth

---

1. Previously published, arranged somewhat differently, in *Romanische Forschungen*, LXIV (1952), 304–364, and LXVI (1955), 1–64. The appendix to the first chapter is a revision of the first pages of the essay "Passio als Leidenschaft," *PMLA*, LVI (1941), 1179–96.

century, is not restricted to the theme of the *sermo humilis*, since thus far little work has been done on the style of the first Christian millennium and a somewhat more general investigation therefore seemed in order. The third paper, "Camilla," which starts from a comparison of a passage in the *Aeneid* with a passage in which it is elaborated by a twelfth-century French poet, deals with an essentially similar problem, for it is an attempt to investigate the decline of the ancient lofty style and its rebirth under different circumstances.

But here we come to the state of affairs which I believe to be the crucial theme of research in the literature of the early Middle Ages—the great hiatus, the period in which there is no literary public and no generally intelligible literary language. It is not an easy matter to present this hiatus and the way in which it was surmounted as a single process; to do so we must hold intently to our goal and fight our way resolutely through the plethora of source material, modern studies, and points of view. These pre-occupations resulted in the fourth paper, whose intentionally para-doxical title ("The Western Public and Its Language") stresses European unity. Here three investigations, which though separate were all undertaken with a view to the same end, are taken as starting points and woven together. The first begins with an anec-dote from Tacitus and deals with "the reader" as he appears in Pliny and Martial; the second deals with the late and fragmentary records of early vernacular literature; the third, with Dante's ad-dresses to the reader. Other starting points are attempted and developed to a certain extent, but these three play a guiding role.

A task of this kind calls for an unconscionable amount of read-ing. Nevertheless I hope that no significant discovery or method in the various fields touched upon has been entirely overlooked. I have used relatively few quotations, and then almost always in order to clarify or document statements of fact. Such a book is bound to be difficult, but it is not intended as a reference work; I should like it to be read as a whole, and with that in mind I have tried to make its form as inviting as possible. I hope my readers will not assume that anything I fail to mention is unknown to me or that I have rejected it. Certain books have helped me more than my quotations show; I have drawn considerable material and also the formulation of certain problems from Ernst Robert Curtius' imposing work on the Middle Ages, although I seldom agree with his judgment as to what is significant and what is not; among Romance scholars I should like to mention Ramón Menéndez Pidal, Alfredo Schiaffini, and Reto R. Bezzola.

Despite its singleness of purpose, this book is a fragment or rather a series of fragments. It lacks even the loose but always perceptible unity of *Mimesis*. It is not brought to a conclusion, but broken off; it achieves no proper integration of its subject matter. Nevertheless, some readers may sense the unity behind it. In his preface to the *Quaestiones in Heptateuchum*, Augustine wrote: *nonnulla enim pars inventionis est nosse quid quaeras* (a considerable part of discovery is to know what you are looking for). What is being looked for in the following pages has, I hope, been made plain enough. But I should have liked to make more evident the connecting thread that unites the whole. In this light the book is still in search of its theme. Perhaps its readers will help in the search; perhaps one of them, by giving more precise and effective expression to what I have tried to say, will find the theme.

I

Sermo Humilis

. . . una voce modesta,
forse qual fu dall' angelo a Maria

(. . . a gentle voice,
Perhaps such as was that of the Angel to Mary)
DANTE, *Paradiso*, 14.35f.

O N AN OCCASION whose date happens to be known to us,[1] Augustine delivered a sermon (numbered 256 in the Maurist edition)[2] beginning as follows:

Quoniam placuit Domino Deo nostro, ut hic constituti praesentia corporali etiam cum vestra Charitate illi cantaremus Alleluia, quod Latine interpretatur: "Laudate Dominum"—Laudemus Dominum, fratres, vita et lingua, corde et ore, vocibus et moribus. Sic enim sibi dici vult Deus Alleluia, ut non sit in laudante discordia. Concordent ergo prius in nobis ipsis lingua cum vita, os cum conscientia. Concordent, inquam, voces cum moribus; ne forte bonae voces testimonium dicant contra malos mores. O felix Alleluia in coelo, ubi templum Dei Angeli sunt! Ibi enim concordia summa laudantium, ubi est exultatio secura cantantium; ubi nulla lex in membris repugnat legi mentis; ubi non est rixa cupiditatis, in qua periclitetur victoria charitatis. Hic ergo cantemus Alleluia adhuc solliciti, ut illic possimus aliquando cantare securi. Quare hic sollicti? Non vis ut sim sollicitus, quando lego: "Numquid non tentatio est vita hominum super terram" (Cf. Job 7:1)? Non vis ut sim sollicitus, quando mihi adhuc dicitur: "Vigilate et orate, ne intretis in tentationem" (Mark 14:38)? Non vis ut sim sollicitus, ubi sic abundat tentatio, ut nobis ipsa praescribat oratio, quando dicimus: "Dimitte nobis debita nostra, sicut et nos dimittimus debitoribus

1. At a council of bishops held in Carthage, on May 5, 418. Cf. A. Wilmart in *Revue Bénédictine*, XLII (1930), 142.
2. *PL*, XXXVIII, 1190f.

nostris" (Matt. 6:12)? Quotidie petitores, quotidie debitores. Vis ut sim securus, ubi quotidie peto indulgentiam pro peccatis, adiutorium pro periculis? Cum enim dixero propter praeterita peccata: "Dimitte nobis debita nostra, sicut et nos dimittimus debitoribus nostris"—continuo propter futura pericula addo et adiungo: "Ne nos inferas in tentationem." Quomodo est autem populus in bono, quando mecum clamat: "libera nos a malo"? Et tamen, fratres, in isto adhuc malo cantemus Alleluia Deo bono, qui nos liberat a malo. Quid circum inspicis unde te liberet, quando te liberat a malo? Noli longe ire, noli aciem mentis circumquaque distendere. Ad te redi, te respice: tu es adhuc malus. Quando ergo Deus te ipsum liberat a te ipso, tunc te liberat a malo. Apostolum audi, et ibi intellege, a quo malo sis liberandus, "Condelector enim," inquit, "legi Dei secundum interiorem hominem, video autem aliam legem in membris meis repugnantem legi mentis meae et captivantem me in lege peccati quae est"—ubi?—"captivantem," inquit, "me in lege peccati quae est in membris meis." Putavi quia captivavit te sub nescio quibus ignotis barbaris, putavi quia captivavit te sub nescio quibus gentibus alienis vel sub nescio quibus hominibus dominis. "Quae est," inquit, "in membris meis." Exclama ergo cum illo: "Miser ego homo, quis me liberabit!" Unde quis liberabit? Dic unde. Alius dicit ab optione, alius de carcere, alius de barbarorum captivitate, alius de febre atque languore: Dic tu, apostole, non quo mittamur, aut quo ducamur, sed quid nobiscum portemus, quid nos ipsi simus, dic: "De corpore mortis huius." De corpore mortis huius? "De corpore," inquit, "mortis huius" (Rom. 7:22–24).

Since it has pleased the Lord our God that we, here present with you in person, and one with you in charity, should sing the Alleluia, which in Latin means, "Praise the Lord"—then let us give praise to the Lord, brethren, by our lives and by our speech, by our hearts and by our voices, by our words and by our ways. For the Lord wants us to sing Alleluia to Him in such a way that there may be no discord [lit., doubleness of heart] in him who gives praise. First, therefore, let our speech agree with our lives, our voice with our conscience. Let our words, I say, agree with our ways, lest fair words bear witness against false ways. O happy

Alleluia on high, where the Angels are the temple of God! For the highest harmony of those giving praise will be found there on high where the joy of those who sing is beyond troubling, where no law in the members struggles against the law of the mind, where no struggle of desire imperils the victory of charity. Let us therefore sing Alleluia here below even though we are still troubled, so that on high we may finally sing it free from care. Why are we troubled here below? How could I not feel troubled when I read, "Is not temptation the life of man on earth" (cf. Job 7:1)? How could I not feel troubled when it is said to me in this life, "Watch ye, and pray, lest ye enter into temptation" (Mark 14:38)? How could I not feel troubled here, where temptation so abounds that the prayer itself warns us when we say, "Forgive us our debts as we forgive our debtors" (Matt. 6:12)? Petitioners daily, debtors daily. How can I feel free from care where I daily ask forgiveness for my sins, help against dangers? For when I have said because of my past sins, "Forgive us our debts as we forgive our debtors," I immediately add, because of the dangers to come, "and lead us not into temptation." But how can a people be in a good state when they cry out with me, "Deliver us from evil"? And yet, brethren, even while we are still in this evil state, let us sing Alleluia to the good Lord, who delivers us from evil. But why do you look around you to see what he delivers you from, when he delivers you from evil? There is no need to go far afield, there is no need to cast your mind in every direction. Return inwards, look within yourself: you yourself are still in this evil state. When, therefore, God delivers you from yourself, then he delivers you from evil. Hear the Apostle, and understand from his words the evil from which you are to be delivered: "For I delight," he says, "in the law of God for the inward man. But I see another law in my members, warring against the law of my mind, and holding me in captivity to the law of sin which is" . . . where? . . . "holding me in captivity," he says, "to the law of sin which is in my members." I had thought that it held you in captivity among some unknown barbarians or other. I thought that it held you in captivity among some foreign nations or other, or under some other men and masters. "Which is," he says, "in my members." Then cry out together with him, "O wretched man that I am! Who shall deliver me?" And who is to deliver me from what? Tell me, from what? One says from arbitrary proceedings, another says from prison, yet another from captivity among the barbarians, and still another from fever and disease. Tell us, O Apostle, not whither we are sent, or whither we are carried off, but what we

bear within ourselves, what we ourselves are. Say it: "From the
body of this death."—From the body of this death?—"From the
body," he replies, "of this death" (Rom. 7:22–24).

The subject of this text is man's bondage to sin, to "the body
of this death." In a subsequent passage (not quoted here) the
author goes on to say that the "body of this death," from which
Paul wished to be delivered, is nevertheless ours: we cannot free
ourselves from it, for even in dying we shall not leave it behind us
forever. It remains with us, we shall be reunited with it, though
it will no longer be the body of death, but a spiritual, immortal
body.

The presentation, as we see at a glance, is rhetorical, almost
theatrical; let us read it slowly and try to hear it as it was spoken
aloud. At the very beginning the *Laudate Dominum*, introduced
merely as a translation of *Alleluia*, finds a forceful, dramatic
response in the *Laudemus Dominum*, followed by the vocative
fratres and the three structurally identical measures *vita et lingua,
corde et ore, vocibus et moribus*. In interlocking antithetical
phrases,[3] the tone rises to the summits of angelic jubilation—
exultatio secura cantantium is contrasted with *concordia summa
laudantium, lex mentis* with *lex in membris* (in the quotation from
St. Paul), *rixa cupiditatis* with *victoria charitatis*—and then falls
to the *Alleluia* on earth, where the earthly theme *solliciti* is introduced in opposition to the heavenly *securi*. A succession of questions, anaphoras, isocola, and antitheses[4] leads on to the source of
all this distress, namely evil, from which deliverance is sought.
The rest of the passage consists largely of questions and answers:
"What do you seek outside of yourself? Look within, you yourself are this evil." Paul is summoned as a witness; his words, which
above were only alluded to, are quoted; but now they are drama-

3. *Laudate/laudemus/laudante/laudantium; corde/discordia/concordent/con-
cordent; voces cum moribus/bonae voces/malos mores.*
4. Anaphoras: *Non vis ut sim sollicitus* (three times), followed by *vis ut sim
securus; Quotidie; noli.* Antithetical isocola, especially *indulgentiam pro
peccatis* opposed to *adiutorium pro periculis.* Also the sonorous echoes
through *quomodo, quando, libera, bono, malo, in te, te, tu,* continuing to
the word *liberandus.*

tized as in a law court, and his testimony provokes repeated expressions of astonishment, doubting counterquestion, and confirmation. From what are we to be delivered? Tell me, from what? One says from this, another from that, and still another. . . . Tell us, O Apostle. "From the body of this death." From the body of this death? "From the body," he says, "of this death."

This rhetorical style, as a whole and in every particular, stems from the ancient academic tradition. Not only the sound patterns, the structurally identical clauses often with rhymed endings, the anaphoras, questions, and antitheses, but also the fictitious dialogues are inherited from the schools of rhetoric. At an early date the Christian sermon began to develop on the model of the diatribe, or moralistic declamation, in which the opinions of others are adduced in imaginary speeches to which the speaker replies,[5] the whole thus forming a dialogue. There are numerous examples, some dating back to the earliest Christian period; characteristic is the *inquit*, which appears several times in our text, in the last line for example.[6]

At Augustine's time (c. 400) the uneducated or semi-educated, un-Greek or un-Latin style of earliest Christian literature, so distressing to the ears of a classically educated public, had long fallen into disuse. In East and West alike a fusion or adaptation had taken place. The authors of Christian sermons drew on the rhetorical tradition that pervaded the ancient world and spoke in the forms to which their audience was accustomed, for in those days almost everyone judged an oration by the ring of the words. Even in Punic Africa, where the Latin spoken was far from pure, the taste for high-sounding oratory had become universal. The congregation clapped and cheered when a rhetorical figure caught their fancy; this is attested by the famous preachers

5. U. von Wilamowitz-Moellendorff, "Der kynische Prediger Tales," 292; E. Norden, *Die antike Kunstprosa*, pp. 129 and especially 556; P. Wendland, *Die hellenistisch-römische Kultur*, ch. V.
6. There is a literary reminiscence in the formulation itself: Seneca writes (*Ad Luc. Epist. Mor.* 75.4): *Quod sentimus loquamur, quod loquimur sentiamus; concordet sermo cum vita* (Let us speak what we feel, let us feel what we speak; let our speech accord with our life).

of the East, John Chrysostom for example, and in the West by Augustine himself. To us rhetorical figures seem artificial, pedantic, and precious; and so they are, but they derive their justification from a universal love of phonetic parallels and plays on words; and moreover, what a given public may regard as the height of art may strike later generations as utterly hackneyed and conventional.

The figures in our text stem from the tradition of the schools of rhetoric; and yet the rhetoric gives an impression of simplicity, it serves no other purpose than effective teaching, and the sentence structure sometimes verges on the colloquial. Compounded of the solemn and the homely, it is the utilitarian rhetoric of a preacher intent on teaching and admonishing. The resounding isocola impress themselves on the hearer's mind; the lyrical outburst *O felix Alleluia in coelo,* with its *ubi* and *ibi,* teaches a lesson in simple childlike terms, and, if not quite colloquial, the anaphoric question *Non vis ut sim sollicitus* (How could I not feel troubled?) is assuredly in the simplest of styles. And undoubtedly the ensuing dialogues with their wealth of gesture, first the search for evil, then the questioning of the Apostle with its threefold repetition, each time with a change of intonation, of the crucial answer, are a kind of didactic play, in which scenes and gestures not only teach a lesson but also embody the response which the lesson is intended to arouse.

The lesson in question is one of the most difficult of Christian doctrines and moreover one of those most at variance with classical modes of thought: although we know and desire the good, we do evil because we have been sold into captivity to sin, to the body; our sound knowledge and will are powerless. It is from ourselves that we must be delivered, from the body of this death; and yet the body is ours, it will be reunited with us at the Resurrection. Here, as in a thousand other passages, the forms of ancient rhetoric are employed [7] to set forth an enormously difficult para-

---

7. Not in every case with the same mastery. In the West there was scarcely another orator such as Augustine, and in the East there were only a few. On the style of Augustine's sermons, see Edith Schuchter, "Zum Predigtstil des hl. Augustinus."

dox as though it were something self-evident and not to be doubted. The audience was equally amenable to these forms and to these ideas; they welcomed both at once. Our question, which many have asked before us, is: what changes did the traditional forms of discourse incur under the stress of such ideas, and can the new Christian discourse still be classified according to the system of ancient rhetoric, based on a graduated series of style levels? Our question, then, becomes: what place does the level of style represented in our text assume in the ancient hierarchy?

Augustine himself spoke of the matter. In *De doctrina christiana* (4.12ff.) he discussed the use of academic rhetoric in sermons. That it had to be used he took for granted; would it not be absurd, he says in substance, to leave the weapons of eloquence in the exclusive possession of the advocates of the lie and to deny them to the champions of the truth? In his conception of the three traditional levels of style (the sublime, the intermediate, and the low, or lowly) he follows Cicero (in particular *Orator* 69ff.). For instruction and exegesis he recommends the low style, which, according to Cicero, should be unadorned but neither slovenly nor uncouth; for praise and blame, admonition and dissuasion, the intermediate (*temperatum*), in which rhetorical figures have their proper place; while for arousing the transports of emotion that move men to action, he advises the sublime, lofty style, which does not exclude rhetorical ornament but has no need of it. Christian writers, Augustine maintains, had already used the three styles in this way. The examples he cites from the Pauline Epistles and the sermons of Cyprian and Ambrose show that he particularly admired passages (in the intermediate style) deriving their movement from short, structurally identical clauses disposed in antithetical pairs.[8] The examples of the lowly style are for the most part

8. *De doctr. chr.* 4.20.40: . . . *illa pulchriora sunt, in quibus propria propriis tamquam debita reddita decenter excurrunt* (. . . those passages are the more beautiful where things properly related flow fittingly from one another as though in payment of what is due). And somewhat later (on Rom. 12:16): *Et quam pulchre ista omnia sic effusa bimembri circuitu terminantur!* (viz., *non alta sapientes, sed humilibus consentientes*): And with what beauty are all those utterances brought to a close by a period consisting of two members (viz., mind not high things, but condescend to men of low estate).

drawn from explanations of Bible passages; those of the intermediate style (two of them are concerned with the praise of
virginity) are descriptive and admonitory, the quotations from
Cyprian and Ambrose being gentle, almost tender in tone. Of
the sublime style he cites examples employing figures of speech
(*granditer et ornate*) and others that are free from ornament;
common to them all is their impassioned tone. He recommends
the use of all three levels in the same discourse for the sake of
variety, and here again the tradition offered precedents (e.g.,
Quintilian, *Inst. orat.* 12.10.58ff.).[9] In Chapters 22 and 23 he indicates how such transitions from one style to another should be
effected and cautions the student against introducing the lofty
style too abruptly or using it at excessive length; he recommends
frequent use of the lowly style, either for purposes of explanation
or to set off ornamented or lofty passages by contrast.

From this it might be inferred that in Augustine's own opinion
our text is chiefly in the intermediate style, with some admixture
of the lowly, didactic style. The profusion of parallels and ornamental figures, the somewhat lyrical, generally descriptive and
admonitory tone of the beginning, point to the intermediate style;
further on, in the imaginary dialogues of the diatribe, we note a
didactic element; here we seem to have the lowly style. Striking
use of similar colloquial forms may be found in the passages from
Galatians (4:21–26) which Augustine, at the beginning of Chapter 20, expressly assigns to the lowly style.

Augustine's views in the matter become readily understandable if we bear in mind that his aim was to provide practical
pointers for the use of the classical style levels and that he closely
followed Cicero, especially Cicero's definition of the low *sermo*,
formulated entirely with a view to political or forensic oratory.
But their basic assumptions were entirely different. When Cicero
(*Orator* 101) writes (as Augustine quotes him in *De doctr. chr.*

9. Cicero at the beginning of *De optimo genere oratorum;* Quintilian 10.2.22
or 12.10.58ff. Cf. also the *eloquendi varietas* in Pliny, *Epist.* 6.33; also 2.5,
3.13, etc.

4.17): *Is igitur erit eloquens, qui poterit parva submisse, modica temperate, magna granditer dicere* (He therefore will be eloquent who can speak of small things in a simple manner, of middling things in the intermediate style, and of great things in the grand manner), he takes these gradations (*parva, modica, magna*) in an absolute sense; *parva* designates something absolutely base, such as the financial transactions and commonplace occurrences that an orator addressing a court of law is obliged to speak of. A Christian orator recognizes no absolute levels of subject matter; only the immediate context and purpose (whether his aim is to teach, to admonish, or to deliver an impassioned appeal) can tell him which level of style to employ. A Christian orator's subject is always Christian revelation, and this can never be base or in-between. When Augustine teaches that Christian themes should sometimes be expounded in the intermediate or lowly style, he is referring solely to the form of presentation, which must be varied if it is to be understandable and effective; the pagan gradations of subject matter have lost their validity. The sublime or pleasingly "middling" subjects of pagan literature are un-Christian and reprehensible; Augustine is visibly embarrassed by a passage in which Cyprian employs an idyllic style in dealing with an "intermediate" theme. But it is in Chapter 18, immediately after the quotation from Cicero, that he takes his most explicit stand against the ancient gradations of subject matter. I shall paraphrase the passage in slightly abridged form.

Cicero's threefold classification, he writes, is appropriate to legal matters, but not to the spiritual matters with which we are concerned. Where financial dealings are involved, Cicero calls the subject matter "low"; he calls it "lofty" where men's lives and well-being are at stake; the intermediate lies in between. We Christians cannot accept such a distinction: for us all themes are sublime, especially when we are addressing the people from the pulpit; for we are always concerned with the welfare of men, and not only their worldly welfare but their eternal salvation; so that even the gain and loss of money become important, regardless of whether the sum involved is large or small; the justice we must assuredly observe even in trifling money matters is of no small importance, for the Lord has said: "He that is faithful in that which is least is faithful also in much" (Luke 16:10). The least is very little; but it is great to keep faith in little things. (Augustine goes on to cite I Cor. 6:1–9, where Paul rebukes the members of the congregation who have laid legal disputes among themselves before the heathen courts). Why is the Apostle indignant? Why does he react so violently? Why does he vituperate, rebuke, and threaten? What is the reason for the agitation manifested by his bitter invective and frequent changes of tone? Why, in short, does he adopt so lofty and impassioned a style in speaking of such insignificant matters? Are earthly affairs so important to him? Not at all. He does so for the sake of justice, charity, piety; no man of sound mind can doubt that these are sublime even in connection with the most paltry affairs. . . . Wherever we may speak of those things that save us from eternal damnation and lead us to eternal beatitude, whether to the people or in private conversation, whether addressing one or many, friends or enemies, in continuous discourse or in dialogue, in sermons or in books, they remain sublime. A cup of cold water is assuredly a small and worthless thing; but does this mean that the Lord said something small and worthless when he promised that whosoever should give a cup of cold water to the least of his servants would in no wise lose his reward (cf. Matt. 10:42)? And should a preacher who refers to this incident in church suppose that because it is trivial he should employ not the intermediate nor the lofty, but the lowly form of discourse? Has it not transpired that while we were speaking of this to the people (and not ineptly because God was with us), there burst from that cold water something akin to a flame, which, through hopes of heavenly reward, fired the cold hearts of men to works of mercy?

Only after this remonstrance, which is itself delivered in an impassioned, lofty style, does Augustine proceed to explain how the doctrine of the three levels may nevertheless prove useful to

a Christian orator. The remonstrance is of fundamental importance: in the Christian context humble everyday things, money
matters or a cup of cold water, lose their baseness and become
compatible with the lofty style; and conversely, as is made clear
in Augustine's subsequent remarks, the highest mysteries of the
faith may be set forth in the simple words of the lowly style
which everyone can understand. This was a radical departure
from the rhetorical, and indeed from the entire literary, tradition.
It was a fundamental tenet of this tradition that each style level
or literary genre must deal with a corresponding level of subject
matter; thus a classification of themes was essential. A wide variety
of subjects were assigned to the lowest class; in general it embraced
factual information, all things regarded as insignificant and unim-
pressive, personal matters, daily life, the comic and frivolously
erotic, the satirical, realistic, and obscene; genres associated with
such subject matter were satire, mime, iambus, legal oratory when
it dealt with private and economic interests, and usually the animal
fable. The dividing line between low and intermediate was fluid.
The descriptions of the lowly style are as varied as the subject
matter, and there are subgradations. As we have seen, Augustine
takes Cicero's account of it in *Orator* as his starting point; Cicero
describes the low style as unadorned yet pure and elegant, seemingly easy but requiring true mastery; his conception of it is
barely distinguishable from the Attic ideal (δηλοῦν: to make manifest—not ψυχαγωγεῖν: to seduce). But in the most widespread view
the low style implied sharp realism and homespun vigor.[10] The style

10. This is not the place to analyze the variants of these conceptions and the
   different opinions and tendencies to be found among ancient writers
   on rhetoric. Among the more recent investigations might be mentioned
   C. Jensen, "Herakleides von Pontos"; and F. Wehrli in the *Phyllobolia
   für Peter von der Mühll.*—Characteristic of the more elegant conception
   of the lowly style is the word *subtilis*, which occurs not only in Cicero,
   Orator 78, but also in the much-cited passage from Porphyrio's commentary on Horace, *Carmina* 4.2.27, where he says that, unlike Pindar, Horace
   in his Odes writes in a style modest and subdued, yet refined and sweet
   (*parva quidem et humilia . . . , sed subtilia ac dulcia*). On the subject of
   the realistic, see another passage in Porphyrio, on Horace, *Satires* 1.10.5.
   For the dramatic style, see the famous and influential passages of Horace's
   Ars poetica, particularly 89ff. and 225ff. An interesting passage concerning

levels are particularly evident in the ancient theater; in comedy persons and events of daily life are treated in the low, and occasionally in the intermediate, style; in tragedy legendary figures, princes, and heroes in extraordinary situations are made to speak with lofty dignity. In every case the greatest importance is attached to compatibility between subject matter and expression. It is held to be ridiculous and in monstrous bad taste (*kakozēlia, tapeinōsis, indecorum*) to treat of sublime matters in base, everyday, realistic words or of commonplace matters in the sublime style. This idea is expressed time and time again by Cicero, Horace, Quintilian, by the author of *Peri hypsous* (*De sublimitate*), and later by the innumerable rhetoricians who copied out the works of the classical theoreticians. The doctrine of the style levels led a phantom existence throughout the Middle Ages and awoke to new life in the era of Humanism. It should not be thought that the great orators and critics of late antiquity were petty pedants; they were flexible enough to recognize that a crass, realistic expression could occasionally be used effectively even in a "sublime" setting;[11] and it was sometimes with admiration that they noted changes of level in a single work with one and the same over-all style. But even this attitude presupposed a gradation of themes and a correspondence between subject matter and expression.

In Augustine, however, the principle of the three levels hinged exclusively on the author's specific purpose, accordingly as he wished to teach (*docere*), to condemn or to praise (*vituperare sive laudare*), or to persuade (*flectere; De doctr. chr.* 19). He found a

---

a realistic painter is found in Pliny, *Hist. nat.* 35.112: . . . *e quibus fuit Piraeicus . . . humilia quidem secutus humilitatis tamen summam adeptus est gloriam. Tonstrinas sutrinasque pinxit et asellos et obsonia ac similia, ob haec cognominatus rhyparographos, in iis consummatae voluptatis, quippe eae pluris veniere quam maximae multorum* (. . . among whom was Piraeicus . . . [who] although he concentrated on humble subjects, nevertheless out of the commonplace attained the peak of glory. He painted barbershops, shoemakers' stalls, and donkeys and fish and the like, earning thereby the nickname "painter of dirt." He provided the highest pleasure from these subjects, and they would sell for more than the greatest works of many other painters).

11. E.g., *On the Sublime* (*Peri hypsous*) 31.1, and Quintilian 8.3.20ff.

similar view in Cicero; but he rejected Cicero's assumption that each level of style corresponded to a class of subject matter. The themes of Christian literature, he held, are all sublime; whatever lowly thing it may touch upon is elevated by its contact with Christianity. Nevertheless, the theory of the three levels of expression is useful to Christian teachers and orators; for Christian doctrine is not only sublime, but also obscure and difficult; yet since it is intended for all, since it is desirable that all should understand it and live in accordance with it, it should be set forth in the lowly, intermediate, or sublime style as the situation requires. Perhaps we shall gain a closer idea of what this meant by an investigation of the Latin word *humilis*, which derives semantic force from the range of contents that converge in it.

Humilis is related to *humus*, the soil, and literally means low, low-lying, of small stature. Its figurative meanings developed in various directions. In general it signifies worthless, paltry, trifling, both in an absolute sense and in relation to other objects. In a social and political context it consequently connotes lowly origin, lack of education, poverty, lack of power and prestige; from an ethical point of view it applies to base, unworthy actions or attitudes, slavishness in words and gestures, vileness; it can also mean dejected, pusillanimous, cowardly. Sometimes, where it refers to sordid, straitened circumstances, to misery and fear, the social and ethical aspects are hard to distinguish. The word can apply to a degraded life and a degrading death; it is frequently synonymous with modest, inelegant, of poor quality, shabby: a house, a doorway, an inn, a garment are said to be *humilis;* in connection with occupations and activities it means "subaltern"; Ammianus Marcellinus (16.5.6–7) seems, in accordance with the Aristotelian tradition, to call poetry and rhetoric *humiliora membra philosophiae* (the humbler divisions of philosophy). In general, the word often indicates inferior rank; even "lesser" vices and crimes are termed *humiliora*. It was not always used in a pejorative sense. From the first its range of meaning included modesty, wise moderation, obedience, pious submissiveness; but in non-Christian literature the pejorative use is strongly predominant. Seneca used it several times to indicate the insignificance of earthly life in comparison with immortality after death.[12]

Because of its connotation of inferior rank, *humilis* came to be one of the terms most frequently used to designate the low style: *sermo humilis*. There were many others, such as *tenuis, attenuatus, subtilis, quotidianus, submissus, demissus, pedester, planus, communis, abiectus, comicus, trivialis, vilis, sordidus;* but most of these are specialized terms, distinctly less satisfactory than *humilis* as designations for the over-all style. Cicero, Horace, Propertius, Seneca, Quintilian, both Plinys, and all the later rhetoricians, commentators, and grammarians make frequent use of *humilis, humiliter, humilitas* in this sense; the word was taken over by Christian and medieval writers; it came to be used in the Romance languages and even in English as a name for the lowly style.

On the other hand (and this is what gives the word the semantic force to which I have referred), *humilis* became the most important adjective characterizing the Incarnation; in all Christian literature written in Latin it came to express the atmosphere and level of Christ's life and suffering. The word "level" seems odd in this context, but I know of no other that encompasses the ethical, social, spiritual, and esthetic aspects of the matter; and as we shall soon see, all of these are involved. It was precisely its wide range of meaning—humble, socially inferior, unlearned, esthetically crude or even repellent—that gave it the dominant position which makes it so valuable as an indicator of trends. Especially in its ethical connotations, but in others as well, the word underwent a re-evaluation; its pejorative implication vanished, and the positive aspect, which had been feeble and infrequent in pagan literature, became dominant. But many of its previous associations remained unchanged: side by side with *humilis* we find, for example, *abiectus* and *con-*

12. And naturally in Christian authors also, but not very frequently nor for very long because in Christian usage, as we shall see, the semantic development took quite another course.—My account of the semantic history of the word *humilis* is based for the most part on the material collected in the *Thesaurus linguae latinae*.

temptus, but also *mitis* and *mansuetus;* and as antonyms *altus* and *sublimis,* though also, to be sure, *superbus.*

The most important passage in this connection is Phil. 2:7f.:

> Sed semetipsum exinanivit, formam servi accipiens, in similitudinem hominum factus, et habitu inventus ut homo. Humiliavit semetipsum factus obediens usque ad mortem, mortem autem crucis.

> But emptied himself, taking the form of a servant, being made in the likeness of men: and was found in fashion as a man. He humbled himself, and became obedient unto death, even death on the cross.

Other such passages are Acts 8:26ff., telling how Philip found an Ethiopian eunuch reading Scripture (Isa. 52:13–53) and converted him, and Matt. 11:29. And there are numerous other passages which, while not expressing the exact same thing directly, contributed, each in its own way, to the development of the above-mentioned attitude. Among these we may include Matt. 11:25; Matt. 23:12 and the corresponding passages in Luke (14:11 and 18:14); Rom. 12:16; I Cor. 1:26–29; Phil. 3:21; and many more.

This theme—the humility of the Incarnation—was elaborated in different directions. The Incarnation as such was a voluntary humiliation illustrated by a life on earth in the lowest social class, among the materially and culturally poor, and by the whole character of Christ's acts and teachings. It was crowned by the cruelty and humiliation of the Passion. In the course of conflict with purely spiritualist tendencies of heretical sects as well as of pagan doctrines, this conception led to an insistence on Christ's corporeality and on the related doctrines of Christ's Resurrection and of universal resurrection. The humility of the Incarnation derives its full force from the contrast with Christ's divine nature: man and God, lowly and sublime, *humilis et sublimis;* both the height and the depth are immeasurable and inconceivable: *peraltissima humilitas.* For the purpose of the present investigation this complex of ideas forms the first foundation of the Christian *humilis* motif; it relates directly to Christ himself. As everyone knows, examples of it are frequent in all Christian literature; in the following we shall cite a few relevant passages from Augustine.[13]

The bodily existence of Christ on earth and after the Resurrection (*verbum caro factum*), upon which earlier writers had already insisted (especially Tertullian in his controversy with Marcion), is spoken of throughout Augustine's writings as *humilitas;* best known perhaps are the polemical passages against Platonism, e.g., *De civ. Dei* 10.29, in which Christ's *humilitas* is contrasted with the Platonists' *superbia*, their contempt for the body: *Christus humilis, vos superbi* (Christ is humble, you are proud). This theme accounts for the fundamental importance accorded to concrete historical events in Christian doctrines; we shall have more to say on this point. In connection with *humilitas passionis*, the most expressive text I can think of, although the word *humilis* does not occur in it, is to be found in Augustine's *Enarrationes in Psalmos* 96.4 (*CCSL*, 39, 1356f. = *PL*, xxxvii, 1239):

> Ille qui stetit ante iudicem, ille qui alapas accepit, ille qui flagellatus est, ille qui consputus est, ille qui spinis coronatus est, ille qui colaphis caesus est, ille qui in ligno suspensus est, ille cui pendenti in ligno insultatum est, ille qui in cruce mortuus est, ille qui lancea percussus est, ille qui sepultus est: ipse resurrexit. Saeviant quantum possunt regna; quid sunt factura Regi regnorum, Domino omnium regum, Creatori omnium saeculorum?

> He who stood before the judge, he who was struck in the face, he who was scourged, he who was spat upon, he who was crowned with thorns, he who was covered with blows, he who was hanged on a tree, he who while hanging on the tree was mocked, he who died on a cross, he who was pierced with a lance, he who was buried: the same is risen. Let earthly powers rage as they may: what can they avail against the King of kingdoms, the Lord of all kings, the Creator of all worlds?

13. For the antithesis *humilis/sublimis* (in place of *sublimis* there may occur also: *altus, exaltatus, excelsus*) there exists the dialectical variant of the exaltation of the cross, for which I will cite Augustine, *In Joannis Evangelium tractatus* 40.2 (pertaining to John 8:28): *illa exaltatio humiliatio fuit* (that exaltation was a humiliation).

Nowhere has the lowliness of the sublime, the historical humiliation of the godhead, been formulated more sharply.[14]

A related field of application is the social and cultural *humilitas* of those to whom the Christian doctrine is addressed and who are prepared to receive it; the most important Bible quotations are Matt. 11:25; Luke 10:21; Acts 4:13; Rom. 12:16; I Cor. 1:18–21; James 4:6. There are also numerous passages in the patristic literature, some merely setting forth the Christian point of view, most of them, however, like many of the Bible passages, taking a polemical stand against the worldly wisdom of those who disdain the gospel of Christ and his apostles as lowly and uncouth. Passages worth considering in this connection are the beginning of Augustine's Christmas sermon 184 (*PL*, xxxviii, 995), *De civ. Dei* 18.49 (*CCSL*, 48.647), and, in the other sermons, such passages as 43.6 or 87.12 (*PL*, xxxviii, 256f. and 537). God, says Augustine, did not elect an orator or a senator, but a fisherman: *non oratorem, non senatorem, sed piscatorem.* He calls the apostles *humiliter nati* (lowborn), *inhonorati* (unesteemed), *illitterati* (unlettered), or *imperitissimi et abiectissimi* (most ignorant and of the lowest condition), or characterizes them as fishermen and publicans. Among earlier authors I should like to mention Arnobius, *Adversus nationes* 1.58 (*CSEL*, IV, 39), and among Augustine's contemporaries Jerome, who devoted a number of long passages to our themes. In 3.5 of his commentary on Galatians (*PL*, xxvi, 401) he writes:

> Quotusquisque nunc Aristotelem legit? . . . Rusticanos vero et piscatores nostros totus orbis loquitur, universus mundus sonat.

> How many read Aristotle today? But the whole world speaks of our country folk and fishermen, the universe resounds with their praise.

14. Cf. also, for example, Hilary, *Comm. in Matt.* 18:3 (on Matt. 18:7 in *PL*, ix, 1019): *Humilitas passionis scandalum mundo est. In hoc enim maxime ignorantia detinetur humana, quod sub deformitate crucis aeternae gloriae Dominum nolit accipere.* (The humility of the passion is a scandal to the world. For on this point especially is human ignorance held fast because under the offense of the cross it refuses to accept the eternal glory of God.)

and in the letter *ad Paulinum presbyterum* 53.3f. (*CSEL*, LIV, 449), after referring to Peter and John as θεοδίδακτοι:

> Hoc doctus Plato nescivit, hoc Demosthenes eloquens ignoravit.

> This the learned Plato did not know, of this the eloquent Demosthenes was ignorant.

Perhaps the idea is most forcefully expressed in the letter *Ad Heliodorum monachum* 14.11 (*CSEL*, LIV, 61), the passage on the Last Judgment:

> Veniet, veniet illa dies. . . . Tunc ad vocem tubae pavebit terra cum populis, tu gaudebis . . . adducetur et cum suis stultus Plato discipulis; Aristotelis argumenta non proderunt. Tunc tu rusticanus et pauper exultabis, ridebis, et dices: Ecce crucifixus Deus meus, ecce iudex, qui obvolutus pannis in praesepio vagiit. Hic est ille operarii et quaestuariae filius, hic, qui matris gestatus sinu hominem Deus fugit in Aegyptum, hic vestitus coccino, hic sentibus coronatus, hic magus daemonium habens et Samarites. Cerne manus, Iudaee, quas fixeras; cerne latus, Romane, quod foderas. Videte corpus, an idem sit. . . .

> The day, the day will come. . . . Then at the voice of the trumpet the earth with its peoples shall quake, and you will rejoice. . . . Plato with his disciples will be revealed as but a fool; Aristotle's arguments will not help him. Then you the poor rustic will exult, and say with a smile: "Behold my crucified God, behold the judge. This is he who once was wrapped in swaddling clothes and uttered baby cries in a manger. This is the son of a working man and a woman who served for wages. This is he who, carried in his mother's arms, fled into Egypt, a God from a man. This is he who was clad in a scarlet robe and crowned with thorns. This is he who was called a magician, a man with a devil, a Samaritan. Behold the hands, ye Jews, that you nailed to the cross. Behold the side, ye Romans, that you pierced. . . ."[15] (Tr. F. A. Wright)

Here again the main idea is the antithesis, not only between *stultitia* and *sapientia* but very generally between the lowly and

15. Cf. the structurally similar passage at the end of Tertullian, *De spectaculis* 30.6.

the sublime. What is set forth in this passage is the *via pietatis, ab humilitate ad superna surgens* (the way of devotion, rising from the lowly to things sublime; *De civ. Dei* 2.7).

The word *humilis* has still a third field of application, which for our purposes is the most important of all, namely, the *humilitas* of the style of the Holy Scriptures. It is so closely related to the second that many of the passages just quoted are equally relevant to it. The *sermo humilis* of the Bible soon came to be an important theme in Christian apologetics. Most educated pagans regarded the early Christian writings as ludicrous, confused, and abhorrent, and this applied to the Latin even more than the Greek versions. The content struck them as childish and absurd superstition, and the form as an affront to good taste. They found this literature gross and vulgar, awkward in syntax and choice of words, and, to make matters worse, riddled with Hebraisms. Certain passages which to us seem undeniably powerful were looked upon as a turbid jumble, the product of fanatical, half-educated sectaries. The educated pagan public reacted with ridicule, contempt, and horror. How could the profoundest of problems, the enlightenment and redemption of mankind, be treated in such barbarous works? In order to eliminate this stumbling block educated Christians might well have decided at an early date (here we are speaking only of the Latin texts) to correct the first translations of Scripture which had been done by men without education or experience and adapt them to good literary usage. But this was not done. The first Latin translations, with their very peculiar style, were never replaced by a Bible text in the classical taste. The texts in the *Vetus latina* had quickly acquired such authority among the congregations, they were so appropriate to the social and intellectual level of the first Latin-speaking Christians,[16] that they soon became a firmly established normative tradition. A more cultivated literary version would never have found acceptance. Jerome's new translation was relatively late (c. 400);

16. Up to the middle of the third century the language of Christians in Rome was Greek. See T. Klauser, in *Miscellanea Giovanni Mercati*, I.

he did not revise all parts of the Bible with equal thoroughness, and where he deviated appreciably from the customary version, the congregations were slow to accept his wording. But above all, the Biblical Latin had long been established by the time Jerome began to write; Jerome himself was so deeply immersed in this style and, generally speaking, in early Christian habits of thought that, even if he had wished to, he would not have been able to modify the early Christian atmosphere of Biblical Latin. For all his merit as a translator, he remained within the limits of a general style that had already been established. We find occasional classical paraphrases of Bible passages in late antiquity; Fulgentius Planciades (*De aetatibus mundi*) paraphrases God's words to Moses, Exod. 3:7, as follows: *Duros populi mei ex operationis ergastulo gemitus intellexi* (I have heard the heavy sighs of my people, rising up from the dungeons of toil). This tendency remained without influence; it reappeared only with the Humanists (Valla, Bembo, Erasmus): Bembo, for example, replaced *Spiritus sanctus* (the Holy Spirit) by *divinae mentis aura* (the breath of the divine mind).[17]

Thus the Holy Scriptures remained a foreign body in Latin literature as long as the classical tradition survived and as long as there were men who preserved a feeling for classical style. In reply to those who looked down on the language of the Bible, the apologists (exemplified by Augustine) never wearied of repeating that the Scriptures also contained rhetorical figures; they even went so far as to say that all the nations had derived not only their eloquence but all the true wisdom in their possession from the Old Testament, which was far older than the heathen cultures.[18]

17. On Biblical language see W. Süss, "Das Problem der lateinischen Bibelsprache" (my Bembo quotation, ibid., 17); and the same author's "Studien zur lateinischen Bibel I." Both studies give bibliography of earlier investigations.—The relevant portions of Norden's *Antike Kunstprosa* are still very informative on patristic Latin.

18. Excellently treated by E. R. Curtius, *Europ. Lit.*, pp. 48f. [Amer. edn., p. 41], in the paragraph on Cassiodorus. The main passage in Cassiodorus is *In Psalterium praefatio* 15 (PL, LXX, 19–22). Cf. also Curtius, p. 445 [Amer. edn., pp. 446f.], where Curtius's remark about Jerome's reference to Peter and John in his Letter to Paulinus does not quite convey its tone

In its application to stylistic questions this argument was none too effective. No one, to be sure, thought of replying that it was relevant only to the original Hebrew text; the Western Church Fathers, with the obvious exception of Jerome, had little feeling for philology and tended to treat the Latin text as though it were *the* Bible. But it was difficult, if not impossible, to find classical eloquence in the Latin Bible. Cassiodorus, perhaps the most consistent Western advocate of the theory that all eloquence (and wisdom) originated in the Bible, still acknowledged the difference between secular and Biblical style: the tropes and figures, he says, are present in the Psalms *in virtute sensuum*, not *in effatione verborum* (embedded in the meaning, not in the actual words).[19] In any case no apologist of late antiquity doubted that Biblical Latin represented a break with the classical tradition. It was only toward 700, when the feeling for this tradition had died out, that Aldhelm and Bede were able to praise the Bible as a model of classical style.

The serious and enduring argument put forward by the Christian writers of late antiquity was a very different one: they recognized the "lowliness" of the Biblical style, which, they pointed out, possessed a new and more profound sublimity. This dialectical position, in which the problem of translation was ignored, carried force because of its inner truth; at once offensive and defensive, it lived through the Middle Ages and into the modern era; it played a significant part in molding later European views on style and style levels. This idea was formulated at an early date; it is expressed implicitly in several of the above-quoted passages from the New Testament, e.g., I Cor. 1:18–21. Early Greek examples, such as Origen versus Celsus,[20] need not be listed here. Latin ex-

---

and context. Actually Jerome is drawing a contrast between spiritually inspired knowledge and profane knowledge. The notion, probably Judaeo-Alexandrine in origin, that profane and, more especially, Greek wisdom was derived from the much older Jewish wisdom is quite general in the West and is voiced with particular frequency by Ambrose. Cf. *De bono mortis*, PL, XIV, 1154. On Aldhelm and Bede, cf. Curtius, pp. 53–55 [Amer. edn., pp. 45–47].

19. *In Psalterium praefatio* 15 (PL, LXX, 21).
20. Cf. W. Süss, "Das Problem der lateinischen Bibelsprache," 5.

amples are frequent throughout late antiquity down to Isidore of Seville (*Sent.* 3.13; *PL*, LXXXIII, 685–688). The most important Latin witness to it is Augustine, because he personally went through the dialectical reversal it implies; before his conversion he himself had been one of those highly cultivated men who thought they would never be able to overcome their distaste for the style of the Bible. In the *Confessions* (3.5; *CSEL*, XXXIII, 50) he relates how, as a young man, fired by Cicero's *Hortensius* with a passionate yearning for wisdom, he had begun to read the Holy Scriptures but had not yet perceived their true worth; they were *res incessu humilis, successu excelsa et velata mysteriis* (a lowly thing at first, but then sublime and veiled in mysteries), but of this he was not yet aware:

> sed visa est mihi indigna, quam Tullianae dignitati conpararem. Tumor enim meus refugiebat modum eius et acies mea non penetrabat interiora eius. Verumtamen illa erat, quae cresceret cum parvulis, sed ego dedignabar esse parvulus. . . .
>
> They seemed to me unworthy to be compared with the majesty of Cicero. My conceit was repelled by their simplicity, and I had not the mind to penetrate into their depths. They were indeed of a nature to grow in Your little ones. But I could not bear to be a little one. . . . (Tr. F. J. Sheed)

It was only much later, after long and painful vicissitudes, that he began, under the influence of Ambrose in Milan, to understand the authority of Scripture and to formulate it as follows (*Conf.* 6.5; *CSEL*, XXXIII, 121f.):

> eoque mihi illa venerabilior et sacrosancta fide dignior apparebat auctoritas, quo et omnibus ad legendum esset in promtu, et secreti sui dignitatem in intellectu profundiore servaret, verbis apertissimis et humillimo genere loquendi se cunctis praebens, et exercens intentionem eorum, qui non sunt leves corde, ut exciperet omnes populari sinu et per angusta foramina paucos ad te traiceret, multo tamen

plures, quam si nec tanto apice auctoritatis emineret nec
turbas gremio sanctae humilitatis hauriret.

Indeed the authority of Scripture seemed to be more worthy of
reverence and of devoted faith in that it was at once a book that
all could read and read easily, and yet preserved the majesty of
its mystery in the deepest part of its meaning: for it offers itself
to all in the plainest words and the simplest expressions, yet demands the closest attention of the most serious minds. Thus it
receives all within its welcoming arms, and at the same time
brings a few direct to You by narrow ways: yet these few would
be fewer still but for this twofold quality by which it stands so
lofty in authority yet draws the multitude to its bosom by its
holy lowliness. . . . (Tr. F. J. Sheed, mod.)

The same ideas, in many variations, occur frequently in his
writings, for example in the first chapter of the first book of *De
Trinitate* (PL, XLII, 820):

> . . . sancta Scriptura parvulis congruens, nullius generis
> rerum verba vitavit, ex quibus quasi gradatim ad divina
> atque sublimia noster intellectus velut nutritus assurgeret—

> . . . Holy Writ, adapting itself to babes, has not been afraid to
> use expressions taken from any kind of thing, from which, as
> though drawing food from it, our understanding may rise grad-
> ually to things lofty and sublime—

There are several similar passages in *De doctrina christiana* (e.g.,
2.42.63) and scattered here and there in the sermons and commentaries. But I find the most complete statement in a letter
addressed to Volusianus:

> Modus autem ipse dicendi, quo sancta scriptura contexi-
> tur, quam omnibus accessibilis, quamvis paucissimis pene-
> trabilis! Ea, quae aperta continet, quasi amicus familiaris
> sine fuco ad cor loquitur indoctorum atque doctorum; ea
> vero, quae in mysteriis occultat, nec ipsa eloquio superbo
> erigit, quo non audeat accedere mens tardiuscula et ineru-
> dita quasi pauper ad divitem, sed invitat omnes humili ser-
> mone, quos non solum manifesta pascat, sed etiam secreta
> exerceat veritate, hoc in promptis quod in reconditis habens.

> How accessible to everyone is the style of Holy Writ, though only a very few can penetrate its depths! Those clear truths it contains it speaks without subterfuge, like an old friend, to the hearts of learned and unlearned alike. But even the truths which it hides in mysteries are not couched in such lofty style that a slow, uncultivated mind would not dare to approach them, as a poor man does not dare to approach a rich one. Rather by its lowly speech it summons all men, not only in order to nourish them by its plain truths, but also in order to form them by means of its secret truth [*exercere* here means at the same time to form, to sharpen, to test], having the same truth both in its open and its hidden parts. (*Epist.* 137.18; *CSEL*, XLIV, 122f.)

It had become clear to him, he writes (*De doctr. chr.* 4.6.9f.), that the Christian authors, inspired by Providence for our salvation, could not have written otherwise than they did. If he cared to take the time, it would be a simple matter to demonstrate that all the figures and ornaments of pagan eloquence were present in their writings; however, what delighted him beyond measure was not what they had in common with the pagan orators and other writers, but the way in which they fashioned new eloquence of their own, *alteram quandam eloquentiam suam*, from the language of the common people.[21]

I shall now try to sum up the ideas contained in these statements. It is recognized that the style of the Bible is "lowly," the word most frequently employed being *humilis*,[22] which also denotes humility. The purpose of this humility or lowliness of style is to make the Scriptures available to all; the humblest of men should be drawn to them, moved by them, at home in them. Yet Scripture is not always simple; it contains mysteries and hidden meaning; much of it seems obscure. But even the difficult ideas are not pre-

21. Cf. Cassiodorus, *Institutiones* (ed. Mynors) 1.15.7 *sub finem: maneat ubique incorrupta locutio quae Deo placuisse cognoscitur, ita ut fulgore suo niteat, non humano desiderio carpienda subiaceat* (let the expression which is known to have pleased God remain everywhere unchanged so that its brightness may shine forth and not be subordinated to the requirements of human wishes).

22. Also found are: *rusticus, communis, simplex,* and *vilis.* Cf., for example, Jerome's commentary on Galatians 3.5; his letter to Paulinus 53.9; from Cassiodorus the passage in his *Institutiones* 1.15.7 (cited above, n. 21) and in *In Psalt. praef.* 15; finally Isidore, *Sententiae* 3.13.

sented in a learned, "haughty" style that would intimidate and repel the simple man. On the contrary, anyone who is not light-minded (hence, superficial and lacking in humility) can find his way to the deeper meaning; Scripture "grows with the children," that is to say, children grow into an understanding of it. Nevertheless, few get to the core of it; the essential is not learning but true humility (*De doctr. chr.* 2.41–42) in keeping with the humility of the style: there is no fundamental difference between the profound, obscure passages and those that are clear and simple; the former merely open up deeper levels of understanding. The consequence is that those who yearn for pious wisdom and are aware of the depth of the mystery are maintained in a state of tension and yearning, for no one can penetrate to the ultimate core. While sometimes useful, learning is by no means essential to profound understanding; true understanding on earth can spring only from a momentary contact (*ictu*), an illumination, which can be preserved for no more than a brief moment, after which one sinks back into one's accustomed earthly state.

Thus the style of the Scriptures throughout is *humilis*, lowly or humble. Even the hidden things (*secreta, recondita*) are set forth in a "lowly" vein. But the subject matter, whether simple or obscure, is sublime. The lowly, or humble, style is the only medium in which such sublime mysteries can be brought within the reach of men. It constitutes a parallel to the Incarnation, which was also a *humilitas* in the same sense, for men could not have endured the splendor of Christ's divinity.[23] But the Incarnation, as it actually happened on earth, could only be narrated in a lowly and humble style. The birth of Christ in a manger in Bethlehem, his life among fishermen, publicans, and other common men, the Passion with its realistic and "scandalous" episodes—none of this could have been treated appropriately in the lofty oratorical, tragic, or epic style. According to the Augustan esthetic, such matters were

---

23. This is an old and significant theme, generally found in connection with the interpretation of the cloud in Isa. 19:1. It already occurs in this form in Tertullian, *Adversus Marcionem* 2.27, and is still frequent in Bernard of Clairvaux, and indeed in Dante (*Purg.* 30.25ff.).

worthy, at best, of the lower literary genres. But the lowly style of Scripture encompasses the sublime. Simple, vulgar, and crassly realistic words are employed, the syntax is often colloquial and inelegant; but the sublimity of the subject matter shines through the lowliness, and there is hidden meaning at every turn. The sublime content (*res excelsa et velata mysteriis, secreti sui dignitas*) is often obscure and hidden, but even then, thanks to the lowliness of the presentation, the common man can partake of it. The common denominator of this style is its humility.

But the Bible is written history; it was read or listened to by the vast majority of Christians. It shaped their view of history,[24] their ethical and esthetic conceptions. Both consciously and by a process of continued unconscious assimilation, Christian writers were influenced by it and modeled their styles on it. To be sure, they soon made a certain adaptation to traditional rhetoric; many of the Church Fathers were schooled in it, some intensively. But the Biblical and Christian substance was so overwhelming that rhetorical considerations became secondary. We have seen in our initial quotation from Augustine how, despite isocola, anaphoras, antitheses, and apostrophes, the dominant tone is peculiarly Christian. The same applies to numerous other texts in patristic literature, such as the above-cited (p. 44) passage from Jerome about the Last Judgment, with its overpowering conclusion: *cerne manus, Iudaee . . . cerne latus, Romane. . . .* Here we have a mixture of sublimity, popular rhetoric, and tender *caritas*, forcefully didactic and dramatically alive, addressed to a general and indiscriminate audience.

24. Especially in connection with the typological exegesis of the Bible, I have written on several occasions on the Christian conception of history (Christ's sojourn on earth as the center of universal history), which in my opinion was a necessary consequence of Christianity. "Figura," reprinted in my *Neue Dantestudien;* "Typological Symbolism in Medieval Literature," which appeared in German (somewhat expanded) as the second fascicle of the *Schriften und Vorträge des Petrarca-Instituts in Köln* [Eng. tr. in *Scenes from the Drama of European Literature,* pp. 11–76; see Auerbach bibliography, end of this vol.]. Cf. also the last pages of my essay "Franz von Assisi in der Komödie" in *Neue Dantestudien,* which appeared in English in *Italica,* xxii; and my *Mimesis,* passim.

As we have seen, the common people were great lovers of rhetoric. But under their influence a more popular rhetoric developed, paving the way for a specifically Christian style of oratory. It is no exaggeration to say that such a rhetoric was first made possible by the Christian spirit and by Christian themes. For what with the political stagnation of the declining Roman Empire, pagan rhetoric had long been deprived of the themes which gave it vitality. Drained of its life blood, it had succumbed to a rigid formalism. Christianity gave it new life, at the same time changing its character. The keynote now was *humilitas*. Augustine recommended the academic forms of pagan eloquence and even made use of them, but what really strikes us and leaves a lasting impression in his sermons is the directness with which, setting aside all barriers between style levels, they speak to each individual soul. Every single auditor is considered as an individual whose salvation is at stake. The consequence is that far more emotion goes into such a sermon than would have been possible in a philosophical discourse or legal exposition. Even didactic passages take on the soul-stirring quality which rhetorical theory identified with the sublime. And teaching lay within the province of the low style not only because rhetorical theory had so ordained but because the heterogeneous character of the congregations made it necessary to teach in a simple style that all could understand.

We have taken a sermon as the basis of our investigation. But the domain of *sermo humilis* in late antiquity includes all the forms of Christian literature. It pervades philosophical disquisitions as well as realistic records of events. We shall cite a few examples to show on the one hand how deeply it affected theoretical literature and on the other what new problems it solved in the realm of narrative.

The Church Fathers wrote little of a serene, purely contemplative, or theoretical nature; their purpose in writing was to disseminate Christian doctrine and to combat the Jews, the heathen, and the heretics. All their theorizing is shot through with polemic or apologetic designs; the intention throughout is to influence as many people as possible, to win souls. Of course sermons addressed to the congregation differ in style level from treatises, commentaries, or letters intended for friends or enemies among the clergy. But even in the latter case the didactic element is so strong, the tone is so personal and animated, that the *sermo humilis* takes on a specifically Christian coloration. In this connection I have chosen another example from Augustine; I thought at first of selecting a polemical text, but then decided that a purely contemplative and theoretical passage would be more characteristic precisely because such writing represents the extreme limit of the domain of *sermo humilis*. The passage occurs in the second chapter of the eighth book of *De Trinitate* (*PL*, XLII, 948ff.). Augustine is trying to explain that God is neither corporeal, nor subject to change, nor created; even were we to conceive of the greatest and most sublime things, the sun for example, as infinitely greater and brighter than they are, or even were we to consider all the angels, *millia millium*, who move the heavenly bodies, as one—we should still not have God. Then he continues:

> Ecce vide, si potes, o anima praegravata corpore quod corrumpitur, et onusta terrenis cogitationibus multis et variis; ecce vide, si potes: Deus Veritas est. Hoc enim scriptum est: "Quoniam Deus lux est" (I Ioan. 1:5)—non quomodo isti oculi vident, sed quomodo videt cor, cum audis: "Veritas est." Noli quaerere quid sit veritas; statim enim se opponent caligines imaginum corporalium et nubila phantasmatum, et perturbabunt serenitatem, quae primo ictu diluxit tibi, cum dicerem: "Veritas." Ecce in ipso primo ictu quo velut coruscatione perstringeris, cum dicitur: "Veritas," mane si potes; sed non potes; relaberis in ista solita atque terrena.

> Behold if you can the soul, weighed down by the body of corruption and by many earthly thoughts of various kinds. And now behold if you can: God is truth. For it is written that God is light; not as the eye sees it, but as the heart sees it when you hear: "He is truth." Do not ask what truth is. For mists of corporeal images and clouds of phantasm will rise forthwith and confuse the clarity that flared up in you in a first impulse when I said: "Truth." When

the word truth is spoken, remain if you can in that first impulse which struck you as a flash of lightning. But you cannot; you fall back into this world of familiar, earthly things. . . .

Immediately thereafter (Chap. 3, par. 4), he tries another approach:

Ecce iterum vide, si potes. Non amas certe nisi bonum, quia bona est terra altitudine montium et temperamento collium et planitie camporum, et bonum praedium amoenum ac fertile, et bona domus paribus membris disposita et ampla et lucida, et bona animalia animata corpora, et bonus aer modestus et salubris, et bonus cibus suavis atque aptus valetudini, et bona valetudo sine doloribus et lassitudine, et bona facies hominis dimensa pariliter et affecta hilariter et luculenter colorata, et bonus animus amici consensionis dulcedine et amoris fide, et bonus vir justus, et bonae divitiae, quia facile expediunt, et bonum coelum cum sole et luna et stellis suis, et boni Angeli sancta obedientia, et bona locutio suaviter docens et congruenter monens audientem, et bonum carmen canorum numeris et sententiis grave. Quid plura et plura? Bonum hoc et bonum illud; tolle hoc et illud, et vide ipsum bonum, si potes; ita Deum videbis, non alio bono bonum, sed bonum omnis boni.

Try once again if you can. Assuredly you love only what is good. For good is the earth with its high mountains and gentle hills and level fields. And good is a smiling and fertile farm, and good is a well-ordered house, spacious and bright; and good are the bodies of living things, and good is mild and wholesome air, and good is pleasant and healthful food, and good is health, free from pain and weariness. And good is a human face with regular features, a cheerful expression, and high color, and good is the heart of a friend for sweet understanding and faithful love. And good is a righteous man, and good are riches, because they make life easier, and good is the sky with sun, moon, and stars, and good are the angels in their holy obedience. And good is speech that instructs the hearer in a friendly way and gives him appropriate counsel, and good is a song of high-sounding melody and weighty meaning. But why go on? This is good and that is good: take away this and that and look upon the Good itself if you can; then you will see God, who is good not by virtue of another good, but is the goodness of all good things.

These ideas are at once Neoplatonic and Christian. Expressed in their simplest form, they are purely abstract; they are among the ideas from which the great game of abstractions developed in the Middle Ages. God is truth; only in momentary illumination can we on earth know Him. God is the absolute good, the source of all particular goods. From this simple statement Augustine made a moving rhetorical drama—in the first passage with the anaphorical, antithetical movement, *ecce vide si potes, ecce vide si potes, noli quaerere, ecce . . . mane si potes, sed non potes;* in the second passage, again anaphorical, with its tender, profoundly earthly enumeration of good things and the sudden, stormy change of tone at the end: *Bonum hoc et bonum illud; tolle hoc et illud.* . . . The dramatic ascent from the lowly world, which remains present even when Augustine rises, carrying his readers with him, to heights of ecstasy and abstraction, the furious urgency of his plea, in which all theory seems forgotten, the direct appeal to the reader, whoever he may be—all these shatter every barrier between you and me: such a style level would have been almost inconceivable at an earlier day. *Ecce vide si potes* and *tolle hoc et illud* are at once rhetorical and colloquial. It has often been noted that Augustine employs vulgarisms, that he relates anecdotes and uses realistic images; [25] and his sermons, like those of Jerome, include satirical passages.

But this is not our central concern at this point. Of course vulgarisms and realism are significant hallmarks of the Christian *sermo humilis,* but only because they are used in speaking of serious and profound matters, and because such "low locutions" are transformed by their contact with the serious and the sublime. The crux of the matter is the extent of the polarity. And the *sermo humilis,* as I am trying to describe it here, has other fea-

---

25. A number of relevant passages are quoted in such recent studies as J.-T. Welter, *L'Exemplum dans la littérature religieuse,* etc.; J. H. B[axter], *ALMA,* III (with a characteristic passage from *Sermo* 5.3); H. F. Muller, *L'Époque mérovingienne,* pp. 41–45. Cf. also P. Charles, "L'Élément populaire dans les sermons de saint-Augustin," and of course also J. Schrijnen, *Charakteristik des altchristlichen Latein,* passim.

tures besides vulgarisms and the like: one is its implication of direct human contact between you and me, a note that was lacking in the sublime style of Roman antiquity; another is its power to express human brotherhood, an immediate bond between men: all of us here and now. Often, to be sure, the expression of warmth and neighborliness degenerated into an empty formula; but time and time again new life was breathed into it. My primary purpose in quoting the passage from the *De Trinitate* was to show precisely that this style also pervaded the most speculative and least popular writing. Joseph Schrijnen, to whom and to whose school [26] we owe the concept of Christian Latin and highly interesting investigations on the subject, overestimates, it seems to me, the difference between the cultivated and the popular Latin of the earliest Christians. Unquestionably there is a difference; Augustine, for example, writes one way in his sermons and another way in his exegetic and dogmatic works. Gregory the Great still used a much more popular style in his dialogues than in the *Moralia*. But the spirit of the *sermo humilis* is everywhere the same. And when Schrijnen claims that the figures of speech employed in Augustine's sermons bear no relation to academic rhetoric, he is merely giving in to a prejudice which he himself expressed in the following terms: "Where the soul rises up to God, whether the language employed be cultivated or popular Latin, there is no room, in the opinion of St. Augustine, for rhetoric or refined artistry; the popular rhythms of everyday human speech are in order." [27] This, it seems to me, is a hypostatization of concepts (cultivated artistry, popular rhythm) which we ourselves have created as a means of classification and provisional orientation but which, in actual practice, can seldom be clearly distinguished. Shakespeare or the Spanish dramatists of the *siglo de oro* show

26. Cf. n. 25. Further references to Schrijnen and his school in Christine Mohrmann, "Le Latin commun et le Latin des Chrétiens," especially nn. 1 and 4. The meticulous and instructive *Manuel du latin chrétien* by A. Blaise appeared only after the publication of the present paper in 1952. See there especially the summary in § 45, pp. 64–66.
27. *Charakteristik d. altchristl. Latein*, p. 21 and passim.

that the subtlest artistry in the use of word or sound can be incorporated in the popular tradition. If rhetorical art ceased when the soul soars to God, we should have to conclude that this experience was unknown to most of the great Christian authors. What of Ambrose and Jerome, of Bernard of Clairvaux, of John of the Cross, of Bossuet? What, for that matter, of the Apostle Paul? Augustine's rhetoric is always grounded in the classic tradition; a writer in "simple popular rhythms" cannot play with antitheses, he cannot oppose or combine pairs of concepts in resounding periods. On the other hand, even the most elaborate rhetoric has its source in the basic human instinct for rhythm and the correspondence between meaning and sound; and in late antiquity the rhetorical art had become a popular heritage at least to the extent that multitudes of people were able to enjoy it. As his early career shows, Augustine was a master of rhetoric; rhetoric had become second nature with him, as it does with great virtuosos. But supreme skill can very well serve the deepest and most sincere feeling; and popular simplicity is no guarantee against emptiness of heart.

It would be a mistake, I think, to speak of a specifically Christian language characterized solely by a popular "earthiness" or "pithiness." "Christian Latin" contains many popular elements; for in so large a movement, embracing many men and finally extending to the whole population, the common people were bound to exert a dominant influence on the language, if only because they are more numerous than the upper classes. But the characteristic feature of this language, I believe, is that many, if not all, the vulgarisms in the use and formation of words, in shifts of meaning, and in sentence structure, ceased to be vulgarisms the moment they became Christian Latin; they entered into another sphere and took on a new dignity. This applies even to such extreme cases as *manducare* and *eructare* (literally "to gobble with much chewing" and "to belch."). Time and again these words were ridiculed, but the congregations did not give them up; they were retained even in such weighty passages as the beginning of the forty-fourth Psalm and in the account of the Last Supper (I Cor. 11:24). Such words were exalted and sanctified, *sanctificantur;* and the same is true of the new compounds, awkward and wooden for classical taste, of which *sanctificare* is but one example among many. Others are *vivificare, honorificare, glorificare; salvator, fornicator, mediator; tribulatio, prostitutio, redemptio; carnalis, spiritualis, inscrutabilis, inenarrabilis, ineffabiliter, inseparabiliter,* to offer only a small selection. Strictly speaking, these are not popular forms; they did not spring from the language of daily life but are intellectual formations devised by writers not fully versed in the spirit of classical Latin, as means of designating the concepts of a new intellectual world. They all have about them something awkward, half-educated, and heavily pedantic; yet at the same time, because of the spirit that emanates from them, a striking homogeneity. They go together, and they also fit in with other, purely popular elements of the Christian language. In each and all of them a new world is expressed, a world powerful enough to create its own special language; but is it not this same language that will soon become the language of all men, or at least saturate the universal idiom with its specific character? It is assuredly of interest to the modern historian to know that this special language was made up of different elements, but this was not true of the people who spoke it; to them it was a matter of indifference whether a particular feature in their language stemmed from everyday speech or from the endeavor of semi-educated men to find expression for new ideas, or whether Greek or Semitic influence was at work; such elements in any case were absorbed into the language of the Christian community. What Paul (I Cor. 12:13) said of men was equally applicable to words and turns of phrase: *Etenim in uno Spiritu, omnes nos in unum corpus baptizati sumus, sive Judaei, sive gentiles, sive servi, sive liberi* (For by one Spirit are we all baptized into one body, whether we be Jews or Gentiles, whether we be bond or free). Tertullian shows at how early a date the Latin-speaking community acquired an individuality of its own.

Our third and last ancient text is drawn from this period. Unlike the passage from *De Trinitate*, it shows the realistic narrative force of the *sermo humilis;* at the same time, it gives an idea of the new kind of realistic narrative fostered by the spread of Christianity. The text in question, the *Passio SS. Perpetuae et Felicitatis*,[28] is one of the earliest martyrologies. The events related took place in Carthage at the beginning of the third century, during the persecutions under Septimius Severus. The narrator (probably not Tertullian) incorporates in his text the notes taken in prison by two of the martyrs, Perpetua and Saturus. In the following we quote the narrator's introduction (2) and the beginning of Perpetua's record (3, 4):

2. Apprehensi sunt adolescentes catechumeni: Revocatus et Felicitas, conserva eius, Saturninus et Secundulus; inter hos et Vibia Perpetua, honeste nata, liberaliter instituta, matronaliter nupta, habens patrem et matrem et fratres duos, alterum aeque catechumenum, et filium infantem ad ubera. Erat autem ipsa circiter annorum viginti duo. Haec ordinem totum martyrii sui iam hinc ipsa narravit, sicut conscriptum manu sua et suo sensu reliquit.

3. Cum adhuc, inquit, cum prosecutoribus essemus et me pater verbis evertere cupiret, et deicere pro sua affectione perseveraret; "Pater," inquam, "vides, verbi gratia, vas hoc iacens, urceolum sive aliud?" Et dixit: "Video." Et ego dixi ei: "Numquid alio nomine vocari potest quam quod est?" Et ait: "Non." "Sic et ego aliud me dicere non possum nisi quod sum, Christiana." Tunc pater motus hoc

28. Text in the *Acta Sanctorum* for March 7th; most conveniently accessible in the *Ausgewählte Märtyrerakten*, ed. by O. L. von Gebhardt or by R. Knopf (3rd edn. by G. Krüger). Most recent edition, *Passio Sanctarum Perpetuae et Felicitatis* by C. J. M. J. van Beek. In English, by E. C. E. Owen in *Some Authentic Acts of the Early Martyrs*, pp. 78–92. I have not seen the German translations by Rauschen (Bibliothek der Kirchenväter) and by Hagemeyer.–Since the discovery of a Greek version in 1839, several scholars have expressed their opinion that the Greek text is the original. I have worked on the assumption that it is the Latin version that is the original, a view that is probably held at the present time by most scholars. Cf. E. Rupprecht in *Rheinisches Museum* (1941). A comprehensive survey and French translation of the *Passio* by H. Leclercq in *DACL*, s.v. "Perpétue et Félicité (Saintes)."

verbo mittit se in me, ut oculos mihi erueret, sed vexavit tantum, et profectus est victus cum argumentis diaboli. Tunc paucis diebus quod caruissem patre, Domino gratias egi, et refrigeravi absentia illius. In ipso spatio paucorum dierum baptizati sumus, et mihi Spiritus dictavit non aliud petendum ab aqua nisi sufferentiam carnis. Post paucos dies recipimur in carcerem: et expavi, quia numquam experta eram tales tenebras. O diem asperum! Aestus validus turbarum beneficio, concussurae militum. Novissime macerabar sollicitudine infantis ibi. Tunc Tertius et Pomponius, benedicti diaconi qui nobis ministrabant, constituerunt praemio uti paucis horis emissi in meliorem locum carceris refrigeraremus. Tunc exeuntes de carcere universi sibi vacabant. Ego infantem lactabam iam inedia defectum; sollicita pro eo adloquebar matrem et confortabam fratrem, commendabam filium; tabescebam ideo quod illos tabescere videram mei beneficio. Tales sollicitudines multis diebus passa sum; et usurpavi ut mecum infans in carcere maneret; et statim convaluit et relevata sum a labore et sollicitudine infantis, et factus est mihi carcer subito praetorium, ut ibi mallem esse quam alicubi.

4. Tunc dixit mihi frater meus: Domina soror, iam in magna dignatione es, tanta ut postules visionem et ostendatur tibi an passio sit an commeatus. Et ego quae me sciebam fabulari cum Domino, cuius beneficia tanta experta eram, fidenter repromisi ei, dicens: Crastina die tibi renuntiabo. Et postulavi, et ostensum est mihi hoc: Video scalam aeream mirae magnitudinis pertingentem usque ad caelum. . . .

The translation that follows also includes some comments; I cannot be certain that I have always hit upon the correct interpretation.

2. The young catechumens [i.e., those still unbaptized but being prepared for baptism] Revocatus and his fellow slave-woman Felicitas were arrested along with Saturninus and Secundulus. And with them also Vibia Perpetua, a young woman of distinguished family, carefully educated, and married in keeping with her station; she had a father and mother and two brothers, one

of whom was also a catechumen, and a child, a boy, at the breast. [There is no mention whatever of the husband.] She was about twenty-two years old. From this point on she herself has narrated the whole story of her martyrdom. Her account, written in her own hand, is quoted as she left it.

3. While we were still—so she relates—under police surveillance [and thus not yet in prison], and while my father was attempting to make me change my mind by his words and, because of his love for me, trying to undermine my decision, I said to him: "Father, do you see, let us say, that vessel standing over there, a small jug or something of the kind?" "Yes, I see it," he said. And I said to him: "Can one call it by any other name than that which indicates what it is?" And he said: "No."—"Nor can I call myself anything else but what I am, a Christian."—Then my father, infuriated by these words, hurled himself at me as if he wanted to tear my eyes out; but he merely shook me and then he went away, vanquished along with his arguments, which were those of the devil. Then I did not see him for a few days, and I gave thanks to God and recovered because of his absence. And during those few days we were baptized, and the Holy Spirit inspired me to ask nothing from the waters of baptism but endurance of the flesh. A few days later we were taken to prison; and I was horrified, for I had never experienced such darkness. What a terrible day! The air was appalling because of the press of people, not to mention the extortions of the soldiers; besides, I was tormented by worry about my child in such a place. Then the venerable deacons, Tertius and Pomponius, who were ministering to us, obtained permission by means of a money bribe for us to recuperate for a few hours in a better part of the prison. Then all of us left the deeper prison and were able to care for ourselves. The child had already become weak from hunger, and I gave him the breast. Full of concern, I spoke about him to my mother, comforted my brother, and handed over my son to them. I also suffered because I saw them suffering on account of me. I bore such hardships for many days. And I succeeded in arranging to have the child remain in prison with me, and at once it recovered, and I was freed from concern and distress about the child; and suddenly the prison became a palace for me, so that there was nowhere I would rather have been than there.

4. Then my brother said to me: "My lady sister, you are now in such an exalted state of grace that you can ask for a vision, so that it may be revealed to you whether this is a martyrdom or a passing ordeal." And I, who was aware that I was speaking with the Lord, from whom I had already experienced so many

benefactions, promised this with full assurance, saying: "To-morrow I will let you know." And I made the request, and this was shown to me: I see a bronze ladder, of enormous size, reaching right up to heaven. . . .

There is no rhetorical art in Perpetua's narrative. The careful education she had received is hardly reflected in her style. Her vocabulary is limited; her sentence structure is clumsy, the connectives (frequent use of *tunc*) are not always clear. A specialist cannot help noting the many vulgarisms (such as *mittit se* for *ruit*) and typically Christian locutions (such as *refrigerare*). The language in general is brittle, quite unliterary, naïve, almost childlike. And yet Perpetua is expressive. She speaks of things that do not occur elsewhere in ancient literature: the obstinate zeal with which, illustrating her argument with her little jug, she explains to her father that she is a Christian and can call herself nothing else; her father's fit of impotent rage; the first hours in prison, in the stifling darkness, among the soldiers, with her famished child; the happiness she comes to experience in prison; and perhaps most striking of all, her dialogue with her brother, both so very young, radiant with ecstasy at the thought of the test ahead: *Domina soror, iam in magna dignatione es.* . . . And her confident "To-morrow I will let you know."

Ancient literature had its Antigone, but there was nothing like this, nor could there be; [29] there was no literary genre capable of presenting such a reality with so much dignity and elevation, and there was no *gloria passionis*. Antigone went to her death full of dignity, but lamenting, not triumphant. Perhaps it will be argued that the Acts of Perpetua are not a literary document. That is true; they were not, like the mimes and satires, conceived as a literary work. But they were destined to circulate widely; hundreds of thousands of people would hear of them; similar things would happen in other places to other people; these in turn would

29. This applies, obviously, only to the question of style that is here discussed. I am aware that many ancient ideas are to be found in the *Passio* of Perpetua. Cf. especially F. J. Dölger, "Antike Parallelen zum leidenden Dinocrates in der Passio Perpetuae," in *Antike und Christentum*, II, 1–40.

be recorded and tales would be spun. A literary genre would develop, and here we see it coming into being. In its beginnings it disclosed the full force of the crude reality in which these plain people who chanced to be called to martyrdom celebrated their triumph of suffering; everything—the persecutors, the scene of martyrdom, the happenings in the wholly or partly pagan families of the martyrs—is treated with unadorned realism. Yet this humble everyday reality is transfigured, it takes on a new *gravitas*. The father with his "diabolical" arguments is a tragic figure; Perpetua senses it and cannot help him. Later (6) at the trial he again tries desperately to make her change her mind, and only the rods of the court attendants can drive him off. Speaking of this incident, Perpetua writes: *et doluit mihi patris mei, quasi ego fuissem percussa; sic dolui pro senecta eius misera* (and I suffered for my father as though I myself had been beaten; I sorrowed for his unhappy old age). In the ensuing account, interrupted by visions, of the events in prison, an entirely new style level develops. The fate of the slave-woman Felicitas, who gives birth prematurely in prison, is interpreted in triumphant antitheses: her fellow prisoners and she herself are filled with joy that she has thus been enabled to suffer martyrdom with them all (18): *a sanguine ad sanguinem, ab obstetrice ad retiarium, lotura post partum baptismo secundo* (from blood to blood, from the midwife to the gladiator, to be washed after her travail by a second baptism). They were all familiar with the idea of baptism by blood. When Saturus, leader of the group who had converted them all, is carried out of the arena covered with blood, the populace shouts: *Salvum lotum, salvum lotum!* (May the bath do you good!) This was the customary good wish proffered after the bath. But the narrator interprets these cruelly ironical words as *secundi baptismatis testimonium. . . . Plane utique salvus erat qui hoc modo laverat* (a testimony to second baptism. . . . Clearly indeed he was fortunate who had washed in this way).

The mixture, discernible in the Acts of Perpetua and related documents, of elements that had formerly seemed incompatible—

that is, the presence of the tragic or sublime in a lowly existence depicted with the utmost realism—has its model, in literature as well as reality, in Christ's Passion as related in the Gospels. This also is the source of the motif of the *gloria passionis*, the triumph of suffering.[30]

Few texts can be compared with the Acts of Perpetua; even the authentic martyrologies of the third century seldom give so detailed and penetrating a description of persons and situations. In most cases it is only the trial that is recorded with dramatic vividness, and sometimes even authentic documents incline toward the conventions of legend. Later, when the persecutions had come to an end, the martyrologies became a distinct literary genre, characterized by the miraculous and by legendary types.[31] But even these schematic works disclose the same spirit, for it is implicit in the subject matter. It is always an ordinary individual who is picked out from his ordinary real-life situation, from his family, social class, or profession—however schematic or legendary the treatment of these circumstances may be—and called upon to bear witness; the holy sublimity of the event is rooted in everyday life, and even amid the trials and torments inflicted on the saint, a kind of realism prevails. It was this realism that I wished to stress by citing the passage from the Acts of Perpetua. It fits in with the previously discussed characteristics of *sermo humilis:* accessible to all, descending to all men in loving-kindness, secretly sublime, at one with the whole Christian congregation. But on the whole, I believe, it can be grasped most easily and concretely in the way here attempted: as a blending of two realms, the sublime and the lowly, expressed in the semantic development of the word *humilis*.

This kind of *sermo humilis* was employed in Christian literature throughout the Middle Ages and even afterward. We shall have frequent occasion to refer to it. The greatest document of this

---

30. See the following Excursus.
31. H. Delehaye, *Les Passions des martyrs et les genres littéraires,* is relevant here.

Christian sublimity is Dante's *Divine Comedy;* for this reason I shall conclude this chapter with a quotation from Benvenuto da Imola, the commentator on Dante, whose words gave me my first idea, many years ago, of how to treat this problem. Commenting on *Inferno* 2.56—*e cominciommi a dir soave e piana:* she [Beatrice] began to speak pleasantly and softly—Benvenuto writes: *et bene dicit, quia sermo divinus est suavis et planus, non altus et superbus sicut sermo Virgilii et poetarum* (and this is well said, for the divine style is sweet and plain, not lofty and proud as that of Virgil and the poets).[32]

32. Cf. my *Neue Dantestudien.*

Gloria Passionis

Originally, and particularly in Aristotelian usage, the word πάθος (Latin *passio*) meant an affliction or seizure; it always implied suffering, passivity, and it was ethically neutral; no one could be praised or blamed for his πάθος. It was under the influence of Stoic ethics that the passions came to be identified with unrest, with an undirected drive that destroys philosophical peace of mind. Thus the word *passio* took on a strongly pejorative meaning, for the Stoic ideal was to remain aloof from the world, *impassibilis:* untouched and unmoved by its strife and bustle. The original opposition to *actio* was overshadowed, and *passio* became the antonym of *ratio;* the turmoil of the *passiones* was contrasted with the serenity of reason. But motion implies a kind of activity. Now for the first time we are justified in employing the English word "passion"; partly by the implication of motion and partly by the violence which the Stoics associated with it. It was then that men began to speak of the "storms" and "whirlwinds" of *passio,* and sometimes the word is replaced by the clearly pejorative *perturbatio.* This is the second stage in the semantic development of the word πάθος/*passio;* it is characterized by violence, an approach to activity, and a pejorative evaluation. This second meaning has had still greater influence than the first—the Aristotelian—conception, for it survives to this day in the popular ethics of the most divergent peoples. In one way or another it has played a part in almost every system of morality since the Stoics. Often, to be sure, the two meanings of *passio,* the Aristotelian and the Stoic, coexist in all manner of combinations, especially in late Scholasticism and the philosophies of the Renaissance.[1]

From the very outset Christian writers of late antiquity were influenced by the Stoic meaning of the word. Ambrose wrote:

1. Cf. my "Passio als Leidenschaft."

caro nostra diversis agitatur et freti modo fluctuat passionibus (our flesh is disturbed by the various passions and is ever restless like the sea; *De Noe et Arca* 15.51; *PL*, XIV, 385). Augustine uses a similar metaphor: . . . *cur* . . . *passionum turbelis et tempestatibus agitentur* (why are they disturbed by the tumults and tempests of the passions; *De civ. Dei* 8.17), and he defines *passio* as *motus animi contra rationem* (a movement of the soul contrary to reason), an unmistakably Stoic definition. In many Christian authors the *passiones* become synonymous with the lusts of the flesh (*concupiscentiae carnis*) and often simply with the sins.[2]

On the other hand, Augustine vigorously rejects the Stoic doctrine of the passions (*De civ. Dei* 9.4ff.). He recognizes good passions (*bonae passiones*), as Ambrose had done in a passage that sounds almost Peripatetic: *omnis enim affectus qui est praeter deformis delectationis illecebram passio quidem est, sed bona passio* (for every desire that exists, excepting the attraction of a deformed love, is indeed also a passion, but a good passion; *De Noe et Arca* 24.88; *PL*, XIV, 423). Even then the two trends converged and combined, as can be gathered from Augustine's remarks. It is clear, however, that Christian ethics was closer to Stoic than to Aristotelian conceptions.

But from the start there was a fundamental difference between them. For what the Christian authors opposed to the *passiones* was not the serenity of the philosopher but submission to injustice—a Christian, they said, should not withdraw from the world in order to avoid suffering and passion; he should transcend the world through suffering. Stoic and Christian flight from the world are very different things. The aim of Christian hostility to the world

---

2. As in the Vulgate: Rom. 1:26; 7:5; I Thess. 4:5. Also, for example, Cassian, *De institutis coenobiorum* 5.2, and *Collationes* 5.19 and 20. A Provençal text translates the word *peccata* of Defensor's *Scintillarum liber* (*PL*, LXXXVIII, 600) by "passios" (K. Bartsch, *Chrestomathie provençale* 6th edn.; col. 258). On the other hand, there is an interesting passage in Augustine's *De nuptiis et concupiscentia* 2.33.55 where he seems to object to the translation of I Thess. 4:5 ἐν πάθει ἐπιθυμίας by "in the lust of concupiscence" (*in passione concupiscentiae*). For, he says, "passion in the Latin tongue, especially in ecclesiastical usage, is not generally understood as having a censorious meaning" (*passio in lingua latina, maxime usu loquendi ecclesiastico, non ad vituperationem consuevit intelligi*). Cf. C. Mohrmann, "Le Latin commun et le Latin des chrétiens," 5.

is not a passionless existence outside of the world, but counter-suffering, a passionate suffering in the world and hence also in op-position to it; and to the flesh, to the evil *passiones* of this world, the Christians oppose neither the apathy of the Stoics nor "good emotions" (*bonae passiones*) with a view to attaining the Aristo-telian mean by rational compromise, but something hitherto un-heard of: the *gloriosa passio* that springs from ardent love of God. Not the impassive man (*impassibilis*) is a saint, but he who is per-fect in all things (*perfectus in omnibus*), says Ambrose (*Expos. Evang. sec. Lucam* 10.177; *PL*, xv, 1848): *quem caro iam revocare non posset a gloria passionis* (whom the flesh could no longer call back from the glory of suffering); [3] and as they were led to their

3. Prior to the Incarnation, Jesus was *impassibilis*. Concerning this Bernard of Clairvaux writes (*De gradibus humilitatis et superbiae* 3.9; *PL*, CLXXXII, 946): *Beatus quippe Deus, beatus Dei Filius, in ea forma, qua non rapinam arbitratus est esse se aequalem Patri, procul dubio impassibilis, priusquam se exinanisset formam servi accipiens* (Phil. 2:6f.), *sicut miseriam vel sub-jectionem expertus non erat, sic misericordiam vel obedientiam non noverat experimento. Sciebat quidem per naturam, non autem sciebat per ex-perientiam. At ubi minoratus est non solum a seipso, sed etiam paulo minus ab angelis, qui et ipsi impassibiles sunt per gratiam, non per naturam, usque ad illam formam, in qua pati et subjici posset . . .* (For the blessed God, the blessed Son of God, in that form in which he thought it not robbery to be equal with the Father, beyond doubt not subject to suffering, before he had made himself of no reputation and taken the form of a servant, just as he had not experienced sorrow or submission, so he had not known sorrow or obedience by way of experience. He knew them indeed through their natures, but he did not know them as something experienced. But when he made himself not only lower than himself, but even a little lower than the angels—who also through grace are immune to suffering, though not by nature—when he lowered himself even to that form in which he could experience suffering and submission . . .). After the Resurrection, Christ is again *impassibilis*. Cf. Bonaventura, *Breviloquium* 4.10 Thesis 2 (*Opera omnia*, v, 251): *Post haec tertia die resurrexit a mortuis resumendo corpus . . . sed non tale, quale prius fuerat; quia prius fuit passibile et mortale, postquam autem resurrexit, impassibile et immortale, vivens per-petuo* (After that, on the third day he rose from the dead by taking up again the body . . . but not such as it had been before; because previously it had been subject to suffering and death, whereas after he rose from the dead it was not subject to suffering and was immortal, living forever). For God's *impassibilitas*, cf. Isidore, *Etym.* 7.1.24, discussed by L. Spitzer in an extremely interesting note, *Romania*, LXV (1939), 123f. *Passibilis* in this meaning is occasionally rendered also by *sensibilis*, both occurring almost synonymously in Bonaventura's *Stimulus amoris* 1.2 (ed. Peltier, XII, 637). Cf. also *Enéas*, 2883-2888: *Sire . . . ge voil savoir, se ce puet estre . . . veir que cil . . . aient forme corporel, passible seient et mortel* (Sire, I would like to know if this may be true, whether these have corporeal form, are subject to suffering and are mortal). Dante, on the other hand, uses *sensibilmente* (*Inferno* 2.15).

death, the Scillitan martyrs (*Analecta Bollandiana* 8 [1889], p. 8)
cried out: *Deo gratias et laudes, qui nos pro suo nomine ad glori-
osam passionem perducere dignatus est* (Thanks be to God, who
for the honor of his name has deigned to bring us to a glorious
passion).[4]

Those who stress the distinction between the two meanings
"suffering" and "passion" have not understood the dialectical relation between them in the Christian use of the word—for God's
love, which moved him to take upon himself the sufferings of
men, is itself a *motus animi* without measure or limit.[5] This dialectic is powerfully expressed long after the age of the martyrs
in the literature of the later Middle Ages, at the beginning of the
second millennium, when literary style had achieved new vigor.

In a once famous passage, quoted by many of his contemporaries (*Serm. in Cant.* 61.8; *PL*, CLXXXIII, 1074), Bernard of Clairvaux speaks of the martyr. The passage should be read aloud:

> Enimvero non sentiet sua, dum illius [Christi] vulnera
> intuebitur. Stat martyr tripudians et triumphans, toto licet
> lacero corpore; et rimante latera ferro, non modo fortiter,
> sed et alacriter sacrum e carne sua circumspicit ebullire
> cruorem. Ubi ergo tunc anima martyris? Nempe in tuto,
> nempe in petra, nempe in visceribus Jesu, vulneribus ni-
> mirum patentibus ad introeundum. . . . Neque hoc facit
> stupor, sed amor.

> For he does not feel his own wounds when he contemplates
> those of Christ. The martyr stands rejoicing and triumphant, even
> though his body is torn to pieces; and when his side is ripped open
> by the sword, not only with courage but even with joy he sees

4. Further examples in *Thesaurus linguae latinae* VI 2 *s.v.* gloriosus (col. 2103,
ll. 62–64).

5. But not, of course, a *passio*, since God is *impassibilis* (*vide supra*). In a
Renaissance dialogue on love, "Il Raverta: Dialogo di Messer Giuseppe
Betussi . . . ," in the *Trattati d'amore del Cinquecento* (ed. G. Zonta),
Raverta declares (p. 39): . . . *quello affetto suo volontario non è suggetto
a passione, come il nostro, non essendo in lui difetto d'alcuna cosa* (this
voluntary love of his is not subject to passion, as is ours, because there is
no defect of any kind in him). See on this problem also Thomas Aquinas,
Summa theologica, P. I, q. xx ("*De amore Dei*"), art. 1 ("*Utrum amor sit
in Deo*").

the blood which he has consecrated to God gush forth from his body. But where now is the soul of the martyr? Truly in a safe place, in the rock [this refers to a commentary on Cant. 2:14, *columba mea in foraminibus petrae:* O my dove, (that art) in the clefts of the rock], in the bowels of Christ, where it has entered, indeed, through his open wounds. . . . And this is the fruit of love, not of insensibility.[6]

It is the open wounds of Christ that provide shelter for the martyr and so kindle the flame of love within him that he triumphs ecstatically over the torments of his own body; they bear witness to him of Christ's love.

Amavit, inquam, amavit: habes enim dilectionis pignus Spiritum, habes et testem fidelem Jesum, et hunc crucifixum.

He has loved, I say, he has loved: for you have the Spirit as the pledge of love. You have, too, the faithful witness, Jesus, and Him crucified. (Bernard, *Epist.* 107.8; *PL,* CLXXXII, 246.)

Bernard developed this Cistercian mysticism, which was to exert an enormous influence on the similar movements of later centuries, within the frame of a commentary on the Song of Songs. A largely allegorical but in part topological and figural interpretation, which a modern reader has difficulty in following, gives expression to an overpowering creative love, so rich and sweet that it almost surpasses our understanding.

Facile proinde plus diligunt, qui se amplius dilectos intelligunt [says Bernard in his book *De diligendo Deo* 3.7; *PL,* CLXXXII, 978]; cui autem minus donatum est, minus diligit. Judaeus sane, sive paganus, nequaquam talibus aculeis incitatur amoris, quales Ecclesia experitur, quae ait

6. Cf. Meister Eckhardt, *Predigt* (sermon) 107 (F. Pfeiffer's 4th edn., 353, 23–26): *Ez wundert vil menschen, wie die lieben heiligen in sô grôzer süezikeit sô grôz lîden getragen haben. Wer des wunders wil ledic werden, der erfülle daz die heiligen mit grôzem flîze erfüllet hânt unde hânt Jêsû Kristô mit inhitziger minne nâch gevolget.* (Many people wonder how the dear saints have borne such great sufferings with such great sweetness. They should not wonder but do what the saints did with such great zeal when they followed Jesus Christ with burning love.)

"Vulnerata charitate ego sum," et rursum: "Fulcite me
floribus, stipate me malis, quia amore langueo" (Cant.
2:5) . . . cernit Unicum Patris, crucem sibi bajulantem;
cernit caesum et consputum Dominum majestatis; cernit
auctorem vitae et gloriae confixum clavis, percussum lancea,
opprobriis saturatum, tandem illam dilectam animam suam
ponere pro amicis suis. Cernit haec, et suam magis ipsius
animam gladius amoris transverberat, et dicit: "Fulcite me
floribus, stipate me malis, quia amore langueo." Haec sunt
quippe mala punica, quae in hortum introducta dilecti
sponsa carpit ex ligno vitae, a coelesti pane proprium
mutuata saporem, colorem a sanguine Christi. Videt deinde
mortem mortuam. . . . Advertit terram, quae spinas et
tribulos sub antiquo maledicto produxerat, ad novae bene-
dictionis gratiam, innovatam refloruisse. Et in his omnibus,
illius recordata versiculi: "Et refloruit caro mea, et ex vo-
luntate mea confitebor ei" (Ps. 27:7); passionis malis, quae
de arbore tulerat crucis, cupit vigere, et de floribus resur-
rectionis, quorum praesertim fragrantia sponsum ad se
crebrius revisendam invitet.

They will easily love more, then, who understand that they are
loved more; but to whom less has been given, he will love less.
A Jew, certainly, or a pagan, is in no way spurred by such
goads of love as the Church experiences, who says, "I have been
wounded by charity," and again, "Stay me with flagons, comfort
me with apples, for I am sick of love" (Cant. 2:5). She sees the
only-begotten of the Father, carrying his cross; she sees the Lord
of majesty, struck and spat upon; she sees the author of life and
glory, transfixed by nails, pierced with a lance, heaped with abuse,
until at last he lays down his dear life for his friends. She sees
this, and the sword of the same love pierces her own soul the
more, and she says, "Stay me with flagons, comfort me with
apples, for I am sick of love." For these indeed are the pomegran-
ates which the bride, brought into the garden of her beloved,
plucks from the tree of life, their own taste changed to the taste
of the heavenly bread, their color to the color of Christ's blood.
Then she sees death dead. . . . The earth, which under the ancient curse had brought forth thorns and thistles, she sees flowering again, renewed by the grace of a new blessing. And in the
midst of all these things she is mindful of that verse (Ps. 27:7):
"Therefore my flesh hath flourished again, and with my will I
will praise him." She desires to grow strong on the apples of the

Passion, which she has taken from the tree of the cross, and on the flowers of the Resurrection, whose perfume particularly invites the bridegroom to visit her more and more.

Just as Christ was drunk with the wine of love (*ebrius vino charitatis*) when he sacrificed himself (Bernard, *Sermones de diversis* 29.3; *PL*, CLXXXIII, 621), so will the soul become drunk that immerses itself in his Passion and Resurrection.

> Suavissimum mihi cervical [as a follower of Bernard [7] writes], bone Jesu, spinea illa capitis tui corona. Dulcis lectulus illud crucis tuae lignum. In hoc ego nascor et nutrior, creor et recreor, et super passionis tuae altaria memoriae mihi nidum libenter recolloco.

> A most pleasant pillow, O good Jesus, is that thorny crown around thy head; a sweet bed, that wood of thy cross. In this am I born and nourished, made and remade, and on the altar of thy suffering will I gladly establish again a dwelling place for my remembrance.

Another passage from the Song of Songs that served as a basis for this Cistercian mysticism of the Passion is 1:12: *Fasciculus myrrhae dilectus meus mihi, inter ubera mea commorabitur* (A bundle of myrrh is my well-beloved unto me; he shall lie betwixt my breasts). In the light of the draft of myrrh before the crucifixion (Mark 15:23) and of the narrative of Joseph of Arimathea and Nicodemus, who took the corpse of Jesus from the cross and wrapped it in linen perfumed with myrrh and aloes, the *fasciculus myrrhae* is taken as a symbol of the crucified body or of the Passion, which like myrrh is bitter and salutary. It should rest forever between the breasts, that is, in the heart of the beloved, or in other words: the Church should meditate unremittingly upon the Passion.[8] Similarly, the cluster of Cyprian grapes in the next verse (Cant. 1:13: *botrus Cypri dilectus meus mihi* . . .) is in-

---

7. Gilbert of Hoyland, *Sermones in Canticum Salomonis* 2.7 (on Cant. 3:1; *PL*, CLXXXIV, 21).

8. For the tradition cf., for example, Bede, *In Cantica Canticorum allegorica expositio* 2.1.4 (*PL*, XCI, 1097).

terpreted, because of its heart-warming sweetness, as a reference to the Resurrection. Bernard's commentary on these verses—which contains a variant, for he interprets only the draft of myrrh as the Passion and the embalming itself as the incorruptibility of the body—must have made a great impression at the time; I have come across the central passage quoted both in Bonaventura and in Suso:

> Et ego, fratres, ab ineunte mea conversione, pro acervo meritorum, quae mihi deesse sciebam, hunc mihi fasciculum colligare, et inter ubera mea collocare curavi, collectum ex omnibus anxietatibus et amaritudinibus Domini mei. . . . Ubi sane inter tot odoriferae myrrhae hujus ramusculos minime praetermittendam putavi etiam illam myrrham, qua in cruce potatus est; sed neque illam qua unctus est in sepultura. Quarum in prima applicuit sibi meorum amaritudinem peccatorum; in secunda futuram incorruptionem mei corporis dedicavit. Memoriam abundantiae suavitatis horum eructabo, quoad vixero; in aeternum non obliviscar miserationes istas, quia in ipsis vivificatus sum.

> And I, brethren, from the beginning of my conversion, in order to store up the merits which I knew to be wanting in me, took care to gather up this bundle of myrrh and to place it in my breast, a bundle gathered together out of all the anguish and sorrows of my Lord. And indeed, among all these sprigs of sweet-smelling myrrh I have been careful not to leave out that myrrh which he drank upon the cross nor that with which he was anointed in the tomb. For by the first he took upon himself the bitterness of my sins; and by the second he proclaimed the future incorruption of my body. I shall proclaim the memory of the abundant sweetness of this myrrh as long as I live; unto eternity I shall not forget these mercies, for in them I have been made to live. (Bernard, *Sermones in Cantica*, 43.3; *PL*, CLXXXIII, 994.)

These quotations show how close together the two meanings of "passion"—"suffering" and "creative, ecstatic love"—had come. A whole book might be devoted to a detailed discussion of the recurrent themes: *ebrietas spiritus, suave vulnus charitatis, gladius amoris, pax in Christi sanguine, surgere ad passionem, calix quem bibisti amabilis* (drunkenness of the spirit, sweet wound of charity, sword of love, peace in the blood of Christ, to rise toward suffer-

ing, the cup worthy of love which thou hast drunk, etc.). In the
following centuries this mysticism of the Passion became still more
pronounced. In Bernard's mysticism, which might be termed classical, the Passion almost always appears in conjunction with other
love themes that vary according to the occasion or context; life
of Christ, the Resurrection, or the power of the Holy Ghost as
witness to Christ's love. There is always a certain restraint in the
description of the Stations of the Cross and the ecstasy they inspire in those who meditate on them.[9] A more concrete view of
the Passion was taken in the ensuing period, and Passion mysticism became far more intense. The miracle of St. Francis' stigmatization seems to have had a good deal to do with this development, and the Franciscans, to judge by the famous *Stabat mater*
of Jacopone da Todi, especially vv. 25ff., played a leading role.
The trend can be noted even in so cool-headed a man as Bonaventura. Of the numerous examples in his work I shall cite only
the most important: Part 6, Chap. 9 of the *Breviloquium;* Chap.
7 of the *Itinerarium* (*De excessu mentali et mystico*); the preface
to the *Lignum vitae;* the sixth chapter of *De perfectione vitae;*
and from the writings formerly attributed to him one might add
Diaeta Salutis, Tit. 7, Chap. 7; the proemium and the sexta feria
of the *Meditationes Vitae Christi;* and the opening pages of the
Stimulus Amoris.[10] In all these passages devoted to the Passion we

9. As striking examples of the shift in the meaning of the word *passio* from
   passive to active, E. Lerch, in his study " 'Passion' und 'Gefühl,' " cites several eighteenth-century texts (Bonnet, Wieland, Choderlos de Laclos)
   which speak of "active passions" (*passions actives*). In *Les Liaisons dangereuses,* Valmont recommends these *passions actives* as the only way to
   happiness. Yet, in a sermon on the Passion, *In Feria IV Hebdomadae Sanctae* II (PL, CLXXXIII, 268f.), Bernard of Clairvaux says of Jesus: *Et in vita
   passivam habuit actionem, et in morte passionem activam sustinuit, dum
   salutem operaretur in medio terrae* (And in life he maintained a passive
   action, and in death an active passion, doing the work of salvation in the
   midst of the earth).

10. In the *Ottimo commento della Divina Commedia* on *Paradiso* 11.118, I find
    the following sentence concerning St. Francis: *Da quella ora innanzi
    l'anima sua fu tutta liquefatta, e la passione del Crucifisso nel suo cuore
    fu mirabilmente fitta* (From that moment on [since Christ himself had
    appeared to him in San Damiano] his soul was completely melted (Cant.
    5:6) and the suffering of the Crucified One was wondrously fixed in his
    heart).

note the growing kinship between the component meanings "suffering" and "passion," *passio* and *fervor.*

> Christus homo hunc [ignem charitatis] accendit in fervore suae ardentissimae passionis—devotionis fervor per frequentem passionis Christi memoriam nutritur—transfige, dulcissime Domine Jesu, medullas animae meae suavissimo ac saluberrimo vulnere amoris tui—animam [Mariae] passionis gladius pertransivit—in passione et cruce Domini gloriari desidero—curre, curre, Domine Jesu, curre et me vulnera.

>> Christ the man kindled this fire of charity in the fervor of his most ardent passion. . . . The fervor of devotion is fed by the frequent recollection of the passion of Christ. . . . Wound, O most sweet Lord Jesus, the inner depths of my soul with the most sweet and salutary wound of thy love. . . . The sword of the passion pierced the soul of Mary. . . . I yearn to glory in the passion and cross of the Lord. . . . Hasten, hasten, Lord Jesus, and wound me.

These are only a few sentences chosen at random. There are many relevant passages that cannot be quoted because they can only be understood in context. *Passio,* to be sure, is often replaced by *crux, vulnera, gladius,* etc., or by one of the innumerable images that a medieval theologian could derive from the allegorical or figural interpretation of the Bible; and in place of *fervor* we often find *ardor, amor, ebrietas, dulcedo, suavitas, excessus,* etc. I should like to cite one more example of the metaphorical language that developed from Biblical exegesis. It is from the sixth chapter of *De perfectione vitae ad sorores.* Addressing a nun, Bonaventura paraphrases Isa. 12 : 3 (*Haurietis aquas in gaudio de fontibus Salvatoris*):

> Quicumque desiderat a Deo aquas gratiarum, aquas devotionis, aquas lacrymarum, ille hauriat de fontibus Salvatoris, id est de quinque vulneribus Iesu Christi. Accede ergo tu, o famula, pedibus affectionum tuarum ad Iesum vulneratum, ad Iesum spinis coronatum, ad Iesum patibulo

crucis affixum, et cum beato Thoma Apostolo non solum
intuere in manibus eius fixuram clavorum, non solum mitte
digitum tuum in locum clavorum, non solum mitte manum
tuam in latus eius [Joan. 20:25 et 27], sed totaliter per
ostium lateris ingredere usque ad cor ipsius Iesu, ibique
ardentissimo Crucifixi amore in Christum transformata,
clavis divini timoris confixa, lancea praecordialis dilectionis
transfixa, gladio intimae compassionis transverberata, nihil
aliud quaeras, nihil aliud desideres, in nullo alio velis con-
solari, quam ut cum Christo tu possis in cruce mori. Et
tunc cum Paulo Apostolo [Gal. 2:19f.] exclames et dicas:
Christo confixus sum cruci. Vivo . . . iam non ego; vivit
vero in me Christus.

"With joy shall ye draw water out of the wells of salvation."
Whosoever desires from God the waters of grace, the waters of
devotion, the waters of tears, let him draw them from the foun-
tains of the Saviour, that is, from the five wounds of Jesus Christ.
Therefore, draw near with the feet of thy affections, O handmaiden, to Jesus wounded, to Jesus crowned with thorns, to Jesus
nailed to the gibbet of the cross; and with the blessed apostle
Thomas, do not merely look at the marks of the nails in his hands,
do not merely put your finger into the place of these nails, do
not merely place your hand into his side, but enter wholly by the
gate of his side right to the very heart of Jesus. And there transformed into Christ by the most burning love of the Crucified,
fastened by the nails of the divine fear, transfixed by the lance of a
heartfelt love, pierced by the sword of the deepest compassion,
seek nothing else, wish for no other thing, and seek no other consolation than to die with Christ on the cross. And then with the
Apostle Paul, cry out and say: With Christ I am nailed to the Cross.
Nevertheless I live; yet not I, but Christ liveth in me.[11]

11. Anyone who is familiar with the predilection for antithetical paradoxes in
European love poetry from the Provençal poets through Petrarch to the
Renaissance (of the type: *Pace non trovo, e non ho da far guerra:* I do
not find peace and I have nothing to make war with) can scarcely avoid
the impression, as he reads medieval mystical texts, that the great paradoxes
of the Passion created the climate in which it was possible for these forms
to develop. While the following text is relatively late (from the *Stimulus
amoris*, second half of the thirteenth century, and thus roughly contempo-
raneous with the rise of the *stil nuovo*), similar themes can be found a great
deal earlier: *Si ergo, anima, carnem diligis, nullam carnem, nisi carnem
Christi ames. Haec enim pro tua, et totius humani generis salute, est super
aram crucis oblata, cujus passionem in corde rumines quotidie. Hujus enim
passionis Christi meditatio continua mentem elevabit. . . . O passio desider-
abilis! o mors admirabilis! Quid mirabilius, quam quod mors vivificet, vul-*

What strikes us as significant in these mystical texts is not only the *rapprochement* between suffering and passion but even more so the yearning for *passio* in both senses, *desiderium et gloria passionis*.[12] In marked contrast to all ancient conceptions and especially to the ideas of the Stoics, *passio* is praised and desired; the life and stigmatization of Francis of Assisi embody this union of passion and suffering, the mystical leap from one to the other. The passion of love leads through suffering to *excessus mentis* and union with Christ; those who are without *passio* are also without grace; those who do not give themselves to the passion of the Saviour, who do not share in his suffering, live in hardness of the heart (*obduratio cordis*), and in a number of mystical treatises we find instructions on how to overcome this state. But important as it is in certain contexts, Lerch's criterion,[13] the activation of the *passio*, should not be overemphasized. The dynamism of the soul

---

nera sanent, sanguis album faciat, et mundet intima, nimius dolor nimium dulcorem inducat, apertio lateris cor cordi conjungat? Sed adhuc mirari non cesses, quia sol obscuratus plus solito illuminat, ignis extinctus magis inflammat, passio ignominiosa glorificat. Sed vere mirabile est, quod Christus in cruce sitiens inebriat, nudus existens virtutum vestimentis ornat, sed et ejus manus ligno conclavatae nos solvunt, pedes confossi nos currere faciunt.—(If therefore, soul, you love the flesh, love no other flesh than the flesh of Christ. For it was sacrificed on the altar of the cross for your salvation and that of all mankind; meditate daily in your heart on its suffering. For constant meditation on this passion of Christ will raise the mind aloft. . . . O passion to be yearned for! O death to be wondered at! What could be more wonderful than that death gives life, wounds heal, blood makes white and cleanses deep within, that a pain beyond measure brings a very great joy beyond measure, that the opening of the side joins heart to heart? But do not cease to wonder further, that the sun covered over should give more light than ever, that the fire when quenched should kindle even more, that a shameful passion should give glory. For it is truly wonderful that Christ thirsting on the cross gives us plenteously to drink, that being naked he clothes us with virtue as with a garment, and that his hands nailed to the wood set us free, his feet pierced through cause us to run—and so on.) This already is excessively full of artifice. (*Stimulus amoris* 1.1: St. Bonaventura's *Opera omnia*, ed. Peltier, XII, 633.)

12. Suso's *Horologium sapientiae*, ch. 14, is also relevant. I have used J. Strange's edition. For an understanding of this passage it should be noted that the rose is a symbol of celestial bliss; cf. M. Gorce (ed.), *Le Roman de la Rose*, pp. 29–36.—The mysticism of the Passion is also highly developed in German women mystics such as Mechtild of Magdeburg and Margaretha Ebner.

13. In his study " 'Passion' und 'Gefühl.' "

is more potential than real; it is receptive and filled with yearning rather than truly active; its attitude is that of a bride. To whatever heights of love and self-abandonment the soul may rise, it is always overwhelmed by the power of Christ or of grace; these are the source of activity. The wounds of love, the *fervor spiritus*, the *unio passionalis* are gifts of grace; the bride can prepare herself for them, she can yearn and pray for them; the power of longing can be so great as to compel fulfillment—just as Jacob's yearning bested the angel. But this only shows that the bride was inhabited by grace to begin with (*Par.* 20.94f.):

> *Regnum coelorum violenza pate*
> *Da caldo amore e da viva speranza,*
> *Che vince la divina volontate;*
>
> *Non a guisa che l'uomo all' uom sopranza,*
> *Ma vince lei, perchè vuole esser vinta,*
> *E vinta vince con sua beninanza.*

The kingdom of heaven suffers violence from fervent love, and from living hope which vanquishes the divine will; not in such wise as man overcomes man, but vanquishes it, because it wills to be vanquished, and, vanquished, vanquishes with its own benignity.

In this sense the *passiones* remain something which the soul suffers, by which it is assailed—and in this sense the root meaning and the Aristotelian tradition are preserved. The new and, in a way, active element in the Christian conception is that spontaneity and the creative power of love are kindled by *passio* (fundamentally, this too is Aristotelian). But *passio* always comes from the superhuman powers above or below and is received and suffered as a glorious or terrible gift.

The "positive evaluation" of *passio* in the mystical ecstasy of love must also be considered with caution. All Christian thinking, and in particular all mystical conceptions, are subject to a polarity. The love of God is also torment, even when it is answered; for God is too mighty for the soul; "if He took it to his heart, it would be overwhelmed by his mightier being" (Rilke)—it would die a love-death, torment and ecstasy in one. Perhaps this thought will be clarified by a few lines from the *Cantico dell'amor super-ardente* by Jacopone da Todi: [14]

> *Amor de caritate,—perchè m' hai sì ferito?*
> *Lo cor tutt' ho partito,—ed arde per amore.*
> *Arde ed incende, nullo trova loco:*
> *non può fugir però ched è legato;*
> *sì se consuma como cera a foco:*
> *vivendo more, languisce stemperato;*
> *demanda de poter figire um poco,*
> *ed en fornace tròvase locato.*
> *Oimè, do' so menato?—a sì forte languire?*
> *Vivendo sì, è morire,—tanto monta l'ardora!*
> *'Nante che el provasse, demandava*
> *amare Cristo, credendo dolzura:*
> *en pace de dolceza star pensava,*
> *for d'ogni pena possedendo altura;*
> *pruovo tormento qual non me cuitava,*
> *che 'l cor se me fendesse per calura:*
> *non posso dar figura—de que veggio sembianza,*
> *chè moio en delettanza—e vivo senza core.*

> Love, that art Charity,
> Why hast Thou hurt me so?
> My heart is smote in two,
> And burns with ardent love.
>
> Glowing and flaming, refuge finding none,
>   My heart is fettered fast, it cannot flee;
> It is consumed like wax placed in the sun;
>   Living, yet dying, swooning passionately,
> It prays for strength a little way to run,
>   Yet in this furnace must it bide and be:
>   Where am I led, ah me!
>   To depths so high?
>   Living I die,
> So fierce the fire of Love.
>
> Before I knew its power, I asked in prayer
>   For love of Christ, believing it was sweet;
> I thought to breathe a calm and tranquil air,

14. *Le Laude*, ed. Ferri (2nd edn. by Santino Caramella), 208.

> On peaceful heights, where tempests never beat.
> Torment I find, instead of sweetness there!
> My heart is riven by the dreadful heat:
> Of these strange things to treat
> All words are vain;
> By bliss I am slain,
> And yet I live and move.
>
> (Tr. Mrs. Theodore Beck)

All these themes of course recur in profane love poetry, sometimes treated with such intensity that one wonders whether the poems are indeed profane. To be without love is unworthy of a noble heart; love is the way to all virtue and knowledge; and yet love is in equal measure torment and delight; suffering and passion are one; not only his yearning but the loved one's presence as well is a source of suffering to the lover; her greeting and her words so overwhelm him that he thinks he is dying. All these are familiar themes of love poetry. Though gradually taking on a secular and often a conventional character, they run from the Provençal poets and Dante well into modern times and awaken to fresh vigor wherever an intense mystical movement makes its appearance. Though often of earlier origin, the mystical images of burning, wounding, piercing, of drunkenness, captivity, martyrdom, etc. retain a specifically mystical coloration wherever they may occur. Fra Francesco Tresatti da Lugnano, who edited the poems of Jacopone da Todi at the beginning of the seventeenth century, cites parallels to his author's verses in later profane poets (Petrarch, Bembo, etc.).

I believe, as the reader has no doubt gathered, that the mysticism of the Passion, with its *rapprochement* between *passio* and ecstasy, also exerted an influence on the development of *passio* in the sense of passion; that it made *passio* more amenable to the modern meaning "passion," and in this respect gave it a head start over the competing term *affectus*. In my opinion, what *passio/* passion derived from the mysticism of the Passion was a deeper, dialectical concept of suffering, a suffering that can also encompass delight and rapture—in short (see n. 6, above) what Eckhart called *inhitzige minne*, "burning love."

2

Latin Prose
in the Early Middle Ages

In THE FIRST HALF of the sixth century, which witnessed the beginning and end of Ostrogoth rule in Italy, Latin literature becomes medieval. Boethius was the last "ancient" author, and the role of Rome as the center of the ancient world, as *communis patria*, was at an end. Although Latin lost none of its universality in the process, although it became more and more exclusively a literary language—the literary language of people who spoke another tongue but could not write it—the first consequence of this "loss of Rome" was a marked provincialism. That was true both of Italy and of the long-Latinized provinces of Spain and Gaul, which amid frequent crises embarked on a political life of their own. Everywhere a fresh layer of Germanic conquerors had to be absorbed, and everywhere elements of the vulgar idiom forced their way more and more into the literary language. As to the British Isles, here Latin had been introduced only as a literary language and for this reason continued to be employed far more correctly, but even so the old Roman tone was lost. In every case the common Roman element became virtually ineffectual, while the common Christian element did not suffice to overcome the prevailing provincialism. Here I am not referring primarily to regional idiosyncrasies but rather to an over-all provincialism, a narrowness of horizon, a preoccupation with local problems, interests, and traditions. Nearly all the texts that have come down to us from between the middle of the sixth and the middle of the eighth century seem provincial and utilitarian in character; even

Gregory the Great and Isidore of Seville are narrower and more pragmatic than the earlier Church Fathers. From the outset, to be sure, a part of Christian literature had been largely utilitarian and popular. But it had been written in the wide Mediterranean world whose parts were still in lively contact with each other. Moreover the earlier writers had taken part in the dogmatic controversies which in the fourth and fifth centuries had produced a literature marked by keen thought and expression. All this was now at an end. Communications between the different regions were greatly reduced where they were not broken off altogether; the theoretical disputes over dogma seemed to be at an end. The Church faced practical tasks which overshadowed all other concerns. Above all, there were the pagan, heretical, or superficially Christianized populations that had been neglected during long periods of crisis. Far more primitive than the inhabitants of the old Mediterranean empire, they often had to be taught not only a Christian way of life but the elements of civilization as well. The resulting problems of education, organization, and adaptation were very different even from those facing the early Christian missionaries.

The Church had long ceased to be a new institution. It already had several turbulent centuries of history behind it. *Vetustam navem, vehementerque confractam, indignus ego infirmusque suscepi* (Unworthy and weak, I have taken over a vessel that is old and exceedingly battered), writes Gregory the Great (*Epist.* 1.4; *MGH Epist.* I, 5, 4f.), after his election, to the Patriarch of Constantinople, and there is no reason, I believe, to relate these words solely to Rome rather than to the whole Roman Church.[1] The two can scarcely be separated, and there was no impiety in the idea that the Church on earth was threatened with destruction, especially when voiced by a man who believed the end of the world to be imminent. In any event the Church already had

1. Compare also Julianus Pomerius, *De vita contemplativa* 1.16 (PL, LIX, 431f.), cited by Boniface in his 78th letter (*MGH Epist. sel.,* I, 164, 27–165, 1). Later on the comparison becomes a *topos;* cf. *Das Register Gregors VII,* 1.42 (*MGH Epist. sel.,* II:1, 64, 31–33).

the dignity, the traditions, the patina, and the weaknesses characteristic of an ancient institution. Its doctrine was a product of the old Mediterranean cultures and, based as it was on a book and the interpretation of a book, markedly literary even by Mediterranean criteria. In the course of the long and difficult debates on dogma, it had become a masterpiece of religious subtlety. But the people to whom it now had to be taught and even the vast majority of the teachers were without subtlety. The problems of the patristic Golden Age were quite beyond them. The extermination of primitive superstition, the restoration and preservation of the barest rudiments of morality and social life, the organization of congregations—these were the tasks to be undertaken not once but over and over again, since every step forward was threatened by the incursion of new populations. Thought structure and linguistic expression became exceedingly simple. The remarkable part of it is that the substance of the doctrine should have suffered no lasting harm. Even the typological explanation of Scripture, which was held to be extremely difficult and beyond the understanding of the average man, proved to be highly effective. Apart from the miraculous tales of saints and martyrs, it constitutes the most important literary genre of this period. We shall speak of it below.

In the sixth century there were still a few authors whose style shows a trace of the classical traditions. Among them we may number Cassiodorus, Avitus of Vienne, Ennodius of Pavia, Arator, and, in the second half of the century, Venantius Fortunatus. Most of them are mannered to the point of absurdity. But in the same period there developed an unadorned, utilitarian prose tending toward colloquial speech in its sentence structure, tone, and choice of words. To my knowledge, Caesarius of Arles was its first important representative; Gregory the Great employed this style; its master was Gregory of Tours. This style, I am convinced, was not a mere product of faulty education or incapacity for classical expression. The main point is that a new situation created a need for a new kind of expression. This writing reflects not so much the decay of the old forms as a new—and deliberately new–style. Of this, modern critics were long unaware, because since the Renaissance the entire Latin literature of late antiquity and the Middle Ages had been judged by the classical criteria of the humanists. Such criticism has its justification; for it is true, of course, that the ancient feeling for style ceased to function as a whole and for a considerable period survived only in fragments comparable to the stones of a demolished building. But these stones went into the construction of a new edifice, and an attempt must also be made to see this edifice for what it is: a new and coherent whole.

Caesarius of Arles was assuredly one of the greatest and most influential preachers the Church ever possessed. A modern scholar, A. Malnory, devoted a large part of his book on Caesarius [2] to his sermons and their influence, which extended far beyond the limits of his time and country. But Malnory harps continually on the corruption of Caesarius' style and almost apologizes for employing the word "eloquence" in connection with it. Obviously something is wrong. Later the works of Caesarius were edited by Dom Germain Morin, one of the subtlest and most learned of Catholic philologists.[3] Morin devoted a large part of his lifework to Caesarius, and his affection for him is unmistakable. Yet his judgment of Caesarius' style (*nitida et simplex beati viri eloquentia*, the clear and simple eloquence of this blessed man) is dictated largely by a humanistic conception of style; he vindicates Caesarius and apologizes for him, but hardly praises him. He did not really appreciate this style, though it would be hard to conceive of anyone better equipped to do so. In his introduction (p. viii) he writes:

> Equidem fateor, nihil in eo affectatae subtilitatis reperiri, quae aliquando in eiusdem aetatis scriptoribus, ut puta Ennodio ac paulo anteriore Apollinare Sidonio vix ferendam esse nemo negabit: at neque incomptae omnino orationis

2. Malnory, *Saint Césaire évêque d'Arles.*
3. *Sancti Caesarii . . . Opera omnia . . .* , 1: *Sermones seu Admonitiones.* Concerning his vocabulary cf. A. Vaccari, "Volgarismi notevoli nel latino di S. Cesario di Arles." On his preaching in general, see also H. G. J. Beck, *The Pastoral Care of Souls in South-East France During the Sixth Century*, p. 357.

culpandus Noster est, quae in suo mox discipulo Cypriano, nedum in Gregorio Turonense episcopo a teretibus sensibus abhorret; ac propterea haud immerito eum dicas inter cultiorum temporum elegantiam ac penitus deflorescentis eloquentiae humilitatem medium quasi locum tenuisse.

> I for my part declare that there is in him none of that studied subtlety which, no one will deny, is sometimes unendurable in writers of the same period; as, for example, Ennodius and shortly before him Apollinaris Sidonius. Yet neither can our author be accused of an altogether inelegant style, free from involved periods, such as that of his future disciple Cyprian, not to speak of Gregory, bishop of Tours. Thus it would not be unreasonable to say that he occupies a place between the elegance of more cultured times and the base style of a wholly withered eloquence.

This is true, no doubt, but such an approach makes it impossible to recognize the individuality of Caesarius' style. These lines also give an idea of Morin's own style, a cultivated Benedictine Latin unobtrusively interwoven with choice classical quotations and presenting an almost ludicrous contrast to the style of his author.

The intention behind Caesarius' style can be gathered from his own words. In his 86th *sermo* (Morin quotes the passage on p. viii of his introduction) he apologizes to the cultivated public for his uncouthness. But such a style, he says, is indispensable if spiritual nourishment is to be made available to all; educated persons would be sure to understand what was written for the simplest of men, but not the other way around. Statements of this kind are frequent in his work, and they in themselves define a certain stylistic intention. But that is not the whole story. From certain passages it can be gathered that his appeals to the cultivated public are no more than polite formulas, that the educated were a vanishing minority and only very relatively educated at that. His first *sermo*, addressed to the bishops, also begins and ends with formulas of modesty:

> Ego enim certus sum quod rusticissima suggestio mea eruditis auribus possit asperitatem ingerere vel fastidium generare.

> I have no doubt that my very crude speech may grate on culti-
> vated ears or arouse distaste (*Sermo* 1.21, p. 19, 20–22).

But he has already remarked that these bishops, whose ears are
so cultivated, preach reluctantly and far too seldom, justifying
themselves by saying: we are not eloquent enough; we are incapable of explaining Holy Scripture in our sermons (*Sermo* 1.12).
A sorry state of affairs when we recall that public speaking had
been the foundation of all ancient education. Obviously there were
by then few hearers for whom a classical style would have had
meaning. And the same can be inferred from Caesarius' rejection of
the bishops' excuses: You have no need of eloquence! On the
contrary, if any of you still has any command of that worldly
eloquence, he will do well to make no use of it, to forswear a
manner *quod vix ad paucorum potest intelligentiam pervenire*
(which at best can reach the intelligence of the few). And then he
breaks out into stormy anaphoras covering several pages:

> Quis enim etiam presbyter, non dicam episcopus, qui non
> possit dicere populis suis: Nolite falsum testimonium dicere,
> quia scriptum est [Prov. 19:5] *Falsus testis non erit impu-*
> *nitus;* nolite mentiri, quia scriptum est [Sap. 1:11] *Os quod*
> *mentitur occidit animam;* nolite iurare, quia scriptum est
> [p. 10, 14–18] . . . ? Quis est, qui non possit admonere [p.
> 10, 26] . . . ? Quis est qui non possit dicere [p. 11, 8–9]
> . . . ? Quis est qui contestari non possit [p. 11, 30] . . . ?

> What priest, not to say bishop, is incapable of telling his people:
> You shall not bear false witness, for it is written, A false witness
> shall not be unpunished; you shall not lie, because it is written,
> The mouth that belieth killeth the soul; you shall not swear, because
> it is written. . . . Who is there who is not able to admonish . . . ?
> Who is there who cannot say . . . ? Who is there who cannot
> call to witness . . . ?

And after this storm of outraged questions, he sums up (p. 12,
13–24):

> Non hic aut eloquentia aut grandis memoria quaeritur,
> ubi simplex et pedestri sermone admonitio necessaria esse

cognoscitur. Si aliquis nobis terrenam substantiam tollat, potentissimos iudices et scholasticos auditores interpellantes cum summa praesumimus auctoritate suggerere, ut rem terrenam possimus ab invasore recipere: et simplicissimam plebiculam nostram communibus verbis dicimus nos admonere non posse! Quare clamamus pro terra? quia diligimus terram. Quare non clamamus in ecclesia? non sum ausus dicere, sed tamen compellit veritas non tacere: ideo in ecclesia non clamamus, quia commissum nobis populum non amamus. Unde vereor ne in futura poena sine ullo remedio clamemus, qui in ecclesia fructuose clamare non volumus.

> This task needs neither eloquence nor a remarkable memory when you know that what is needed is a simple admonition in plain language. If anyone takes a piece of land from us, we are quick to bring in the most capable judges and rhetorical scholars to intercede before the highest authority, so that we can get those goods back from him who has taken them. And yet we say that we cannot admonish our simple people in plain everyday language! Why do we raise our voices over a piece of land? Because we love a piece of land. Why do we not raise our voices in church? I have not dared to say this, yet truth compels me to speak; we do not raise our voices in church because we do not love the people who have been entrusted to us. And so I fear that we who are not willing to raise our voices to good effect in church may raise them to no avail in the punishment to come.

It is well known (and the point has recently been reiterated by E. R. Curtius) that in the authors of late antiquity such protestations of inadequacy in education and eloquence are *topoi*, mere formulas. This is especially obvious in the present case. Caesarius' apologies are essentially a demand: sermons should be simple and forceful. Caesarius was not exactly known for his modesty. He led an austere life and his Christian humility was sincere. But clearly he was a man of strong will, accustomed to giving orders and to speaking plainly. He was an exacting administrator and surely not an easy man to work under. The tone in which these words must have been spoken is almost audible. The pious and learned bishops were being raked over the coals by their humble and uncultivated primate. He does not say that he regrets his lack of cultivation; on the contrary, he says that if anyone is versed in classical culture and eloquence he should refrain from using them, for none of his listeners would understand him. Refined oratory is useless in the present situation. In his youth Caesarius had studied classical rhetoric. It is related in his *Vita* that a vision which came to him in a dream moved him to abandon these studies.[4] Whether true or not, the story characterizes his attitude. But it would surely be one-sided to attribute such an attitude to hatred of ancient culture. Men seldom hate and combat what has lost its power and ceased to be dangerous. The heritage of antiquity that was still effective and worth combating in Caesarius' day was not its culture but a residue of base superstition. He despised classical eloquence because in his world it was useless. He needed a new way of expressing himself, and it can scarcely be denied that this new style was powerful and persuasive, that it deserved the name of eloquence.

All this however is not to deny the classical features in Caesarius' style. The materials from which the new edifice was built were taken from ancient rhetoric. The passage quoted above consists of rhetorical questions and anaphoras; there are frequent isocola, often rhymed, of the same type as *quare clamamus*. Here is another example from *Sermo* 6.3 (I, 34, 1–2), concerning the ability of men to remember prayers and love songs (*cantica diabolica amatoria et turpia*): *Ista possunt tenere atque parare, quae diabolus docet: et non possunt tenere, quod Christus ostendit?* (Can it be that they are able to learn and retain what the devil teaches and unable to retain what Christ makes known?) Caesarius had no need to learn these and similar forms from profane literature; he found them in the Church Fathers, especially Augustine, whom he knew thoroughly and sometimes copied out word for

---

4. *Opera* (ed. Morin), II, 300: *Igitur contempsit haec protinus, sciens quia non deesset illis perfectae loquutionis ornatus, quibus spiritalis eminet intellectus* (He therefore thoroughly despised all this, recognizing that those who excelled in the understanding of spiritual things would not lack the ornament of perfect style). For dreams of this kind, cf. Jerome, *Epist.* 22.30 (*PL*, XXII, 416).

word. But in Caesarius the effect is entirely different. The magic
of oratory meant little to him; he was practical, precise and concrete, concerned with the real life around him. He addressed a
specific group, provided definite answers to definite questions,
and drew clear conclusions from a concrete situation (the example of the piece of land). His rhetorical questions (*quis est qui
non possit*) sum up the ethical doctrines that are the substance
of his sermon, and each one is illustrated by an appropriate quotation from Scripture ("for it is written"). Criticism is combined
with counsel. The over-all tone is ironical; but this irony is not
witty or elegant; it is simple and pedagogical, and carries the ring
of outraged authority. Caesarius is not always so severe, but he
is always pedagogical, simple, and practical. Many of his sentences
can be translated almost literally, with little change in the concepts
or structure, into modern colloquial speech—an operation that
can seldom be performed on a serious classical text; even in the
case of Augustine, such a translation would seem unnatural. Let
us consider some of the sentences quoted above: "What priest,
not to say bishop, is incapable of telling his people: You shall
not bear false witness, for it is written. . . ." Or: "Why do we
raise our voices over a piece of land? Because we love the land.
Why do we not raise our voices in Church? I have not dared to
say this, yet truth compels me to speak; we do not raise our
voices in church because we do not love the people who have
been entrusted to us. . . ." In Caesarius we often come across
mordant sentences of this kind, intended to jolt the listener and
shake him out of his thoughtless, impious indifference. An example
from *Sermo* 37.2 (1, 155, 23–26):

> Sed dicit aliquis: "Nulla ratione possum inimicos meos
> diligere." In omnibus scripturis sanctis Deus tibi dixit quia
> potes: tu e contra te non posse respondes. Considera nunc,
> utrum Deo an tibi debeat credi.

> But someone says: "I simply cannot love my enemies." Through-
> out Holy Writ God tells you you can; but you answer that you
> cannot. Consider, then, who is to be believed, God or you!

He is never cold; there is a frank cordiality in his admonitions to his flock, which are largely concerned with practical morality: people should not cheat each other, nor commit acts of violence, nor get drunk, nor practice heathen magic, nor perform abortion, nor engage in sexual irregularities; for grave sins they should do the penance imposed by the Church and not postpone repentance and atonement until the hour of death.[5] They should pay their tithes to the Church and give their excess wealth to the poor. They should concern themselves no less with their souls than with their bodies and earthly possessions. The study of this age, when the problems of the patristic period had been well-nigh forgotten, when few men could understand Augustine's spiritual inwardness, when nothing remained of those inner conflicts but their simplified conclusions presented as dogmas, makes it clearer than ever before that no ancient literary genre is comparable to the sermon as a means of direct intervention in the daily lives of men. It was the expression of a mass movement, but of a mass movement in which every man is taken as an individual. Throughout the sermons of Caesarius we note a mixture of authority and personal warmth, as when he gives advice about the reading of the Bible (*Sermo* 6) or when he explains that those who find it hard to digest an entire sermon should tell each other what each has remembered (*Dicat unus alteri: Ego audivi* . . . , Let one say to the other: I have heard [1, 37, 26–27]). Other striking examples are 13.3, on the conduct of the Church, with its reference to the piety of the Jews and its many simple figures of speech; or the sermon at the burial of the rich man, with its dramatic use of the *topos* of the transience of life (31.2); or the harangue about drunkards:

> se dicunt esse viros, qui in ebrietatis cloaca iacent; et illos dicunt non esse viros, qui honesti et sobrii stant. Iacent prostrati, et viri sunt; stant recti, et viri non sunt?

> They say that they are men when they lie in the sewer of drunkenness; and they say that they who stand up honest and

5. *Cras, cras! O vox corvina!* (Tomorrow, tomorrow. O voice of the crow! *Sermo* 18.6.)

sober are not men. Are they who lie in the dirt men, while they
who stand upright are not men? (*Sermo* 47.1)

Or finally *Sermo* 154.2 with its detailed account of the practices
by which a poor neighbor is swindled out of his land. It is only
natural that this homespun eloquence, concerned with the affairs
of everyday life, should be rich in descriptions of specific social
situations. Caesarius is not a literary man; no more than Jerome did
he aim at a literary or realistic picture of manners and customs.
The effect should merely be realistic enough to make his hearers
feel that this applied to them. But that is what gives these sermons
their note of earnestness. His realistic pictures of manners and
morality are not meant to entertain his listeners or move them to
laughter, but to threaten and goad them, not to please them but
to shake them to the depths of their being. This is a serious and
dignified undertaking, and it is this earnestness, this dignity, which
raises this realistic comedy of manners far above the comic, satirical
style.

Half a century later, at the end of the sixth century, the Germanic kingdoms were well established. Most of Italy was ruled
over by the Longobardi, all Gaul was Frankish, Spain was in the
hands of the Visigoths. The last vestiges of the Arian churches were
disappearing. Irish as well as Roman missionaries had begun to
convert the Anglo-Saxons; Columban and his fellow workers were
engaged in their important missionary work on the Continent.
Both politically and spiritually the dominant figure of the period
was again a Roman, Pope Gregory; the other Gregory, Bishop of
Tours, was almost exactly his contemporary; somewhat older was
Bishop Martin of Braga (Bracara, in northern Portugal, then under
Swabian rule), author of the informative sermon *De correctione
rusticorum*; Bishop Isidore of Seville was a few years younger.

Pope Gregory the Great came of a noble and wealthy family.
Before becoming Pope, he was prefect of Rome and himself papal
ambassador (*apocrisiarius*) in Constantinople. As Pope he maintained contact with all Christendom and proved a great statesman

and organizer under the most difficult circumstances. The economic administration of the Church in Italy, which was of the
utmost importance for the practical welfare of the country, must
have been an enormous undertaking. He was a great theologian
whose influence lasted throughout the Middle Ages; as early as
the eighth century he was recognized as one of the four great
Doctors of the Western Church. A man of enormous energy, he
allowed neither the often desperate situation of Rome and all
Italy nor the prevailing apocalyptic mood with which he himself
was sometimes infected to distract him from his grandiose plans.
As far as we know, his breadth of outlook was unequaled in his
day. In disregard of his own ascetic, contemplative bent, he was
constantly involved in affairs which brought him face to face with
the crudest and most ruthless historical reality. And yet, in addition to his great theological works and his extensive and significant
correspondence, he wrote a book of miracles, the *Dialogues*,[6] in
which the supernatural continually, even on seemingly trivial occasions, takes a hand in everyday life. Of course it was not unusual
to believe in miracles; a belief in certain supernatural events is an
essential component of the Christian faith. What is striking is the
scope and character of this belief in miracles in a man of Gregory's
stamp. The dialogues disclose an almost childlike, fairy-tale world.
This state of mind, to be sure, had long been widespread. Supernatural gifts of all sorts were attributed not only to the early
martyrs but also to men of more recent times and even to saintly
contemporaries; written two centuries earlier in excellent classical Latin, Sulpicius Severus' biography of St. Martin of Tours,
with whom the author was well acquainted, was already full of
miracles. And it is perfectly natural that miracles should have
occupied so prominent a place in the Christian world, for it was
important to show the large number of barbarians and semibar-

6. *Dialogorum libri IV, de vita et miraculis Patrum Italicorum* . . . (PL,
LXXVII) or in U. Moricca's edition. The fine Old French translation (twelfth
century), *Li quatre livre des dialoges Gregoire lo pape del borc de Romme
des miracles des peres de Lumbardie*, has been published, together with the
Latin text, by W. Foerster under the title *Li Dialoge Gregoire lo Pape*.

barians then pressing into the Christian world that the Christian God was more powerful than the old pagan gods.

The *Dialogues* consist of four books. They are short stories related to a listener, a deacon named Peter, who makes comments which sometimes give rise to short discussions. The second book is devoted entirely to St. Benedict; the three others deal with a large number of persons. The purpose is stated in the beautiful and very personal introduction, namely, to show that holy men, authors of signs and wonders (*signa et virtutes*), lived and are still living in Italy. It is often stressed that the events are recent and reliably attested; time and time again we read such statements as: "This was told me by the venerable Bishop X himself, who is still living and whom you know," or: "Many reliable persons of the region declare it to be so." [7] Peter, the listener, is insatiable, and on one occasion Gregory feels obliged to tell him that miracles are not everything (1, 12), that some holy men do not possess such powers: Peter walked over the water, but Paul suffered shipwreck, and yet their rank in heaven is equal. The listener agrees that we should inquire into their lives rather than their miracles (*vita et non signa quaerenda sunt*). But this concession is expressed in a breath with the desire to hear more miraculous tales.

Many of the stories are extremely naïve. I shall cite a few examples; the first (1.4) is about the abbot Equitius (*PL*, LXXVII, 168f.):

> Quadam vero die una Dei famula ex eodem monasterio virginum hortum ingressa est: quae lactucam conspiciens concupivit, eamque signo crucis benedicere oblita, avide momordit; sed arrepta a diabolo protinus cecidit. Cumque vexaretur, eidem Patri Equitio sub celeritate nuntiatum est, ut veniret concitus, et orando succurreret. Moxque hortum idem Pater ut ingressus est, coepit ex eius ore quasi satis-faciens ipse qui hanc arripuerat diabolus clamare, dicens:

---

7. The "indications of sources" have been assembled by Moricca, preface to his edition, pp. xxiii ff.

"Ego quid feci? Ego quid feci? Sedebam mihi super lactucam; venit illa, et momordit me." Cui cum gravi indigna-
tione vir Dei praecepit ut discederet, et locum in omnipo-
tentis Dei famula non haberet.

One day a handmaiden of God from the same convent went
into the garden. Seeing a head of lettuce, she wanted to eat it,
and forgetting to bless it with the sign of the cross, bit greedily
into it; but straightway she was seized by a devil and fell flat on
the ground. And as she was shaken to and fro, the news was
quickly brought to Father Equitius, that he might come at once
and help her with his prayers. The good father had scarcely
entered the garden when the devil who had seized the nun, as
if to justify his action, began to scream out of her mouth: "What
have I done? What have I done? I was merely sitting on the head
of lettuce when she came along and bit me." With great indignation the man of God ordered him to depart and cease to reside
in a handmaiden of almighty God.

Another incident (3.20) involves a priest called Stephanus:

. . . Qui quadam die de itinere domum regressus, man-
cipio suo negligenter loquens praecepit, dicens: "Veni,
diabole, discalcea me." Ad cujus vocem mox coeperunt se
caligarum corrigiae in summa velocitate dissolvere, ut
aperte constaret quod ei ipse qui nominatus fuerat ad extra-
hendas diabolus caligas obedisset. Quod mox ut presbyter
vidit, vehementer expavit, magnisque vocibus clamare
coepit, dicens: "Recede, miser, recede. . . ."

Returning home one day from a journey, he heedlessly ordered
his servant: "Come, you devil, take off my shoes!" No sooner
had he said this than the straps of the shoes began to unfasten
themselves with the utmost speed. Obviously the devil he had in-
voked was obeying his order to take off his shoes. As soon as the
priest saw what was happening, he was overcome by terror and
began to cry loudly: "Go away, you wretch, go away. . . ."

One can hardly fail to note the grotesque humor: the little
devil, whimpering in self-justification like a little boy after he
has been bitten along with the lettuce, the shoe straps that untie
themselves with the speed of lightning. These devils are comical

goblins. The miraculous is often mingled with the grotesque. The dead are awakened; one man, in response to his own fervent prayer to be freed from the temptations of the flesh, is castrated by an angel; at the request of a pious monk, a snake guards a vegetable garden against a thief; a Jew obliged by chance to spend the night in an abandoned temple of Apollo (he makes the sign of the cross as a precaution) witnesses a gathering of demons, and from their conversation learns all about the sexual temptations of a bishop; after the untimely death of her husband, a young woman of noble family (*Symmachi consulis ac patricii filia*, daughter of Symmachus, the consul and patrician) decides to become a nun and is not deterred even when the doctors tell her that, unless she marries again, she will, because of her overly ardent disposition, grow a beard in defiance of nature; which is exactly what happens (*quia nisi ad amplexus viriles rediret, calore nimio contra naturam barbas esset habitura, quod ita quoque post factum est;* iv.13). The following lively scene (1.5; *PL*, LXXVII, 180) is realistic in a different way: a peasant has come a long way to visit a man named Constantius, sexton in a church near Ancona, who is famous far and wide for his piety. Constantius is standing on a wooden ladder filling the oil lamps:

> Erat autem pusillus valde, exili forma atque despecta. Cumque is qui ad videndum eum venerat quisnam esset inquireret, atque obnixe peteret ut sibi debuisset ostendi, hi qui illum noverant monstrarunt quis esset. Sed sicut stultae mentis homines merita ex qualitate corporis metiuntur, eum parvulum atque despectum videns, ipsum hunc esse coepit omnino non credere. In mente etenim rustica inter hoc quod audierat et videbat, quasi facta fuerat quaedam rixa; et aestimabat tam brevem per visionem esse non posse, quem tam ingentem habuerat per opinionem. Cui ipsum esse dum a pluribus fuisset assertum, despexit et coepit irridere, dicens: "Ego grandem hominem credidi, iste autem de homine nihil habet." Quod ut vir Dei Constantius audivit, lampades quas reficiebat protinus laetus relinquens, concitus descendit, atque in ejusdem rustici

amplexum ruit, eumque ex amore nimio constringere coepit brachiis, et osculari, magnasque gratias agere quod is de se talia judicasset, dicens: "Tu solus in me apertos oculos habuisti."

> But he was quite a small man, slight and insignificant in appearance. When the man who had come to see him inquired who he was and repeatedly asked to be introduced, those who knew him pointed him out. But as people of limited intelligence judge of a man's worth by his physical appearance, and he found him so small and insignificant, he absolutely refused to believe that this could be the man he was looking for. For a kind of struggle was taking place in his rustic intelligence between what he had heard and what he saw; and it seemed to him impossible that a man with so great a reputation could look so small. When several people assured him that this was indeed the man, he scorned him and made fun of him, saying, "I thought he was a great man, but there is nothing resembling a man about him." When Constantius, the man of God, heard this, he joyfully left the lamps he was trimming and rushed down to embrace and kiss the peasant with the utmost affection, and thanked him repeatedly for having judged him in this way, saying, "You alone have looked at me with your eyes open."

These are types of popular short story; the naïve love of the miraculous shown in them and the narrowness of their horizon should not make us forget that they are inspired by a spiritual ideal of humanity which they portray with a heart-warming directness. In almost every line the language of the people rings through,[8] not only in such obvious turns as those employed by the goblin in the lettuce (*Ego quid feci? Ego quid feci? Sedebam mihi super lactucam . . .*), but in the whole manner of exposition, which is often awkward and sometimes exceedingly broad. The

---

8. In his introduction Gregory says: *Hoc vero scire te cupio, quia in quibusdam sensum solummodo, in quibusdam vero et verba cum sensu teneo; quia si de personis omnibus ipsa specialiter verba tenere voluissem, haec rusticano usu prolata stylus scribentis non apte susciperet* (But I would like you to know that in some things I retain only the sense, in other things the sense and the language as well. For if I had decided to keep the exact words of every person, the low manner of speech this would have required would have been incompatible with my style of writing). This interesting passage, if I am not mistaken, indicates that Gregory strove as far as possible to reproduce common speech, and that he gave up only when it was too difficult to reproduce in writing. A comparison with Gregory's other works shows that he did his best, in the *Dialogues*, to remain close to the popular tongue.

tone is often that of a pious fairy tale; grotesque humor is frequent. Yet in a number of the tales, as in the passage about the un-prepossessing sexton who is a great saint and wonder worker, Gregory achieves the simplest possible expression of a fully matured human ideal. *Suaviter et luculenter scripti* (written in a pleasant and bright style) says the *argumentum* of the Roman edition of 1591 of the *Dialogues*,[9] and it is easy to see that they must have exerted an enormous influence. This was true even in their own time, as the Pope intended, especially on the Longobardi who were still Arian. Gregory himself was said to have sent them to Queen Theodelinda, who was veering toward Catholicism. But for a thousand years thereafter the *Dialogues* remained famous and widely read. They were early translated into Greek, Arabic, Anglo-Saxon, Old French, and Italian, and we possess them in numerous incunabula.[10] They became a "chapbook," one of the earliest and most typical. An essential factor of the European chapbook was the Christian *sermo humilis*, which provided the mixture from which its style was compounded: intimate and simple, at once matter-of-fact and miraculous, entertaining and didactic, capable of rising up abruptly from the trivial and com-monplace to the earnest and the sublime, the good and the wise; even in its late, corrupt products, the original impulse is still dis-cernible. Gregory's attitude in the *Dialogues* is that of a pious educator and storyteller; he tells stories which, while entertaining and holding his audience, redound to their eternal salvation and no doubt to their earthly welfare as well. His superiority to the listener, the tone of a man who is teaching something he knows, can be felt throughout. He speaks as though to children. He knows what is good for his hearers; he does not tell them everything he knows, and what he does say he says in such a way that they will understand it.[11] But it would be overhasty to infer that he some-

9. Reprinted in *PL*, LXXVII, 127–130. Already found in Paulus Diaconus, *His-toria Langobardorum* 1.26: *suavi sermone*.
10. Cf. Moricca, preface to his edition, p. lxxix, in which, however, Foerster's edition (cited above, n. 6) is not mentioned.
11. Cf. the letters he wrote to Mellitus and Augustine in England, quoted by Bede, *Hist. eccl.* 1.30 and 31.

times does not believe what he says. The society he lived in had little earthly hope to offer; the prospect of a better order of life here below had all but vanished. The world was beset by famine, plagues, natural catastrophes, and aimless brute force. In such a world visions and miracles were indispensable. And from the realization that it is necessary to present a highly simplified picture of God's omnipotence and justice, it is only a short step to an inner adjustment that stifles all critical doubts as to whether such things really happened. And what possibilities the saint blessed with miraculous powers offered! He captured the imagination, aroused the desire for emulation; his example offered the simplest way of demonstrating the power of the spirit. Here was a man who, staking his own life, had gained power over life, vanquished evil, transformed it into good, and moved the wicked themselves to insight and repentance. The almost joyful freedom and assurance that the saint achieves by his voluntary self-sacrifice, the power over life that he gains by it, are often beautifully expressed in the *Dialogues;* an example is the story of Paulinus of Nola (III.1), who to save another lets himself be sold into slavery.

Caesarius, the energetic preacher, and the Pope with his miraculous tales have in common the importance they attached to the concerns of everyday life; to them nothing was insignificant. Their purpose—to teach Christianity—enabled them to raise the simplest matters to a new style level and speak of them in a tone that would not formerly have been possible; this was a far cry from the moralistic philosophizing of late antiquity. Another feature common to Caesarius and Gregory is that their Latin tended toward the vernacular. In the sixth century, to be sure, it would have been difficult to develop a style responding to the traditional classical requirements in respect of grammatical correctness, choice of vocabulary, and balanced sentence structure. Such a style had become exceedingly rare, and moreover, the last representatives of the classical tradition were exceedingly mannered. Nevertheless, we may be certain that what drove Caesarius or the Gregory of the *Dialogues* toward the spoken language was not incompetence, but a very deliberate intention. In connection with Gregory, we have definite evidence of this: his theological works and letters are written in a very different, far more literary style; he still had the power to vary his manner, as the classical tradition prescribed, according to the nature and purpose of the work in hand. For the *Dialogues* he chose the most popular form of which, to his mind, written Latin was capable. It would be inappropriate to speak of artistic purpose in connection with such men as Caesarius and Gregory, but expressive purpose there assuredly was, which in practice amounts to the same thing. Thus they did not deviate from the classical literary style because of incapacity, or reject it out of hatred for pagan culture; they discarded it in the knowledge that it could not serve their purpose, not only because their audience was too uncultivated, but also because the topics and ideas they wished to deal with could not have been expressed in the classical forms.

Already in Caesarius (see pp. 88ff., above), I believe that I can demonstrate a definite stylistic intention, and it is evident that Pope Gregory deliberately wrote the *Dialogues* as he did. But it is in Gregory of Tours,[12] the most individual of the sixth-century writers, that the drive to write in a colloquial style seems most intense. I have dealt elsewhere with the character of his writing and the trend it embodies (*Mimesis*, ch. IV [Amer. edn., pp. 77–95]), but at the time I did not realize how emphatically he states his stylistic intention. He does so in the same way as Caesarius, by an affectation of humble apology. His syntax is far less classical and coherent than that of Caesarius or, as far as we know, of any earlier or contemporary author of comparable origin and position. His phonetics and morphology have also begun to waver, obviously under the influence of the vernacular, and it is by no means certain that he could have written much more correctly

12. Gregory of Tours, *Opera* (based on Ruinart's 1677 edition) in *PL*, LXXI; also *MGH Scr. rer. Mer.*, I, by Arndt and Krusch. A new edition of the *History of the Franks*, following H. Omont and G. Collon, by R. Poupardin. German translation by W. von Giesebrecht, 4th edn. by S. Hellmann. On his Latin, see M. Bonnet, *Le Latin de Grégoire de Tours*.

even if he had wished to. But he was quite aware of the incorrectness of his style; he apologizes so often, at such length, and with such exact knowledge of his failings, that his excuses must be regarded as something more than conventional formulas. Such protestations were a conventional form, but in this case they are sincere. In the preface of his hagiographic work *In gloria confessorum* (*MGH Scr. rer. Mer.*, I, 2, pp. 747f.), he writes:

> Sed timeo, ne, cum scribere coepero, quia sum sine litteris rethoricis et arte grammatica, dicaturque mihi a litteratis: "O rustice et idiota, ut quid nomen tuum inter scriptores indi aestimas? Ut quid opus hoc a peritis accipi putas, cui ingenium artis non subpeditat, nec ulla litterarum scientia subministrat? Qui nullum argumentum utile in litteris habes, qui nomina discernere nescis; saepius pro masculinis feminea, pro femineis neutra, et pro neutra masculina conmutas; qui ipsas quoque praepositiones, quas nobilium dictatorum observari sanxit auctoritas, loco debito plerumque non locas. Nam ablativis accusativa et rursum accusativis ablativa praeponis. Putasne: videtur, ut bos piger palaestrae ludum exerceat, aut asinus segnis inter spheristarum ordinem celeri volatu discurrat? . . . Nempe, ut ista fieri possibile non est, ita nec tu poteris inter scriptores alios haberi." Sed tamen respondebo illis et dicam, quia: "Opus vestrum facio et per meam rusticitatem vestram prudentiam exercebo. Nam, ut opinor, unum beneficium vobis haec scripta praebebunt, scilicet ut, quod nos inculte et breviter stilo nigrante describimus, vos lucide ac splendide stante versu in paginis prolixioribus dilatetis."

> But I fear that when I begin to write, since I am without learning in rhetoric and the art of grammar, the learned will say to me: "Uncouth and ignorant man, what makes you think that this gives you a place among writers? How do you suppose critics will receive this work, which is neither provided with artistic skill nor helped out by any knowledge of letters? You who have no useful foundation in letters, who do not know how to distinguish between nouns, who often put feminines for masculines, neuters for feminines, and masculines for neuters; who often, furthermore, do not put even prepositions in the place where the authority of the more celebrated mentors has decreed that they belong. For

you use accusatives for ablatives and again ablatives for accusatives. Does it not occur to you that a dull ox is playing at school games, or a sluggish donkey is racing about among a group of ball-players? . . . And indeed, just as these things cannot be done, so neither can you be counted with the other writers." Yet I shall reply to them, saying: "I do the same work as you and by my very roughness will provide matter for your skill. For, as I think, these writings will bring you one benefit, namely, that what we describe rudely and abruptly in our turgid style you may enlarge in verse standing clearly and sumptuously in more ample pages.

This is clear and detailed self-criticism; its very precision shows that it is not a mere formula. But at the same time he vindicates himself, and the tone in which he makes his learned critics speak seems to imply not only an appreciation of his own literary failings but also a certain irony toward his detractors. He concludes by inviting them to make use of his rough prose productions as raw material for great poems, polished in form and adorned with all the arts of rhetoric. This he means seriously; the poetic paraphrase and amplification of prose works had been taken over by Christian literature from the ancient academic tradition,[13] and it was perfectly natural that such an idea should occur to Gregory, for the biography of Martin, his famous predecessor, written in prose by Sulpicius Severus, had been versified by Paulinus of Périgueux. He also wished his own four books on Martin's miracles to be put into verse, and in another passage that we shall speak of later, he invites future readers to paraphrase parts of his *History of the Franks* in verse. But the present passage can only be addressed to contemporaries, and to whom among them can he attribute such abilities? In the preface to the *History of the Franks* he laments the decline of the liberal arts in the cities of Gaul and goes so far as to say:

nec repperire possit quisquam peritus dialectica in arte grammaticus, qui haec aut stilo prosaico aut metrico depingeret versu.

13. On this, see E. R. Curtius, *Europ. Lit.*, pp. 155f. [Amer. edn., pp. 147f.].

> Neither can any grammarian be found skilled in the art of dialectic to depict these things [contemporary events] either in prose style or in measured verse.

In the preface to his book on Martin he can call to mind no writer superior to himself among his contemporaries in Gaul except for Fortunatus, and even today we can think of no other likely candidate.

In another, far more earnest passage (from the last chapter of the *History of the Franks*), written toward the end of his life,[14] he lists all his writings and implores those who come after him to make no changes in his text:

> Quos libros licet stilo rusticiori conscripserim, tamen coniuro omnes sacerdotes Domini, qui post me humilem ecclesiam Turonicam sunt recturi, per adventum Domini nostri Iesu Christi ac terribilem reis omnibus iudicii diem, sic numquam confusi de ipso iudicio discedentes cum diabolo condempnemini, ut numquam libros hos aboleri faciatis aut rescribi, quasi quaedam eligentes et quaedam praetermittentes, sed ita omnia vobiscum integra inlibataque permaneant, sicut a nobis relicta sunt. Quod si te, O sacerdos Dei, quicumque es, Martianus noster septem disciplinis erudit,[15] id est, si te in grammaticis docuit legere, in dialecticis altercationum propositiones advertere, in rethoricis genera metrorum agnoscere, in geometricis terrarum linearumque mensuras colligere, in astrologiis cursus siderum contemplare, in arithmeticis numerorum partes colligere, in armoniis sonorum modulationes suavium accentuum carminibus concrepare; si in his omnibus ita fueris exercitatus, ut tibi stilus noster sit rusticus, nec sic quoque, deprecor, ut avellas quae scripsi. Sed si tibi in his quiddam placuerit, salvo opere nostro, te scribere versu non abnuo.

14. The authenticity of the final pages of the tenth book has at times been questioned because of a somewhat irregular transmission, but today it is generally accepted. It seems very unlikely that anyone else should have found reason or opportunity to add this particular passage.

15. He is referring to Martianus Capella, author of *De nuptiis Philologiae et Mercurii.*

Although I have written these books in a rough style, yet I adjure all the priests of the Lord who will govern the Church of Tours after my humble self, by the coming of our Lord Jesus Christ and the day of judgment terrible to all sinners, if you wish not to depart in shame from that judgment, to be condemned with the devil, never to let these books be destroyed or rewritten, picking some parts and leaving out others, but to let them all remain with you, whole and undiminished just as they were left by us. But even if, priest of God, whoever you may be, even if our Martianus has taught you the seven arts, that is, if he has taught you to read by means of grammar, to recognize propositions in an argument by means of dialectic, by rhetoric to recognize the various meters, by geometry to compute the measurements of lands and boundaries, by astronomy to observe the courses of the stars, by arithmetic to calculate the parts of numbers, by music to harmonize the modulations of sound with songs of pleasing accent; if you are thus trained in all these things, so that our style is crude to you, even so, I pray, do not tear out anything of what I have written. But if anything has pleased you in these things, I do not forbid you to write it in verse, as long as you leave our work whole.

This is a solemn plea, voiced in the strongest terms at Gregory's disposal. Such attempts at rhetorical expression and high-sounding eloquence are rare in Gregory, but there are other examples, especially in his prefaces. The listing of the liberal arts is clearly rhetorical in intention; the effect is awkward, but moving. Why did he attach so much importance to his text? Was he aware of his distinctive worth? It seems likely, when we consider the strength of his personality and the extent of his gifts. Moreover we have evidence of his self-awareness. In his preface to *De virtutibus beati Martini episcopi* (*MGH Scr. rer. Mer.*, 1, 2, pp. 585f.) he tells how his misgivings about undertaking this work were overcome by a vision. In a dream he sees great numbers of the sick and ailing being healed in the basilica of St. Martin. Whereupon his mother appears to him and asks why he hesitates to write down what he has seen. And he answers: "I am without literary training. How can an ignorant, dull-witted man like me dare to present such amazing miracles to the public? If only Severus or Paulinus were still alive, or at least Fortunatus!" To which she replies: "Can't you understand that we prefer the way you speak (*sicut tu loqui potens es*) because people understand it?" Comforted by his mother's words, he finally downs his misgivings and sets to work:

> Sed quid timeo rusticitatem meam, cum Dominus Redemptor et Deus noster ad distruendam mundanae sapientiae vanitatem non oratores sed piscatores, nec philosophos sed rusticos praeelegit?
>
> But why should I fear my rough style, since, when the Lord our Redeemer and God wished to cast down the vanity of worldly wisdom, he chose not orators but fishermen, not philosophers but yokels?

This is an old and familiar theme (see above, pp. 89ff.).

He makes similar statements elsewhere, for example, in the preface to the *History of the Franks: Philosophantem rhetorem intellegunt pauci, loquentem rusticum multi* (Few understand a philosophizing rhetorician, but many understand when a rustic speaks). However, his mother's assertion that his way of speaking—*sicut tu loqui potens es*—is better than that of famous authors means still more because it was not addressed to a rustic but to Gregory himself. Not every rustic was able to do what Gregory, according to his mother, could do: to speak and write so effectively that the subject matter came alive for his audience, and, most particularly, to relate events in such a way as to lend them concrete reality not only for the common people of his own day but even for any halfway receptive modern reader (provided, of course, that he can read Gregory's Latin). Gregory was conscious of his abilities; the popularity of his work among his contemporaries was indication enough. But he also knew that his manner of writing was a departure from the literary tradition and that certain guardians of this tradition, more learned than astute, might fail to appreciate his methods; hence his earnest plea to change nothing and delete nothing.

By the force of his personality Gregory developed a form of written Latin suitable for historiography, or more exactly, for the narration of concrete events; it was related to the language of the people, from which in all probability it was intuitively developed. Many turns, many word meanings, much of the rhythm, especially in the frequent direct discourse, were unquestionably taken over directly from the language that he heard around him and himself spoke every day of his life. Still, needless to say, his written Latin is not identical with the language spoken at the time. For all the wealth of material that historians of Vulgar Latin have found in his work, he could not, in particular, take account of the colloquial phonetics, for that would have required a system of transcription; and besides, it never entered his head to break with the tradition in this respect. Moreover, his material obliged him to employ words having little currency in the spoken language and sometimes to resort to a concentrated sentence structure, seldom used in speech and in those days probably never. Yet a good deal of the popular language is there. As far as possible with the means at his disposal, he committed the spoken language of his environment to writing; it is certain that almost everyone could understand what he had written and that his readers felt no appreciable change from their accustomed idiom. From this point of view one can hardly ask for more in a written language. In this respect he far surpasses Caesarius and the Gregory of the *Dialogues*, if only because frequently, especially in the *History of the Franks*, the narration of events becomes for him an end in itself. Of course, he too aims to instruct and to educate, but time and time again he is carried away by the concrete event and by his own expressive talent; he tells us what happened [16] "hot off the fire," as I once wrote,[16a] and the words come to mind whenever I read him.

16. This has no bearing on his reliability as a historian. For our present purpose it would be irrelevant to ask how far he may have been led astray by a defective memory, a lively imagination, or partisanship.

16a. [*Mimesis*, p. 93 (Amer. edn., p. 90).]

Whether one is justified in calling him a historian it is hard to say; the political context is often muddled, an over-all picture must be painstakingly reconstructed, and for this the annal form is not solely to blame. Even a single episode, if it consists of several parts, is seldom coherently organized; the sequence and development are often hard to follow. But each living moment is magnificent. And impressive, too, is the way in which he compels the reader to take for granted the astonishing mentality of the upper classes in the Merovingian kingdom. Examples of this may be found throughout; I have assembled and tried to analyze a few in the above-mentioned chapter of *Mimesis*. A good example that is not cited in *Mimesis* is the story about the *cubicularius* (room servant) Eberulf who, suspected of having murdered King Chilperic, takes refuge in St. Martin's basilica.[17] In reading it, one should note the vivid detail with which Gregory describes a number of scenes and conversations that are quite irrelevant to the historical or political context. Thus, though the sequence of events is not always clear, the whole episode lives and breathes. One among many incidents is the scene at night in the church, where Eberulf, furiously drunk, pours abuse on Gregory, who, accompanied by a priest, has come in singing to perform the night office. It ends with a sentence so succinct as to be almost worthy of Tacitus: *Nos vero cum vidissimus eum, ut ita dicam, agi a demone, egressi a basilica sancta, scandalum vigiliasque finivimus* (When we had seen him, driven as it were by the devil, we left the holy basilica, so ending the scandal and the night service as well). Or the following scene, in which Gregory tells Eberulf a dream, which gives rise to a discussion. If we read it slowly (*Et quid providit cogitacio tua?:* and what do your thoughts portend?), the two of them seem to stand before us in the flesh.

The Bishop of Tours is inferior to the Pope, his namesake and contemporary, in intellectual stature, breadth of horizon, and moral authority. But his gift of expression is incomparable for

17. *Historia Francorum* [Histoire des Francs] (ed. Poupardin) 7.21f. and 26 (29).

his day, and in this respect his originality is unsurpassed. His models—if the term is permissible—were probably ecclesiastical and above all Biblical. They showed him how to bring realistic everyday material into his historical work; and they taught him his rich use—quite unrhetorical in the classical sense—of direct discourse, particularly as a means of revealing motives or character in soliloquy.[18] But whatever he may have learned comes to life through contact with concrete events and the spoken language of the time, of which unfortunately we know little more than what we can infer from the written language that Gregory made of it.[19] If we put overselves into the situation of the time, we realize what strength of character, what courage, and what an overpowering desire for expression his achievement required. Pope Gregory had written simply in the *Dialogues;* sometimes he had tried to reproduce the wording of the popular tales, but often he had decided not to because *haec rusticano usu prolata stylus scribentis non apte susciperet* (the low manner of speech this would have required would have been incompatible with my style of writing [see n. 8, above]). The Bishop of Tours created a literary language with which the colloquial tongue had been fused. One can only wonder what would have happened if he had had imitators, if at this stage of development a literary language, a Romance koine, had developed from the Vulgar Latin. But as far as we know he had no successors. The seventh century produced none on the European continent, and written Latin became utterly formless. But then came the Carolingian reform; the foundation of its educational program was a correct Latin for use both in the liturgy and

---

18. For instance, *Hist. Franc.* 3.14: *Mundericus igitur, qui se parentem regium adserebat, elatus superbia, ait: "Quid mihi et Theudorico regi? . . ." Et egressus coepit seducere populum . . .* (Munderic, therefore, who claimed to be of royal lineage, puffed up by pride, said: "What have I to do with Theodoric the king?" And when he had gone forth he began to lead the people astray . . .).

19. In the matter of the relationship between spoken and written language during the Merovingian and Carolingian epochs, I am largely in agreement with the conclusions of Dag Norberg in the introduction to his syntactical investigations, "Syntaktische Forschungen."

in writing. This meant a definite break with the vernacular languages of the Romance countries.

In the nineteenth chapter of the *Vita Karoli Magni*, written most probably in the third decade of the ninth century, Einhard speaks of the Emperor's relation to his family: [20]

Mortes filiorum ac filiae pro magnanimitate, qua excellebat, minus patienter tulit, pietate videlicet, qua non minus insignis erat, conpulsus ad lacrimas. Nuntiato etiam sibi Hadriani Romani pontificis obitu, quem in amicis praecipuum habebat, sic flevit ac si fratrem aut carissimum filium amisisset. Erat enim in amicitiis optime temperatus, ut eas et facile admitteret et constantissime retineret colebatque sanctissime quoscumque hac adfinitate sibi conjunxerat. Filiorum ac filiarum tantam in educando curam habuit ut numquam domi positus sine ipsis caenaret, numquam iter sine illis faceret. Adequitabant ei filii, filiae vero pone sequebantur, quarum agmen extremum ex satellitum numero ad hoc ordinati tuebantur. Quae cum pulcherrimae essent et ab eo plurimum diligerentur, mirum dictu quod nullam earum cuiquam aut suorum aut exterorum nuptum dare voluit, sed omnes secum usque ad obitum suum in domo sua retinuit, dicens se earum contubernio carere non posse. Ac propter hoc, licet alias felix, adversae fortunae malignitatem expertus est. Quod tamen ita dissimulavit ac si de eis nulla umquam alicujus probri suspicio exorta vel fama dispersa fuisset.

He bore the death of his sons and daughter less patiently than might have been expected in view of his greatness of soul: his regard for his family, for which he was no less renowned, impelled him to tears. When he was also informed of the death of Hadrian, the Roman pontiff, whom he regarded as his closest friend, he wept as though he had lost a brother or his dearest son. For he was indeed well tempered in his friendships: he formed them freely, held to them most firmly, and treated respectfully those with whom he had formed this relationship. He devoted so much care to the education of his sons and daughters that he would never dine without them when he was at home nor go on a journey without them. His sons used to ride alongside

20. Quoted from L. Halphen's edition: Éginhard, *Vie de Charlemagne*.

him, while his daughters followed behind. The rear of the column
in which they rode was protected by a number of guards selected
for this duty. Since his daughters were extremely beautiful and he
loved them dearly, he did not, strange as it seems, wish to give any
of them in marriage, either to any member of his own household
or to an outsider. To the day of his death he kept all of them in
his own home, saying that he could not do without their com-
panionship. And for this reason, although otherwise happy, he
experienced the malignity of an adverse fortune. Nevertheless he
pretended that no suspicion of any wrongdoing on their part had
ever arisen, or any such report been spread abroad.

This is much better Latin, or at least it is far closer to classical
taste than anything that has come down to us from Merovingian
times. Einhard is one of the foremost stylists of the Carolingian
period. Eduard Norden writes (*Kunstprosa*, 749) that there are
sentences in Einhard of which Caesar and Livy would not have
been ashamed, and all authorities are of pretty much the same
opinion. Like most writers of this and the following period, Einhard adheres closely to the old models, in the present case to Suetonius. Suetonius treats a similar theme in the *Divus Augustus* (65,
2–4):

Aliquanto autem patientius mortem quam dedecora suorum tulit. Nam C. Lucique casu non adeo fractus, de filia
absens ac libello per quaestorem recitato notum senatui
fecit abstinuitque congressu hominum diu prae pudore,
etiam de necanda deliberavit. Certe cum sub idem tempus
una ex consciis liberta Phoebe suspendio vitam finisset,
maluisse se ait Phoebes patrem fuisse. Relegatae usum vini
omnemque delicatiorem cultum ademit neque adiri a quo-
quam libero servove nisi se consulto permisit, et ita ut
certior fieret, qua is aetate, qua statura, quo colore esset,
etiam quibus corporis notis vel cicatricibus. Post quinquen-
nium demum ex insula in continentem lenioribusque paulo
condicionibus transtulit eam. Nam ut omnino revocaret,
exorari nullo modo potuit, deprecanti saepe p. R. et perti-
nacius instanti, tales filias talesque coniuges pro contione
inprecatus. Ex nepte Iulia post damnationem editum infantem adgnosci alique vetuit. Agrippam nihilo tractabilio-

rem, immo in dies amentiorem, in insulam transportavit
saepsitque insuper custodia militum. Cavit etiam s.c. ut
eodem loci in perpetuum contineretur. Atque ad omnem
et eius et Iuliarum mentionem ingemiscens proclamare
etiam solebat: αἴθ' ὄφελον ἄγαμός τ' ἔμεναι ἄγονός τ' ἀπολέσθαι
[after the *Iliad* 3.40], nec aliter eos appellare quam tres
uomicas ac tria carcinomata sua.

He bore the death of his kin with far more resignation than
their misconduct. For he was not greatly broken by the fate of
Gaius and Lucius, but he informed the senate of his daughter's
fall through a letter read in his absence by a quaestor, and for
very shame would meet no one for a long time, and even thought
of putting her to death. At all events, when one of his confidantes,
a freedwoman called Phoebe, hanged herself at about that same
time, he said, "I would rather have been Phoebe's father." After
Julia was banished, he denied her the use of wine, and every form
of luxury, and would not allow any man, bond or free, to come
near her without his permission, and then not without being informed of his stature, complexion, and even of any marks or scars
upon his body. It was not until five years later that he moved
her from the island to the mainland and treated her with somewhat less rigour. But he could not by any means be prevailed upon
to recall her altogether, and after the Roman people several times
interceded for her and urgently pressed their suit, he in open as-
sembly called upon the gods to curse them with like daughters
and like wives. He would not allow the child born to his granddaughter after her sentence to be recognized or reared. As Agrippa
grew no more manageable, but on the contrary became madder
from day to day, he transferred him to an island and set a guard
of soldiers over him besides. He also provided by a decree of
the senate that he should be confined there for all time, and at
every mention of him and of the Julias he would sigh deeply
and cry out: "Would that I ne'er had wedded and would I had
died without offspring!"; and he never alluded to them except
as his three boils and his three ulcers. (Tr. J. C. Rolfe)

The imitation is most apparent in the first sentence: it would
be even more striking if the chapters fully corresponded, but some
of Einhard's themes occur in Suetonius' preceding or following
chapter. The content, of course, is entirely different. Charlemagne
is represented as a spontaneous, emotional type, though, to be sure,

his lack of self-control is praised as *pietas*. He disregards the immorality of his daughters, for which he himself, with his emotional egotism, seems partly to blame. This is a very different man from Augustus, self-controlled, conscious of, and vulnerable in, his dignity, sternly punishing the offenses of his progeny and suffering deeply from their scandalous behavior.

A comparison of the two very similar opening sentences indicates the looser structure of Einhard's thought and syntax. He describes the emotional Charlemagne, who bursts into tears over the death of his dear ones. Because his ideas of style had been developed on the basis of classical models, Einhard felt the need of antithetical movements. This is what led him to introduce the abstract terms *magnanimitas* and *pietas*, each with its corresponding relative clause (*qua . . .*). And the repetition of *minus* was no doubt suggested by similar stylistic considerations. The effect is not very impressive. Suetonius' *patientius mortem quam dedecora suorum* shows by contrast what could be done with true classical form: the whole of Augustus' misfortune lies in that hard, succinct antithesis. By comparison Einhard is lame and feeble; he would have done better merely to describe Charlemagne's proneness to tears and omit the abstractions, which in this case are mere classicistic ornaments. In the ensuing sentences he strays off into another theme. Charlemagne's grief at the death of his friend Pope Hadrian beguiles Einhard into general reflections on Charlemagne's friendships—a theme which Suetonius treats far more appropriately and concretely in a different passage (ch. 66). Going back to Charlemagne's family, Einhard employs a result construction (*tantam curam ut*) describing Charlemagne's eagerness to educate his children at meals and on journeys. From the standpoint of meaning, the nexus is feeble and lacking in precision. The corresponding passage in Suetonius occurs at the end of a detailed account of the children's education. This too Einhard imitated, though much less sharply and concretely, but at the beginning of the chapter, with the result that the parts which hang naturally together in Suetonius are torn apart. Suetonius' account of the meals and journeys in common concludes his remarks on Augustus' education of his children. It runs as follows (64):

> Filiam et neptes . . . extraneorum coetu . . . adeo prohibuit, ut L. Vinicio, claro decoroque iuueni, scripserit quondam parum modeste fecisse eum, quod filiam suam Baias salutatum venisset. Nepotes et litteras et notare aliaque rudimenta per se [that is, he himself] plerumque docuit, ac nihil aeque elaboravit quam ut imitarentur chirographum suum; neque caenavit una, nisi ut in imo lecto assiderent, neque fecit, nisi ut in vehiculo anteirent aut circa adequitarent.

He forbade his daughter and granddaughters to meet with strangers, so much so that he once wrote to Lucius Vinicius, a young man of good family and character, that he considered him to be lacking in proper respect because he had come to Baiae to call on his daughter. He taught his grandsons, for the most part in person, reading, writing, arithmetic, and the other elements of learning, and he made every effort to have them imitate his handwriting. When he dined with them, he insisted that they sit beside him on the lowest couch, and he would not go on a journey unless they went before his carriage or rode alongside it.

We see at a glance that the characterization is incomparably sharper and more genuine.[21] But Einhard is no more astute in imitating Suetonius' style. The first thing that strikes us is the limp result clause. And why, at the end, does he forgo the impressive *neque . . . nisi . . . neque . . . nisi,* and substitute *numquam . . . numquam . . . ?* Perhaps in order to make room for the traveling emperor's long retinue, which, it must be admitted, may give an attentive reader some slight notion of the Carolingian atmosphere. But this is not justification enough.

Einhard's loose, halting sentence structure parallels the vagueness and lifelessness of his content. In comparing these accounts of two emperors' domestic misfortunes, we should not be misled by conventional notions of Germanic purity and late-Roman de-

---

21. The question of the truth and credibility of Einhard's statements is irrelevant to our present study. Cf. L. Halphen, *Études critiques sur l'histoire de Charlemagne,* pp. 92ff.

cadence into attributing the thinness and unconcreteness of Einhard's narrative to discretion or delicacy of feeling. Einhard states the essentials of the distressing situation very clearly, so clearly that one is inclined to doubt whether he realized how damaging a picture he was painting of his hero—it is quite possible that in the Carolingian period such goings-on aroused less indignation than in the age of Augustus. And actually nothing that Suetonius says offends against the strictest exigencies of discretion or good taste. The reason for the poverty of Einhard's picture is rather that, whenever he sets out to say anything concrete about human behavior or human relations, his linguistic instrument is not equal to his material. He knew Charlemagne and his family intimately, while Suetonius was several generations removed from Augustus. Yet Suetonius continually cites characteristic utterances of Augustus, while in Einhard Charlemagne never speaks; in our quotation, the clause introduced by *dicens* is obviously not an authentic and characteristic quotation. It is impossible to doubt that Einhard had often heard Charlemagne speak and that the Emperor's somewhat too highly pitched voice (ch. 22) still rang in his ears. But his Charlemagne does not live. We know the legendary figure of the *Song of Roland;* but the historical Charlemagne, whom Einhard set out to describe, remains a shadowy abstraction. This view does not necessarily conflict with Paul Lehmann's high opinion of Einhard's *Vita.*[22] In the Carolingian period, with its hagiographical tradition, Einhard's imitation of Suetonius was a significant achievement. Suetonius had assuredly opened Einhard's eyes to much of what was important in the portrayal of a secular ruler. And it is also certain that Einhard was remarkably independent; he really tried to portray Charlemagne and not some literary model. But his work, it seems to me, cannot be termed "a living development and original creation in keeping with the new times." [23] That would have required a new style, appropriate to

---

22. Lehmann, "Das literarische Bild Karls des Grossen."
23. See also H. Löwe's estimate of Einhard in the new revised 1953 edition of Wattenbach-Levison's *Deutschlands Geschichtsquellen im Mittelalter: Vorzeit und Karolinger,* pp. 275ff., which seems to be essentially at

the age. It was not possible to render the living words of the Carolingian world in Suetonian Latin. Suetonian Latin is suited to the society that Suetonius portrayed (here the changes that had taken place in the century separating Augustus from Suetonius can be left out of account). This society was steeped in a literary tradition, the very foundation of which was precise expression— something that every child learned. A clear-cut style, elegant yet forceful, measured yet rich in shadings, was second nature with Augustan society, so much so that these people *felt* as the language required. The spirit of the language so pervaded all life, even in its crises, that speech as it poured forth was highly stylized, sharply formed, often ironic, often tending to circumlocution, intimation, and understatement. That a young admirer should visit his daughter at Baiae strikes Augustus (ch. 64) as *parum modeste* (roughly, "unseemly"); he wishes Julia had had dignity enough to die rather than survive the scandal that had forced him to take action, but all he says is that he would rather have been Phoebe's father (hence, a slave); in reference to the misfortune that had befallen him in his family he employs a line from Homer, striking for its play on sounds. Even his grim words about the three ulcers form a stylized metaphor. In treating this material, Suetonius views his facts as a coherent whole and orders them into comprehensive periods. Einhard was unable to follow Suetonius in his sharpness and firmness of outline. He tried to. But the whole structure of Carolingian life—its personalities, institutions, and happenings—was different. All the popular poems and legends, all the Latin chronicles showing an approach to the vernacular, present their characters in isolated gestures; events or relationships are set forth singly, successively or side by side, in unbending simplicity; the descriptions of manners and customs are at once rigid and unclear. Einhard's Suetonian Latin enabled him to organize and relate events and to note universal traits of character. It also enabled him—and

variance with our own. But this is explained by our different approaches to the question. Löwe is interested in political attitudes and *Weltanschauung*, whereas I am concerned with sensuous figures and human individuality.

this is what is most significant in his achievement—to set forth the political attitude of his hero. But the moment he tried to deal with the details of life, his instrument failed him. It was not possible, in Suetonian Latin, to show how men lived in the Carolingian period, how they looked and moved, and above all how they spoke and reacted. The rhythm is wrong, the words are wrong, and the sentence structure is incompatible with the structure of a genuine Carolingian sentence or conversation. It is never an easy matter to narrate the events of life in a language other than the one they happened in. But when the style of another age, the language of a culture long dead, is employed, the narrative is bound to be lifeless. What are we to make of Einhard's description of Alcuin, whom he knew well—and whom he refers to as *Saxonici generis hominem, virum undecumque doctissimum* (of the Saxon race, as learned a man as ever lived [ch. 25])? [24] His Latin is correct, it may even be said to be relatively elegant, but it is lifeless. There is much more life in Gregory of Tours and sometimes even in Bede and Paulus Diaconus.

This brings us to the problem of the Carolingian reform, which irreparably severed the bond between written Latin and the popular Romance tongue. For the next three centuries all intellectual life in the West, and most of it over a much longer period, was expressed in a dead language, almost entirely cut off from the life of the populations and understood by very few. This development, to be sure, had been long in the making. Even in the Golden Age of classical literature, literary Latin had led a far more independent life than a modern literary language, and its isolation had been further increased in the post-classical period by archaism and other manneristic fashions. Nevertheless, certain outstanding Christian writers had remained close to the language of the people, and at the beginning of the Merovingian period the catastrophic decline of Latin culture seemed to be paving the way

24. I am indebted to Luitpold Wallach for the information that *undecumque doctissimus* is a *topos* often applied to Varro (for the first time, probably, by Terentianus Maurus). See, for example, Augustine, *De civ. Dei* 18.2.

for a compromise.[25] The Carolingian reform put an end to this development.

In Germany there was no possibility of a compromise. Here Church Latin was a foreign tongue, unrelated to the language of the people. The Latin culture of the Church had not interfered with the budding literary development of the Germanic languages and had sometimes favored it. However, such was its intellectual and political superiority that Latin remained the universal literary language as long as in the Romance countries, relinquishing its hold only very gradually.

Even in connection with the Latinized countries of the Frankish Empire it would be absurd to find fault with the decision of the Carolingian reformers. Only a modern philologist would think of saying that a universal written language should even then have developed from the Romance vernaculars; Charlemagne and his advisers could not have conceived of any such idea, and if they had, it would have been of no use to them. The confusion of the liturgy and the imprecision of the administrative language had become intolerable; unity and order had become a necessity. In painstakingly [26] restoring a halfway correct Latin for use in the liturgy, the administration, and literary expression, the reformers took the only course that was natural and possible in view of the circumstances and the prevailing tradition. No one possessing the power to act could reasonably have done anything else.

But now, for the first time, the use of Latin was everywhere and irrevocably narrowed down to liturgy and the written word. Now that the institutions of Latin learning (the Carolingian pal-

25. In the kingdom of Leon a semivernacular intermediate tongue survived until the end of the eleventh century (Lapesa, *Historia de la lengua española*, pp. 114f.).

26. For the difficulties involved in the reform in the administration, cf. F.-L. Ganshof's highly informative "Charlemagne et l'usage de l'écrit en matière administrative." In Italy the Carolingian reform made slow headway. Cf. H. Bresslau, *Handbuch der Urkundenlehre*, II: 1 (2nd edn.), 344–349; or the style of the Ravenna historian Agnellus, *MGH Scr. rer. Lang.*, pp. 265–391. Concerning Lothar's attempt at reform (capitulary of 825), see U. Gualazzini, *Ricerche sulle scuole preuniversitarie del medioevo*, pp. 1–23.

ace school, the monasteries and episcopal schools) became islands in a sea of vernacular speech, Latin took on the exclusively learned and literary character which it was never to lose. From this time writers of Latin were obliged to rely on models which (though not identical with those prized by the Humanists of later days) [27] derived from a remote past and an alien culture. The consequence was that development became virtually impossible. But since Latin was the only written language, the events and ideas of the day could only be recorded in a medium that was almost wholly sealed off from the life of the time. Nevertheless, thanks to the development of scholastic philosophy and jurisprudence, Latin was to embark on a last renewal at the end of the eleventh century, concurrently with the first effective literary use of the vernacular languages. But this movement came too late and covered too small an area; Latin could no longer become the universal literary language even of the Romance world.

In the period that will now concern us, namely the ninth and tenth centuries and the first half of the eleventh, Latin was a purely artificial language, written according to ancient models and often degenerating into a kind of pedantic puzzle. Yet it was the sole medium of intellectual life. During the Carolingian period a good deal of German poetry was committed to writing and Latin works were translated into German, but this activity, carried on largely by the clergy, had little influence. For even reading and writing could be learned only in Latin: the vernaculars with their many dialects were without unified spelling or grammar.[28]

This state of affairs must be borne in mind if we wish to understand the intellectual activity of those centuries or even the

27. See E. R. Curtius, *Europ. Lit.*, pp. 56ff. [Amer. edn., pp. 48–53], and passim.
28. Alcuin, *Grammatica* (PL, ci, 854): *Quatuor sunt differentiae vocis . . . litterata, illitterata. . . . Litterata, quae scribi potest; illitterata, quae scribi non potest* (There are four different kinds of words . . . literate, illiterate. . . . Literate those which can be written, illiterate those which cannot be written).—Old English forms an exception, but its literary flowering was prevented by the Norman invasion.—On this whole problem, see M. Bloch, *La Société féodale*, pp. 121–126 [Eng. edn., pp. 75–81], and ch. 4 below.

characteristic features of the subsequent European development, which were largely brought about by the circumstances we have been discussing. Dependent on the study of a dead language, elementary education was long at a standstill. Europe had universities long before elementary education in any of the current languages could even be conceived of. The Carolingians have justly been praised for preserving the ancient heritage and perhaps for saving it from total destruction. But the cost of this achievement was very high.

Because Latin ceased to develop, it is hard to distinguish styles characteristic of the subdivisions of this period of roughly three hundred years (from the eighth to the middle of the eleventh century). We know the centers of learning; the tendencies they exemplified, their spheres of influence, and the relations between them have been investigated; we know what ancient authors were imitated and in what ways, what ancient cadences and rhetorical forms were preserved and what gradual changes they underwent. But these investigations have not produced any sense of an overall style, such as we possess for the periods of antiquity, or for those of later times beginning with the twelfth century. The documents are reticent; they do not readily yield what is needed for a synthetic picture. Neither the men who wrote them nor the men represented in them stand out clearly; blurred figures such as these are hardly accessible to our sympathy or understanding. For when we do understand the past, what we understand is the human personality, and it is through the human personality that we understand everything else. And to understand a human existence is to rediscover it in our own potential experience (*dentro le modificazioni della medesima nostra mente umana*, as Vico [29] puts it). But in those centuries the personality is hidden from us by the veil of scholastic Latin.

Long before the period with which we are dealing, roughly since the fourth century, we discern a schematization, a sclerosis in the representation of the human person; it was due chiefly to

29. *Scienza nuova* (ed. Nicolini, 1928), p. 331.

the inundation of society, in late antiquity, by new populations
of a far lower cultural level: prerational legal concepts and "pre-
historic" ornaments, often deriving from the animal world, make
their appearance and create an image of man that is more alien to
us than that of antiquity.[30] Still, this image speaks to us; in its own
way it has gradually taken on meaning for us. But it is not this
form of primitive rigidity that confronts us in the literary documents, particularly the Latin ones, of the ninth and tenth century.
The *Hildebrandslied* had already been composed, there was already an Anglo-Saxon literature; I have no doubt that certain of
the monuments of Romance literature were already in existence,
but here I shall speak only of the Germanic documents, which
have been reliably dated. In them the human personality is portrayed simply, but forcefully and without ambiguity; we can understand it. The blurred, lifeless quality of the figures we encounter in the Latin literature of the Carolingian and post-Carolingian
periods is not a product of barbaric primitivism; primitivism has
nothing to do with it; the Latin is simply incapable of expressing
the life of the times. And furthermore, until the investiture conflict broke out, there was no generalized and deeply stirring movement that might have given content and direction to literary effort.

I have selected a few prose texts to demonstrate my point. They
are by important and relatively original writers. I have selected
them because they seemed unusually alive for the period.

The first is by a younger contemporary and friend of Einhard,
Abbot Lupus of Ferrières (who died late in life, probably toward
the end of 862). Lupus was definitely what we would call a philologist, full of enthusiasm for humanistic studies, a collector of
manuscripts; he even engaged in textual criticism. He was also an
important theologian; his influence was responsible for a tradition
of humanistic and theological learning that lasted into the Ottonian period. He belonged to the group associated with the Empress Judith and her son, Charles the Bald, and was involved on

30. Cf. H. Focillon, *L'An mil*, pp. 14ff.

a number of occasions in the stormy events of his times. The most valuable of his extant works is probably a collection of some 130 letters. One of the earliest medieval collections of this kind,[31] it is significant both as a historical source and as an example of style. Modern critics are full of praise for his style, and it is true that he created a natural and almost spontaneous utilitarian Latin. He used classical models but did not slavishly imitate them—an enormous achievement at the time. Nevertheless his style is not, by any stretch of the imagination, classical. Anyone who wishes to convince himself of this need only read his long letter of condolence to Einhard on the occasion of his wife's death.[32] The second sen-

31. I use Levillain's two-volume edition of Lupus. It is probably best to consult E. von Severus, *Lupus von Ferrières*, where there is further bibliographical material. For his style see Z. C. Snijders, *Het Latijn der brieven van Lupus van Ferrières*. On Lupus and the Carolingian authors one may also consult: M. L. W. Laistner, *Thought and Letters in Western Europe A.D. 500 to 900*, and J. de Ghellinck, *Littérature latine au moyen âge* (to the end of the eleventh century).

32. Levillain 4; I, 18 and 20. The sentence reads: *Et quamvis, qui me longe praestent, amicorum solacia temptaverint hunc tantum levare dolorem, nec tamen ob eam rem profecerint, ut litteris vestris satis eminet, quod ipsi casus vestri considerationem non satis ad se admiserunt, eo usque ut eorum quidam super excessu gratissimae quondam uxoris gratulandum monerent, quod, ut opinor, nihil ad consolationem pertinet, non tam aetatis levitate vel ingenii, quod exiguum sentio, confidentia quam proni erga vos amoris magnitudine, haec rursum, qualiacumque sint, in vestri solacium non sum veritus cudere, siquidem conscius mihi sum, intimum me nobilissimae illius feminae morte cum vestra tum etiam ipsius vice traxisse dolorem, quem atrociter exasperantem vestrae litterae, fateor, recrudescere coegerunt.*
(And although friends far worthier than I have endeavored to alleviate your heavy sorrow—unsuccessfully, to be sure, as your letter amply indicates—because they failed to put themselves in your place in considering your misfortune, some of them going so far as to advise you to look upon the death of your dearly beloved wife as an occasion for rejoicing—advice which to my mind is far from consoling—nevertheless, impelled not so much by the light-mindedness of old age or confidence in my talents, which I know to be small, as by my great love for you, I have not hesitated to employ my gifts, however meager, in an attempt to comfort you, because I myself was deeply afflicted by the noble lady's death, and your letter, I must own, has caused my bitter sorrow to burst forth afresh.)
      The corresponding passage in Servius Sulpicius runs (*Ad fam.* 4.5.1): *Etsi genus hoc consolationis miserum atque acerbum est, propterea quia, per quos ea confieri debet, propinquos ac familiares, ii ipsi pari molestia adficiuntur neque sine lacrimis multis id conari possunt, uti magis ipsi videantur aliorum consolatione indigere quam aliis posse suum officium praestare tamen, quae in praesentia in mentem mihi venerunt, decrevi brevi ad te perscribere, non quo ea te fugere existimem, sed quod forsitan dolore*

tence in the letter is a long concessive period (*Et quamvis . . .*) in which he explains why he is writing. It so happens that one of the opening sentences in the letter of condolence which Servius Sulpicius wrote Cicero from Athens on the occasion of his daughter Tullia's death (*Ad fam.* 4.5) includes an explanatory concessive period (*Etsi genus hoc consolationis . . .*). If we compare the two sentences for structure and content, we cannot fail to note how awkward and unclassical even a writer of Lupus' distinction seems beside such models. He was a practical man, and his writing is interesting and meaningful when it deals with practical matters. Even his long struggle over the *cella Sancti Judoci* (Saint-Josse, a small abbey on the Straits of Dover, which Louis the Pious had donated to the monastery of Ferrières and which had later been arbitrarily taken away) arouses our interest, and it is with mingled pleasure and sympathy that we read his complaint to the king, saying that because the *cella Sancti Judoci* had been given to a layman,[33]

> Dei servi, qui pro vobis assidue orant, hoc triennio consueta vestimenta non accipiunt et, quae ferre compelluntur, attrita et pleraque resarta sunt, leguminibus empticiis sustentantur, piscium et casei consolationem rarissime consequuntur. . . .
>
> The servants of God [the monks of Ferrières], who diligently pray for you, have been for three years without their usual garments, and those they are obliged to wear are worn out and covered with patches; they live on vegetables which they have to buy, and rarely do they know the consolation of fish and cheese.

For all these good things were received from Saint-Josse.

impeditus minus ea perspicias. (Consolation of this kind, it is true, is thankless and of little value, because those who ought to be offering it, the friends and relatives, are themselves afflicted with a like sorrow and cannot make the attempt without many tears, so that they themselves seem more in need of receiving consolation from others than able to discharge their duty of offering solace to them; yet I have decided to write to you briefly what has occurred to me at the present juncture, not that I think you have overlooked it but because in view of your grief you may not see it so clearly.)

33. Levillain 42; 1, 176.

The next passage I wish to quote is an account of a dramatic occurrence in Lupus' own life. After studying for some years in Fulda, he had returned in 836 to his home monastery of Ferrières (south of Fontainebleau). He was already a respected scholar, with good connections at court, especially with the Empress Judith, mother of Charles the Bald. It is possible that he owed these connections to Odo, his abbot; it is certain in any case that Odo encouraged him to teach, put important business matters in his hands, and entrusted him with the writing of certain important letters. It is safe to say that their relationship was one of trust and friendship.

Louis the Pious died in the middle of 840. Immediately after his death the old conflicts between his sons burst into the open. Odo seems to have inclined toward Lothar's party, which stood for the unity of the Empire—or at least to have wavered at a decisive moment. In any case, he fell into disfavor with King Charles the Bald, then seventeen years of age, and was deposed; Lupus, who was at Charles' court at the time, was appointed in Odo's place and ordered to attend to his removal from the monastery. In November 840 Lupus was actually elected by the monks. He described his part in these events in a letter (Levillain 24; I, 114–120). This letter, which must have been written shortly after the events, is addressed to Bishop Jonas of Orléans, a learned theologian with whom Odo as well as Lupus had formerly been on friendly terms. But the tone of the letter is one of annoyance, even in the first lines, which deal with a relative of Bishop Jonas, who, it appears, had illegally taken possession of some property near Orléans belonging to the monastery of Ferrières. Jonas had taken no action, and Lupus, though expressing himself with ecclesiastical unction (*quod cupio vos episcopaliter accipere:* which I want you to receive in your capacity as a bishop), is unmistakably indignant. He continues as follows (I, 118–120):

> Ceterum de abbate quondam nostro falsa nescio quae vobis relata esse audio, et ne apud vos ea ulterius praeva-

leant, quae super eo gesta sunt quam verissime sanctitati
vestrae significo. Dominus noster ne in monasterio nostro
esse permitteretur jussit, praefatus de eo talia quae melius
reticentur. Id reversus ad monasterium quam mollissime
eidem abbati edixi atque, illi hominibus qui eum deducerent
deputatis, equis et vestimentis et argento ad viaticum con-
cessis, cum jussu domini regis II kalendas decembris pro-
moverem, constitui ut intra III nonas memorati mensis
monasterio decederet, quod eo die ante dominum regem
me venturum sperarem. Quod enim cum juxta meam opinionem fecissem, post sollemnem exceptionem quaesivit
quidnam de praefato abbate fecissem. Ego, qui crederem
sic eundem abbatem gessisse, ut nobis convenerat, praeceptum ejus me super eo complevisse respondi. Accepta
igitur licentia, cum pridie idus decembres monasterio pro-
pinquassem, comperi saepedictum abbatem ibi adhuc mo-
rari. Hinc vehementer anxius, quod aliter domino nostro
dixeram, aliter inveniebam, praemisi nocte qui ei honeste
diceret ut primo diluculo egrederetur: non esse honestum
ut aut ego meum differrem ingressum aut illum ibi contra
domini nostri praeceptum invenirem. Cumque ille mandasset se in crastinum exire disposuisse, ne aliquam inimicis
calumniandi ansam relinquerem, remandavi me non ante
ingressurum quam ipse egrederetur. Ita ille coenobium
egressus est, permissis sibi omnibus quae illi ante largitus
fueram et nonnullis insuper attributis. Quam rem aulicis
familiaribus meis continuo significavi et oportune egomet
domino nostro exposui et mendacia quae inde sererentur
declaravi. Non aliter me facere debuisse eis concorditer
visum est. Viderint qui alia inde sparserunt, an perperam
fecerint. Ego certe simplicem in hac parte oculum habens
lucidum fore corpus meum divina autoritate confido (cf.
Matth. 6:22).

Here is an English rendering of the passage, with a few addi-
tions and paraphrases:

   I have heard that false rumors have come to you concerning our
   one-time abbot; lest you give them credence I will give you a truth-
   ful account of what took place. Our lord [King Charles the

Bald] ordered [me, as I happened at that time to be at court] [34] that Odo should no longer remain in our monastery, and in doing so said things about him best left unrecorded. After my return to the monastery I conveyed the news to the abbot in as considerate a way as possible. I designated men to accompany him, and saw to it that he should have horses, apparel, and money for the journey. Since in accordance with the king's command I had to set off again for the court on the thirtieth of November and expected to see the king on the third of December, I stipulated that by this day at the latest Odo should have left the monastery. All this I had arranged according to my best judgment. After my official reception the king inquired what I had done about the abbot. Since I naturally assumed that the abbot had kept the terms of our agreement, I replied that I had carried out the king's orders. I was given leave to withdraw. On the twelfth of December I approached the monastery and learned that the abbot was still there. This greatly perturbed me, because the situation as I found it did not correspond to the assurances I had given the king. That very night I sent a messenger on ahead to request the abbot politely to leave by daybreak; it was not fitting that I should postpone my arrival, and equally improper that, in defiance of the command of our liege lord, I should still find him there. When he sent me the message that his departure was set for the following day, I had him informed that I would not enter the monastery until after he had gone—this I did to avoid giving my enemies any opportunity to slander me. In these circumstances he left the monastery, taking with him everything I had previously bestowed on him and various other things besides. I at once acquainted my friends at court with the facts in the matter, and at the next opportunity informed our lord personally of them, making it clear what false rumors would be put in circulation on the strength of this incident. All were agreed that I could not have acted in any other way. Whoever spreads any other account concerning it should ask himself whether he is not acting wrongly. As for myself, since my eye is single in this matter, I have faith in the divine word that my whole body shall be full of light (cf. Matt. 6:22).

The structure of this passage is clear, the vocabulary is rich and properly employed; there can be no mistaking Lupus' mastery of syntax and rhetoric. Of course this passage cannot be mistaken for

34. Presumably in the middle of November 840, in Orléans. See F. Lot in *Romania*, LXV (1939), 149.

a classical text. Such forms as *sanctitati vestrae, dominus noster, eidem abbati, praefato abbate, saepedictum abbatem,* make it clear that we are in the early Middle Ages. Nor would any classical author have made such liberal use of personal and demonstrative pronouns (illi *hominibus qui* eum *deducerent deputatis; praeceptum* eius me *super* eo *complevisse*), and the use of words is sometimes unclassical (e.g., *exceptio* in the sense of "reception").[35] But there can hardly be any objection to such deviations from classical usage; they contribute to the naturalness and ease characteristic of Lupus' style. Classical and sharply contrasting with Gregory of Tours and other Merovingian authors is the way in which the language—clear, free, and sometimes elegant—follows the subject matter. The whole account of the measures taken by Lupus between his two trips to the monastery, complete with particulars and motivations, forms a single period, so that we gain a quick over-all view of a situation calling for prudence and circumspection but also for a quick decision. Contrastingly, the break between Charles' question and Lupus' answer (*quaesivit, quidnam . . . fecissem;* new sentence: *Ego, qui crederem . . . respondi*) and the causal subjunctive *crederem* convey a sense of danger and uneasiness. Further on, the whole sentence structure reflects Lupus' anxiety: *Hinc vehementer anxius quod aliter domino nostro dixeram, aliter inveniebam, praemisi nocte . . . non esse honestum. . . . Cumque ille mandasset . . . remandavi. . . .* And the parallel between subject matter and sentence structure might be carried still further. Apart from his other qualities, Lupus was unquestionably a gifted writer who spontaneously transferred the rhythm of events to the rhythm of his language. In this respect he equaled the best Latin authors.

However, the clarity of presentation applies only to external movements and countermovements. There is not so much as an

---

35. Also unclassical are probably *juxta* used in place of *secundum*, and *super*, "concerning," with persons, instead of *de*. Z. C. Snijders, *Het Latijn der brieven . . . ,* p. 87, also mentions *nobis convenerat* instead of *inter nos convenerat,* but the construction is well attested and is at worst a little careless.

intimation of the human relations between characters. But in reading about an incident of this sort, we demand to learn something about the human element; without it we understand nothing, for all the clarity of the syntax. This is a story about human beings; it becomes intelligible only if we know something about the characters, temperaments, motives, and reactions of the *dramatis personae*. By way of suggesting what is missing, I shall venture a few conjectures. They are without value as an explanation of the incident, for they cannot be proved, but they do show what is lacking in Lupus' account.

What were his relations with Odo, his former abbot, whose intimate and protégé he had been until very recently? Writing to Jonas of Orléans, who knew both of them well, he obviously wishes to defend himself against the charge of ruthlessness in turning Odo out of the monastery. He calls Jonas' attention to the danger facing him at court, where his enemies asked nothing better than an opportunity to slander him for treating the disgraced abbot too gently. It is quite conceivable that Odo and Lupus had fallen out long before, or that Lupus had secretly plotted Odo's downfall. In a letter which Lupus, in Odo's name, had recently written to a powerful figure at court (Levillain 16; 1, 94 and 96), Odo expresses his fear that certain ecclesiastics at court might lay claim to his monastery, and begs for protection. Lupus had connections at court. But would Odo have had Lupus write such a letter if he had held him in suspicion? Odo seems to have trusted Lupus implicitly up to the time of his deposition. Did Lupus betray this trust by making it known that Odo favored Lothar's faction? Quite possibly. But it is equally possible that he did nothing of the sort but merely proceeded with caution; that thanks to his friendly relations with the Empress Judith he was generally regarded as a supporter of Charles, or actually had been from the first. But it does not follow that he necessarily denounced Odo. And perhaps, on the strength of his reputation for learning, his friends at court had arranged for his appointment as successor to the hopelessly compromised Odo—perhaps not without difficulty, for he too had enemies who wished to involve him, as a known friend of Odo, in Odo's disgrace. King Charles, then aged seventeen, had grown up amid the vilest intrigues. It is quite conceivable that, in appointing the celebrated Lupus abbot of Ferrières and at the same time ordering him to expel his luckless predecessor, he was motivated by sadistic duplicity—for at one stroke he was promoting him, tormenting him, putting him to the test, and discrediting him with his former friends. This conjecture would explain a number of things: it would show, for example, why, instead of giving Lupus detailed instructions, Charles left him free to carry out the order *juxta suam opinionem*—but at the same time summoned him back to court to ask him (as Lupus had foreseen) how he had managed. The same conjecture would also make it clear that Lupus had no way of sidestepping this painful mission, because any attempt to do so would only have made him more suspect.

These questions can no longer be clarified. One would like to see the face, the gestures, of Charlemagne's young grandson, to hear his words. We never see anything of the sort. Far less than Gregory of Tours or even Paulus Diaconus does Lupus or any other Carolingian author convey such impressions.

And what happened at the meeting between Odo and Lupus, when Lupus was obliged to tell Odo *quam mollissime* to leave as soon as possible? There is not one word in our text or in any of Lupus' earlier letters to tell us what kind of man Odo was. How did Odo take the news? Was there hatred between the two men or a certain amount of secret but helpless understanding? And why did Odo delay his departure? Did he wish to create difficulties for Lupus? Did he still hope for a change in his fortunes or perhaps for an intervention on the part of Lupus himself? Lupus' remark that Odo had taken more with him than he had received permission to is unkind and betrays irritation. But no inferences can be drawn from it.

It might be argued that Lupus had no need to fill in these gaps because Jonas was familiar with the situation and knew the persons involved. But this argument is refuted by experience. In any other period a writer capable of composing so well-turned a letter would have woven certain glimpses of personal attitudes, words, gestures, and motives into his account. Such sidelights are of particular interest to an addressee acquainted with the persons and circumstances; they support the narrative and make it clear to him by relating it to his own experience. This is known to everyone who has corresponded regularly with his close friends or read such correspondences. It might also be argued that Lupus had to be careful. He could not entirely trust Jonas, and he did not know into whose hands his letter might fall. Any expression, however indirect, of sympathy for Odo, any characterization of Charles' conduct that might be interpreted as criticism, was dangerous. This argument is justified. But where living experience finds living expression no amount of discretion can hide it completely. Lupus could have said more about Charles' attitude and Odo's reactions without endangering himself in the least. Actually, the concrete personal touches that bring the correspondents and the persons mentioned in their letters to life are nowhere to be found in Lupus' correspondence, even when there is nothing in the circumstances to hamper his freedom of expression. He speaks a little more freely of the king in later letters to Paschasius Radbertus (Levillain 52; I, 212: *Ille quo solet vultu cum gratiosus apparet*, the expression customary with him when he is in a good humor); to Markward, abbot of Prüm (83; II, 68), and to Aeneas, bishop of Paris (122; II, 186), in which he would seem, not perhaps without irony, to be advising the prelate on how to persuade the king to support learned endeavors or at least to tolerate them. But these passages are all unclear and add up to very little. There is never a concrete picture. Lupus is not without humor or vigor of expression. When one has read him through a few times, the historical landscape in which he lived gradually takes form. More than any other Carolingian author known to me, he manages to convey in Latin a picture of his own existence, to describe its material aspects as well as the underlying strivings and inclinations,

his struggles, concerns, and desires. He is one of the first to succeed, now and then, in wresting a glimmer of living expression
from the school Latin established in the Carolingian period. But
this is not very much. For all the events that pressed in upon him,
for all his cultivation, he does not stand out as a coherent, dynamic
figure capable of moving us.

Such figures, otherwise so plentiful in the history of the Christian Middle Ages—the preceding century had known Bede and
the mighty Boniface—do not appear in the Carolingian period.
With the sole exception of the strange and problematic Gottschalk, none of the Carolingian scholars or poets was of a nature
to arouse direct interest in his existence. The many violent and
disastrous events that burst in on the Carolingian Empire after
the death of Louis the Pious seem confused; they led to no deep-
seated movement; the theological problems of the day aroused
learned polemics but no profound or widespread interest.

Probably late in 926, Hilduin, bishop of Liège, was driven from
his see by political events. He went to the court of Pavia, where,
shortly before, his relative the margrave Hugo of Provence had
been proclaimed king of Italy. A member of Hilduin's retinue
was Rather, then about thirty-five, a learned monk from the
monastery of Lobbes in Hainaut. King Hugo received them both
with favor. He put Hilduin in temporary charge of the bishopric
of Verona, and when the archbishop of Milan died in 931, appointed him his successor. He had promised the bishopric of
Verona to Rather when this long-expected event should occur but
hesitated to keep his promise; there were other candidates whose
support for his political designs was more important to the king.
By a skillful but untimely intrigue Rather and his friends created
a situation in which it was well-nigh impossible for Hugo to
ignore his promise. Rather became bishop of Verona, but his relations with his protector suffered in the process and further deteri-
orated in the ensuing years. Rather opposed the king's suggestion
that he forgo a part of the revenues of his bishopric. With his exaggerated zeal for reform, he also antagonized the Veronese

clergy, who may have distrusted him as a foreigner to begin with. In 934 Duke Arnulf of Bavaria tried to seize the kingdom of Italy. He took Verona but had to withdraw in haste when by a swift and skillful maneuver Hugo threatened to cut off his lines of communication. Count Milo of Verona and Bishop Rather had given Arnulf a friendly reception; Liudprand of Cremona goes so far as to say that they had sent for him (*Antapodosis* 3.48). When Hugo approached Verona, after the withdrawal of the Bavarians, Count Milo made submission and was pardoned. Certain members of the Veronese clergy, who were themselves gravely compromised, managed to put all the blame on Rather. He was deposed without a trial, imprisoned in Pavia, and some two and a half years later exiled to Como.

While in prison in Pavia he wrote his longest and best-known work, the *Praeloquia* (*PL*, cxxxvi, 145–344), a moral treatise replete with autobiography and self-justification. It has often been consulted as a source for the social and economic life of the early tenth century but is far from having been fully exploited. From Como Rather wrote a letter to a cleric named Ursus, who had played a prominent part in his deposition and imprisonment and who was still agitating against him. From this letter, which Rather later inserted in the *Praeloquia* (3, 25–28), we learn that Ursus had publicly referred to him as "a stinking corpse." Rather's letter runs as follows: [36]

36. Rather's complete works were edited by the two Ballerini brothers, ecclesiastics of Verona, in 1765; their edition is reprinted in *PL*, cxxxvi. A new edition of the letters was prepared by F. Weigle, *MGH Briefe*, i. For Rather's biography see: the Ballerini in their edition of his works and in *PL*, cxxxvi, 27–142; A. Vogel; G. Pavani; G. Monticelli. Other publications or significant references: A. Hauck in *Kirchengeschichte Deutschlands*, iii, 284–295; B. Schwark, *Bischof Rather von Verona als Theologe*; A. Adam, *Arbeit und Besitz nach Ratherius von Verona*; N. Jorga in (Rumanian) *Revista istorică*, xiii, reviewed by R. O[rtiz] in *Studi medievali*, N.S. i; and especially the work of F. Weigle in *Quellen u. Forsch. aus ital. Arch. u. Bibl.*, xxviii and xxix, and in *Deutsches Archiv für Gesch. d. MA*, i and v, 347–386. This last study contains a new interpretation of the events in Verona during the Bavarian occupation, i.e., of Rather's letter to Ursus, which is our only source. It strikes me as more plausible than the studies of earlier scholars, although it, too, leaves a good deal unexplained.—For the letters I generally follow Weigle's text, for other passages, the Ballerini

Heu me, fili mi, quid agam? Quem primum plangam, me mortuum an te mortuo insultantem—quasi et tibi eadem non sit conditio moriendi—immo, quod est multo miserius, fetores mortui naribus trahentem, ore aspirantem pulmonibusque longe peius moriturum mittentem et, quod est gravius, aliis hoc, ut simul possint commori, propinantem? An nescis, fili, quoddam supra tibi contiguum mare Commacla dici castrum, in quod fertur mortuus occidere vivum?

Quantum vero, preter innumerabilia et non solum tibi, sed etiam mihi et omnibus preter soli Deo cognita non minusque lugenda, in ipsis etiam, quae a te—et utinam falso—proferuntur, me iure lugendum censeam, tibi, fili, caritative, ut sepe, confabulando referrem, si locum colloquendi haberem. At cum omnimodis desit, breviter hinc aliquid pro tempore fabor.

Primum me lugeo, quod talis inveniri quiverim, qui a te talis dici possim; secundo, quod te ad hoc meo, ut tu alios modo, instruxerim exemplo, siquidem te presente multis—heu dolor—mei oblitus et etiam melioribus sepe derogavi et ego. Tertio auditorum terreor nece, qui tam tuo quam meo periclitantur fetore.

Sed desine me, fili, hac in parte non minus, quam accusare, imitari, qua noxius cum mihi, si ita est ut asseris, magnopere fuerim, maxime fui tibi. Habes sanum super hoc, quod sequaris, consilium, quandoquidem, non defutura huiusmodi cadaverum male olida presciens busta, tale quid, ne horum foetore necarentur, vivis consulens divina pietas dixit: "Que dicunt, facite; que autem faciunt, facere nolite." Nam etsi ego tibi causa, quia materies fui mortis, tamen scito, quia quovis ordine, cuiusvis scelere moriaris, inter mortuos mortuus deputaberis. Sic enim dicit Deus: "Ipse quidem in iniquitate sua morietur, sanguinem autem eius de manu tua requiram." Et revera quid profuit Eve

---

edition, which I quote as reproduced in *PL*, cxxxvi.—H. Silvestre has recently published "Comment on rédigeait une lettre au Xᵉ siècle," an analysis of a very manneristic letter written to Rather in 968 by a former pupil, Bishop Everaclus of Liège. This analysis is very meticulous and informative. Silvestre has rediscovered a number of quotations and allusions, and he justly underlines the influence of Juvenal and, more especially, of Persius on the mannerism of the early Middle Ages. Nevertheless, I am not in complete agreement with all of Silvestre's interpretations and judgments.—Rather's letter, which I am discussing below, is the first in Weigle's edition.

dixisse: "Serpens decepit me"? Et utique dum hec tibi, ut compescaris, tui sollicitus scribo, id studiosissime ago, ut et tu a morte libereris et ego reus tui non tenear sanguinis. Potest autem fieri; nec enim id fieri posse despero ab eo, cui idem est posse quod velle, nec tu quoque hinc debes desperare, cum eum quatriduanum legeris suscitasse. Nec ego meminerim me id te dedocuisse in eo, quem manibus scripsisti, de parricidio sermone, ut ego iam ad vitam clamer cum fremitu pietatis divinẹ, licet tu me adhuc, quod ille melius novit quam tu, utpote quatriduanum dicas foetere. Nam nec desunt super me pie flentes sorores, inter quas, rogo, et tu annumereris, id est, ut sit in te sororius, et non parricidialis, affectus. Quo si me foetere, quia potes, confitearis vere, non succenseo, immo omnimodis postulo, dummodo mellifluam illam Domini merear audire vocem, resurrectionem mihi, tibi miraculum promittentem.

Few readers will fully understand this text at first or even second reading. Rather's Latin is extremely difficult for many reasons, chiefly because, not content with employing the inversion (hyperbaton, or *scinderatio*) and parenthesis characteristic of the Liège school, he is led by his involuted thinking and sensibility to exaggerate these devices in a private way of his own. The present text is by no means one of the most difficult; in the *Praeloquia*, and even more so in later works such as the *Phrenesis* (PL, cxxxvi, 365–392) or *Qualitatis coniectura* (PL, cxxxvi, 521–548), there are much worse passages; indeed, it is seldom that two successive sentences can be read at sight. The difficulty is increased by the plethora of allegorical Bible references that are never explained and by the dialogue form, employed almost throughout, in which it is often necessary to guess who is speaking and who being spoken to. In their footnotes the Ballerini brothers, the first editors of Rather's collected works, provide a good deal of help in construing sentences and reproduce a number of them with a more conventional word order. But sometimes they too are silent or in doubt, while later editors, such as Monticelli and Weigle, do not always agree with them or with each other. In the following attempt at translation, my sole concern has been clarity; accordingly I have occasionally paraphrased. No attempt is made to imitate the style. Those readers who are sufficiently interested in Rather and his style will do well to read the original aloud.

Alas, my son, what shall I do? Whom shall I first lament, myself who am dead or you who insult the dead—as if you too were not mortal—and, far worse, who draw the stench of the dead into your nostrils, breathe it with your mouth, and carry it to your lungs, so that you will die a far more hideous death, and who, which is much more serious, transmit it to others to breathe in, so that they too may die at the same time? Do you not know, my son, that above the sea [the Adriatic] not far from you there is a fortress named Comacchio, where, as they say, the dead kill the living? [37]

I have done countless things which not only in your eyes but in mine as well—not to mention innumerable others known only to God—are no less deplorable than what you accuse me of. Yet how much of what you adduce (oh, if only it were not true!) I feel bound to deplore, I would tell you in a spirit of love, dear son, as often in the past, in friendly conversation if such conversation were possible. But since it is altogether out of the question, I will write you briefly of these things.

First of all I deplore that men could judge me to be such [namely, dead] as you now call me. Secondly, that by my example I led you astray as you are now leading others astray— since unfortunately I, frequently in your presence, have so far forgotten myself as to speak ill of many, including better men than I. Thirdly, I am appalled to think of the possible death of the listeners, exposed to peril as much by your stench as by mine.

But cease, dear son, to accuse me and at the same time to imitate me in this matter, in which, if what you say is true, I have assuredly done myself great harm, and greater still to you. In this connection you have at your disposal a salutary counsel, which you ought to follow, for God in his divine mercy, foreseeing that there would be no lack of stinking corpses [Isa. 34:3] and concerned lest the living should perish from the stench, has said: "All therefore whatsoever they bid you observe, that observe and do; but do ye not after their works" [Matt. 23:3]. For although I was the cause of your death because I furnished

37. This allusion has never been explained. The fortress of Comacchio, often mentioned in our sources, is situated near the then important port of Comacchio, at the mouth of the Po, not far from Venice and Ravenna.

the diseased matter [38] that led to it, know that in whatever order [i.e., in whatever company], through the crimes of whomsoever you may die, you as a dead man will be counted among the dead [i.e., the damned]. For God has said: "He himself [namely, Ursus] will die in his sin, but his blood I will demand from your [Rather's] hand" [Ezek. 3:18]. And verily, what did it avail Eve, that she said: "The serpent beguiled me" [Gen. 3:13]? And in any event, in writing this, in thus attempting out of solicitude for you to restrain you, I am striving zealously to save you from death and to prevent your blood from being upon my head [echo of Num. 35:31]. This [the object of his efforts] may come to pass; I am not without hope that it can be brought about by Him for whom there is no distinction between will and power; nor should you despair of it, for you have read how he waked the man who had lain four days in the tomb.[39] And I remember too that I taught you this, in my sermon on parricide, which you wrote down with your own hands.[40] May I yet be awakened to life by the excitation [41] of divine mercy, although you say—and God knows it better than you do—that I stink like a four-day-old corpse. For around me there is no lack of sisters weeping in sympathy, among whom, I beseech you, count yourself, that is to say, let there be no homicidal, but only sisterly feelings [see n. 40]. If

38. I hope I have not gone too far in this interpretation of *materies*. The passage, I might add, is not hard to understand if we bear in mind the identification of death with sin. More on this below.

39. From this point to the end of the passage Rather uses the images with which the fourth Gospel relates the resurrection of Lazarus, who was a stinking corpse, having lain for four days in his grave (John 11). This is the source of *quatriduanus, fremitus pietatis divinae* (John 11:33 and 38), *ad vitam clamare* (ibid. 43), *foetere* (ibid. 39), *pie flentes sorores* (ibid. 31 and 33). *Sorores* refers first of all to Mary and Martha, but figuratively to those who lament Rather's sins in a spirit of love and who hope for his spiritual salvation and resurrection; he asks Ursus to take his place among them.

40. We do not possess this sermon, which Ursus must have taken down from dictation or after Rather's notes, and do not know what was in it. Perhaps it was not about murder in general but about the murder of close kin. For in the ensuing passage of his letter, not reproduced here, Rather accuses Ursus of having cursed (i.e., slandered) father and mother—i.e., Rather himself as his spiritual father and the Church (the bishop's mystical bride) as his mother. This helps us to understand *parricidialis affectus* in the next line of our text.

41. *Fremitus* is untranslatable, for it implies at once the inner trembling of Jesus' mercy and the roaring and rumbling of His might, as revealed in the miracle of the resurrection of the dead man. In any case, Luther's *ergrimmen* can hardly be regarded as a satisfactory translation. ["Excitation," above, translates Auerbach's *Erregtwerden*. The standard English Biblical tr. is "groan."—TRANS.]

with such feelings you declare, as you may do in all truth, that
I stink, I shall not be angry. On the contrary, I bid you do so,
provided only that I may be held worthy to hear the mellifluous
voice of the Lord,[42] promising to me resurrection and to you
a miracle.

The Christian or, more precisely, Pauline identification of death
with sin is a *topos;* it may have been expressed or implied in Ursus'
original insults. But what Rather made of it! Without introduction, like Cicero in his first oration against Catiline, he launches
into his questions in the very first paragraph—questions which
for all their rhetorical devices, for all their similarly constructed
clauses, rhymes and assonances, studied word order, and graduated comparisons,[43] seem overpoweringly spontaneous and almost
excessive in their passion. This impression comes from the content which has created its form. This content is an intimate mingling of accusation and self-accusation, which is indeed the content of all Rather's writings. His way of expressing it is almost
always impressive and moving, though occasionally he carries it
to the point of absurdity and wearies even the most patient of
readers. The image of the stinking corpse that runs through our
whole text, owes its poignancy to this mingling of accusation and
self-accusation, which makes possible a wide range of tone, for
without losing force the accusation is interrupted and softened
by the urgent, appealing, almost intimate, and often lyrical out-
bursts of brotherly love and hope in divine mercy. Yes, I stink,
like the corpse that I am; you too are dead, I have infected you,
now you are infecting others, and for all that I am to blame. But
perhaps God, He who *cum fremitu pietatis divinae* awakened the
stinking corpse of Lazarus, will yet call me (and you too) back
to life. To be sure, the style is sometimes rendered almost unin-
telligible by its many clauses within clauses—not only for the
modern reader but even for Rather's contemporaries, as may be

42. An allusion to the Promised Land (flowing with milk and honey); typo-
logically the Kingdom of God.
43. *me mortuum—quod est multo miserius—longe peius moriturum—quod est
gravius.*

gathered from certain of his own statements.[44] Yet it is rewarding to decipher him. His word order and plays on sound are exaggerated, but they are not meaningless: they serve to accentuate the significant feature, and they give an effect of power, sweep, and rhythmic variety. In the second paragraph (*Quantum vero*) the long, comprehensive, and carefully subdivided panorama of self-accusation (down to *me iure lugendum censeam*) is followed by a period which surprises us by the friendliness and gentle sadness of its cadence as well as its content (*tibi, fili, caritative, ut saepe, confabulando referrem si . . .*).

The third paragraph brings in the sharp division of *me, te, auditores*; the antithetical parallels—*talis inveniri quiverim qui a te talis dici possim; te ad hoc meo, ut tu alios modo; tam tuo quam meo*—and the sentence endings—*derogavi et ego; periclitantur fetore*—are magnificent. Similar features may be found throughout the long fourth paragraph (*Sed desine*); there is no need to list them. Here the theme of redemption by divine mercy, enriched by typological images, is set forth in a grandiose rhythm. It is already foreshadowed in the words *non defutura presciens . . . vivis consulens divina pietas.* It gains full force with the strikingly simple *potest enim fieri; nec enim id fieri posse despero ab eo . . . nec tu quoque hinc debes desperare, cum eum. . . .* Then comes the hopeful, almost exultant *ut ego iam ad vitam clamer cum fremitu pietatis divinae . . . utpote quatriduanum dicas foetere* (although you say I stink like Lazarus). And in conclusion, introduced by the allusion to the stinking corpse (rhymed cola: *Quo si me foetere/quia potes, confitearis vere*), the ecstatic and almost lyrical *dummodo mellifluam illam Domini merear audire vocem . . .*, in which we already seem to hear the voice of Bernard of Clairvaux.

In spirit this strange masterpiece—it is only a small part, perhaps a quarter, of the letter to Ursus—is Pauline and Augustinian, more

44. Especially in the introductory letter to Rather's *Phrenesis*, §§ 3 and 9: PL, cxxxvi, 369 and 376; Weigle, *MGH Briefe*, i, pp. 58f. and 65f. More on this below.

particularly Augustinian. Rather was well acquainted with the other Church Fathers; he often quotes Gregory. He also knew and made use of numerous classical authors. But in manner and temperament Augustine was closest to him; from Augustine comes the constant self-accusation, and it is Augustine who probably exerted the strongest influence on his style. Occasionally we find Augustinian turns of phrase, the origin of which Rather himself had forgotten.[45] But as a writer Rather lacked Augustine's balance, just as Rather the man lacked Augustine's assurance and dignity. He seems also to have been wanting in inner freedom and purity of will, for time and time again he was carried away by political ambition and literary vanity. He was only too well aware of these weaknesses and probably exaggerates them in his confessions, which are always accompanied by attacks on others. The result was an almost clownish exhibitionism, more suggestive of Rousseau or Strindberg than of Augustine, which became more and more prevalent as he grew older. Rather is often undignified and grotesque, but always expressive.

Such events as his first expulsion from Verona were frequent in his long life (he lived to be about eighty-five). He was twice reappointed bishop of Verona, in 947 and 965, the second time by Otto I; in between, in 953, also at the instigation of Otto's court, he became bishop of Liège. Each time Rather got himself into trouble, each time his protectors were ultimately compelled to drop him, and each time he was more or less forcibly removed. He spent the last years of his life in his native region of Liège (with occasional stays in Lobbes), and even then there were stormy conflicts.[46] It is understandable that, especially in view of his noble birth, so unusually gifted a man should have risen to high posi-

---

45. In the dedicatory epistle of the *Vita Sancti Ursmari*, addressed to the monks of Lobbes, there are found the words: *bona est locutio plane et suaviter congruenterque movens audientem*, as Rather says, *iuxta cuiusdam sapientis sententiam* (speech simply and agreeably and fittingly moving the hearer is good, according to the opinion of a certain wise person); *PL*, cxxxvi, 346 = Weigle, letter 4, p. 29, 6f. This is a reminiscence of Augustine, *De Trinitate* 8.3.4.

46. Folcuin, *Gesta abbatum Lobbiensium* 28 (*MGH Scr.*, iv, 69f.).

tion, and equally natural that the higher he rose, the more the instability of his character made itself felt. He saw the increasing corruption and secularization of the Church, and was keenly aware of their economic and psychological causes. His accounts of the mentality and economic situation of the Veronese clergy are remarkably penetrating.[47] He also had a wide knowledge of canon law and its tradition (including the famous forged decretals, which he, quite naturally, regarded as authentic), and took a lofty view of his episcopal office. He tried with the utmost zeal to reform his diocese. But he was never able to gauge the forces for and against him or to take a sound view of his own position. He had been appointed by secular rulers, first by King Hugo, then by Otto I. The secular rulers, especially the Ludolfings, built their political and military power on bishops devoted to their cause. If this situation called for concessions he could not accept, Rather should have resigned or become a martyr. He felt—perhaps his attachment to power had something to do with it—that it would be wrong to resign (and no amount of unfortunate experience could ever deter him from accepting a bishopric). On the other hand, his martyrdom was never very impressive because time and again, however protesting and reluctant, he would accept the helping hand that brought him to safety. He was lacking in poise and dignity, he did not know how to inspire esteem, and he was unable to make friends among the clergy or even to make his enemies respect him. Erudite and passionate, pedantic and vain, solitary and moody, a man of tenacious vitality—so we see him in his writings, which are our chief source for his biography: far more a petulant crank than a martyr. He has occasionally been called a forerunner of the Reformation, or even of Hildebrand (Gregory VII). This is true in regard to certain of his ideas, but not to his intellectual and moral attitude as a whole. He not only

47. See, for instance, *De contemptu canonum* (letter to Hubertus of Parma, I.4; *PL*, cxxxvi, 491ff. = Weigle, letter 16, pp. 76ff.) or *Discordia* (letter to Ambrosius; *PL*, cxxxvi, 617ff. = Weigle, letter 29, pp. 159ff.).

(like Bede and Boniface before him) [48] castigated the corruption
and secularization of the clergy but also developed ideas about
the primacy of the spiritual function, the celibacy of the clergy,
and Church property, which later became part of the reformers'
program. But in the situation of the Church and the Papacy at his
time, such statements were empty words. An ecclesiastical attitude or spirit had still to be created. Alarm at the dependence,
feudalization, and secularization of the clergy became widespread
with the monastic reform movements, which were founded in
Rather's day; Cluny had been in existence since 910, Gorze since
933. He seems to have had little contact with these movements;
but it was in them and not in isolated individuals like Rather that
the spirit of Church reform, the spirit that was to lead to the
investiture conflict, had its beginnings.[49]

But as I have said, Rather is always expressive, and unquestionably the mannerism of his language is something more than learned
ornamentation, namely an authentic reflection of his nature: as
far as I know, he is the first author of the Middle Ages in whom
mannerism became a genuine style, but it was rooted in his being,
which he could not have expressed in any other way. Rather was
very proud of his style (though he also felt guilty over his pride),
and it was not only in its erudition—which also demanded erudition of the reader—that he took pride. He sensed that there was
something more in this style. There is an interesting passage on
the subject in the introduction to *Phrenesis* § 3 (*PL*, cxxxvi, 369
= Weigle letter 11, pp. 58, 13–59, 13):

> Generat praeterea hoc et difficultatem intellectus eis,
> quos fecit, libellis, quod creberrime posita illic cernitur
> parenthesis et, ut liquidam faciat orationem, mirabilem dic-
> tionum facit saepius ordinationem, difficillimam quae pariat,

48. The former in the letter to Ecgbert, *Hist. eccl.* (ed. C. Plummer), I,
    410–417. For Boniface, see his letters edited by M. Tangl, *MGH Epist.
    sel.*, I, 82f. and 163f.
49. Rather's adventures in Verona were not unique; Gerbert of Aurillac, as
    abbot of Bobbio, had very similar experiences.

optimam licet intelligentibus, constructionis materiem. Fe-
fellerit sane plurimos ne eius improvide considerata loquacitas, morum ipsius uti et qualitas, fateor magis eum
intellectu viguisse quam arte, exercitio quodam scribendi
quaeque, non vero copiose dicendi quam privilegio plura
sciendi, quem priscorum magis exploratio curiosa quam
ipsa artis dictare docuerint praecepta. Pauca a magistris,
plura per se magis didicit praesumptione temeraria compa-
rando, quae a doctoribus praecipuis alii maximo vix per-
cepissent labore. Unde et quidam sapiens pariterque religio-
sus, inflatilis ne illum subverteret caritate minime subnixa,
apostolus ut praemonuerat, scientia, relectis quibusdam
opusculis ait: In eo gratiam vigere quam sapientiam magis
mirandusque magis quam laudandus videtur, miranda potius
et praedicanda misericors, quae talia tali deserendo utique
sese deserentem non deserens, non deserendo deserens con-
tulit, gratia.

I have attempted a translation accompanied by the necessary
commentary:

> The difficulty of understanding his [Rather's] writings is
> further increased by his frequent use of parentheses; furthermore,
> he employs an astonishing word order, which is exceedingly diffi-
> cult to construe, but altogether excellent for those who under-
> stand it. Lest many be misled by a superficial view of his writing,[50]
> as they have been in judging his character, I own that he is dis-
> tinguished more by innate ability than by theoretical training,
> more by a certain ease, though not prolixity, in writing than by
> extensive knowledge; for he learned to write more by ceaseless
> study of the Ancients than by following the actual rules of
> rhetorical theory.[51] He learned little from teachers and much
> more by himself, acquiring more by his own presumptuous bold-
> ness than other men are able to absorb by painstaking effort under
> the most distinguished preceptors. Thus, after reading several of

50. *Loquacitas* occurs in a favorable sense in Sidonius, *Carm.* 14.7 and *Epist.*
5.5.2. Cf. also Du Cange.
51. Reference is made here not only to the authors of antiquity but also to
the Church Fathers; in another passage, however (*Praeloquia* 6.24) Rather
calls the latter *moderni* in contrast to the *antiqua* or *prisca exempla* of
Holy Writ. On all this see E. R. Curtius, *Europ. Lit.*, pp. 257ff. [Amer.
edn., pp. 251–255].

his works, a man as wise as he is pious spoke to him as follows, fearing that he might be corrupted by such inflated knowledge, unsustained by Christian love, against which the Apostle has warned us [I Cor. 8:1]: In him grace is mightier than wisdom; he is more to be wondered at than praised. Far more to be wondered at *and* praised is the merciful grace that has granted such things to such a man; to one whom in truth it should forsake, because he forsook it, but which it did not forsake; and yet in not forsaking him it did forsake him [by exposing him to literary vanity? The Ballerini brothers omitted the final words, *non deserendo deserens;* Weigle restores them, but in my opinion without sufficiently explaining his grounds].

I am not sure that I have always hit on the right meaning, though a certain amount of explanation is provided by a somewhat later, hardly less difficult passage.[52] Rather held that his obscurity contributed to a higher clarity, which to be sure is made manifest only to those who make an effort (*ut liquidam faciat orationem . . . optimam licet intelligentibus*).[53] In this other passage he cites the example of the Holy Scriptures and of Augustine's commentaries on them (from *De doctrina christiana*) in justification of his obscurity. This may be taken as a traditional gesture.

But in both passages he shows that he regards himself as a superior writer who, precisely because of his superiority, is exposed to envy and incomprehension (in this connection he cites Horace, *Epist.* 2.1.13f.). In the passage we have just quoted, the accent is on his independence: he tells us that he did not learn most of what he knew from teachers of rhetoric but from independent study of the great authors of the past. In conclusion he introduces a wise and pious man to certify (in Christian terms, but very plainly) that Rather is what would later be known as a genius,

---

52. *Phrenesis* prooem. 8f. (Weigle, pp. 64–66): *Vos, o neniae . . .* to the end of the letter.

53. He concludes a letter to Bruno, the brother of Otto I, written between 942 and 946, with an apology for not including any verses as was customary; he explains that he is no poet although he understands the rules of prosody (Weigle, letter 6, pp. 32f.): *Diffusiorem namque sum semper amplexus sermonem, obscuritatis odio diffugiens contractiorem* (I have always embraced a more diffuse style, shunning a more compact one out of a hatred for obscurity).

distinguished not by school learning and acquired skill but by his own experience and inspiration.

In this he is right; he was a literary genius, though a very odd one. This oddness, however, did not reside only in his temperament but also in the linguistic material he worked with. It is a Latin which had long been withdrawn from the daily usage that ordinarily creates language and gives it life; and which had not yet been renewed, as it would be later on, by living intellectual currents. He stood alone. It is not in the least surprising that the flowers of human expression that bloomed on such a soil should have a strange look. Rather drew on the ancient tradition, on the Bible with its typological and ethical images, and on the *sermo humilis* of the Church Fathers: all that he himself could add with a view to expressing his own originality was a kind of expressionistic ornament, based on word order and a combination of tone color, rhythm, and striking accents. In this he followed the mannerist tradition, especially of the Liège school, from which he is distinguished, however, not only by his extreme exaggeration but above all by the subservience in his writing of technique to content: it is the meaning that determines the accents; word order and phonetic figures are treated as instruments.

In the treatise *Qualitatis coniectura cuiusdam* (a title characteristic of Rather), written during his last years in Verona when he was almost seventy-five, he uses a new device in his self-portrayal (he finds a thousand different pretexts for talking about himself): he makes his Veronese adversaries talk about him and records their seemingly haphazard chatter. A few excerpts may give the reader an idea of this remarkable piece: [54]

... Nasum semper tenet in libro, inde garrire non cessat. Omnino redarguit omnes, contiguus nulli cujus mores placeant illi. Quem vero laudat, qui seipsum semper vituperat? ... Quae dicit, scribit, legendaque posteris, prae-

54. *Qual. coniect.* 2–9 (*PL*, cxxxvi, 524–534).

sentibus ut derogent, linquere gestit. Chronographiam,[55]
graecizando vanus, cum non sit saltem Latinus, hujusmodi
sui temporis vocat scripturam, quae utique contemporalium
sibi contineat vitam; se primum, se mediastino, se rodens
ipsum postremo, inde omnes suopte more viventes, genui-
num in eis figere non desinit dentem, intactum deserens
neminem. Unde quia contra omnes lingua ejus, lingua
merito est omnium contra eum (Gen. 16:12). . . . Nil
quod gloriae pertineat in eo videtur, nil quod honori.
Manus tantum et labia cibum lavat sumpturus, necnon et
sumpto; faciem raro. Forsitan in patria sua fuerat bacularis,
ideo illi tam honor omnis est vilis, longe aliter saepe licet
dictum sit frequentius nobis, fillus carpentarii; ideo tam
gnarus, tamque voluntarius est basilicas struendi vel re-
struendi; lapides semper versat et reversat, ipse eos saepe
connectit. (3) Quae sunt servorum agere non dedignatur;
dominorum adeo negligit usum, ut posthabito curule pon-
tificali frequentius decubet humi; Epicurus ac veluti alter,
summum in voluptate bonum qui censeat esse, si ventri
bene est, si lateri, si pedibus, si sibi est suisque sufficiens
soli, contentus. Non curat sibi manducanti utrum quilibet
assideat coetus . . .

There follows a passage which it would be tedious to explain
on the basis of the text, because of the difficult metaphors employed; the gist is that the only inference to be drawn from
Rather's eccentricity is that he had committed particularly abomi-
nable sins. The speaker adds that he is often heard moaning and
lamenting when alone.

Non desunt enim qui saepissime audiant eum solum quasi
cum altero rixari, et aliquando dicere: "Quid vis iterum,
diabole? Nonne jam consenuisti in talibus mecum; effeta
membra et enerves cur adhuc laceras artus? Nonne tibi
satis sum traditus? Nonne satis gehennam habeo emptam?

55. Like Weigle (letter 26, p. 146, 12 and n.4) I suppose that *chronographia* is
not the name of a lost work by Rather, but designates collectively those
of his works which deal with the contemporary period.

Quid amplius pretii quaeris? Minoris potuit vita perennis emi. Si non sufficiunt vero quae sunt in libro *Confessionis* meae descripta, recurre, maligne, ad tuum, ubi utique scio nihil malorum meorum omissum. Sufficere, sed fateor, poterant tantummodo illa quae Italia, Francia cantat, et Norica, quae non ignorat Burgundia, recolit Provincia, meminit Septimania, Suevia recordatur. Inveteratum dierum malorum (Dan. 13:25) me nominari valere, sufficere tibi, maligne, poterat jure. . . . (5) . . . Solus, si liceret, tota die sederet, libros versaret vel reversaret. Frequentiam odit, solitudinem diligit, trocho non ludit, aleam fugit, de canibus nil curat, de accipitribus nihil. Interdum loquacissimus, interdum est quasi mutus; risu dissolutus, subindeque tristissimus, rixarique actutum paratus; scurrilitatem vero vel verba otiosa, risumque moventia, omni proferre, sive sit laetus sive iratus, paratissimus hora. . . . (8) . . . Psalmos se dicit non ideo cantare, quod noverit exaudibiles eos, cum semper aliud cogitet, esse; sed quia cum sentiat se illos perinvitum canere, ipsam vim quam, contra voluntatem eos recitans, sibi ingerit, putet ad hoc aliquid valere quod contra Deum volens actitat ipse, sive ut labia saltem ipsa compellat Deo servire, etsi corde vagante, caeterisque Deo rebellantibus membris, cum et in nullo eorum magis sit ad irritandum Deum quam in excessibus linguae proclivis. . . . (9) . . . Mirum qualiter saltem vivere talis sinitur diabolus. Quis ergo talem amare queat adversarium? Qui tamen si forte placet alicui, magis pro scurrilitate quam pro sua illi placet aliqua bonitate; qua utique scurrilitate gratus probatur ipsis etiam inimicis existere.

He always has his nose in a book and he never stops chattering. He is always finding fault and is satisfied with none of those around him. Whom indeed can a man who is always reviling himself be expected to praise? . . . He writes down everything he says, wishing to bequeathe it to posterity and give them a poor opinion of his contemporaries. Writings of this kind, which describe the life of the times, he calls *chronography*, pleased as Punch with his Greek when he hardly knows Latin; he flays himself at the beginning, himself in the middle, himself at the end; then he goes on to take bites at others who live in the same way as he does, and spares no one. Since his tongue is against everyone, every man's tongue is quite justly against him. . . . Nothing conducive to his good name can be found in him, nothing that is in keeping with his dignity [i.e., the requirements of his position]. Before and after meals he washes only his hands and lips, his face but seldom. It seems likely that he was a mere beadle in his own country, and that is why all dignity means so little to him, although we have often been told a very different story about his origins [namely, that he was of noble birth], or perhaps the son of a carpenter; that must be why he knows so much about the building and remodeling of churches and takes so much interest in such things; he is always turning the stones this way and that, and sometimes he himself fits them into place. (3) He does not consider it beneath him to do the work of a servant; he is so indifferent to the ways of the upper classes that he makes no use of his bishop's chair and often sits on the floor; like a second Epicurus, who finds the greatest happiness in comfort; satisfied if his belly, his hips, and his feet are at ease, if he has enough for himself and his household. He desires no company at mealtimes. . . .

He has often been heard to speak when alone as though quarreling with someone, saying: "What do you want now, devil? Haven't you grown old along with me in such temptations? Why do you continue to afflict these weak and powerless limbs? Am I not yet sufficiently in your power? Haven't I bought a sufficient share in hell? What greater price do you expect? I could have bought eternal life for less. If what is described in the book of my confessions is not enough for you,[56] look, evil one, into your own book, which, I am certain, omits none of my evil deeds. Besides, you ought to be satisfied with what Italy, France, and the Noric regions are telling each other, with what Burgundy knows, Provence remembers, Septimania does not forget. Wicked one, it should really be enough for you to know that I have earned the name of a man waxen old in wickedness. . . ." (5) If he had time, he would sit alone all day thinking through his books. He detests company, loves solitude, plays no games of chance,[57] keeps away from dice, takes no interest in dogs or in falcons. At times he chatters endlessly, at times he doesn't say a word; he can laugh immoderately, grow sad for no reason, or suddenly begin to quarrel; but regardless of the mood he is in, he is always glad to make others laugh with his jokes and idle chatter. . . . (8) He says that he chants the Psalms not because he knows they are worth hearing, since he is always thinking of something else at

56. Rather's work: *Excerptum ex dialogo confessionali* (PL, cxxxvi, 393–444).
57. In the view of my colleague Oystein Ore, who is an authority, *trochus* probably refers to a kind of wheel of chance.

the time, but because he is aware that he sings them most un-
willingly and believes that the very constraint he puts upon himself in reciting them against his will may count toward his salvation and counterbalance his customary godless actions; in other
words, he compels his lips at least to serve God, though his heart
may stray and his other members rebel against Him; he well
knows that through no other of his members is he so prone to
arouse God's wrath as by his over-ready tongue. . . . (9) One
cannot but be amazed that such a devil is even allowed to live.
Who could love such a fiend? If anyone really likes him, it is
more for his clownishness than for any good quality; with his
clownery he amuses even his enemies.

That in the tenth century this man should have achieved, and succeeded in expressing, such self-awareness seems a miracle that can
be explained only by an overpowering need and genius for expression—the two go hand in hand. In the last quotation there are a
few simply constructed, quite colloquial sentences (*nasum semper
tenet in libro,* or *quid vis iterum, diabole*)—their style is in keeping with the person he is describing. But we also perceive the
tragic, perverse complexity of this person, his profound sadness, his
loneliness, his uneasy conscience, his vanity, and his shame at being
so vain. Rhetorical artifice plays a dominant part almost throughout, and, as usual with Rather, the finest effects are achieved by
the idiosyncratic word order; it seems to me that for all its oddity,
it springs directly from his nature. Of course he molded his nature
in this way; but once he had done so, it was *his* nature, and the
expressive sentences flow spontaneously from his pen: *se primum,
se mediastino, se rodens ipsum postremo . . . intactum deserens
neminem;* the whole sentence containing the comparison with
Epicurus; the questions addressed to the devil, with the climax
minoris potuit vita perennis emi; and the sentence ending (in § 5)
omni proferre, sive sit laetus sive iratus, paratissimus hora. In this
last case the whole sentence (*scurrilitatem vero . . .*) is a kind of
interpretive summary of the previously described eccentricities
and contradictions; *scurrilitatem* is strongly emphasized, it is the
key word; the somewhat less accented rhymed couplet *vel verba*

otiosa/risumque moventia serves to analyze it, and this *scurrilitas*, which dominates and subordinates the whole period, is again stressed by the new beginning, in which *omni* and *hora*, which properly belong together, bracket the words *sive sit laetus sive iratus*, while *paratissimus* serves as a pedestal for *hora*. Into this sentence, which as a whole forms a coherent summary, Rather has managed to put two strong accents which do not interfere with but complement each other: first *scurrilitatem*, then *omni hora*.

Rather is an outstanding example of literary talent, and clearly this talent drew its nourishment from the tradition that we have called *sermo humilis*. True, he had learned a good deal from the authors of antiquity, but so had the Church Fathers. Like them he combines the sublime with the lowly, the urgency of his Christian message with the trivia of everyday life; he speaks at once as a sinner and as a preacher. This tradition had never been lost; even in the theological writings of the Carolingian era, in Alcuin for example, or in Paschasius Radbertus and in a number of others, it is unmistakable, for the influence of such Church Fathers as Augustine and Gregory was still at work. But in the Carolingian era there was no original development, the tradition had become rigid and sterile. In Rather it takes on new life, developing in a characteristically mannered style which already foreshadowed the flowering that was to come in the eleventh and twelfth centuries.

If we attempt to formulate the new element introduced by Rather, what first comes to mind is his buffoonery, *scurrilitas*. It springs from Rather's own temperament and consequently need not have been significant for any further development; but we know that the farcical element had its place in medieval sermons and religious life in general (especially among monks, and Rather was already thirty-five when he left the monastery), and it seems to me that this combination was important for the subsequent development in Europe of the tragic fool, a figure not cultivated in antiquity. Mannerism is related to *scurrilitas* but goes far beyond it. Rather knew all the rhetorical devices of his day, but there was one to which he was particularly given: ingenious word order. He carries it to the point of absurdity, often obliging the reader to work out puzzles. But even so, it is a more human device than arrangements of letters and plays on sound. Rather favors intricate word order because of the expressive possibilities it offers. Stylistic mannerism is of course an ancient heritage, as Curtius has brilliantly shown. It goes back at least to such late Latin authors as Sidonius Apollinaris or Fortunatus, or perhaps even to Persius, and can ultimately be traced to far earlier currents in the Greek rhetorical tradition. Manneristic fashions are known to have existed also in Irish, Anglo-Saxon, and Carolingian Latin; they were inherited by the Liège school, in which Rather received his training. In any event he did not invent strange glosses or complicated sentence structure, or the use of rhymes and other plays on sound. But whereas in the three centuries preceding Rather these and similar devices may be regarded as sterile, pedantic games, he (as far as I know) was the first to have lent such mannerism the dignity of a style. With him for the first time mannerism is subordinated to expression; it becomes an instrument suited to what he has to communicate; and what he has to communicate is his very own existence.

Rather, I believe, is by far the most interesting and important Latin writer of his time; but in the tenth century a certain vividness of portrayal and originality of style were making their appearance among other writers. The foundation is the mannerism inherited from late antiquity; but new subject matter gave rise to a new form.

Liudprand,[58] who became bishop of Cremona in 961, lived ap-

---

58. *MGH Scr.*, III, 264–363. I have used the edition *in usum scholarum*, 3rd edn. by J. Becker, which contains a bibliography. German translation by K. von der Osten-Sacken, 2nd edn. by W. Wattenbach, in the series Geschichtschreiber der deutschen Vorzeit. Liudprand wrote the *Antapodosis*, an international chronicle chiefly concerned with Germany, Italy, and Byzantium; the *Historia Ottonis*, which is in the main a justification of the Italian policy of Otto I during 963 and 964; and *Relatio de legatione Constantinopolitana*, an account of his second mission to Constantinople in 968.

proximately from 920 to 972. He came of a distinguished Lombard family. As a boy his fine voice won him favor at the court of King Hugo of Pavia. In 949 Berengar II sent him to Constantinople as his ambassador; later he incurred Berengar's disfavor, and in 956 he entered the service of Otto I, in whose behalf he was active in Italian politics during the sixties as a diplomat and publicist. In 968, as Otto's ambassador, he went a second time to Constantinople. Courtier and diplomat, he was an ecclesiastic only in name; his literary talent was considerable but superficial, journalistic, and anecdotic; as a man he was vain, vengeful, and indiscreet. He often made an absurd display of his erudition and knowledge of Greek. And he did not, like Rather, compensate for all these unpleasant traits by the substance of his character.

Nevertheless he is an important figure: he is, I believe, the first medieval writer whose works show a breadth of horizon and give a living picture of a wide variety of places. He knew Italy, Germany, and the Byzantine Orient; he was on terms of friendship with a Spanish bishop, at whose behest he wrote his main work, the *Antapodosis*. And he had many other connections of all sorts; he was, as we should say today, "open to the world," and he was a gifted, though not exactly natural, storyteller. There had already been a few well-traveled writers—Rather, for example, or Gerbert of Aurillac—but none of them had the will or talent to give a lively account of what he saw or heard. In addition to traveling widely and meeting everybody, Liudprand had a taste for satirical anecdote. His malicious and certainly exaggerated, but striking and amusing picture of the Byzantine court at the time of Nicephorus (*Legatio*) is probably the best known piece of prose that has come to us from the tenth century; it is to be found even in school anthologies. Though sometimes spoiled by stilted speeches, most of Liudprand's anecdotes and tales are highly effective, and there is little to compare with them in the early Middle Ages. Let us discuss at least one of them. He tells the following story about Willa, a Tuscan princess and wife of Berengar II (*Antap.* 5.32):

Habuit ea presbiterulum capellanum, nomine Dominicum, statura brevem, colore fuligineum, rusticum, seti-
gerum, indocilem, agrestem, barbarum, durum, villosum,
cauditum, petulcum, insanum, rebellem, iniquum, cuius
magisterio duas Willa commendaverat gnatas, Gislam scilicet atque Girbergam, ut eas litterarum scientia epotaret.
Occasione itaque puellarum, quas presbiter Dominicus,
hirsutus, inlotus facete docebat, mater ei propitiaverat,
tribuens delicatum cibum vestesque preciosas. Mirari
omnes, cur cunctis invisa, ingrata tenax huic existeret larga.
Sententia tamen veritatis, quae ait: "Nihil opertum, quod
non reveletur, et occultum, quod non in publicum veniat"
(Matt. 10:26), diu mirari homines passa non est. Nam cum
nocte quadam Berengario absente ad cubile dominicum
more solito hirsutus isdem vellet accedere, canis isthic ade-
rat, qui latratu horribili circumiacentes excitavit huncque
morsu vehementi laniavit. Consurgentes denique, qui in
domo erant, cum eum conprehenderent et, quo iret, inter-
rogarent, apologeticum istud anticipando domina dedit:
"Ad mulieres nostras ibat perditus." Sperans itaque presbiterulus sibi lenius fore, si teneret sententiam dominae: "Ita
est, inquam." Coepit itaque domina vitae eius insidiari
praemiumque promittere, si esset, qui ei vitam auferret.
Sed cum timerent Deum omnes et mors eius differretur,
pervenit ad Berengarium sermo. Willa vero coepit aru-
spices maleficosque inquirere, quo eorum carminibus iuva-
retur. Utrum autem horum carminibus an Berengarii sit
adiuta mollicie, nescio; adeo mens eius est inclinata, ut
sponte *maritali porrigeret ora capistro* (cf. Juvenal 6.43).
Presbiterulus itaque, quia dominae asseculas adhinnivit,
virilibus amputatis dimittitur; domina vero a Berengario
magis diligitur. Dixerunt autem, cui eum eunuchizaverunt,
quod merito illum domina amaret, quem priapeia portare
arma constaret.

For her chaplain she had a priestling named Dominic, short of
stature, soot-colored, rustic, bristly, uncouth, ill-mannered, rough
and shaggy, with a mighty rod, aggressive, mad, stubborn, and
unrestrained.[59] To him Willa had entrusted the education of her

59. The collection of epithets is derived for the greater part from a poem
of late antiquity on Pan (Riese, *Anth. lat.*, carm. 682 = Baehrens, *Poet.
Lat. min.*, III, 170). Liudprand uses them in a similar way for Nicephorus
also in his *Legatio* 10.

two daughters, Gisla and Girberga, in order that the science of letters might intoxicate them. Through these daughters, who were instructed in an entertaining fashion (or, ironically, graciously) by the disheveled and unwashed priest Dominic, the mother also acquired a liking for him; she saw to it that he had choice victuals and costly clothing. Everyone was amazed that she, so hateful, unfriendly, and miserly toward all others, should be so generous to him. But the maxim which says: "Nothing is hidden that shall not be made manifest, etc.," saw to it that they did not wonder for long. For one night, when Berengar was absent and the disheveled rogue was making his way as usual to the princely chamber, a dog set up a horrible barking that woke up everyone in the vicinity, and began to tear him apart with powerful bites. Everyone in the house got up. Seizing him, they asked him where he was going. The princess answered in his behalf: "The wretch was on his way to my women." The priestling, hoping to get off more lightly if he accepted the noble lady's explanation, said: "That is the truth." Whereupon the lady began to plot against his life and to promise a reward to anyone who would kill him. But since they all feared God and consequently his death was not encompassed, the story came to Berengar's ears; Willa, however, called in soothsayers and magicians to help her by their spells. Whether it was their incantations or Berengar's weakness that came to her help, I cannot say. At all events, his mind was so affected that of his own free will he "offered his snout to the marital muzzle." Whereupon the priestling, for having neighed [60] at the women in the queen's retinue, was castrated and driven away; but Berengar loved the lady more than ever. But those who had castrated him maintained that the lady had loved him according to his merits; for beyond a doubt he had possessed weapons excellently suited to love.

Neither the content nor the style of this story requires an extensive commentary. Those who question its credibility should bear in mind that Liudprand hated Berengar and Willa and was eager to connect them with any evil or ridiculous actions that he could make halfway credible; and, on the other hand, that the details of the story—the dissoluteness of the priest, the uncouthness of the sovereigns, the recourse to sorcerers, the nature of the punishment—are quite in keeping with the times. But there was no other comparable storyteller at the time, and assuredly not in

60. *Adhinnire* had been already used in this sense by Plautus.

the preceding Carolingian period. The epithets with which Liudprand describes the priest are, to be sure, borrowed from late antiquity; but how skillfully he chose what to borrow! No one will
contest Liudprand's literary verve—lively tales of this kind remained very rare for several centuries, down to the thirteenth
century. Though in the detail we find a good deal of high-flown
mannerism (not only a number of Latin expressions such as *litterarum scientia epotare, latratu horribili excitare, priapeia arma
portare*, but the whole sentence with the Bible quotation seem inappropriate to the subject matter), this is attributable less to bad
taste than to conscious irony; in this and similar tales it is precisely by his mannerism that Liudprand obtains his grotesque effects.

Different as they are, Rather and Liudprand have something
in common: mannerism, which to be sure was already widespread in Carolingian Latin and universal in that of the tenth century, and above all a certain eccentricity and unevenness of style.
Their works are full of *scurrilitas*, indiscretion, and immoderation,
though in the one these spring from a heartfelt need, in the other,
from rancor and self-importance. Both lack the sense of the appropriate, the control and harmonious form which lend unity and
dignity to literary expression.

In the tenth century we also find—north of the Alps, at the
Ottonian court—a solemn, homogeneous, and almost official mannerism. This was the style cultivated by the historians who wrote
panegyric biographies of the leading members of the imperial
family, stylized in the manner of lives of the saints.[61] This period
witnessed the beginnings of a more rigorous piety which paved
the way for the reform movements of the ensuing century. Asceticism, the cult of the saints, and belief in relics achieved an intensity unknown in the Carolingian era. The new ideal of piety
colored men's actions and gave rise to a new way of life.

61. There is an excellent monograph on *Das Heiligenleben im 10. Jahrhundert*
by Ludwig Zoepf.—The traditional features of the panegyric, especially
of rulers, are described by E. R. Curtius, *Europ. Lit.*, pp. 161ff., 183ff.
[Amer. edn., pp. 155–162; 176–178], and passim.

Among the Ottonian biographers this pious style is highly political, panegyric, and manneristic—this last if only because the
most suitable models were to be found in the mannerism of late
antiquity. Long passages from writers of antiquity are woven into
the texts. The best example is the *Vita Mahthildis,*[62] wife of Henry
the Fowler and mother of Otto I. This work is a kind of mosaic,
containing long passages from earlier writers: Sulpicius Severus,
Venantius Fortunatus, Boethius, Terence, Virgil, Prudentius; and
yet the style is perfectly homogeneous. When these many borrowings were first noted, their importance, it seems to me, was
overestimated. This work is a panegyric on the ancestress of a
royal family; even if a reader does not recognize the borrowings
as such, the general tone must make it clear to him that this is a
ritual stylization; in a composition of this kind, intended to establish or reinforce a myth, it would be quite naïve to look for reliable information even if the author had used fewer models for
his ornaments. On the other hand, to reject the work as worthless because of its so-called plagiarism is to close one's eyes to
the artistry with which these ancient jewels were selected, refur-
bished, and fitted into a new setting. All this adds up to a conscious stylistic intention which has created a new and homogeneous work. In the fifth paragraph, which both in its wording and
its themes is taken over largely from Fortunatus' life of Radegundis, the sainted Merovingian queen, we find a sentence which
starts out with an echo of Fortunatus but soon turns in another
direction:

> Nam quanto sibi accessit potestas sublimior, tanto se
> humiliavit devotior; et quod perraro evenit, dignitatem
> seculi sine superbia possedit. In publico processit ornata
> gemmis et serico, sed interius gerebat pretiosius ornamen-
> tum, cor acceptabile Deo; tantamque sibi subditis exhibebat

62. *MGH Scr.,* IV, 282–302. There are two versions, the first from the standpoint of the Ludolfingian main branch, the second revised under Henry II
to match the outlook of the then ruling Bavarian branch. German translation by P. Jaffé, 2nd edn. by W. Wattenbach. See there, too, the preface
by Jaffé, who was the first to call attention to these borrowings.

humilitatem et in vice matris caritatem, ut omnibus esset
amori pariter et honori.

> For the higher she rose in authority, the more devoutly did she
> humble herself; and she possessed that very rare thing, dignity of
> place without pride. She appeared in public adorned with jewels
> and clothed in silk; but inwardly she bore a more precious orna-
> ment, a heart pleasing to God. And so much humility did she
> show to those beneath her and so great a charity in her role as
> mother that she was equally loved and honored by all.

The brief passage is easy to understand, the manneristic ornaments are obvious. It gives us an impressive picture, a living image of queenly dignity (*in publico processit* . . .), or it might be
more accurate to say an idealized portrait of a womanly dignity
that is both regal and Christian. The *dignitas seculi* is sanctified
and exalted by the dignity of the heart. The splendor of this
woman's jewels and raiment is enhanced by the realization that
beneath them lies the costly jewel of a heart pleasing to God. The
biographer is far from suggesting that this woman might wish to
cast off her secular dignity—Mathilda is the ancestress of the imperial house and symbol of its often menaced unity. The situation
of Fortunatus' heroine is very different.[63] Poor Radegundis had
been obliged to marry the man (Chlotar I) who had laid waste
her Thuringian homeland and deposed her family—even after her
marriage to him, he had put her brother to death. Everything we
know of her leads us to suppose that her most fervent desire was
to escape from her marriage, her royal position, and from worldly
life in general—which in the end she succeeded in doing.

   In the ensuing sentences of both these works (*Vita Mahthildis*
5, pp. 286f., and Fortunatus' *Vita S. Radegundis* 14f., p. 40) we
read that both queens often left their marriage bed at night in

63. Venantius Fortunatus, *Vita Sanctae Radegundis* 9 (*MGH AA*, IV: 2, 39):
   *Nubit ergo terreno principi nec tamen separata a caelesti, ac dum sibi
   accessisset saecularis potestas*, magis quam permitteret dignitas *se plus
   inclinavit voluntas* . . . (She was, therefore, married to a worldly prince
   yet not separated from heavenly life. And even as worldly power came
   to her, she humbled her will *more than her rank permitted*). The emphasis is mine.

order to pray. But Fortunatus is rich in details: Radegundis uses the call of nature as a pretext for slipping away; she prays so long that she can scarcely be warmed when she gets back to bed, and King Chlotar expresses his incomprehension and disapproval in no uncertain terms. Mathilda's biographer mentions no such particulars and sticks to elegant generalities. He insists explicitly and at length that harmony reigned between the queen and her husband. Obviously he borrowed themes and turns of phrase from Fortunatus. But whereas in his life of Radegundis Fortunatus seems to employ his manneristic style out of mere habit, often drops it entirely, and never makes deliberate use of it to express royal splendor, Mathilda's biographer shows a constant preoccupation with his ornate, ceremonious style, which he often employs to remarkable effect—it sparkles brightest when he wishes to bring out the power and magnificence of the imperial house. In footnote 63 we have reproduced Fortunatus' sentence *Nubit ergo terreno principi,* etc. The corresponding sentence in the *Vita Mahthildis* reads:

> Cum igitur regalis solii ascendisset gradum venerabilis regina, illustris maritali potentia et illustrior religione divina, in coniugii foedere manebat pudica.
>
> When therefore the worthy queen ascended the steps of the royal throne, illustrious by the authority of her marriage and still more illustrious by her holy religion, she remained chaste in the conjugal union.

Another well-known example is the *Vita Brunonis,* a biography of Archbishop Bruno of Cologne, written immediately after his death. It was written at the behest of Bruno's successor by Ruotger, a learned cleric. It, too, is full of literary reminiscences. But the stylization as a whole is unmistakably Ottonian. Bruno, Mathilda's younger son and younger brother of Otto I, was the mainstay of imperial policy. He seems to have been a highly intelligent man, who matured early and never indulged in the crude and unpredictable excesses that characterized most of the mighty of those times. He had been carefully educated; when scarcely more than a child he had held high secular and ecclesiastical positions; he became archbishop of Cologne at the age of eighteen and at the same time, under the most difficult conditions, administrator of the duchy of Lorraine. It was not unusual at the time for youthful scions of great families to attain to such positions. Children became bishops, and John XII was not much older when he was elected Pope. The astonishing part of it is that Bruno, displaying extraordinary independence, proved equal to these and other difficult political tasks. He was successful also in the administration of his archbishopric, where he introduced important reforms. He died at the age of forty-one. Unquestionably he was pious and free from petty self-seeking, but above all he was an adroit, realistic politician, conscious of his aims. As such he had enemies. Undoubtedly his ambiguous position as a high ecclesiastic with ascetic leanings and as a powerful representative of Ottonian policy exposed him to attack. Ruotger's biography of him is at once a political apology and the life of a saint, a combination characteristic of the period. As an example of the style, I cite the description of Bruno's way of life, from the thirtieth chapter: [64]

Iuvenis ut erat omnique pompa circumfluus, audeo dicere, *dissolvi* vellet, tantum ut *cum Christo esset* (Phil. 1:23). Hinc lacrime assidue, suspiria fere continua, furtive orationes et singultus in ipso etiam lecto clarius perstrepentes, ut testantur, quos id minus celare poterat, etiam dum latere volebat. Quotiens diem mortis posuit ante conspectum cordis! Quotiens ad hoc vocis quoque officio prorupit, quod corde molitus est! Quotiens audivimus eum vehementi gemitu preoptasse id, quod futurum non tamen sine gravi trepidatione speravit, ut estuosum mundi huius naufragium in Dei sola misericordia tutus evasisset et in littore tandem securitatis intime constitisset! Elapsurus quodam modo putabatur, ut quasi mortem aufugeret totum, quod ei in huius mundi deliciis blandiebatur. Testes supersunt conversationis eius quam plurimi; quoties eum in se-

64. *MGH Scr.*, IV, 252–275. A new edition, with a good introduction and extensive bibliographical references, by Irene Ott, *Ruotgers Lebensbeschreibung des Erzbischofs Bruno von Köln.*

cretis corde contrito et spiritu humiliato persenserant, mirari plus poterant quam imitari. Nam illi popularis plerumque quasi solitarius vixit; mirum dictu inter convivas letissimos letior ipse frequenter abstinuit. Molles et delicatas vestes, in quibus nutritus et ad hominem usque perductus est, etiam in domibus regum multoties declinavit; inter purpuratos ministros et milites suos auroque nitidos vilem ipse tunicam et rusticanas ovium pelles induxit. Lectuli delicias vehementer aspernatus est. In balneis cum lavantibus cutisque nitorem querentibus vix aliquando lotus est; quod eo magis mirum est, quia ab ipsis cunabulis eiusmodi munditiis et pompa regia educatus est. Haec autem pro tempore et loco modo palam, modo secretius egit, ut et laudem humanam subterfugeret et tamen subditis exemplum hoc agendo preberet. Multi enim verbis, plus exemplis proficiunt plerique. Apud mites et humiles nemo humilior, contra improbos et elatos nemo vehementior fuit. Hunc terrorem, qui beneficio obligari non potuit, indigena eque et alienigena formidavit, et recto convenientissimoque ordine omnis, ad quem magnitudinis eius fama pervenit, primo eum timere, postea consuevit amare.

He was a young man, surrounded by all luxury; and yet I dare to assert that he would gladly have been dissolved, if he might be with Christ. Hence the many tears, the almost unceasing sighs, the secret prayers and the sobs which could be heard distinctly from his bed; this being attested by those from whom he was unable to hide it, although he wished it to remain unknown. How often did he place the day of his death before the eye of his heart! How often also did what was moving him in his heart burst forth in his words! How often did we hear him, amid violent lamentations, long for what nevertheless he could not anticipate without a fearful trembling: that he might take flight from the storm-bound shipwreck of this world into the salvation of God's mercy alone and stand at last on the shore of innermost safety! And it was believed also that he would somehow escape, for he avoided like death itself all the delights of this world that might tempt him.[65] Many witnesses to his way of life are still alive. How often did they behold him, in secret, with a contrite heart and humble spirit! They were better able to admire than to

65. In my rendering of this sentence, which is not quite clear, I follow the new translation of Ruotger by Irene Schmale-Ott in the *Geschichtschreiber der deutschen Vorzeit*, xxx, 57.

imitate him. Although he was much in the company of men, he lived for the most part like a hermit; it is amazing how, while often with joyous table companions, and even more cheerful than they, he practiced abstinence. Even in the palaces of kings he scorned to wear soft and elegant attire, to which he had been accustomed from childhood and into maturity; among court officials in their crimson garb and warriors resplendent with gold, he would often appear wearing a poor garment and rustic sheepskins. He despised the luxury of a comfortable bed. He almost never made use of the baths where bathers strive for a glistening cleanliness of the skin; and this was all the more astonishing in view of the fact that he had been raised from the cradle to enjoy this kind of elegance and, in general, a regal luxury. As circumstances permitted, he did all this at times openly, at times in secret, in order on the one hand to avoid men's praise, yet on the other hand in order to set an example for his subordinates by such behavior. For while many learn through words, many more learn from the force of example. No one was more humble toward the meek and humble, and no one more terrible against evil and presumptuous men. This severity, from which there was no way to purchase exemption, was feared equally by natives and by strangers; whoever heard tell of his greatness learned, in proper and very fitting order, first to fear him and later to love him.

The reader will have no difficulty in noticing the rich ornamentation, the anaphoras, and assonances. In her edition Irene Ott lists the literary reminiscences. They come from Claudian, Sulpicius Severus, Prudentius, the Benedictine rule; in this paragraph they are not very numerous and always short. It is evident, however, that even when there is no specific borrowing, many of the themes stem from a very old tradition.

Ruotger starts with Bruno's asceticism and unworldliness. These are strict and fervent, but secret; only his intimates were aware of them. They are described with great rhetorical display; such turns as *ut estuosum mundi huius naufragium in Dei sola misericordia tutus evasisset*, etc. (note the rhyme and the ensuing colon) are heavily ornamental. Here we encounter one of the main themes: the contrast between Bruno's asceticism and his youth, upbringing, origin, and position—a typically, though of course not exclusively, Ottonian conception. Then Ruotger describes the as-

cetic features of Bruno's behavior; these descriptions are effective
and rich in imagery (his simple dress amid the exaggerated splendor of his retinue). The contrast with his upbringing and position
is brought out over and over again. But even in his ascetic practices Bruno is discreet: he makes a display of them only when he
wishes to teach others by his example. He is friendly to all those
who are themselves modest, but—and this takes us rather by surprise—*contra improbos et elatos nemo vehementior.* Here we see
the powerful prince and administrator, whose very name inspires
terror. Those who hear it learn, *recto convenientissimoque ordine,*
first to fear him then to love him. A striking combination: ascetic
unworldliness and iron severity in the exercise of power! The connecting link between the two is rigor.

There can be little doubt that by and large the account comes
close to the truth. It is not possible, in writing of a man who has
died only recently and who was widely known, to make statements that conflict with his reputation. And there are numerous
indications that Bruno was excellently suited to the role which the
circumstances imposed on him; he adapted himself to it quickly,
and the attitude it required came naturally to him. For him there
was nothing paradoxical about it. The currents of reform and asceticism emanating from Cluny and Gorze influenced him at an
early date, and he was born into Ottonian politics. The two impulses were compatible; their interaction [66] forged a self-discipline
which provided excellent material for ornate characterization. In-
wardly to renounce the world, while outwardly acting as an administrator and organizer; to carry on an inner life of the utmost
humility, to forgo the pleasures of the senses, though engaged unremittingly in earthly activities, earthly calculations, and the exercise of earthly power: this was all the more impressive in that—if
I am not mistaken—it was new. Up until then the great Germanic
princes had not been ascetics, and in general the rulers of the early
Middle Ages had been far from distinguishing themselves during

---

66. Concerning the relations between the Ottonian family, especially Bruno,
and Gorze, cf. K. Hallinger, *Gorze-Kluny*, pp. 99–106.

their reigns by moderation, self-discipline, and spiritual dignity. The Ottonian myth, which certain contemporary historians [67] endeavored to create, was—by dint of its dignity, rigor, and spirituality—something new, and achieved a considerable influence. Inevitably its style was the traditional rhetorical mannerism—but this mannerism has its own peculiar contemporary content and consequently its own characteristic form.

In this period when the reformers of Burgundy and Lorraine were embarking on their work and a desire for purity and rigor was arising in other quarters as well, there were many saints, and accounts of their lives were written. Zoepf devoted a study to the tenth-century lives of saints (see n. 61), which remains an outstanding work although it was published in 1908, before the author had espoused the idea that every epoch has its characteristic overall style. Many of these works are related in style and spirit to the Ottonian *vitae;* of course the mythical treatment of the ruling house is absent, but the rigor and ornamental mannerism show a marked resemblance.

The life of Blessed John of Gorze (died 976),[68] one of the most influential of the Lorraine reformers, contains any number of passages that would be worth quoting: the prologue, with its reflections on John's cruel death; the scene about the young girl's hair shirt, which leads to her conversion (17); the section about his studies (83); certain passages about the economic management of the monastery (95–114); and of course some part of the consistently interesting account of his embassy to Caliph Abderrahman in Cordova. Although the author's style is less manneristic than awkward, the figure of John stands out clearly: his severe humility, his energy in practical matters, and the unyielding consistency

---

67. Widukind of Corvey reveals little of this, but it can be clearly felt in Hrotswith. On the concept of the ruler as the preserver of peace through justice (Augustinian), see L. Zoepf, *Heiligenleben,* pp. 86f. But it is difficult to discern the characteristic features of the tenth century in an analysis of the underlying concepts, because these concepts are traditional.

68. Compiled some years after his death by his friend Johannes, Abbot of St. Arnulf; incomplete. Text in J. Mabillon, *Acta Sanctorum Ordinis S. Benedicti,* v, and in *MGH Scr.,* iv, 335–377. I use the latter.

of his conduct in every situation. I have finally selected a short scene from his early days in the monastery, when he worked under an impatient superior (74). It runs:

> . . . Preposituram monasterii vir venerabilis Fridericus . . . , et sub eo hic domnus Iohannes gerebat. Ille ut superior, hunc gravibus verborum contumeliis persepe etiam publice et praesentibus secularibus irritabat. Illo diutius perstrepente, hic tantum item itemque ad satisfaciendum terrae se sternens, perpetuum tenebat silentium. Cum ille crebro eadem clamore ingeminans, ira fessus iam et in verba deficeret, Iohannis acsi simulacrum sine voce diu immotus persisteret, ad ultimum columpnam vel parietem tangens, et ut eis potius verba quam sibi faceret dicens, e conspectu se proripiebat. Ille eo tamquam contemptus incensior, quolibet forte residebat. Inde post paululum motu subsidente, ubi placidior ad se mentem redierat, secrecius eodem Iohanne abducto, pedibus eius advolutus: "Occidisti me!" aiebat. Cum Iohannes: "Ego in quo? Patientia tua me," dicebat, "occidit."—"Non ita," inquid iste, "sed animositas vestra vos occidit." Nec pluribus, lites ilico rumpebantur.

The office of provost was occupied by the venerable Frederick, and our lord John worked under him. As his superior he [Frederick] irritated him by using violent terms of abuse, even publicly and in the presence of laymen. Now while the other never ceased his clamor, John begged his pardon and threw himself time and again on the ground, remaining completely silent. When finally the other, continuing to shriek, and exhausted by rage, could find no more words, John, who had long stood as dumb as a statue and motionless, finally said, at the same time touching a column or the wall, that the other had better speak to these than to him, and he withdrew from his presence. The other, still more furious because he believed himself to be despised, went off somewhere by himself [?].[69] When after a little while his emotions had become more moderate and his spirit was calm again [?], he led John to a place where they were alone and threw himself at his feet. "You have killed me!" he said. "How have I done that?" John answered. "Your patience," said

69. *Or perhaps:* sat down somewhere.

the other, "is killing me." "Not at all," said John, "it is your violence that is killing you." And with that the quarrel was over.

The Latin style is clumsy, but it is not simple; there is too much
circumlocution (*gravibus verborum contumeliis irritabat*, etc.) and
condensation; both make for stiffness. The simple incident has
difficulty, as it were, in disentangling itself from the language. Only
the dialogue at the end produces a direct effect. The incident, as
we have said, is very simple; the biographer tells a few similar
stories and says he would be able (and glad) to tell many more.
Why did such incidents stick in the memory of his associates, and
why were they held worthy, several decades later, to be included
in the biography of a man regarded as a saint? The answer is plain,
the author himself gives it; he included such incidents in order to
show John's patience, humility, and self-abasement, his love of
God and his fellow men. But the stories show more than that.
They show superior strength and discipline. This cannot be ade-
quately gathered from the one anecdote we have quoted, but it
follows from the *vita* as a whole. In his own way John is shown
to be very similar to Bruno. His ascetic humility is combined with
extreme rigor in earthly life. The rigor of his asceticism and humility is assuredly genuine, but it is a rigor that governs his whole
being. *Fortitudo* is John's dominant virtue. The biographer suggests as much in the above-mentioned passage (at the beginning
of 74) when he says:

> Pacientiam, humilitatem, seu abiectionem, et quae omnia
> superat caritatis in Deum et in omnes fervorem, incredible
> dictu est, quanta fortitudine servaverit.
>
> It is hard to believe with what fortitude he practiced patience,
> humility, or lowliness, and the fervent love of God and all men
> that surpasses all other virtues.

Of course there were men of very different character among
the saints of those days; and toward the end of the century, at
the time of Otto III, we often find an unstable fanaticism that may

be exemplified by the strange figure of the martyr Adalbert of Prague, a close friend of Otto III.[70] The tendencies to strict asceticism and a manneristic ornamental style are in any case universal. They are combined in the person of Otto III.

I have not yet mentioned the most remarkable figure of the period, Pope Sylvester II, in collaboration with whom Otto tried to work out his plans for a supranational empire. His name was Gerbert, known as Gerbert of Aurillac from the monastery where he spent his youth. He was the richest mind and most celebrated teacher of his day; the only outstanding mathematician, astronomer, and natural scientist in the Christian world of the time, he had studied mathematics and natural science in Catalonia, not far from Islamic territory; and he was also a humanist, an impassioned collector of manuscripts, and an excellent writer. It was to these intellectual attainments (he was of lowly birth) that he owed the beginning of his career, but it soon became clear that he also possessed great political gifts. As cathedral schoolmaster in Rheims, friend, secretary, and adviser to the powerful Archbishop Adalbero, who was a member of the house of Luxemburg and had been educated in Gorze, he played a decisive role in the complex and treacherous struggles of the late Carolingian period. A few years after the death of Adalbero he himself became archbishop of Rheims but in the end proved unable to maintain his position in that city. He made his way to the imperial court in Germany and, having long been a supporter of Ottonian policy, became closely associated with Otto III. Otto made him archbishop of Ravenna and soon afterward Pope. He died in 1003, not long after the emperor. He lived on in legend as a magician who had sold his soul

70. The most interesting of his *Vitae* is by Bruno of Querfurt, who a few years later, like Adalbert, was put to death by the pagan Prussians as an apostle of Christianity. This *Vita*, which dates back to the beginning of the eleventh century, displays many realistic traits along with its extreme mannerism. Bruno of Querfurt was also close to Otto III. Another of his works, *Vita quinque fratrum* (of the "Polish brothers"), contains many personal details and a great deal of information about the young Emperor. Bruno of Querfurt provides perhaps the best example of a manneristic *sermo humilis* in the late Ottonian period.

to the devil. Even this very incomplete summary of his biography reveals a rich and many-sided nature.

The chronicler Richer, a monk at Saint-Rémy near Rheims, describes Gerbert's method of teaching.[71] He tells us in this connection that Gerbert caused his students to be instructed by a "sophista," *apud quem in controversiis exercerentur, ac sic arte agerent, ut preter artem agere viderentur, quod oratoris maximum videtur* (with whom they engaged in controversy and spoke with so much art that they seemed to be speaking without art, which strikes us as the height of eloquence; 3.48). This is highly characteristic. We possess a collection of Gerbert's letters, some of which he wrote in his own name and some for others, and which he himself gathered for publication.[72] Perhaps no work of the period is less mannered. Gerbert writes easily and elegantly, sometimes with an almost Ciceronian *aisance;* he moves gracefully from one style level to another, and even today it is almost always easy to read him, when the text is not corrupt or incomplete. To be sure, we sometimes find turns of phrase that would be incorrect by classical standards, and we also find the usual flourishes of court and ecclesiastical style—but nowhere do we find glosses or involved word order, and conspicuous plays on sound are rare. Even when his writing is highly rhetorical, the rhetoric is Ciceronian rather than manneristic, and the authors he quotes are almost exclusively classical. His style is sharp and clear but at the same time flexible and subtle, incomparably more elegant and richer in feeling than that of Lupus of Ferrières, for example. He stands by himself in a period otherwise characterized by awkward or

71. *Richeri Historiarum* 3.46–54 (Scr. rer. Germ. in usum scholarum, 2nd edn. by G. Waitz).

72. *Lettres de Gerbert,* ed. J. Havet. On the very complicated questions of transmission and dating, the most recent writer is K. Pivec, "Die Briefsammlung Gerberts von Aurillac." Of the very extensive literature on Gerbert I shall mention F. Lot, *Études sur le règne de Hugues Capet,* and the early as well as the concluding chapters of his book, *Les Derniers Carolingiens.* On the whole, his portrayal of Gerbert seems to me the best I have come across. On Otto III and Gerbert, see P. E. Schramm, *Kaiser, Rom und Renovatio,* especially I, 92ff.; C. Erdmann, "Das Ottonische Reich als Imperium Romanum"; and finally the last two chapters of H. Focillon's *L'An mil.*

manneristic writers. Unfortunately I am unable to judge whether this classical, almost Attic spirit had come down in any school tradition (deriving perhaps from Lupus) that Gerbert could have drawn on. But it seems likely that in this respect as in others he went his own way, that—like Rather, despite their very different tastes—he was self-taught as a stylist and drew inspiration directly from no classical author.

It is hard to select examples because most of the texts require an understanding of extremely involved political events. I have chosen a short letter, written in 989. Gerbert's situation was rather difficult at the time. At the beginning of the year his friend and protector, Archbishop Adalbero of Rheims, had died. Gerbert believed that he had a claim to the succession. The decision rested with the king, and Gerbert had played a considerable part in the elevation of Hugh Capet (987). But Hugh distrusted Gerbert— perhaps because of his Ottonian connections—and in any case believed that there was no need to show him any consideration now that Adalbero was dead. Instead, in the illusory hope of conciliating or at least splitting the last remnants of Carolingian opposition, he preferred to appoint a certain Arnulf, a young Carolingian of illegitimate birth. Gerbert submitted and stayed on in his old position under Arnulf. Yet he wrote letters to influential persons at the Ottonian court, describing his situation, demanding a reward for his services, and sometimes uttering veiled threats.[73] But he received no satisfactory answer. And then a very strange thing happened. By an act of treason Rheims fell into the hands of the Carolingian pretender, Duke Charles of Lower Lorraine, an uncle of Arnulf's. For a time Arnulf affected surprise and at first was actually treated as a prisoner; but it soon became evident that he was in league with his uncle, as he himself later admitted. After a time Gerbert offered the two Carolingians his services and, veering from his previous political position,[74] wrote anti-Capetian let-

73. Havet, letter 158, at end.
74. He had, however, already been in contact with Charles of Lorraine in the time of Adalbero; cf. Havet, letter 122.

ters. He soon repented and was received by King Hugh with
open arms. A few months later Rheims was retaken by Hugh—
again through treachery. The two Carolingians were captured and
imprisoned; Arnulf was deposed by a French synod, and Gerbert
became archbishop of Rheims, a position from which he was to
reap little joy.

Shortly after Duke Charles' seizure of Rheims, Gerbert wrote
the following letter to the abbot of his home monastery of Aurillac: [75]

> Domino et reverentissimo patri Raimundo, G(erbertus)
> filius. Quo in portu agam navim gubernatore amisso, scire
> vis, dulcissime pater, et quinam sit status in Francorum re
> publica. Ego cum statuissem non discedere a clientela et
> consilio patris mei beati Ad(alberonis), repente sic eo pri-
> vatus sum, ut me superesse expavescerem, quippe cum esset
> nobis cor unum et anima una (Acts 4:32), nec hostes ejus
> eum putarent translatum, cum me superesse viderent. Me
> ad invidiam K(aroli), nostram patriam tunc et nunc vexan-
> tis, digito notabant, qui reges deponerem, regesque ordi-
> narem. Et qui rei publicae permixtus eram, cum re publica
> periclitabar, velut in proditione nostrae urbis pars praedae
> maxima fui. Eaque res iter meum in Italiam penitus distulit,
> ubi et organa conservantur, et optima portio meae sup-
> pellectilis. Non enim potuimus obsistere praecipiti fortunae,
> nec divinitas declaravit adhuc, quonam in portu me sistere
> velit. Igitur de me ac de meis fortunis gavisuri expectent
> exitum instantis fortunae. Dabo operam pro viribus, nec
> quicquam eorum quae fieri oporteat intermittam, donec
> optatis perfruar sedibus, reddamque Deo vota mea in Sion
> (Ps. 64:2).
> Vale, amantissime pater. Valeat frater Ayrardus. Valeat
> sanctissimum collegium tibi subjectum. Meique sitis me-
> mores in contemplativis, cum patre meo Adal(berone).

To my lord and most venerable father Raymond, his son Gerbert. You wish to know, my dear father, into what harbor I
will bring my ship, now that the helmsman is lost, and what the
situation is in the Frankish [French] State. I had resolved never

75. Havet, letter 163.

to depart from the service and counsel of my blessed father
Adalbero, and now I was suddenly deprived of him in such a
way that I was filled with terror at the prospect of surviving
him, for we had one heart and one soul; even our enemies could
not believe that he had departed this life, when they saw me survive. Appealing to the envy of Charles, who then as now was
troubling our country, they denounced me as a man who deposes
kings and names kings. And since I was involved in the fortunes
of the State, I found myself in danger along with the State, just
as in the betrayal of our town [Rheims] I was an important piece
of booty. This happening delayed my journey to Italy, where the
organs and the greater part of my household goods are still ly-
ing.[76] For we were unable to withstand the sudden change in fortune, and God has not yet revealed in what harbor He wishes me
to come to rest. Therefore let those who take interest in my fortunes [or, more precisely: who will rejoice over my good for-
tune] await the outcome of the present crisis. I will do everything
in my power and neglect nothing that the situation demands, until I go to my longed-for home and fulfill my vow unto God in
Zion (Ps. 64:2).

Farewell, beloved father. Greetings to brother Ayrard. Greetings to the holy community that is subject to you. Think of me
in your prayers, and of my father Adalbero also.

The Latinist will admire the clarity and soft rhythmic elegance
(*suavitas*) with which the themes are woven together: his grief
for Adalbero, his indirect reference to his own prestige, the dangers of his present situation, the postponement of his trip to Italy,
his doubts about the immediate future, and the pious formula with
which he concludes. Our admiration is increased when we read
other contemporary authors. Gerbert's art is masterly in its simplicity. The graceful rhythm of the first sentence, for example,
rests on his separation of the two indirect questions by the main
clause *scire vis, dulcissime pater*. Apart from this everything is
perfectly natural. The image of ship and harbor is a common
topos, used in the simplest way. And how clearly he describes
the situation, neither expatiating nor unduly condensing. There is

76. Gerbert had earlier been named abbot of Bobbio by Otto II but, unable
to hold this position after Otto's death, had returned to Rheims. Some
of his possessions were still in Bobbio, and he continued to use the title
abbot of Bobbio.

nothing forced about the isocola and antitheses, the transitions are smooth, the rhythmical rise and fall are gentle and consummately graceful. The spirit of this style is classical; the admixture of pious cordiality and warmth yields an over-all style which in later times, particularly in France, came to be identified with Christian humanism.

The reader will also note that Gerbert postpones answering the question as to what he himself intends to do. The letter speaks of crisis and troubled times, but obviously the man who writes it is not greatly troubled. He surveys the situation and asks himself what profit can be drawn from it. Perhaps he has already made up his mind, but does not yet see fit to disclose his conclusions. He still calls Duke Charles the man who "torments," or "troubles," the country, and refers to the surprise attack on Rheims as "treachery." Nevertheless, he does not count Charles among his "enemies"—his enemies are those who slander him in Charles' presence. And above all he is uncertain *quonam in portu divinitas me sistere velit,* and pious flourishes take the place of further information. It may be presumed that he had already received offers from the Carolingian party. Hugh had made a mistake in supposing that after the death of Adalbero, who was supported by the nobles of Lorraine, he could neglect Gerbert. It would have been unnatural if Charles and Arnulf had not tried to benefit by this mistake and to procure the services of a man whose skill as a diplomat and publicist bordered on the miraculous. Their efforts were at first successful. A few weeks or perhaps only days after the letter to the Abbot of Aurillac, Gerbert embarked on his activity in the service of Charles. But meanwhile the opposing party had realized its blunder; negotiations were begun with a view to winning back Gerbert. Whether the offers of Hugh's party were more attractive, whether Gerbert lacked confidence in the cause of Charles and Arnulf, whether he was overcome by remorse, as he himself insists, it is hard to decide; perhaps all these factors played a part. In any case his defection to the Carolingians was only a brief episode.

The letter shows Gerbert's character very clearly: nowhere is he more sincere and confidential than in his letters to his friends in Aurillac. He is sensitive, expressive, tender; conscious of his superiority but never unpleasantly vain; extremely natural yet at the same time only too adroit and calculating. Here it is important to note that his adroitness and calculation did not serve a cause in which he deeply believed, but his own advantage. It can scarcely be denied that almost throughout his life Gerbert was a political intriguer without political ideas. He was capable of personal affection: it seems safe to say that he would not have betrayed Adalbero under any circumstances, and from the start he showed a certain devotion to the Ottonian house; but within these limits he was an ambitious gambler, who made use of ideas for the personal advantage they seemed to hold out to him. It is hard to determine exactly what political affairs he had a hand in; but in general it is certain that he was an unscrupulous schemer, so much so that certain of his failures can be attributed to the complexity of his scheming. He captivated his students and friends by his intelligence, but elsewhere, even in his own entourage, he was an object of hatred and envy. His intellectual superiority and his career, amazing for a monk of humble origins, were in themselves enough to arouse hatred and envy; but a man of his gifts might have possessed a radiant wisdom and purity that would have countered such sentiments. This was not the case. Nor did he possess Rather's sensitive conscience, that would have enabled him to see through himself. At times, especially in his struggle over the archbishopric of Rheims, we have the impression that, like so many lesser minds, this wonderfully gifted man, with a naiveté that was almost sincere, looked on what served his purposes as right and proper. He fell short of being great for lack of something that is hard to define, but even beside the clownish and scurrilous Rather he seems insubstantial and somehow superficial.

Luckily for him, or so it seems to me, he was finally defeated in his struggle for Rheims, made his way to Germany, and became the friend and adviser of Otto III. From this time on his letters and other writings acquired what up until then they had largely lacked, namely, unity and stature. To my mind there can be no doubt that it was Otto who cast a spell on the old magician and courtier and gave his work a content that had hitherto been lacking. Otto, the Saxon and Greek, was only seventeen at the time; his character was still uneven; he was too absolute in his ideas and goals and dangerously subject to strong emotions; but his life and the few, sometimes awkward and often mannered utterances that may safely be attributed to him bear witness to a generous and lovable, bold and passionate heart. Gerbert's influence upon him was assuredly great; Gerbert's almost classical gift of style enabled him to formulate certain of Otto's central ideas as Otto himself could scarcely have done. But without Otto, Gerbert would never have conceived such ideas. As Otto's adviser, on the other hand, Gerbert was far more than a skillful courtier: the enthusiasm with which he supported Otto's ideas is unmistakable and moving. It becomes apparent at the very beginning of their collaboration. Otto had written Gerbert a letter of invitation, asking him to instruct and advise him, to develop the spark of Hellenism in him. This letter is mannered to the point of absurdity but at the same time delightful for the modest, shy, discreetly humorous way in which Otto seems to woo Gerbert.[77] Gerbert's answer runs:

> Ubi nescio quid divinum exprimitur, cum homo genere Grecus, imperio Romanus, quasi hereditario jure thesauros sibi Greciae ac Romanae repetit sapientiae. Paremus ergo, Cesar, imperialibus edictis cum in hoc, tum in omnibus quecumque divina majestas vestra decreverit.

> Something divine is realized when a man, Greek by birth, Roman by rule, claims for himself as it were by hereditary right the

77. This is courtesy, for Gerbert had offered his services.—Otto was particularly eager to receive instruction in the Arithmetic of Boethius. The words *Romanae . . . sapientiae* allude chiefly to this; but in intention they go much further.—Text in Havet, letters 186 and 187.

treasures of Greek and Roman wisdom. We obey, therefore, O Caesar, your imperial commands in this as in all things, and shall do whatsoever your divine majesty may decree.

The phrase *genere Grecus, imperio Romanus,* and indeed the whole first sentence is consummate; Otto must have taken as much pleasure in reading it as had Gerbert himself in writing it. In addition, it is interesting to note how Gerbert throughout the letter, but especially in the beginning, adapts his expression to the hieratic pomp of the Ottonian style. He preserves his usual clarity, but the words and cadences begin to sparkle:

> Supereminenti benevolentiae vestrae qua in sempiternum digni vestro judicamur obsequio, fortasse votis, sed respondere non valemus meritis . . .

> To your supereminent benevolence by which we are continually deemed worthy of your indulgence, we are enabled perhaps by our prayers, though not by our merits, to respond . . .

Still more characteristic is another famous passage. It is from the dedication,[78] addressed to the Emperor, of Gerbert's book *De rationali et ratione uti,* which he had written at Otto's request. It runs (Havet, p. 237):

> . . . quae de hac quaestione concepi, breviter describo, ne sacrum palatium torpuisse putet Italia, et ne se solam jactet Grecia in imperiali philosophia et Romana potentia. Nostrum, nostrum est Romanum imperium. Dant vires ferax frugum Italia, ferax militum Gallia et Germania, nec Scithae desunt nobis fortissima regna.[79] Noster es, C(aesar), Romanorum imperator et auguste, qui summo Grecorum sanguine ortus, Grecos imperio superas, Romanis hereditario jure imperas, utrosque ingenio et eloquentia praevenis.

78. Havet, Appendix ii, 236–238.
79. The homage of the nations can also be found in Ottonian art. For example, in the *Gospels* (Munich, *Staatsbibl. cod. lat.* 4453) of Otto III and in the portrait of Otto II on a single page, now in Chantilly, Musée de Condé. Reproductions in H. Jantzen, *Ottonische Kunst,* figs. 87 and 88; also in H. Focillon, *L'An mil,* p. 131, Pl. 19. In this connection see also C. Erdmann, "Das Ottonische Reich," particularly pp. 424ff.

I shall briefly set forth my thoughts on this question, lest Italy should think that her sacred palace has grown mute, and lest Greece boast herself alone in philosophy of empire and Roman power. Ours, ours is the Roman Empire. Italy fruitful in things of the soil, Gaul and Germany fruitful in soldiers, give us strength, nor do the mighty realms of Scythia escape our influence. You are ours, Caesar, emperor of the Romans and Augustus, who, sprung from the noblest Grecian blood, rule over the Greeks by right of dominion, over the Romans by right of inheritance, and tower over both in talent and eloquence.

The hostile reference to the Byzantine court, which refused to recognize the Ottonian Empire,[80] prepares the way for the cry of triumph with its repeated first word: ours, ours, is the Roman Empire—not only because it is we who possess the most celebrated provinces of the empire,[81] but also because you, O Caesar, sprung from the noblest Grecian blood, by inheritance Roman Emperor, tower over Romans and Greeks alike by your greatness of mind. What a document to the rich historical consciousness that lived in the Ottonian Empire! Here the archbishop and future Pope neglects the Christian aspect of this historical consciousness completely. In the present case this is an accident, but in actual fact Gerbert/Sylvester took less interest than others among the Emperor's friends in this aspect of the mystical *renovatio*.

Here Gerbert's style has become Ottonian; *suavitas* and classical grace have vanished, the loftiness no longer reminds one of Cicero. Luminous allegories and abstractions accompanied by glittering epithets produce the effect of precious stones in a diadem, the clauses have a mighty roll, the dominant note throughout is one of ecstatic majesty. The triumphal outcries (*nostrum est, noster es*) are followed by ornamental enumerations; the first intro-

---

80. The rivalry between the cultures of the Western and the Byzantine empires naturally dates back to Carolingian times. I came upon a characteristic passage from the time of Charles the Bald, by Heiricus of Auxerre (*MGH Poet.*, III, 429), cited by R. R. Bezzola, *Les Origines et la formation de la littérature courtoise en Occident*, I, 202, n. 1: *Luget hoc Grecia novis invidiae aculeis lacessita* (Greece, wounded by new stings of envy, mourns this thing).

81. *Scitha* (the Scythian) refers to the Slavic expansion of the Ottos; *Gallia* refers to the Duchy of Lorraine, between the Meuse and the Rhine.

duces a list of countries, beginning with the verb for emphasis and continuing anaphorically: *Dant vires ferax . . . ferax . . . nec desunt . . .* ; the second, addressed to the Emperor, prepares the way for an accumulation of titles in the vocative and a eulogy in the form of a triple relative clause, intensified by an adjectival colon.

Situated as it is between the Carolingian flowering and the great period of reform, the tenth century was rather neglected until quite recently; interest in it has now revived. Against a background of late Latin, characterized by stiff and often empty rhetorical pedantry and a dependence on the academic precepts of antiquity and late antiquity, a new style was beginning to emerge. It is not easy to appraise and describe this development, because writers were few in this period, and there was no coherent movement. Dispersed through the whole of what had been Carolingian Europe, they constituted an international but not very numerous class, and there was little homogeneity in the strivings which led them to speak. We find no clearly definable common trend. Who will claim to formulate with any precision what is common to Rather, Liudprand, the Ottonian biographers, the Lorraine reformers, and Gerbert—not to mention those authors whom we have named only in passing or not at all? No unified trend of thought holds them together or divides them into opposing fronts; nor were they sustained by any far-reaching popular movement. In the course of our exposition we have stressed asceticism, reform, and mannerism. But Rather is not really an ascetic, Liudprand is neither an ascetic nor a reformer, and Gerbert was not originally a mannerist.

We shall have to take something very general as our starting point, namely, the fact that all the tenth-century authors discussed here were concerned with the contemporary scene, either attacking and satirizing corruption or praising those whom they believed to have triumphed over corruption. This amounts to saying that after the collapse of the Carolingian order certain individuals at least began to develop an eye for contemporary conditions and that this period saw the beginnings of an insight that was to dominate European thinking for centuries, the insight that actual conditions in Christendom were a far cry from the ideal of a Christian society deriving its political organization—this in the last analysis could not have been otherwise—from the Roman Empire, on whose soil and within whose institutional framework Christianity had spread. In the tenth-century writers we discern only the first beginnings of such an awareness, often intermingled with an egotistical particularism or related only to the special situation in which the author found himself, and not yet involving a general plan of reform; and even where such a plan was conceived, it was not yet based on an over-all view of the problems. In many cases we find little more than an awareness that sharpens perception and stimulates expression. That it should have arisen when it did, at a time marked by a general setback, the loss of something already achieved, namely, the Carolingian order, seems only natural. Sometimes, as in the Italian Liudprand, the moral dissatisfaction is slight, resulting in little more than polemics and satire; sometimes it is so powerful that it leads to a radical asceticism. But everywhere the foundation is a sharpened insight into contemporary conditions, which was particularly stimulating to the more gifted writers of the time.

The instrument of this new expression was Latin—at least, all the documents that have come down to us are Latin. The words that were actually spoken (at the synods, for example, the vernacular languages were already used extensively) are unknown to us; they were recorded only in Latin. The subject matter was of immediate interest and was often crude and extreme, involving immoderate emotions and fantastic happenings. This subject matter sought expression in Latin, and the Latin tradition was not necessarily an obstacle; it offered great freedom in word order, rhetorical models for the use of this freedom, a rich vocabulary permitting of surprising effects, and an abundance of phonetic figures. In addition Latin had the advantage of offering stylistic models from antiquity and late antiquity, and above all the text of the

Bible, with its inexhaustible opportunities for typological and allegorical interpretation. Erudition was required for the mastery of all these instruments; expression was possible only where learning and spontaneous drive went hand in hand. Only a very few writers achieved true originality; and it seems perfectly natural that under such circumstances most authors should have written an artificial and intricate style, the understanding and appreciation of which require a considerable erudition. But remarkable effects were obtained where, as in the case of Rather, personal originality or the passion aroused by the subject matter molded the rhetorical mannerism to its designs.

It remains to be said that nearly all the persons and trends we have dealt with in this connection were in some way related to the Ottonian court. Not only was it the sole center of power—France was much more profoundly disunited, the papal court was impotent and discredited—it was also, beginning with Otto I and Bruno of Cologne, a source of cultural radiation. There was no hostility between the Ottonian house and the religious reformers —on the contrary, the influence of the reformers on the spirit of the court is deep and significant. The court gave the manneristic style of the period a kind of unity. This style was not static; Otto III and his friends introduced a new tone. Nevertheless it is convenient and not without justification to designate the literary style of the second half of the tenth century as Ottonian. Of course the choice of term is not very important; the word merely has the advantage of bringing under one head a style which could otherwise be characterized—and still not fully—only by a large number of epithets (ascetic, ornamental, manneristic, etc.).

3

Camilla,
or, The Rebirth of the Sublime

῞Υψος μεγαλοφροσύνης ἀπήχημα
(Sublimity is the echo of elevation
of thought.)

Peri hypsous 9.2

WHEN, AT THE END of the seventh book of the *Aeneid*, the allies whom Turnus has summoned to battle with Aeneas enter the city of King Latinus, the last to appear is an Amazonian figure, Camilla, the virgin queen of the Volscians. The lines describing her arrival complete the descriptive enumeration of the Ausonian heroes and tribes, and with them the book ends. They read as follows (7.803–817):

Hos super advenit Volsca de gente Camilla
agmen agens equitum et florentis aere catervas,
bellatrix, non illa colo calathisve Minervae
femineas adsueta manus, sed proelia virgo
dura pati cursuque pedum praevertere ventos.
Illa vel intactae segetis per summa volaret
gramina nec teneras cursu laesisset aristas,
vel mare per medium fluctu suspensa tumenti
ferret iter, celeris nec tingeret aequore plantas.
Illam omnis tectis agrisque effusa iuventus
turbaque miratur matrum et prospectat euntem,
attonitis inhians animis, ut regius ostro
velet honos levis umeros, ut fibula crinem
auro internectat, Lyciam ut gerat ipsa pharetram
et pastoralem praefixa cuspide myrtum.

Beside all these there came from the Volscian nation Camilla
Leading a cavalry column, squadrons petalled with bronze:
A warrior maid, her woman's hand unaccustomed to womanly
Tasks—to the distaff, the basket of wool; a girl, but hardy
To face the horrors of battle and to catch up with the winds.

She could have skimmed along the blades of an unmown corn-crop
Without so much as bruising their tender ears as she ran:
She could have flitted over the waves of a swelling sea
Without so much as wetting the quicksilver soles of her feet.
From field and cottage the young came running, the housewives
   gathered
To stare at this Camilla and marvel as she went by,
Gaping, struck with amazement to see how nobly sat
The cloak of royal crimson on her smooth shoulders—see
The gold clasp in her hair, the Lycian quiver she carried
And the spear-shaft of country myrtle with its warhead.
                                        (Tr. C. Day Lewis)

This piece of classical poetry is carefully constructed and rich
in phonetic and syntactic devices. After the two opening lines,
which state Camilla's origin, name, and present activity (passing
by at the head of her horsemen), it describes her in three anaphoric periods: *non illa . . . illa . . . illam . . .*, introduced by
the forcefully isolated apposition *bellatrix* at the beginning of the
third line, which states the theme. The first anaphoric period (*non
illa*) comments directly upon the theme with a sharp antithesis
(*non illa colo . . . sed proelia virgo / dura pati*). The position
of these last four words in the sentence and line achieves a maximum of concentration; they introduce the development (in the
second anaphora) of the motif of movement (*cursuque pedum
praevertere ventos*) already sounded in the assonance evoking her
riding past in the second line (*agmen agens equitum . . .*).
   This anaphora is in the subjunctive, for it deals with the possibilities of movement suggested by the vision of Camilla; it consists of two similarly constructed but slightly varied clauses (isocola), wonderfully balanced in their rhythm: *Illa // vel . . . per
summa volaret . . . nec teneras . . . laesisset . . . / vel . . . per
medium . . . ferret . . . celeris nec tingeret. . . .* From here on
the viewpoint changes. The third anaphoric period seems to deal
not directly with the vision, but with its effect on the viewers
who hasten to the spot. But the motif of movement persists, *prospectat euntem*, and the poet does not dwell on the feelings of the

onlookers; we are merely told that they are amazed and what they see in their amazement: Camilla riding by, the royal purple over her delicate shoulders, the golden fibula in her hair, her Lycian quiver, and her shepherd's staff of myrtle with its iron lance head. Then all is still; Camilla has passed.

The reader—whom I expect to read the foregoing with attention in order that he may also read Virgil's lines carefully—will have noticed that this passage is not a systematic description detailing Camilla's personal traits. On the contrary, very few particulars are given. On other similar occasions Virgil, while not piling up individual features, tends to say something of his heroes' origin, previous history, and mythological connections. This was in keeping with the epic tradition, and he does so even in the preceding description of Turnus' other allies. But not in connection with Camilla, not in this passage, at least; he makes up for the omission later, in the eleventh book (lines 535ff.), where the information is supplied by Diana, Camilla's tutelary goddess. But here Virgil, assuredly by design, has only related what fits in with her appearing and riding past and what enhances the power and lightness of her movement. The passage shows her coming into view, evokes possible movements that do not touch the ground, tells us a little of what the onlookers see, and closes with the tranquil strength of the line about the virginal shepherd's staff with the lance head. Both by its content and its rhythm this last line seems to recapitulate the stirring paradoxical grandeur of the whole. The movement of these lines is light yet forceful, like Camilla's own movement. Yet the whole is quiet, self-contained, pure unreflecting epiphany; and this pure epiphany in turn embodies the character and quite unmistakably, though indemonstrably, the destiny which belongs to the character. The passage is a perfect example of classical poetry.

Such lines cannot come into being without artistry and planning, but it should not be supposed that every detail was calculated. Virgil was an experienced writer, deeply involved in his

subject matter. The numerous scenes and figures which he depicted so successfully are integral parts of a single over-all conception—his poem was written in one piece, though selection and
emendation must also have played a part. All this abundance is a
unity, which seems simple as such; but simplicity is an achievement, not a beginning.

Almost twelve hundred years later, between 1150 and 1160, a
gifted and well-educated man, of clerical schooling, living in Nor-
mandy, wrote a poem about Aeneas in rhymed French octosyllabic couplets. We do not know his name, but it is certain that
he was close to the Plantagenet court, where the courtly epic was
developing and where it found patrons. In this early period of
courtly literature ancient themes were extremely popular; later
they gave way to subjects from Celtic legend. The earliest works,
the three classical *romans* that have come down to us,[1] make it
very clear that the literature of the feudal elite could not have
come into being without the help of clerics; for only poets who
had enjoyed a clerical education could have been so well versed
in literature. Laymen, even those belonging to the highest circles
of feudal society, were virtually unlettered; in the middle of the
twelfth century only a very few were able to read and write.

The Old French *Enéas* is a significant work and exerted great
influence; the court poets of the second half of the twelfth
century, Chrétien de Troyes, Gautier d'Arras, Marie de France,
learned a great deal from it, and in the same century Heinrich
von Veldeke, founder of the German court epic, paraphrased it
still more extensively. But the influence in France of the author
of the *Enéas* consists not so much in his imitation of Virgil as in
his treatment of the love episodes, modeled not on Virgil but on
Ovid. It is here that an important feature of the court epic, the
playful, coquettish casuistry of love, deriving from Ovid, makes
its first appearance.

The entrance of Camilla appears also in the Old French *Enéas*

1. In addition to the *Enéas*, the probably somewhat older *Roman de Thèbes*
and the somewhat later *Roman de Troie*.

(lines 3959–4106).² The scene is very long. Here I shall quote the beginning:

> *Enprés i vint une meschine,*
> *qui de Vulcane estoit reïne;*   3960
> *Camille ot nom la damoisselle,*
> *a mervoille par estoit bele*
> *et molt estoit de grant poeir;*
> *ne fu feme de son savoir.*
> *Molt ert sage, proz et cortoise*   3965
> *et molt demenot grant richoise;*
> *a mervoille tenoit bien terre;*
> *el fu toz tens norrie an guerre*
> *et molt ama chevalerie*
> *et maintint la tote sa vie.*   3970
> *Onc d'ovre a feme ne ot cure,*
> *ne de filer ne de costure;*
> *mialz prisoit armes a porter,*
> *a tornoier et a joster,*
> *ferir d'espee et de lance:*   3975
> *ne fu feme de sa vaillance.*
> *Lo jor ert rois, la nuit raïne;*
> *ja chanberiere ne meschine*
> *anviron li le jor n'alast,*
> *ne ja la nuit nus hom n'entrast*   3980
> *dedanz la chanbre ou ele estoit;*
> *tant sagement se contenoit*
> *n'en darriere ne en davant,*
> *que ne en fet ne en sanblant*
> *i peüst an noter folie,*   3985
> *ja tant n'eüst vers li envie.*
> *De biauté n'ert o li igaus*
> *nule feme qui fust mortaus;*
> *lo front ot blanc et bien traitiz,*
> *la greve droite an la vertiz,*   3990
> *les sorciz noirs et bien dolgiez,*
> *les ielz rianz et trestoz liez;*
> *biaus ert li nes, anprés la face,*

---

2. Two-volume edition by J.-J. Salverda de Grave in the series Classiques français du moyen-âge.

car plus blanche ert que nois ne glace;
entremellee ert la color   3995
avenalment o la blanchor;
molt ot bien faite la bochete,
n'ert gaires granz, mes petitete,
menu serrees ot les denz,
plus reluisent que nus argenz.   4000
Que diroie de sa bialté?
An tot lo plus lonc jor d'esté
ne diroie ce qu'en estoit,
de la biauté que ele avoit,
ne de ses mors, de sa bonté,   4005
qui vallent mielz que la bialté.
  Molt par ert bele la raïne.
Vers l'ost chevalche la meschine;
chevous ot sors, lons jusqu'as piez,
a un fil d'or les ot traciez; . . .   4010

Then came a young girl who was queen of Vulcania. The maid
was named Camilla, she was wondrously beautiful and had very
great power; no other woman was so learned. She was wise, brave,
and chivalrous, and had very great wealth; she governed her
country marvelously well. She was ever accustomed to war and
greatly loved chivalry and upheld it as long as she lived. She
never busied herself with women's work, neither with spinning
nor sewing; she preferred to bear arms, to joust and break lances,
to strike with sword and lance. There was no woman with courage equal to hers. By day she was king, and by night queen. There
was no lady-in-waiting or serving maid near her by day, nor at
night had any man the right to enter her room; so wisely did she
comport herself in private as well as in public that neither in fact
nor in appearance could any folly be noted in her, not even by
the envious. No mortal woman was her equal in beauty. Her
forehead was white and beautifully shaped, her head sat straight
on her neck [her hair parted straight over her spine?], her eyebrows were black and delicately drawn, her eyes were laughing
and very gay; fair was the nose in her face, for it was whiter
than snow or ice; her rosy coloring was pleasantly blended with
the white. The mouth was very well-shaped, and small rather
than large; her teeth were close together, gleaming brighter than
silver. What shall I say of her beauty? The longest summer day
would not suffice for me to speak of the beauty that was hers,

nor concerning her character and her goodness, which are more
precious than beauty.
  The queen was very beautiful; the virgin rode with the army;
her hair was blond and reached to her feet; through it she had
woven a golden thread. . . .

The next thirty-six lines are devoted to her raiment and thirty-
nine more to a description of her horse, saddle, and trappings.
Marvelous exotic splendor is the dominant note, and in the description of Camilla's horse the marvelous borders on the grotesque. After this interlude the episode is concluded as follows
(lines 4085–4106):

> *Camille vint molt richement*   4085
> *an l'ost et amena grant gent:*
> *bien ot o soi de chevaliers*
> *desi que a quatre milliers.*
> *Quant a Laurente vint errant,*
> *temolte ot an la vile grant,*   4090
> *borjois monterent sus as estres,*
> *dames, meschines as fenestres,*
> *et esgardoient la pucelle*
> *qui tant ert proz et tant ert bele.*
> *A grant mervoille lo tenoient*   4095
> *tote la gent qui la veoient,*
> *qu'el se deüst onques combatre,*
> *joster ne chevalier abatre.*
> *Parmi Laurente trespassa,*
> *de l'autre part se herberja;*   4100
> *soz la cité a une part,*
> *la fist fichier son estandart;*
> *une liue tot anviron*
> *tienent li tref, li paveillon*
> *et les tentes as chevaliers*   4105
> *et les herberges de lorers.*

In such splendid array Camilla came to the army and brought
along many followers; she had with her almost four thousand
knights. As she proceeded on her way to Laurentum, there was
a great tumult in the town. The citizens climbed on their roof-

tops, the women and girls went to the windows, and gazed upon the maid who was so brave and so beautiful. All who saw her thought it amazing indeed that she should ever fight, break lances, and hurl riders to the ground. She rode straight through Laurentum and took up quarters on the other side; there she had her standards set up: the space occupied by the tents of the knights and the groom's quarters [?] measured about one league around.

It is immediately evident that though the Norman poet deals with the same incident as Virgil, he does so in an entirely different way. The main difference, from which all the others follow, is that he destroys the happening by continually interrupting it. In Virgil the references to Camilla's person are brief and so selected as to fit into the flowing movement. In Virgil, Camilla comes into view and rides past; not for a moment do we lose sight of this happening. The French poet interrupts it in the second line (3960); goes back to it almost fifty lines later (line 4008: *Vers l'ost chevalche la meschine*), but very briefly; and finally completes it, after a further interlude of almost eighty lines, in lines 4085–4106, without further interruption but with a leisurely garrulousness that contrasts sharply with Virgil's pace. The interstices are filled in with moralizing descriptions, and it is to these that the poet obviously attaches the greatest importance. Most modern critics find them overlong, inappropriate, and somewhat ridiculous.[3] But whether or not this style appeals to us, it is consistent in its own way: it moves back and forth between narrative, description, and moralizing on an easygoing middle level of feeling.

This takes us a step further: the author of the *Enéas* moves on a different level of feeling and tone, hence of style from that of Virgil. In the *Aeneid* Virgil does not employ a quiet middle style. He is grand and sublime. These are technical terms with the an-

3. Cf. J. Crosland, " 'Eneas' and the 'Aeneid,' " p. 285. Her article provides a useful compilation of the main differences. Her view that, in the course of his labors, the author's taste veered away from Virgil and turned to Ovid may be correct, but it scarcely takes account of what is essential. A. Pauphilet, "Eneas et Énée," is more subtle and shows far greater understanding; but he too fails to examine the problems which interest us here.

cient writers on style. For them, as we have seen above, the grand and sublime contrast with the pleasing middle level (and also with the low or factual or commonplace). The sublime is intended to carry the reader away, to overpower him; rhetorical devices may be employed, but then in such a way that the overpowering quality of the whole prevents the listener from singling them out and relishing them as such. The middle level, on the other hand, is meant to be quietly diverting; here the rhetorical devices should be so distributed that the reader can dwell on them; here wit, psychology, elegant sensibility, and charming detailed description are in order. With their unapproachable and undeviating perfection, their unbroken action and movement, Virgil's lines on Camilla are a model of the lofty style. When Poseidon descends from the mountain crag to his palace (*Iliad,* beginning of Book 13; *Peri hypsous* 9.8), the effect is more powerful but scarcely more perfect in its unapproachable loftiness. Indeed, there are none too many passages in classical Latin literature that express the noble and arouse a sense of participation in it with such magical simplicity.

The French poet has utterly destroyed all this by diluting it with long moralistic and ornamental descriptions. In so doing, as we have said, he has descended to a style level which in antiquity would have been termed middle, or "pleasing." Why, we may ask, did he make this change? It can hardly have been a free individual decision, for he knew his model thoroughly; and it seems doubtful that anyone, knowing such verses well, should not have felt their power. Or can it be that he despaired of imitating Virgil with the vocabulary, syntax, and prosody of the Old French, a language that was barely awakening to literary expression, and therefore chose a simpler style? That would be more plausible. But obviously he did not see the problem in this light; he had no need to make a personal decision. He moves with great assurance and ease in what is clearly an established stylistic tradition, to which the ancient conception of the sublime had become alien.

How was this possible? We shall try to account for it by summing up and interpreting the results of a number of specialized investigations. But since even this summary will be rather complex, I shall try to simplify matters by anticipating the most important conclusions. In late antiquity, first of all, the classical, Virgilian conception of the sublime was vitiated by the excessive use of rhetorical forms, among which ornamental description may be included; at the same time a growing weariness corroded men's feeling for the grandeur and tragedy of human events. This exaggerated use of rhetoric carried over into the medieval Latin tradition of the Church schools, for which, moreover, "grandiose subjects" in the ancient sense were virtually nonexistent. Finally, the penchant for rhetoric was inherited by the vernacular poets of the twelfth century, who were almost all clerics or educated by clerics. Of course a good many of the old rhetorical devices were inapplicable to the still undeveloped vernacular languages; but rhetorical description found fertile soil in the moralizing, erudite, and sometimes grotesquely humorous school tradition.

Even in the classical period rhetoric had begun to play a dominant part in literature, a development implicit in the nature of ancient letters. Literature and oratory were closely related, both being arts of linguistic expression.[4] Conceived as a preparation for a political career, the education of the ruling classes was based on the study of oratory; eloquence was the first prerequisite for success in public life. At an early date this made for the development of a very precise and, to our way of thinking, pedantic rhetorical technique. It was only natural that this technique should have influenced literary production and at the same time that the rhetoricians should have looked to literature for striking illustrations of their principles. Despite frequent warnings, despite occasional countermovements, which were effective for a time, the two arts merged almost completely in late antiquity. The traces of this fusion may be found throughout the Middle Ages and be-

4. Some formulations from antiquity have been assembled by E. de Bruyne, *Études d'esthétique médiévale*, pp. 45f.

yond, both in literature itself and in the terminology of literary esthetics. Dante called his treatise on writing in the mother tongue *De vulgari eloquentia;* and in several countries the late medieval teachers of writing still called themselves rhetoricians.

The first generation of Augustan poets, among whom Virgil and Horace were the most prominent, acted as a countermovement to the increasing use of rhetoric in poetry. This antirhetorical reaction was far from radical; even our brief analysis of the Camilla passage has shown that rhetorical devices are not lacking in Virgil. Nevertheless Virgil and his contemporaries preferred the great literature of the earlier Greeks to the highly rhetorical Hellenistic works, and he himself wrote the only Latin epic with a lofty style in which rhetoric does not play a preponderant part. The reaction was brief; despite his wonderful gift for form, Ovid allowed himself to be beguiled by rhetorical devices and tricks. In the course of the first century even the sublime style became completely rhetorical; Seneca in tragedy, Statius in the epic, and the short-lived Lucan created a kind of rhetorical sublimity. Seneca and Lucan were effective writers and exerted a considerable influence for many centuries. They developed a style level of gruesome high tragedy, which is quite compatible with heavy rhetorical ornamentation. Its effect, to be sure, is more static than dynamic, more crushing than moving, and in reading long passages it is hard to dispel a feeling of weariness and surfeit. The persistently elaborate formulations become particularly tedious in connection with grandiose events which are expected to arouse tragic sympathy in the reader. Rhetorical excess is very dangerous in treatments of the passions and the sublime; it destroys all immediacy and movement, especially when the reader has the feeling that the scene did not spring from a single impulse but was carefully pieced together with the help of traditional devices. The leading theorists of ancient eloquence were well aware of this and said as much. Many of their less inspired fellows copied the idea from them, but no remonstrances could prevent the invasion of rhetoric from destroying the sublime style.

The most important among the theorists of the Imperial Age, the unknown author of the Greek treatise *On the Sublime*, who probably lived in the first half of the first century A.D., spoke impressively on the matter. The lofty style, he says in substance, is not, like the middle style, intended to please and persuade but to fire with enthusiasm and to carry away; if ornamental figures are used in it, they should be imperceptible, submerged by the great, passionate movement, otherwise they produce an effect of sophistry and triviality. Grandeur should not be confused with inflated bombast (αὔξησις, Latin *amplificatio*); and passionate movement (πάθος) is just as essential to the sublime style (ὕψος) as the description of manners (ἦθος) to the pleasing middle style (ἡδονή).[5] It is an old tradition that the middle style is the proper medium for figures of speech and description of manners; it is still to be found in Augustine's *De doctrina christiana* (see above, pp. 33f.), and still in characteristic form in the compiler Julius Victor (fourth century),[6] who takes it, in part verbatim, from Cicero's *Orator* (91–96).

But even during the first century of the Imperial Age, the trends in public life were such as to provide fewer occasions for grand and impassioned oratory. According to the old tradition, oratory has three functions: political, legal (though most of the great trials had a political background), and ceremonial. During the Imperial Age the first two gradually lost their meaning, and the third alone, the "epideictic" genre, the ceremonial address or

5. *On the Sublime (Peri hypsous)* 1.4; 3.4; 12.1; 17; 29.2. The last named passage reads: πάθος δὲ ὕψους μετέχει τοσοῦτον, ὁπόσον ἦθος ἡδονῆς (passion is as much a part of the sublime style as the description of manners is part of the entertaining style). Here ἦθος means (as in 9.15) "description of manners." In a highly interesting passage in Quintilian (6.2.8ff.) it means "feeling," likewise in opposition to πάθος. In the same passage Quintilian admits that there is no Latin word for "feeling."

6. Halm, *Rhetores latini minores*, p. 438, 22–25: *Medio autem generi dicendi omnia ornamenta conveniunt, plurimum suavitatis, multum sententiarum, latae eruditaeque disputationes, et communes loci sine contentione dicentur. Hoc solum totum genus e sophistarum fonte defluxit in forum* . . . (For the middle style all kinds of ornament are suitable: the highest degree of sweetness, a wealth of aphorisms, extended and learned arguments, and commonplaces freely accepted will be propounded. This style alone in its entirety flowed into the forum from the fountain of the sophists . . .).

panegyric, remained. Here again the author saw the essential: he concedes that the ceremonial address may have dignity and weight but denies that passion has any place in it (*Peri hypsous* 8.3); he even goes so far as to say that passionate orators are the least suited to this kind of address.

In literature as well, lack of subject matter and the influence of rhetoric brought about a decline in the sublime style, which gave way to pompous epideixis. In the crisis provoked by Stilicho and Alaric, at the beginning of the fifth century, there was a brief revival. There is no denying that Claudian, the great poet of the day, was excessively rhetorical and pompous, but we still perceive some of the old grandeur, a certain amount of passion and immediacy. Claudian's somewhat older contemporary Prudentius might be mentioned here, but he far more distinctly than Claudian must be put down as a Christian writer, and we prefer not to deal with Christian literature in the present context. Even then, as we have shown in the first chapter, Christian writers were beginning to fashion a sublime style of their own, far simpler and less rhetorical than its pagan counterpart; and though the formal style of Prudentius was a transitional phenomenon and cannot wholly be identified with *sermo humilis*, it nevertheless has a good deal in common with it. Here we wish to discuss only those writers who employed a Latin in the strict ancient tradition, without Christian admixture. Among these, to be sure, I include certain Christians such as Claudian himself and Sidonius; and as late as the sixth century we find numerous Christian authors who show only the barest suggestion of *sermo humilis*, principally Boethius, and still later certain passages in Fortunatianus. It is precisely within the ancient tradition, already declining but highly influential even in the ensuing centuries, that the impassioned and dynamic sublime style was replaced by a ceremonious epideixis, which is rhetorical, moralistic, static, descriptive, and didactic.

Of particular interest to us here is description, the "ethical," [7]

7. See above, n. 5. Many rival forms for description are employed by the ancient theorists: *diatyposis, ecphrasis, energeia, descriptio, illustratio,* and many others. In this connection, *ethos* really designates the permanent dis-

as the ancient rhetoricians called it. Above we have cited a passage from *Peri hypsous*, according to which "ethical" themes are
suited to the middle style.[8] This is an exaggeration; the great epic
is not entirely dramatic and impassioned, and the radicalism of
his position compels the author of *Peri hypsous* to call the *Odyssey*
a work of Homer's old age. But it is certain that when ornate
description becomes too detailed and long-winded, it destroys the
great sweep of the grand style.

The great model for epideictic description was Sidonius (late
fifth century), the gaudy peacock, as Alan of Lille [9] called him.
Actually it is unfair to Sidonius to regard him solely as a rhetorical
mannerist; and if we take the trouble to read our way into his
letters and poems, we find great wit and charm. His style expresses what it is meant to express. The many figures and the
difficult order, which combines profusion with condensed syntax,
are often, though not always, well adapted to the content; and
what he has to say is worth reading, for he provides the last picture of ancient society and its life. He was a grand seigneur of the
Gallo-Roman aristocracy; his father-in-law Avitus was for a brief
time Western emperor; he himself was, also briefly, prefect of
Rome; and at the time of his death he was bishop of Clermont.

---

position, the character, in contrast to *pathos*, the passionate movement of
the moment. Thence it came to mean the portrayal of customs. Cf., for
instance, Fortunatianus, *Artis rhetoricae* (Halm, *Rhet. lat. min.* 88).—The
whole matter is treated at length by H. Brinkmann, *Zu Wesen und Form
mittelalterlicher Dichtung*, pp. 54ff., and E. R. Curtius, *Europ. Lit.*, passim;
see ibid., index, s.v. *Ecphrasis.*

8. It also finds a place in comedy, satire, and the like. Horace, too, warns
against descriptions in the major epic, at the beginning of his *Ars poetica.*
The *Ars poetica* was known and much cited in the Middle Ages; but the
humorous cast of the lines in question is intended only for Horace's contemporaries, who would appreciate the allusions. It is not surprising that
in later times it was no longer understood. Even Sidonius was unable to
understand the lines about the "crimson patches." Cf. E. R. Curtius, *Europ.
Lit.*, p. 525 [Amer. edn., p. 539].

9.   *Illic Sydonii trabeatus sermo refulgens
Sydere multiplici splendet gemmisque colorum
Lucet et in dictis depictus pauo resultat.*
                                        Anticlaudianus 3.240–242.

(There the radiant word of Sidonius, dressed in a robe of state, shines like
a many-pointed star, gleams with gems of color, and portrayed in words
comes out in the form of a peacock.)

In his work we find the earliest known example of a personal description [10] that is not only static and detailed but methodical and in a way complete: first a piece by piece description of the body from head to foot; then an account of how this individual spends his day, covering the "ethical" element, that is, his mode of life and character. Medieval theorists of style cited it as a model. The portrait in question is that of Theodoric II, king of the Visigoths, at whose court in Toulouse Sidonius was active over a period of years as a young man. Though markedly manneristic in style, it is not schematic and "epideictic," but a comparatively individualized and vivid portrait of an actual human being whom Sidonius knew well. Moreover, it occurs in a letter to a friend, a form of literature in which one expects no high pathos but a middle, pleasing, familiar style. But this consideration soon came to be disregarded, since ornate discourse was sought for its own sake, and where the old stylistic distinctions survived, they were misrepresented and misunderstood.

In order to understand the Latin literature of the early Middle Ages, we must form an idea of its situation. The society on which the ancient literary tradition and, in practice, all literary life depended, was disintegrating; the institutions and views at the base of its subject matter, forms of expression, and entire purpose were disappearing. Latin literature on the ancient model lost its public and its function. The old techniques of dissemination were also disappearing (Sidonius still speaks of the "publication" of his writings, *Epist.* 1.2.1). Since Merovingian times in Gaul and the Lombard period in Italy there had been no educated public. We shall speak of this at length in the next chapter.

The tradition of Latin literature survived only in the Church schools. Christianity itself, it must be remembered, had arisen

10. *Epist.* 1.2; reproduced in part by E. Faral, *Les Arts poétiques du XIIe et du XIIIe siècle*, pp. 8of.—Noteworthy descriptions of personages are also to be found elsewhere in Sidonius; in particular I shall mention the Christian gentleman Vectius (4.9), the youthful sexagenarian Germanicus (4.13), and the pedantically hyperrealistic figure of the traitor (3.13). On this, see E. Faral, "Sidoine Apollinaire et la technique littéraire du Moyen Age."

within ancient culture. Its doctrine was a book; it possessed a steadily developing literature of exegesis, polemics, propaganda, and liturgy. Quite as a matter of course it had taken over its instruments of expression from ancient literature. Of course, as we have tried to show in the first chapter, it had adapted them in its own way, but the fact remains that Christian literature had been built up from the materials provided by the literature and rhetoric of late antiquity. It was generally recognized that Christian authors had every right to make use of ancient rhetoric and ancient culture in general, as Augustine and other Church Fathers had done. Thus the older Christian works, which in monasteries and episcopal schools were handed down to a small minority of students, and the commentaries, the polemical, hagiographic, and liturgical works that the clerics of the early Middle Ages produced, all drew on the literary heritage of late antiquity. The clerical schools did not break loose from the pagan schools until relatively late and were obliged, for their very existence, to carry with them the ancient tradition, though of course in a drastically reduced, simplified, and petrified form. It was individuals and groups in these schools who preserved what love and admiration for the ancient forms still survived. Though distrusted by the rigorists, ancient culture enjoyed high prestige. Neither tendency, it seems to me, was really crucial. The rigorists could not destroy the ancient tradition without at the same time making it impossible to transmit the Christian tradition, and the humanists of the early Middle Ages could not conjure up out of nothing the society needed for a new flowering of ancient culture.

In any event, the ancient tradition survived; not only hidden away in the strictly Christian literature of the Bible commentaries, the holy books, the homiletic, polemical, apologetic, and liturgical works, but also in works of wholly or semiprofane character: chronicles, lives of rulers, letters, pedagogical treatises, the documents and correspondence of the chancelleries, and profane literary works. Rhetorical theory was busily studied as part of the trivium; we find traces of it in Isidore of Seville, Bede, Alcuin,

Lupus of Ferrières and his students, Rather of Verona, Gerbert of Aurillac, Meinhard of Bamberg, and many others; beginning at the end of the eleventh century (Marbod von Rennes), it experienced a kind of revival.

But the classical conception of grand, sublime, impassioned style which rhetoric serves as a mere handmaiden was lost. All the theoretical statements of the period show that elevation of style was equated with wealth of ornament. Through the inbreeding of the schools, the lofty style degenerated irrevocably into mannerism. And in many quarters this high rhetorical style was held to be contrary to the Christian tradition, unfit for the treatment of Christian subjects. Even in the early Middle Ages, to be sure, in Rather of Verona and in late Ottonian mannerism (Bruno of Querfurt) we find a few texts which do justice to specifically Christian preoccupations in an extreme mannerist style, in other words, a Christian mannerism; but, generally speaking, the style of Christian writing throughout this period is only moderately rhetorical: such classical and, one might say, natural devices as anaphora, rhetorical question, isocolon, antithesis, apostrophe, and homoeoteleuton (rhymed prose played an important part) had their place in it, but mannerism proper, specifically, phonetic tricks and intentional obscurity in sentence structure and the choice of words, is avoided. The style level of Christian literature, as we have attempted to show in the preceding chapter, is principally determined by the conception of *sermo humilis*, which may be said to be implicit in it—and though this *sermo humilis* is by no means free from rhetoric, it is nevertheless *simplex* and *apertus*.[11] The truly rhetorical style was regarded as ornamental and profane.

These two observations—first, that the lofty style of early

---

11. The words *simplex, apertus,* and *humilis* to designate what is appropriate to Christian themes are used by Meinhard of Bamberg in a letter which, although much more specific than the summary given above, may nevertheless be cited in evidence. It was not written, however, until the end of the eleventh century. It may be found in C. Erdmann and N. Fickermann, *Briefsammlungen der Zeit Heinrichs IV.,* p. 175.

medieval Latin is essentially ornamental and manneristic, and second, that as such it is not suitable for Christian subjects—are crucial for our investigation. The authentic lofty style of the classical period, ὕψος, is appropriate only to sublime subjects that stir the heart; but early medieval Latin possessed only one such subject. It had neither tragedy nor great epic poetry and could not have them, for its one lofty concern was the story of Christ, which embraced the entire tragedy of man. But the story of Christ and everything connected with it had its own style, which we have called *sermo humilis.*

A new flowering of learned Latin literature set in toward the middle of the eleventh century; at the same time the Romance vernaculars began to awaken, first, it would seem, in Gallo-Roman territory. In the course of this medieval renaissance epic poetry in the grand style was also attempted in Latin hexameters. The most significant examples are Walter of Châtillon's *Alexandreis* and Joseph of Exeter's *De bello Troiano;* both authors belong to the Anglo-Norman cultural sphere, and both wrote in the second half of the twelfth century. The moralistic satires which Walter of Châtillon wrote in medieval rhymed verse are a good deal more lively, but despite certain trivial or excessively didactic passages, the *Alexandreis* is also an interesting achievement; Joseph of Exeter was one of the subtlest and most ingenious technicians of Latin rhetoric and obtained strong sensuous effects with his mannerism.[12] Such works, however, are little more than proficient technical exercises; outside of the schools there was no public for them, they had no bearing on the great intellectual movements of the day, and they do not, like Petrarch at a later age, express any particular attitude toward art and life.

We shall probably never gain a clear view of the earliest devel-

12. On the *Alexandreis*, see F. J. E. Raby, *A History of Secular Latin Poetry in the Middle Ages*, II, 72–79; on Joseph of Exeter, ibid., 132–137. As an example of the style of *De bello Troiano*, see the description of Helen, the end of which is cited by Raby, p. 135. The whole work, which deserves to be read in full, is to be found in *Dictys Cretensis* (ed. S. Dresemius), II, 474–476.

opment of vernacular literature in Gallo-Roman territory. Fortunate accidents have preserved a few documents from the first two centuries of this development, but they are insufficient. The earliest of them date back to the ninth century. The two poems of the Clermont-Ferrand manuscript (the *Passion* and the life of St. Léger), probably dating from the end of the tenth century, already disclose a certain routine, as though work of this sort were already customary and widespread at the time; and from the middle of the eleventh century on we have numerous literary works on the most divergent style levels. Not all of them can be dated with precision, but in any case they show that in this period there were ample possibilities of expression. Let us consider, for example, the oldest version of the *Chanson de Saint-Alexis*, the Provençal fragment about Sainte Foy d'Agen, the beginnings of the *chanson de geste*, and the beginnings of Provençal lyric poetry. All these should probably be assigned to the eleventh century. It becomes apparent that since the poems of the Clermont-Ferrand manuscript or the Provençal Boethius a powerful movement has occurred in the vernacular. Richness of form, depth and refinement of feeling, elegance and verve—all these have developed enormously.

In the *chanson de geste*, the earliest authenticated examples of which were probably written about 1100, a special variety of lofty epic style makes its appearance. The influence of ancient models can be demonstrated; undoubtedly certain ancient themes still carried on a shadowy existence among the minstrels and jongleurs, and the ancient learning of the clerics who wrote them down also played a part. But on the whole the *chansons de geste* have a style of their own, which, it seems to me, is fundamentally different from that of the classical or postclassical epic. To my mind, the old romantic theory of the folk spirit, from which these works sprang, is essentially sound, in spite of numerous mistakes in its application and the vague way in which the word "folk" was used. It has not been possible to controvert the proofs

and indications favoring an early dating of the *chansons de geste;*
on the contrary, new evidence of it has come to light. The historical tradition underlying certain *chansons de geste* and the course
of their transformation into legend have been traced in a number
of recent works.[13] But my conviction is also based, for want of
compelling proofs, on a feeling for what is natural and plausible.
It is not natural and plausible that a people should have possessed
no poetry in its own tongue over a period of centuries, especially
a people living in a country where there had once been a great
literary culture, which would in all likelihood have perpetuated
itself in subliterary forms, a people, moreover, whose neighbors,
who had several times subjugated them and with whom communication was never broken off, possessed a heroic epic. Furthermore,
the *chanson de geste* unmistakably describes ways of life and contains stylistic peculiarities which were already archaic in 1100: the
paratactic structure, the abrupt leaps from one part of an action
to the next, each sentence amounting to a fresh beginning, and the
frequent repetition of set locutions, whose typically "formulaic"
character suggests strongly that they originated in an oral tradition. Finally, the lofty tone of the *chanson de geste* breaks with
the classical tradition by its impurity, that is, the constant admixture of grotesque and farcical elements. All this can be traced
back to no Latin tradition; nothing in any period of classical,
postclassical, or medieval Latin literature (except perhaps for the
Waltharius or *Ruodlieb*) resembles this style, nor does any Latin
hagiographic text. The only early life of a saint to show any resemblance to the *chanson de geste* is the old French version of
the *Chanson d'Alexis.* (I cannot support the opinion, often met
with today, that in respect of form this poem served as a model
for the *chanson de geste.*) The *chanson de geste* is also fundamentally different from the didactic works, rhymed chronicles,
and *romans* in French octosyllabic couplets that sprang up in the
course of the twelfth century; beside the graceful lightness and

13. See the investigations of René Louis, Rita Lejeune, Martin de Riquer,
Maurice Delbouille, Dámaso Alonso, and others.

the fluid easy articulations that developed in the *roman*, the structure of the *chanson de geste* seems unmistakably archaic.

In any case it is certain that the lofty style of the *chanson de
geste* did not exert an influence for long. The material lived on,
took on new forms, and finally merged with that of the courtly
roman; but the old lofty style of the heroic epic—with its heavi-
ness, its parataxis, and its folk-song-like formulas—disappeared as
soon as a society of the elite, expressing itself in the vernacular,
made its appearance. In this new society there arose a new French
style which, while not lofty, was elegant and conversational. We
shall describe more fully in the next chapter how in the west of
present-day France and in England the first social elite since
ancient times grew up in the course of the twelfth century. It
was still a very small class, consisting almost exclusively of the
high Anglo-Norman nobility; but the Anglo-Norman cultural
sphere included Anjou and, after the accession of Henry II of
Anjou and his queen, Eleanor of Aquitaine, to the English throne
(1154), the most important parts of Provence. The verse form
employed almost exclusively in the new epics composed for this
aristocratic society was the octosyllabic couplet. Octosyllabic
verse was probably taken over from hymns and was also used in
hagiographic works; it had been introduced into the vernacular
by clerics, who exchanged the stanza, in which it originally appeared, for the rhymed couplet, better suited to narration. The
aristocratic ladies and gentlemen needed clerics—those who were
highly educated and socially presentable—to organize their literary
entertainment. At first it was these clerics alone who were capable
of providing the material and the form or of carrying out the
ideas of their patrons. Anglo-Norman culture sprang from an
association of the high aristocracy with cultivated and worldly
clerics who, though trained in Church schools, were not so much
ecclesiastics as courtiers—the type is exemplified by Benoît de
Sainte-Maure and probably by Chrétien de Troyes. Hardly a
trace remains of the jongleur, with his popular verve, buffoonery,

and uncouthness. There had still been a good deal of the jongleur in the gifted William of Poitou, duke of Aquitaine, though he was a great lord and precursor of the courtly style—but by now the jongleur type had all but vanished.

P. A. Becker [14] and others have expressed the opinion that the octosyllabic rhymed couplet was meant to be read. This is true to the extent that the courtly poems written in the great period beginning in 1150 were not intended to be recited by professional singers with instrumental accompaniment before a large and nondescript public. On the other hand, it should not be supposed that these poems served predominantly for the private reading of individuals; in the twelfth century we cannot yet speak of a reading public or of "publication." Courtly literature was meant to be read aloud. Even among the Anglo-Norman aristocracy there were very few persons who could read quickly and easily enough to enjoy doing so, and up until the end of the century the difficulty and expense involved in acquiring manuscripts were such that laymen (with the possible exception of certain noble families) were unable to collect books in any considerable number. The collecting of books began in the following century, and even then the development was exceedingly slow. The courtly works were read aloud in select gatherings, at courts and in castles, either by courtly clerics (from whose ranks the authors themselves came) or nobles, often women skilled in reading aloud. The length of these works [15] fits in with this manner of reading, a poem providing entertainment for several evenings; and only when read aloud do their charm, grace, suppleness, elegance, and the sometimes didactic, often somewhat ironical or flippant, but always pleasing play of the rhymes achieve their full effect.

Thus the poets who first used the rhymed octosyllabic couplet for courtly narrative were clerics; they knew the ancient themes and, as has been amply proved, were versed in ancient rhetoric. But their use of it was very simple and moderate. The French

14. "Der gepaarte Achtsilber in der französischen Dichtung."
15. Some twelve hundred octosyllables can easily be read aloud in one hour.

language of the time and the society for which they wrote were quite unprepared for a more thoroughgoing application of ancient rhetoric. Even then effects could be obtained in French with certain sound patterns, with anaphora, apostrophe, antithesis, isocolon, and various types of amplification. But ancient rhetoric, especially in poetry, obtains its really characteristic effects by inversions of word order (hyperbaton), the possibilities of which are exceedingly limited in French, and by long, intricate periods, favored by the richness of Latin in inflection and connectives. At that time the use of elaborate periods was out of the question in any of the vernacular languages, and the octosyllabic line does not lend itself to it. As far as I know, there is virtually no example of intricate sentence structure in French prose before Alain Chartier and before Scève and the Pléiade in poetry; it was not fully developed until the seventeenth century. In the twelfth century a poet addressing himself to the laity was limited to simple sequences of short sentences; what long sentences can be found are enumerations. Subordinate constructions had to be used simply and sparingly. The octosyllabic *romans* had lost the harsh, block-on-block character of the *chansons de geste;* they were fluent, without abrupt breaks, gracefully modulated in their transitions. But on the whole the structure is simple and, despite a number of elegantly employed rhetorical figures, quite unrhetorical.[16]

Yet the courtly *roman* remained in the tradition of the middle style. Though it could not do much with its rhetoric, it adopted its leisurely pace, its diffuseness, its moralistic amplification, and its main instrument: detailed description. The *roman* took its themes (Greco-Roman and Celtic legends) from the heroic past, but unlike the heroic or grotesque *chanson de geste*, it treated them in a pleasing and elegant middle style. Its creators were clerics trained in rhetoric, and they created it for a highly aristocratic public which had just emerged as a distinct class with its own highly evolved social mores, a public in which women set the

16. Compare, for example, the *Roman de Troie* of Benoît de Sainte-Maure with Joseph of Exeter's *De bello Troiano*. On the latter writer, see n. 12.

tone, inclined toward a rather precious elegance and given to self-portrayal.

The earliest themes treated derived from English history. The twelfth century, the century of the Crusades, was marked by a lively interest in historiography. This period produced a number of significant historians who wrote in Latin; Otto of Freising, the richest mind among medieval chroniclers, wrote in the first half of the century. It is easy to understand that the Norman Conquest should have stimulated historiography in England: the dramatic events of the conquest and the conflicts arising from Norman rule aroused an awareness of the country's special character, deriving from its still distinct ethnic groups. Several important chroniclers wrote in this period, in particular, William of Malmesbury in the first half of the century, somewhat later Roger of Hoveden and William of Newbury. But it was not these historians (whose method, for their time, was critical) who appealed to the need of entertainment of the aristocratic groups, but an imaginative compiler of the legendary early history of Britain, Geoffrey of Monmouth, whose *Historia regum Britanniae* made its appearance in the late 1130's and soon became famous. He made some use of sources and probably also of Celtic folk traditions, but he combined his materials arbitrarily and seasoned them very considerably with his own inventions. It is difficult to determine exactly how much of his "history" was the product of his imagination, since we have no way of knowing what earlier documents have been lost. But in any case, he gave legendary early history the form of an adventure story, not only absurdly falsifying historical events but ignoring all concrete historical problems or possible historical structure. In Geoffrey's work the history of peoples breaks down into a sequence of individual passions, heroic deeds, and crimes. But precisely in the form of such luxuriant, colorful tales, the legends served to entertain courtly society. In this case, one might say that the stage of popular lofty style was passed over. Where a vernacular attains to literary expression by a natural, unimpeded progression, the sifting of its legends goes hand in hand with the genesis of a national written language, and they are committed to writing in a form which preserves their true historico-political core and is significant to the linguistic community. But in the Middle Ages the literary pre-eminence of Latin at first impeded the literary development of the vernacular tongues,[17] just as the orientation of men's inner life and social consciousness toward universal Christianity was to inhibit the rise of a national feeling. An additional factor in the Anglo-Norman cultural sphere was the recent superimposition of the French Normans upon the native population. The vernacular of the aristocracy was not that of the country, and national unity was a long way off. It was during this very period that a feudal class composed of Anglo-Norman and other West-French landed gentry developed a need for entertainment. The legends offered them by Geoffrey's work were not those of their own past; they themselves were predominantly dynastic and feudal in their political feeling. Clearly these fanciful, ahistorical legends, attaching to no national myth, situated in a remote historical past but readily lending themselves to elegant modernization, offered them just what they needed: literary entertainment and self-portraiture. Geoffrey's Latin chronicle was a great success; it was freely rendered into French octosyllables by Wace, a middle-aged cleric from Jersey, already known for his French lives of saints; it was no doubt in the early 1150's that he completed his work and dedicated it to the young Queen Eleanor. At about the same time other courtly clerics, only one of whom, Benoît de Sainte-Maure, is known to us by name, attempted to achieve similar effects with the ancient themes familiar to them. They seem to have been successful at first, but in the long run the Celtic themes proved more fruitful for a fashionable court literature.

The first elegant and pleasing middle style to be met with in a European vernacular occurs in the courtly *roman*. Inferior to its

17. Later, to be sure, this was to be a great advantage to them; it "loosed the tongue of French," as E. R. Curtius once put it: *Europ. Lit.*, p. 388 [Amer. edn., p. 384].

ancient forerunners in rhetorical subtlety, it compensates by the charm of its rhymes. Its handling of its themes is also typical of the middle style. On the one hand there is a strong accent on remoteness in space and time, on the exotic, miraculous, and adventurous; on the other hand the treatment is so rich in psychological aperçus and social and vestimentary detail that the characters lose their legendary remoteness and superhuman stature and become members of contemporary feudal society, fashionable ladies and gentlemen, good to tell stories about. For our present purposes what chiefly interests us in these *romans* is their description of characters, and this brings us back to the text that was our starting point, the description of Camilla in the French *Enéas*.

All *romans* of the period dealing with ancient themes (three have come down to us; see note 1 above) contain such descriptions, some of which the authors found in their sources; the descriptions are done with great care and show a love of concrete observation. Some of them are lifted completely out of the action; this is true of the portraits of the Greek and Trojan heroes in Benoît (borrowed from Dares), who offers a veritable portrait gallery similar to those of Theophrastus or La Bruyère. Benoît's portraits are all the more lively and amusing in that they are not disfigured by pedantic completeness and excessive length; amplification, the most important device which the clerics derived from their training in rhetoric, and which is so well suited to octosyllabic verse because it helps the poet to evade many difficulties in rhyming,[18] remains within tolerable limits. It is pleasing to read that Helen had a beauty spot between her eyebrows (an ancient tradition), that Hector had a slight stutter, that Aeneas was short and fat; the portraits of women—Helen, Briseis, Hecuba, Polyxena, etc.—are delightful; and it is interesting to observe that a portrait such as the following could have been written in French in the middle of the twelfth century:

18. Even Dante still gets around difficulties of rhyming by amplification. With him this often leads to unexpectedly splendid effects, but also results in occasional oddities.

> *Polidarius ert si gras*
> *Qu'a granz peines alot le pas.*
> *En plusors choses ert vaillanz,*
> *Mais toz jorz ert tristes pensanz.*
> *Ainz cerchast l'om par mainte terre,*
> *Qui plus orgoillos vousist querre.*

Polidarius was so fat that he had great difficulty in walking. He had great skill in many matters, but he was always filled with gloomy thoughts. Anyone wishing to find a haughtier man than he would have had to search in many lands.

There are also portraits that are worked adroitly and smoothly into the action and do not unduly interrupt it—for example, the description of the two daughters of Adrastus (*Roman de Thèbes* 927–984) at the moment when their father summons them to the banquet; by describing them not separately but both together, the author obtains a highly voluptuous effect, which was just what he intended, for he says (979f.):

> *Guari serront et retenu,*
> *Quis porront tenir nu a nu.*

They will be healed and accepted for service,
Who manage to hold them flesh to flesh.[19]

Charming and elegant examples such as these show us that it was quite unnecessary to be so complete, methodical, and pedantic as the author of the *Enéas*,[20] that there were other writers who

---

19. The lines 971f., *Mieus vaut lor ris e lor baisiers / Que ne fait Londres ne Peitiers* (Their laughing and kissing are worth more than London or Poitiers), clearly show that the poem was a product of the circle around Henry II and Eleanor of Aquitaine.

20. Later he describes them once again, 6907–6934.—For the origin of the amplifying description of Camilla in contemporary and older theory, see E. Faral, *Recherches sur les sources latines*, pp. 101–109.—E. Langlois, "Chronologie des romans de *Thèbes*, d'*Enéas* et de *Troie*," and also E. Faral, op. cit., pp. 93ff., have shown furthermore that the description of Camilla's arrival and of the bridling of her horse bears some resemblance to the arrival of Antigone in the *Roman de Thèbes* (3807ff.). But in view of the prevailing taste for stately arrivals and the fact that both authors wrote in the over-all style of their time, this resemblance, which applies only to a few lines and even then not to the wording, may well have

did not follow the rhetorical precepts and models so faithfully. Penthesilea, queen of the Amazons, for example, is introduced quite briefly and naturally in the *Roman de Troie*.[21] The author of the *Enéas* is particularly pedantic in his descriptions. He delights in the moralistic, didactic underpainting which these detailed descriptions make possible, and above all he loves to describe raiment and horses with an abundance of marvelous exotic detail that enables him to display his recondite erudition. But the other poets of the *triade classique* were also far removed from the classical sublime style. For them the ancient themes were primarily materials to be adapted to the expressive possibilities of the French language and the needs of a feudal society. If any ancient poet known to them could serve them as a general model of style, it was Ovid. Ovid was far closer to the diffuse storytelling style of these poets than were the classical epic poets. But to a humanist the whole idea of treating such subjects as Troy, the Seven against Thebes, or the Aeneid in the style of Ovid is a mistake. Well versed as they were in certain parts of ancient literature, the courtly clerics of the twelfth century were not humanists.

Even as imitators of Ovid, they had no classical feeling for the different levels of subject matter and style. Faral (*Sources* 109–157) showed great astuteness in compiling the borrowings from Ovid in the *Enéas*, but he points out only the echoes and parallels, without examining their implications. Yet often it is precisely the parallels that show the enormous gulf between the courtly clerics of the twelfth century and their model. I shall cite a single example to make my meaning clear. At the beginning of the eighth book of the *Metamorphoses* Ovid tells the story of Scylla, the Megarian princess who, looking down from the tower of her

---

been fortuitous. In other respects the two passages are radically different. The one from the *Roman de Thèbes* is much shorter and more vivid, and is organically connected with the action. It tells how the three women (Antigone with her mother and sister) set out on their mission to the army of the besiegers.

21. The legend that Eleanor of Aquitaine liked to see herself in the role of the Amazon queen Penthesilea in the Second Crusade, in which she participated as the wife of Louis VII of France, is not implausible, though it is not exactly substantiated by any of the sources.

father's beleaguered city, falls so desperately in love with King
Minos of Crete, the enemy leader, that in the following night she
cuts off the lock of red hair on which depend her father's strength
and life, and offers it along with herself to King Minos as a gift.
But Minos rejects her with horror. Ovid describes the awakening
of love in accordance with a familiar pattern; [22] she sees Minos
from her tower, his attitudes and activities are described; in each
and every one she finds him enchanting and lovable. Her reflections end on a markedly erotic note (*Metam.* 8.32–54), culminat-
ing in her terrible decision:

> *Cum vero faciem dempto nudaverat aere*
> *purpureusque albi stratis insignia pictis*
> *terga premebat equi spumantiaque ora regebat,*
> *vix sua, vix sanae virgo Niseia compos*
> *mentis erat; felix iaculum, quod tangeret ille,*
> *quaeque manu premeret, felicia frena vocabat.*
> *Impetus est illi, liceat modo, ferre per agmen*
> *virgineos hostile gradus, est impetus illi*
> *turribus e summis in Gnosia mittere corpus*
> *castra vel aeratas hosti recludere portas,*
> *vel siquid Minos aliud velit. Utque sedebat*
> *candida Dictaei spectans tentoria regis,*
> *"laeter" ait "doleamne geri lacrimabile bellum,*
> *in dubio est; doleo quod Minos hostis amanti est;*
> *sed nisi bella forent, numquam mihi cognitus esset.*
> *Me tamen accepta poterat deponere bellum*
> *obside; me comitem, me pacis pignus haberet.*
> *Si quae te peperit, talis, pulcherrime rerum,*
> *qualis es, ipsa fuit, merito deus arsit in illa.*
> *O ego ter felix, si pennis lapsa per auras*
> *Gnosiaci possem castris insistere regis*
> *fassaque me flammasque meas, qua dote, rogarem,*
> *vellet emi;*

But when he took off his helmet and showed his face and sat in
purple garb on the back of a white horse resplendent with its
painted trappings and controlled its foaming muzzle, then the

22. The *seu . . . seu . . .* construction; cf. Horace, *Carm.* 3.12.

Niseian maiden was scarcely herself—scarcely possessed any longer a sane mind. Happy she named the missile that he touched, and happy the reins he held in his hand. She feels a tempestuous desire in her, if only it were permissible, to direct her maiden steps through the hostile ranks; she longs to hurl her body from the top of the tower into the Gnosian camp, or to open the bronze gates to the enemy, or whatever else Minos may demand. As she sat there, gazing upon the white tents of the Dictaean king, she spoke: "Should I rejoice or be grieved over this lamentable war? I cannot say. I grieve, because Minos is an enemy of her who loves him [namely, of myself]. But had it not been for the war, would I ever have known him? Yet if he were to take me as hostage, he could desist from the war. He would have me in his company, as a pledge of peace. If the woman who gave you birth resembled you, most beautiful one, then rightfully was a god inflamed with love for her. Oh, thrice happy would I be, if gliding through the air on wings I could appear in the camp of the Gnosian king and ask, making myself and my passion known, with what dowry he would wish to be bought . . .

The author of the French *Enéas*, who knew this passage (cf. Faral, *Sources* 130), has added the story of the love between Lavinia and Aeneas to the Aeneid. It starts out very similarly to Ovid's passage about Scylla. Lavinia, too, stands on the tower of her father's castle, looking down at the enemy army in the plain (8047ff.):

> *Lavine fu an la tor sus,*
> *d'une fenestre garda jus,*
> *vit Eneam qui fu desoz,*
> *forment l'a esgardé sor toz.*   8050
> *Molt li sanbla et bel et gent,*
> *bien a oï comfaitemant*
> *lo loënt tuit par la cité*
> *et de proëce et de bialté;*
> *bien lo nota an son corage*   8055
> *la ou al fu an son estage.*
> *Amors l'a de son dart ferue;*
> *ainz qu'el se fust d'iluec meüe,*
> *i a changié cent foiz colors:*
> *or est cheoite es laz d'amors,*   8060

voille ou non, amer l'estuet.
Quant voit que eschiver n'en puet,
vers Eneam a atorné
tot sun corage et son pansé:
por lui l'a molt Amors navree;   8065
la saiete li est colee
desi qu'el cuer soz la memelle.
Tote ert sole la damoiselle,
l'uis de la chanbre ala fermer,
revient a la fenestre ester   8070
ou al reçut lo cop mortal;
d'iluec esgarde lo vasal.
Ele comance a tressüer,
a refroidir et a tranbler. . . .

Lavinia was up in the tower. She looked down from a window, she saw Aeneas who was down below, she singled him out and looked at him closely. Very handsome and noble he seemed to her; she had heard how in the city all praised him, and this she noted in her heart. In the high place where she stood, Cupid struck her with his arrow; before stirring from the spot, she changed color a hundred times. Now she has fallen into Cupid's snare; she must love him willy-nilly. Aware that she cannot help herself, she turns all her heart and thought to Aeneas. For his sake Cupid has wounded her deeply. The arrow has pierced her heart beneath her breast. The maiden was all alone; she shut the door of her room and went back to the window where she had received the fatal blow. Thence she looked on the knight. She begins to perspire, then a chill runs through her and she shivers.

This passage is followed by a soliloquy of over three hundred lines, in which she analyzes her state and situation; then come forty lines describing a restless night, and a conversation with her mother that takes up some two hundred lines. She confesses her love for Aeneas, and her mother, who favors the suit of Turnus, accuses Aeneas and the Trojans of homosexuality in very plain language. Then her mother leaves her, and after fainting several times, Lavinia goes back to the window:

El s'an rala a la fenestre,   8666
la ou amors l'avoit seisie;

> *la tente Eneas a choisie,*
> *molt volantiers la regarda,*
> *droit cele part son vis torna.*   8670
> *El n'en pooit son oil torner;*
> *bien tost, s'ele poïst voler,*
> *fust ele o lui el paveillon;*
> *ne pooit panser s'a lui non.*

She went once more to the window, where love had seized hold of her; she sought out Aeneas' tent, she was glad to look upon it, she looked straight in that direction. She could not avert her eyes from it; very quickly, if she could have flown, she would have been with him in the tent. She could think of nothing but him.

At this point she launches into a new soliloquy about the new idea that has come to her of sending Aeneas a message. In the end she carries out her project by having one of her father's archers shoot a letter into the Trojan camp. This takes us approximately to line 8840.

Here again the observation we made in connection with the passage from Virgil is in order; the author of the *Enéas* has completely demolished the unity and tension of Ovid's piece of virtuosity. In a single rising movement Ovid passes from description to monologue, from the eruption of Scylla's passion to her terrible decision, which is carried out at once. The French poet creates a wide gap between the two events, the outburst of love and the sending of the message; and moreover, he so dilutes the events themselves with moralizing and descriptive amplification that they lose all dramatic effect. But what concerns us here is not the *fact* of amplification, but the *material* employed in it. Almost all of it is derived from the casuistry of love: the arrow of love (8067, *desi qu'el cuer soz la memelle*), its effect (how she sweats and shivers, trembles and faints, weeps and sobs), the long soliloquy with its varied presentation of the problem, the self-reproach, accusations, lamentations, the night made sleepless by the torments of love, and so on. All this is directly or indirectly Ovidian, but treated at such length such matters are not in keeping with the style of the *Metamorphoses*—they suggest the courtesan poetry of Ovid's youth, the love poems in distichs.[23] The casuistry of love occurs only seldom and sparingly in the *Metamorphoses*. Even in the passage on Medea (*Metam.* 7.11–71), which Faral (quite rightly in other respects) compares with a section of Camilla's monologue (*Sources* 152–154), the erotic element is treated in a few sharp and brief antitheses. The *Metamorphoses* move on a higher style level than the love poetry of Ovid's youth; they approach the epic. But the author of the *Enéas* worked the love casuistry of the courtesan books into the epic material (cf. Faral, *Sources* 133–143).[24] He could not have used it in any other way; for the society for which Ovid's erotic poetry (and Augustan love poetry in general) was written did not exist in the twelfth century—there were no fashionable courtesans, forming a kind of second society and endowed with literary taste (one need only recall *Amores* 2.4). Later, in the Renaissance proper, such a class was to make its appearance. And so the author of the *Enéas* transposed Ovid's love casuistry into another social class and another style, in which it seems—at least to me—rather out of place. But in so doing he paved the way for a development that was soon to become still more pronounced and that was also present in germ in the poetry of the Provençal troubadours: the elevation of love to a theme worthy of the sublime style, indeed, to its principal theme. This is one of the most important developments in the history of European literature.

Chrétien de Troyes seems to have played no part in this blending of ancient themes with Ovidian love casuistry, though we cannot be sure, for his paraphrases of Ovid have not come down to us; the titles listed in the opening lines of the *Roman de Cligès* seem to indicate that he treated the themes from the *Metamor-*

23. Ovid, *Amores, Heroides, Ars amandi, Remedia amoris.*
24. Something of the kind might have been said about the portrait of Camilla, for this type of woman's portrait is also derived from erotic literature. Freshly seasoned with sensuality and irony, but possessing many traditional traits, this same love casuistry appears at the beginning of Adam de la Halle's *Jeu de la Feuillée.*

phoses and the love poetry separately.[25] In his later works, in any case, he developed a definitely courtly and contemporary style of his own, still looking to antiquity for instruction in the use of language but not for his themes and over-all plan of composition. This independence, this beginning of liberation from clerical Latin culture, was needed to complete the development of the courtly style, the first style of a social elite to emerge since ancient times. We cannot be sure to what extent this is due personally to Chrétien de Troyes; in Marie de France a lofty style, independent of classical models, is also fully developed, and among her contemporaries there were several poets who are insufficiently known to us. But we do know that the style of this court poetry was something absolutely new: it raised storytelling in verse to the level of high art, but made no attempt to imitate the over-all plan and absolute remoteness from everyday life that are characteristic of the great ancient models. It was from Celtic legend that this new genre first derived a frame, namely, an imaginary world within which it was possible to picture human relations in all their concrete detail and richness of feeling. Undoubtedly courtly art was the product of an elite culture: the conceptions of the perfect knight, of adventure and quest (*queste*), the choice of a particular man to confront a particular adventure and in succeeding to win liberation and redemption—all these motifs bear witness to high cultivation and a desire for lofty poetry. But, as the French language of the period shows, this cultivation and dignity did not confine themselves to a lofty, exclusive mode of expression, or even necessarily to a lofty and exclusive sensibility or principle of selection. In this elevated style there is room for amiable warmth, friendly playfulness, an irony implicit in things and happenings, a mildly didactic humor, and even a certain crudeness. By ancient standards such a style would have to be regarded as a hybrid, halfway between the middle and the sublime. But such

25. If, however, the *Philomena* from the *Ovide moralisé* (separately edited by C. de Boer) should be Chrétien's poem *De la hupe et de l'aronde*, it would have to be recognized that at least in this instance he interspersed the old epic themes with moralistic digressions on love.

formulations are not very helpful. This manner of treating serious human events with naïveté, warmth, and occasional humor bears no relation to ancient art; it is something new, the origins of which we can scarcely hope to lay bare. Assuredly a kind of popular love poetry, of which we possess too little, and the Christian *sermo humilis* have something to do with it. But that is about all we can say, and even this little is only dimly discernible. All the courtly epics we possess are written in rhymed octosyllables. The rhymed octosyllable is neutral in regard to style level; it lends itself to the telling of any kind of story and may be adapted to any content.

The beginning of the *Perceval*, for example, is full of warm humor; this applies not only to the meeting with the knights, whom Perceval takes for angels and to whose questions he replies with counterquestions, but also to the other scenes leading up to his arrival at King Arthur's castle: his entrance into the tent where he finds the *damoiselle;* his words in the tent as he steals a kiss, her ring, and her breakfast; the return of the knight who sits down to breakfast after reproving the *damoiselle* (933, *Atant s'asist et si manja:* At once he sat down and ate); the ensuing quick change of scene, and the dialogue with the charcoal burner (837f. *"Vilains," fet il, "ansaingne moi, qui l'asne mainnes devant toi . . .":* "Tell me, churl," he says, "you who are driving the donkey before you . . .")*, or the exchange with the red knight.[26] In all this the young man's dauntless energy, his victorious radiance and vision of the future, are clearly and beautifully brought out, although they are never directly mentioned. At the same time we know that his mother dies of grief over his depar-

26. 885–888:

> *"Ou iras tu, vaslez, di va?"*
> *"Je vuel," fet il, "a cort aler,*
> *Au roi cez armes demander."*
> *"Vaslez," fet il, "tu feras bien.*
> *Or va donc tost et si revien . . ."*

(Tell me, young man, where are you going?—I am going to court, he says, to ask the king for those arms [those of the knight!]—Young man, he says, you will do well, go quickly now and return . . .)

ture. This in itself would be serious enough; but we also know that this young man will search for the Grail, that the youth is the chosen one through whom the adventure story of the Breton *roman* is put into the service of eschatology and the drama of redemption.

The rapid but easygoing rhymed octosyllable embraces all these themes and levels of feeling; it can be broadly descriptive or moralistic or didactic, it can be moving and vibrant with feeling or ironic and almost flippant, but it never attains to the tragic and sublime. For that it is too naïve and short-winded; it never rises above the pleasing. Even the procession of the Grail in the castle of the Fisher King is far too naïvely descriptive to produce an effect of sublime solemnity. But in dealing with human situations and relationships, which are described so sparsely and stiffly in the earlier medieval epic and didactic literature, both Latin and vernacular, this courtly Breton poetry achieves an unprecedented sweetness and richness of feeling. In this connection I might cite, also from the beginning of *Perceval*, the night meeting between Perceval and Blancheflor, and countless other passages from Chrétien or Marie de France. But the greatest heights are probably attained in the poems dealing with Tristan, and here the most moving passage I can recall is the long scene from the *Folie Tristan* (MS Douce, ed. Bédier), in which Isolt refuses to recognize Tristan, dressed as a jester and also disguising his voice, even when he reminds her of all the events and adventures of the days of their love, which cannot be known to anyone but her and Tristan; a magnificently constructed scene, from the dog's recognition of Tristan[27] to the climax, when Isolt bursts into tears and faints at the sight of the ring.

Not only would such intensity of feeling have been inconceivable in the Middle Ages before the days of chivalric love; in connection with such a theme it is not to be met with in antiquity. Assuredly Eros is a mighty god, perhaps the mightiest of all

27. This dog is, if we like, a classical *topos* (*Odyssey*). But here he has his place in a love tragedy.

(Soph. *Antig.* 781: ἀνίκατε μάχαν), but in ancient literature little weight is attached to the vicissitudes of lovers. At best they are treated in the middle style, and only when seen as a link in a chain of destiny, as in the case of Medea or Dido, can a love affair become tragic.[28] Otherwise love was not regarded as a fitting subject for the sublime style. Here it might be argued that, as we have stressed in the preceding pages, the courtly Breton *roman* exemplifies not the lofty but the pleasing middle style, and that it is closely related to such tales of love and adventure as *Floire et Blancheflor* or the chantefable *Aucassin et Nicolette*, which definitely suggest the style level of their ancient forerunners. Nevertheless the intricacy of the Breton epic is different, more profound, its passion is more inward and fervent. In this connection we might recall certain of the *lais* of Marie de France and at a later date *La Châtelaine de Vergi*, a masterpiece of early storytelling. Here a serious and high-minded narrative art is in the making, and its central theme is love: the fires of passion, love unrequited, or the perils of lovers. And soon the sensual aspect of love will be transcended. The utterly unclassical notion of the beloved as sovereign commander over her lover's thoughts and destinies originated in Provençal love poetry; it makes its first ap-

28. Love as a major theme does not occur in the earlier tragic literature; it was introduced by Euripides. In the epic, to the best of our knowledge, it first appears in the third book of the *Argonautica* of the Alexandrian poet Apollonius Rhodius. It deals with the beginnings of Medea's passion for Jason, the enemy of her father. Through Virgil and Ovid this model was to exert an enormous influence. The style of this significant episode in Apollonius is strongly affected by the way in which it is introduced: by almost playful scenes among the gods, between Hera and Aphrodite and between Aphrodite and Eros; a capricious child, Eros is persuaded by his mother to wound Medea with his arrow. To our way of thinking, however, the style of Virgil's Dido episode is unquestionably lofty. But even this was not universally recognized by the critics of antiquity. Servius writes on *Aen.* 4.1 (ed. Thilo-Hagen, I, 459, 2–5): *est autem paene totus in affectione, licet in fine pathos habeat, ubi abscessus Aeneae gignit dolorem. Sane totus in consiliis et subtilitatibus est; nam paene comicus stilus est: nec mirum, ubi de amore tractatur* (It is written almost entirely in a studied manner, although it displays passionate feeling at the end, where the departure of Aeneas gives rise to sorrow. Indeed it is made up entirely of contrivances and subtleties; for it is almost in the style proper to comedy; nor is this to be wondered at in a passage that deals with love).

pearance in epic in Chrétien's Lancelot fragment; and through the
prose *Lancelot*, which made a deep impression on Dante,[29] this
lofty, humble, adulterous love became a European ideal. In the
Italian *stil nuovo* the beloved becomes an incarnation of the divine; love is represented as the appanage of the noble heart, a way
to virtue and knowledge; indeed, the terminology and even the
reality of its torments and transports came to be associated with
the ecstasy of *unio passionalis*.[30] Although Platonic motifs are
clearly at work in it, this spiritual-sensual form of love is entirely
modern and could have had no place in ancient literature.

Paradoxically enough, it was this chivalric love, this ideal-sen-
sual worship of the poet's lady, that gave rise to the first sublime
style since antiquity—the *stilus tragicus*, as Dante was to define
it in his *De vulgari eloquentia*:[31] *Stilo equidem tragico tunc uti
videmur, quando cum gravitate sententiae tam superbia carminum,
quam constructionis elatio et excellentia vocabulorum concordat*
(We are employing the tragic style when weight of subject-mat-
ter is matched by sublimity of verse form, sweep of sentence
structure, and excellence of vocabulary). This smacks of pedantry, but it covers the ground completely: the lofty subject; a
meter that has nothing trivial, hurried, or playful about it (in this
respect Dante's precursors had already discovered the dignity of
the hendecasyllabic line, which he praises in the ensuing fifth chapter); further, a sentence structure that is neither primitive and
paratactic nor, like nearly all the Latin rhetoric of his time (*ars
dictaminis, stilus altus*), purely pedantic and epideictic, but richly
diversified, grand, and passionate; and finally, a noble, strong, high-
sounding vocabulary, neither crude, nor childish, nor too glib.
The example that he cites for his third requirement, noble sentence structure (namely: *Eiecta maxima parte florum de sinu tuo,*

29. The Paolo and Francesca episode in *Inferno* 5, and *quella che tossio* (*Par.*
    16.13ff.).
30. Cf. the excursus on *Gloria passionis*, p. 79, above.
31. *De vulg. eloqu.* 2.4.7. By this he means the lofty style (*superiorem stilum*),
    ibid., 5. Like many other medieval authors, he was unaware that the words
    "tragedy" and "tragic" referred only to dramatic poetry.

Florentia, nequicquam Trinacriam Totila secundus adivit: After
the greater part of thy flowers, O Florence, had been cast out
of thy bosom, the second Totila assailed the land of Sicily in
vain. *De vulg. eloqu. 2.6.5*), strikes us, to be sure, as almost absurdly rhetorical; the metaphoric play on sound—*flores—Florentia*—is heavy; the farfetched circumlocution *Totila secundus* for
Charles of Valois distracts one from the subject and mars the intended effect of sublimity. To understand why this sentence appealed to Dante we must bear in mind, first that it does not mor-
alize or express ironical and epideictic praise like the two previously cited sentences, which he esteems less highly and which may
even have been parodies,[32] but communicates an event deeply felt,
namely, the desecration of Florence by Charles of Valois and his
ensuing defeat in Sicily (*Trinacria*); secondly, that the event is
temporally articulated into two antithetical parts containing an almost equal number of syllables, divided by the vocative *Florentia*; and thirdly, that the choice and order of the words give the
first part a tone of sorrow and lamentation, while the second, in
sharp contrast, is harshly triumphant.[33] It will be helpful, even for
an understanding of the *Divine Comedy*, if we try to feel how,
coming as it does after an almost elegiac beginning, the clause
nequicquam Trinacriam Totila secundus adivit charmed Dante's
ear. In general, this combined mastery of meaning and sound,
which is hard to explain systematically because of the great variety of factors and the wealth of shadings that enter into it, but

32. "*Piget me, cunctis pietate maiorem, quicunque in exilio tabescentes patriam
tantum sompniando revisunt*"—this is (*gradus*) *pure sapidus, qui est
rigidorum scolarium vel magistrorum;* and "*Laudabilis discretio marchionis
Estensis et sua magnificentia preparata cunctis, cunctis illum facit esse
dilectum*"—this is (*gradus*) *sapidus et venustus, qui est quorundam super-
ficietenus rethoricam (h)aurientium.* ("I, who surpass all in dutiful affection, sorrow for those who, languishing in exile, revisit their country
only in dreams"—this is the level of simple good taste, which is that of
the strict scholars or masters; "The praiseworthy discernment of the
Marquis of Este and his all-encompassing magnificence make him beloved
of all"—this is the level of taste and elegance characteristic of those who
have taken a shallow draught from the well of the rhetoricians.—*De vulg.
eloqu. 2.6.5.*)
33. Cf. the excellent analysis in A. Marigo's edition of Dante's *De vulg.
eloqu.* 211f.

which a sensitive ear has no difficulty in perceiving, is the decisive element in Dante's literary taste—I am convinced that his predilection for Arnaut Daniel can best be understood on this basis.[34] In any event, the authentic characteristics of the ancient lofty style, namely, loftiness of subject matter and elevation of form, are here for the first time discussed with understanding and true perceptiveness: a feeling had awakened for the levels of dignity implicit in the various meters; and above all the art of the articulated period is discussed in practical terms, entirely on the basis of examples, without recourse to the petrified rhetorical apparatus. The most important of these examples are the vernacular *canzoni* cited in the second book of the *De vulg. eloqu.* (chapters 2; 5; 6; and further on, passim). Most of these are Provençal and Italian; only one French poet, Thibaut de Navarre, is represented. Indeed, it was certain Provençal poets and the Italians of Guinizelli's school who first met with Dante's stylistic requirements.

These *canzoni* are all lyric poems in a lofty tone. Dante writes (*De vulg. eloqu.* 2.2.8) that there are three sublime themes which may be treated in such *canzoni*, namely *Salus*, *Venus*, and *Virtus*, that is to say, feats of arms, love, and virtue. He himself seems to have developed this grouping from scholastic psychology—it does not stem from antiquity.[35] In Dante's day such *canzoni* as those of Bertran de Born, celebrating feats of arms, were no longer being written; and since Guido Guinizelli (though this development had begun with the Provençal poets), virtue had become closely associated with love. Thus the love of the Provençal poets and of the *stil nuovo* became the central theme of the first lofty European poetry since antiquity. Its earliest embodiments were Guinizelli's *Al cor gentil ripara sempre amore* (Love always comes home to a gentle heart), the great *canzoni* of Guido Cavalcanti, Cino da

---

34. On Dante's predilection for Arnaut Daniel, see Sir Maurice Bowra, "Dante and Arnaut Daniel."
35. In the German translation of *De vulg. eloqu.* by Dornseiff and Balogh (p. 96) attention is called to the resemblance of the group *Salus Venus Virtus* to a line in the hymn *Pange lingua* by St. Thomas Aquinas: *Salus honor virtus quoque.*

Pistoia, and Dante. Not only was love admitted among the themes of the lofty style; it was the most important of the themes that made possible a revival of this style. But the new love is not purely a matter of sexuality. It awakens the powers of the "noble heart" and puts them to the test; through trials and suffering it leads to fulfillment. This fulfillment may be of very different kinds, for at first there were many variants of lofty love: one in which the sensual element is paramount, though sublimated by social forms and the participation of the spirit; a second in which sensuality is nothing, or at most a pretext for didacticism; and finally a third in which, barely intimated but never forgotten, it becomes a path leading through suffering and passion (*fervor passionis*) to *caritas* and the highest ecstasy and insight. This is the form for which the *stil nuovo* prepared the way; it produced the first *suprema constructio* in European literature since antiquity, and it is in this light that Dante wrote, in what is one of his last utterances on the subject (*Purg.* 24.52–54):

> *I' mi son un, che quando*
> *Amor mi spira, noto, e a quel modo*
> *ch' e' ditta dentro vo significando.*

I am one who, when Love inspires me, take note, and go setting it forth after the fashion which he dictates within me.

In this lyrical "love" poetry there is an element of feminine sweetness that cannot readily be reconciled with the pure ancient concept of the sublime. Dante himself was aware of this quality. In the *Divine Comedy* he calls the *stil nuovo* "sweet" (*Purg.* 24.57; cf. also 26.99 and 112), and in *De vulg. eloqu.* 1.10.4 he boasts that Cino da Pistoia and himself have written vernacular poetry sweeter and more refined (*dulcius . . . subtiliusque poetati vulgariter*) than that of any French or Provençal poet. But in ancient criticism both words, singly and even more so in combination, are customary terms for light or middle-level poetry. We have quoted Porphyrio's paraphrase of Horace, to the effect that Horace, in contrast to Pindar's sublimity, wrote *parva quidem et humilia, sed subtilia ac dulcia* (in a style simple and modest, but refined and sweet).[36] Gradually and imperceptibly the words had changed in rank and meaning: *subtilis*, which had formerly denoted the refinement and elegance of simple things, still meant refined, elegant, carefully conceived, but it had taken on an overtone of significant, difficult to understand, obscure; Dante wrote, for example, of *amore* (*Vita nuova* 42, sonnet 25): *Io no lo intendo, sì parla sottile* (I do not understand it, so subtly does it speak); or in the *canzone terza: Le dolci rime d'amor* (12–14), explained in the fourth treatise of the *Convivio:*

> *e dirò del valore,*
> *per lo qual veramente omo è gentile,*
> *con rima aspr' e sottile*

and, in verse harsh and subtle, I shall speak of the worth which makes a man truly noble.

Here the juxtaposition of terms is also significant, for *aspro*[37] is an antithesis to *dolce*. As for *dulcis*, the antonym of *amarus* and *asper*, it rose in rank in connection with mysticism and the dialectic of love (*dolci tormenti*); it became loftier and more ardent, though without entirely losing its old connotation of pleasing charm. The *stil nuovo* is a sublime style, as the tone and content unmistakably show; but its components are different from those of the ancient sublime style; it is "sweeter" and occasionally more didactic and more obscure than any ancient example could be. And it is also, up to Dante's *Divine Comedy*, far more limited in subject matter and form. Love and the noble heart are its only themes, and the *canzone* or sonnet its only forms. It seldom goes beyond the lyrical and didactic.

36. It is unlikely that Dante was acquainted with the *Odes* of Horace (although they were occasionally quoted in the Middle Ages, for example, by Meinhard of Bamberg). Cf. H. Hauvette, "L'Antiquité dans l'œuvre de Dante."

37. On *aspro* cf. G. Contini's preliminary remarks to *Rima* 103: *Così nel mio parlar voglio esser aspro* (And thus in my speech I wish to be harsh), in his 2nd edn. of the *Rime*, p. 162.

The *Divine Comedy* broke through this limitation, vastly extending the subject matter of the *stil nuovo;* the subject of the *Divine Comedy*, *status animarum post mortem* (the state of souls after death), embraces the whole of creation. The personal element, the individual human being, the poet himself who is saved by love, is still the occasion of the vast action; but this action is greater than any conceivable theme of antiquity, for it encompasses all happening in the universe. The *Divine Comedy* is the first and in certain respects the only European poem comparable in rank and quality to the sublime poetry of antiquity. Many passages in the work express Dante's awareness of this; but the word "comedy" and Dante's remarks in his letter to Can Grande show that he never freed himself from the purist views on rhetoric which he sets forth in *De vulgari eloquentia*. There is no point in inquiring here whether it was the vernacular language or the realism of his poem (or its happy ending) that prevented him from assigning it to the highest stylistic class. To me it seems unquestionable that by modern standards he equaled and even surpassed the sublimity of the ancients. In conclusion, let us compare a few of Dante's lines with an ancient model in order to gain a closer idea of the similarities and the differences.

As an example of sublimity in the treatment of the divine the author of *Peri hypsous* (9.8) cites a number of lines from the *Iliad*, obviously from memory, for they are put together from different passages. His text is as follows:

. . . τρέμε δ' οὔρεα μακρὰ καὶ ὕλη	13.18
καὶ κορυφαὶ Τρώων τε πόλις καὶ νῆες Ἀχαιῶν	20.60
ποσσὶν ὑπ' ἀθανάτοισι Ποσειδάωνος ἰόντος.	13.19
βῆ δ' ἐλάαν ἐπὶ κύματ', ἄταλλε δὲ κήτε' ὑπ' αὐτοῦ	13.27
πάντοθεν ἐκ κευθμῶν, οὐδ' ἠγνοίησεν ἄνακτα.	13.28
γνηθοσύνῃ δὲ θάλασσα διίστατο, τοὶ δὲ πέτοντο.	13.29

The first three lines read in translation: "The high mountains and the wood, the peaks and the city of the Trojans and the ships of the Achaeans shook beneath the immortal feet of striding Poseidon." In Homer they describe the scene in which the god, overcome with indignation at the defeat of the Greeks, descends to his palace from the peak of the mountain on Samos, whence he had watched the battle of the ships. Longinus [38] has omitted the scene in the palace and placed the god's second journey over the sea in his chariot immediately after his descent from the mountain on foot.[39] In Homer the succeeding lines (13.27–29) refer to the god's chariot ride over the sea. They may be translated roughly as follows: "He guided the chariot over the waves; below him the sea monsters sprang up from their clefts on all sides and recognized their lord; joyously the sea parted; but they [the steeds] surged onward. . . ." Longinus has made the scene even more grandiose and long-rolling than it is in Homer by skipping the relatively tranquil interruption in which the palace, the horses, Poseidon's garment and scourge, are described; probably not by design but unconsciously in his enthusiasm for the sublime, he has ignored the contradiction in the wording, which in the first lines refers plainly to a journey on foot and in the others to a chariot ride.

Let us take the text as Longinus gives it to us. It clearly corresponds to an ideal conception of the grandiose and sublime, of which Homer assuredly provides many examples, though they are rarely pure, for Homer tends to intersperse his sublime passages with lighter touches. The scene shows the power of the god through his swift-moving epiphany, through pure appearance in movement; he does not yet exert his power. Its sheer presence suffices to produce the effects due to it. Under the god's footfalls the countryside trembles far and wide; its trembling parts, high mountains, cities, etc., are enumerated; they roll along in the wake of the short verb; the description of the earthquake ends with its

38. For the sake of brevity we shall continue to designate the author of *Peri hypsous* as Longinus, although this attribution was long ago proved false.
39. This also enables him to insert *Iliad* 20.60. It could never have occurred to Homer to make anything more than the mountains and woods of Samos tremble under Poseidon's steps. The first journey on foot takes only three steps and does not affect Troy or the ships of the Achaeans.

cause in the powerful line about the god's immortal feet, marked by the spondee in the middle of the name and the assonance at the end (Ποσειδάωνος ἰόντος). Next come three lines describing Poseidon's journey over the sea as a triumphal procession; both the words and the rhythm represent the tumult, suddenly aroused and rapidly stilled, of the mythical spirits offering their services. The tumult is announced by the two short cola of 13.27, beginning with the verbs (βῆ δέ and ἄταλλε δέ); it takes on order in the middle line and dies down in the last, where the sea opens and the horses surge through.[40]

This passage, says Longinus, is one of those in which the greatness of the godhead is represented without blemish or mixture, that is, free from the all-too-human moods and passions which usually inhabit the gods in Homer. This assertion is acceptable only if, as Longinus does, we ignore the context of the passage. For what launches Poseidon on his journey is his passionate partisanship for the Achaeans and his rage against Zeus. And yet Longinus is not wrong, for Homer too seems to forget the context. He surrenders to the moment, and the reader is entitled to do the same. No one reading the passage relating how Poseidon descends from the mountain and rides over the sea, whether in Homer's original text or in Longinus' version, has any need to remember that Poseidon is full of rage and bitterness. One feels nothing of the sort. The power of the god is manifested in all its purity, first in the trembling of the earth, then in the colorful tumultuous procession. One tends to think of him as conscious of his power, serenely enjoying it in the knowledge of his eternal youth and intactness. In Homer the present moment is everything. And so Longinus is right in praising Poseidon's striding and riding as a pure representation of divine sublimity. In its pure *appearance* it is free from all passion or purpose. We know, to be sure,

40. In Homer (*Iliad* 13.29f.) the sentence does not end here. It reads:
τοὶ δὲ πέτοντο
ῥίμφα μάλ', οὐδ' ὑπένερθε διαίνετο χάλκεος ἄξων
(But they flew swiftly on, and the bronze axle beneath did not become wet.)

that the god is hurrying to the battlefield to help the Greeks. But for the moment this knowledge is set aside. What the reader or listener enjoys is a vision of the life of the blessed gods, joyfully obeyed by the elements who are their servants. And he is overwhelmed by the powerful sweep of the verse, the sharp changing images, and the magnificent brevity of the conclusion with its galloping horses.[41]

To these lines I should like to compare the epiphany of the *Messo del cielo* in the ninth canto of Dante's *Inferno*. The spirits of hell have barred the way of Dante and Virgil to the *Città di Dite*, and have even tried to turn Dante to stone by showing him Medusa's head, so that Virgil shields Dante's eyes with his hands. But now the expected help arrives (9.64ff.):

> *E già venia su per le torbid' onde*   64
> *un fracasso d'un suon, pien di spavento,*
> *per che tremavano amendue le sponde,*
> *non altrimente fatto che d'un vento*   67
> *impetuoso per li avversi ardori,*
> *che fier la selva e sanz' alcun rattento*
> *li rami schianta, abbatte e porta fori;*   70
> *dinanzi polveroso va superbo,*
> *e fa fuggir le fiere e li pastori.*
> *Gli occhi mi sciolse e disse: "Or drizza il nerbo*   73
> *del viso su per quella schiuma antica*
> *per indi ove quel fummo è più acerbo."*
> *Come le rane innanzi a la nemica*   76
> *biscia per l'acqua si dileguan tutte,*
> *fin ch' a la terra ciascuna s'abbica,*
> *vid' io più di mille anime distrutte*   79
> *fuggir così dinanzi ad un ch' al passo*
> *passava Stige con le piante asciutte.*

And now there came, upon the turbid waves, a crash of fearful sound at which the shores both trembled; a sound as of wind, impetuous for the adverse heats, which smites the forest without any stay; shatters off the boughs, beats down, and sweeps away; dusty in front, it goes superb, and makes the wild beasts and the

41. Though it is a conclusion only in Longinus. See preceding note.

shepherds flee. He loosed my eyes, and said: "Now turn thy nerve
of vision in that ancient foam, there where the smoke is harshest."
As frogs, before their enemy the serpent, run all asunder through
the water, till each squats at the bottom: I saw more than a
thousand ruined spirits flee before one, who passed the Stygian
ferry with soles unwet.   (Tr. Wicksteed)

Here, it seems to me, Dante equals or perhaps even surpasses
the sublimity of the ancients. In these lines appearance and movement carry the same power as in the passage from Homer; they
equal the Greek model in the articulation of expression, richness
of sentence structure, and above all in what for us is the essential, namely, unity of tone. The two passages are comparable
chiefly for their sustained rolling movement, which Longinus intensified by his intercalation of a line, and which in Dante first
runs through the three tercets ending in line 72 but is then (as
in Homer's original text) interrupted; further, in the construction
by which in both cases this thundering effect is obtained, that is,
the anticipation of a comparatively short and unaccentuated gov-
erning verb (τρέμε; *e già venia*), followed by long and weighty
subjects. In Homer there are several subjects, followed by a single but powerful adverbial phrase (ποσσὶν ὑπ᾽ ἀθανάτοισι), while in
Dante there is only one (*fracasso*), whose modifiers, articulated in
a relative clause, culminate in a simile that takes up two tercets
(*non altrimente fatto . . .*). There is no extended simile of this
sort in the Homer passage, but the form is classical,[42] and Dante
was probably the first writer to venture to employ it in a vernacular language. In this simile Dante uses a figure similar to a
polysyndeton (it is not a real polysyndeton, for it is twice interrupted, once rather drastically):

> *che fier la selva e sanz' alcun rattento*
> *li rami schianta, abbatte e porta fori;*   70
> *dinanzi polveroso va superbo,*
> *e fa fuggir le fiere e li pastori.*

42. The comparison with the storm, used here, is also frequent in the literature of antiquity, for instance, Virgil, *Aeneid* 2.416–419.

Longinus smuggled the polysyndeton into the subject of the first sentence: οὔρεα . . . καὶ ὕλη καὶ κορυφαί. . . . The effect is powerful in both cases; but Dante in addition, by means of pace, syntax, and distribution of sounds, obtains a driving movement which strikingly brings out the progress of the storm.

Unmistakable in both cases is the artistic intelligence with which the great effects are achieved. Both employ rhetorical figures. The linking of the words, the versification, and the structure of the periods reveal painstaking artistic practice based on tradition. It can be demonstrated that Dante—and he himself tells us so—studied the ancient poets and the rhetorical arts of his time with great care in order to develop his own style. But it is equally evident that in both passages rhetoric does not govern but serves. There is nothing petty, erudite, or bombastic in this rhetoric; there is no exaggeration of the rhetorical that would destroy the effect of the sublime; on the contrary, what Longinus demanded of the sublime style is achieved, namely, that any rhetorical devices employed be submerged by its overwhelming power.

The most striking difference between the two passages is that Homer introduces the striding and riding Poseidon at once, while in Dante's lines everything is mere preparation down to the last two lines where, finally, the long-awaited bearer of divine power appears—but how briefly and simply! At first Dante, whose eyes Virgil has covered, hears only a raging and crashing, which he compares skillfully and in detail to the sound of a storm before which beasts and shepherds take flight. Then comes an interruption, in which Virgil removes his hands from Dante's eyes (since evidently the Gorgon's head has disappeared) and enjoins him to look upon the dense fog over the Styx. After the interruption the new movement sets in. As in the image of the storm whose fury Dante had only heard, the animals and shepherds take flight, Dante *sees* thousands of fugitive souls. They too are not introduced directly, but through the comparison with the frogs which scatter through the water at the approach of the snake. Only then do the fleeing souls of the damned appear, and finally he from whom they are fleeing (80f.): *un ch' al passo / passava Stige con le piante asciutte.* After the richness of the preparatory images this is very simple, but no less powerful. Homer puts in the name of his striding god at the end of the first two lines, Ποσειδάωνος ἰόντος, with a great rhythmic movement, but there is no tension in this movement; everyone knows in advance who it is. But Dante does not know, even now he does not know, nor does the reader. He who appears at last is "one." [43] But both poets slacken the pace somewhat at this point; they compel the reader to scan the syllables, and they use similar figures—Homer the spondee and the assonance referred to above, Dante a genuine *figura etymologica* (*passo, passava*). And the dry-shod crossing of the water also occurs in Homer, though somewhat later.

Striking as the difference between the passages may be—namely, that Homer, as we have just pointed out, introduces his striding god at once, while Dante refers to his only briefly, after a long preparation—this in itself is not the decisive factor. Decisive is what underlies this difference. Homer narrates an event in which he himself does not participate. His human beings and his gods as well may rejoice or suffer, smile or grow angry, he himself is not involved; and although he may raise or lower the level of style a little according to the changes in subject matter (which takes in assemblies of the gods and battles as well as domestic life and the description of utensils), the underlying tone always remains the same: it is the tone of narrative neutrality, a kind of sublime serenity, equable, untroubled, almost playful, and by virtue of its evenness and unbiased serenity, almost divinely sublime; it has the sublime serenity that his gods are not always able to maintain. Dante, on the other hand, is not only the narrator; he is at the same time the suffering hero. As the protagonist of his

43. The various conjectures concerning the identity of the *messo del cielo* will not be discussed here; in any case he represents the figure of Christ and symbolizes Christ's descent into hell. Cf. the Church office for the *dedicatio ecclesiae*, with Psalm 23[24]:7, *Tollite portas,* and Aaron's rod, which is at the same time the cross (see Karl Young, *The Drama of the Medieval Church,* I, and Bowen in *Speculum,* XVI [1941], 469–479). But *Aeneid* 6.136ff. also plays a part.

poem which, far greater in scope than the Homeric epics, encompasses all the sufferings and passions, all the joys and blessings of human existence, he himself is involved in all the movements of his immense action. In our passage, it is he himself who, held fast in the depths of hell, awaits the savior in a moment of extreme peril. What he relates, accordingly, is not a mere happening, but something that happens to him. He is not outside, contemplating, admiring, and describing the sublime. He is in it, at a definite point in the scene of action, threatened and hard pressed; he can only feel and describe what is present to him at this particular place, and what presents itself is the divine aid he has been awaiting, preceded by the signs of its coming. The interruption while Virgil calls Dante's attention to the blanket of mist over the Styx, out of which the divine messenger steps, intensifies the element of expectation and Dante's involvement in the action. For here the figure of the sublime is not universal and unrelated to the narrator as in Homer; it concerns Dante; the *messo del cielo* has been sent in his behalf and acts to insure his success on the way to salvation.

It is easy to see that the implications of our comparison between these two passages are not limited to the passages themselves; they are more general. Dante revived the ancient conception of the sublime in a European vernacular language; he created a sublime poetry on a level with the great models of antiquity. This could scarcely have been done by any earlier writer. It could not be done in Latin, which had no great and timely theme or genuine public, for schools in themselves can never constitute a public, and moreover, rhetorical excesses had extirpated the concept of the sublime from the school tradition. And it could not be done in the vernacular languages, which before Dante lacked sufficient freedom and richness of expression, not to mention a public capable of understanding such poetry. Quite apart from Dante's genius, the turn of the thirteenth century in Italy was marked by a concurrence of factors favorable to the revival of ancient sublimity in a new creation.

For it is a new creation, not an exact imitation like the epics of Walter of Châtillon or Joseph of Exeter. Dante's poem is not an epic, it does not relate the past deeds of men, like the *Iliad* or the *Aeneid*, the *Chanson de Roland*, the *Nibelungenlied*, or the *Cantar de mio Cid*. His theme is something new and incomparable. The framework, to be sure, the journey to the other world, is far from new, and we know how much material Dante adapted from pagan, Christian, and even Mohammedan predecessors; the whole Mediterranean world of myth and legend is contained in his poem. But the journey to the other world is not a poetic genre; and if it were, we would have to say that it came into existence with Dante. For only Dante treated it in such a way as to make everything previously written on the subject seem fragmentary and episodic. The *Divine Comedy* teaches the physical, ethical, and historical unity of the world, grounded in the spirit of divine love; but this doctrine is not expounded with objective universality as in a didactic poem. It is represented as the experience or vision of a particular man, Dante, in a particular historical moment; its universality is the Christian embodiment of all time in the here and now; and the here and now, the most actual inner history, is also contained in the other world, as I have attempted to show in my earlier Dante studies.[44] Dante's poem is a work of art, but it is at the same time a revelation; to the poet, who at the same time is the traveler through the three realms, divine love, which grew out of his earthly love, has sent in his extreme need the vision that has saved him. This most personal element, supremely universal precisely because it is so personal, is what distinguishes the *Divine Comedy* from all previous epic poetry, and it creates a new relationship between the poet and his subject matter as well as his reader.

Thus the sublime style of antiquity was not revived by pure imitation, but sprang anew from a new world of which the ancient masters knew nothing. In this new world it was able, transformed and yet the same, to play a living and indeed decisive role.

44. More particularly *Dante: Poet of the Secular World* and the chapter on Dante in *Mimesis*.

4

The Western Public
and Its Language

*Lector, opes nostrae; quem cum mihi Roma
dedisset,*
"Nil tibi quod demus maius habemus," ait.

(Reader, you are my riches; when Rome
had given you to me, she said: "We have
nothing of greater worth that we could
give you.")

Martial, *Epigr.* 10.2.5f.

ONE DAY at the games—so we are told by Pliny the Younger —Tacitus struck up a conversation on literature with a member of the equestrian order who was sitting next to him. After a time the knight asked: "Are you from Italy or one of the provinces?" Tacitus answered: "You know me by my writings." Whereupon the knight: "Are you Tacitus or Pliny?" [1]

In relating this anecdote, with which he was understandably delighted, Pliny quite unintentionally gives us certain information about the literary public at the height of the empire. The two gentlemen did not know each other. Even before the first words were spoken, each must have gathered from the other's dress and bearing and from the situation of their seats in the circus that he was addressing a member of the highest social class. From the first words Tacitus must have gained the impression that his neighbor was worth talking to; otherwise he would hardly have gone on with the conversation. The knight on the other hand was presumably not a resident of Rome; if he had been, he would surely —especially in view of his interest in literature—have known the famous Tacitus at least by sight. But he was familiar with the writings of Tacitus and Pliny. Quite certainly he was aware that this was no ordinary man. He gave vent to his curiosity by asking whether the other was from Italy or from one of the prov-

1. *Epist.* 9.23.2: [Tacitus] narrabat sedisse secum circensibus proximis equitem Romanum. hunc post varios eruditosque sermones requisisse: "Italicus es an provincialis?" se respondisse: "Nosti me, et quidem ex studiis." ad hoc illum: "Tacitus es an Plinius?"

inces. Of course the question was a feeler, couched in such general terms only for reasons of discretion. Even so, it cannot have been utterly meaningless. There must have been enough highly cultivated provincials to make it seem plausible that quite by chance one might be sitting next to one of them at the circus. And moreover, the speech of these cultivated provincials must have been such that it would be difficult or impossible to determine their origin from their accent.

We have ample other evidence to the wide range of the literary public after the republic. Horace, Propertius, and Ovid [2] already boasted that their poems were known in the remotest parts of the earth. Horace also says, in a very down-to-earth passage,[3] that successful books crossed the seas. Martial's books were to be had in Vienne,[4] and Pliny's could be purchased from a bookseller in Lyons.[5] Juvenal, in his typical manner, compared the current ubiquity of culture with the simplicity of the old days:

> . . . sed Cantaber unde
> stoicus antiqui praesertim aetate Metelli?
> Nunc totus Graias nostrasque habet orbis Athenas,
> Gallia causidicos docuit facunda Britannos,
> de conducendo loquitur iam rhetore Thule.[6]

But where, in the days of old Metellus, could you find a Cantabrian Stoic? Now the whole globe possesses Greek and Roman culture; eloquent Gaul has trained Britons as lawyers, and in Thule they already talk of engaging a professor of rhetoric.

The conversation at the circus outranks all the other evidence at our disposal, because the truth it contains for us is purely implicit. We see the two gentlemen, who had never met, brought together by common social and literary interests; and behind them we see many others, who might have taken part in the same scene

2. Horace, *Carm.* 2.20; Propertius 2.7; Ovid, *Tristia* 4.9.21 and 10.128.
3. *Ars poetica* 345.
4. Martial 7.88.
5. Pliny, *Epist.* 9.11. Nevertheless he is surprised that there are booksellers in Lyons.
6. Juvenal 15.108–112.

or one like it: not millions, not even hundreds of thousands, perhaps at the height of Roman civilization no more than a few tens
of thousands. Still, this literary public—hearers and readers, admirers and critics of the various authors, purchasers of books—
was a large enough minority to sustain a literature. This large
anonymous minority—we call it anonymous because the overwhelming majority of its members remained unknown to the authors—had probably come into existence in the fifth century in
Athens and in the third century in the Hellenistic world, above
all in Alexandria. In Rome it took form only late and slowly; we
perceive it clearly only toward the end of the republic, in the
generation to which Cicero and Atticus belonged.[7] It was a social
group corresponding to what in modern times is termed the literary public in contrast on the one hand to the great mass of the
uneducated and on the other hand to those who made literature
and learning their profession.[8]

The core of the ancient public was supplied by the well-to-do
classes, who held a relative monopoly on higher education; that
is, in Rome, by those who after their elementary schooling had
at least gone on to study grammar and rhetoric. In the first centuries of the empire this was a large and quickly changing group,
since childlessness was frequent in the leading families and new
members were continuously pouring in from the provinces and
from the Italian business world. The public also included other
groups which may be regarded as appendages to the upper classes.
There were first of all the educated slaves, who served their literary masters as secretaries, correctors, and librarians. They were

7. A passage from Lucilius (592, ed. Marx, p. 41), cited by Cicero, De orat.
2.6.25, may be interpreted in this sense.
8. Tacitus is no more a professional than Churchill. During the first century
of the Empire, almost the only intellectuals whose activities provided them
with a livelihood were the teachers, especially the professors of rhetoric.
They had no social standing; cf. Juvenal 7.150ff.; Juvenal also refers
(7.188–202) to the one celebrated exception, Quintilian, on whom Vespasian
had conferred the public professorship of rhetoric in Rome which he had
founded. Cf. also the account of the former senator Licinianus, who had
fallen to the rank of a professor of rhetoric, in Pliny, Epist. 4.11; cf. ibid.,
2.3, 3.3, and 4.13. The social position of the professors, at least of the more
prominent among them, improved in the later period of the Empire.

often of Greek origin; many were set free but kept on doing the same work for their masters. The most celebrated example of this is Cicero's chief secretary and friend Tiro, but similar cases of slaves belonging either to him or to others are frequently mentioned in Cicero's correspondence.[9] Pliny had several secretaries and readers,[10] and even Martial laments the death of a nineteen-year-old assistant whom he had freed during his last illness.[11] At this time, of course, the educated public included women, and these were not all members of high society; there were also the *puellae* of the elegies. It would no doubt be pedantic to make precise sociological inferences from passages in elegiac poetry; and yet such lines as Propertius 3.3.19f. or Ovid's *Amores* 2.4 could hardly have been written if the situation they refer to had not been a reality.[12]

In general it would be unwise to draw too sharp a dividing line between the educated public and the "people." The transitions were fluid, and without constant contact with the lower levels no literary public can maintain its function and character. Under the empire, everyone took an interest in the rhetorical prowess of the lawyers in the great trials (the entire public life and rhetorical training of the ruling classes centered round the legal profession). Pliny speaks of the ragged, filthy crowd, *sordidi pullatique*,[13] who gave him stage fright on such occasions, although he does not give them credit for much judgment. To what degree the entire population was accustomed to rhetoric can be gathered from the Christian sermons of the first centuries—though the diatribes of the street orators may have contributed more directly to this development than the orations of lawyers before the *centumviri*.

9. Cf. the interesting chapter "Atticus libraire-éditeur" in J. Carcopino, *Les Secrets de la correspondance de Cicéron*, II, 305–329 (Amer. edn., II, 467–481).
10. *Epist.* 8.1; 9.34 and 36.
11. Martial 1.101.
12. Propertius: . . . *libellus, / quem legat exspectans sola puella virum* (a little book which a lonely girl may read while she is waiting for her man). Ovid: *Est quae Callimachi prae nostris rustica dicat / carmina* (There is a girl who tells me that the songs of Callimachus are crude alongside mine).
13. *Epist.* 7.17.

Still more popular than legal proceedings was the theater, which the masses attended and loved. It had ceased to be exactly literary; early in the empire a decline had set in. Tragedy became a lyrico-choreographic pantomime, and comedy a farcical, realistic mime. But in both the tradition lived on. In these productions histrionic genius, musical inventiveness, and choreographic elegance survived, still inspired by themes and forms that had been created by great literature and appealing no less strongly to the masses than to the educated public.[14]

Though on the whole it is correct to say that literature proper was written for the educated public, this should not be interpreted in too narrow a sense. Even then, thanks to their popular appeal, arresting lines of poetry spread far beyond the educated classes.[15] But in the main it was the educated elite which by its interest, its understanding, and its wealth made possible the continued existence of literature.

Yet authors were not, as in modern times, supported by the

---

14. For an over-all view of the development of the theater during the Empire, see the work (with many source references) by J. Carcopino, *La Vie quotidienne à Rome à l'apogée de l'Empire*, pp. 255–267 (Amer. edn., pp. 221–231). Pliny's letter 7.24 on the testament of Ummidia Quadratilla tells us a good deal about the relationship of educated people to the theater.

15. Martial 11.3.1–6:

> *Non urbana mea tantum Pimpleide gaudent*
> *otia, nec vacuis auribus ista damus;*
> *sed meus in Geticis ad Martia signa pruinis*
> *a rigido teritur centurione liber.*
> *Dicitur et nostros cantare Britannia versus.*
> *Quid prodest? Nescit sacculus ista meus.*

(Not city ease alone delights in my poems, nor do we give them to idle ears. But my book is worn away by the stern centurion alongside the standards of Mars amid the Thracian frosts. Britain, too, is said to sing our verses. What good is it? My purse knows nothing of these things.) There is no doubt that at this time the centurions were already persons of importance, but they can scarcely have belonged to the cultivated elite.— Cf. also 7.97.11–13:

> *Te convivia, te forum sonabit,*
> *—aedes, compita, porticus, tabernae.*
> *Uni mitteris, omnibus legeris.*

(You will be recited at banquets, in the marketplace, in temples, at crossroads, covered walks, shops: sent to one, you will be read by all.)

anonymous public as such. No ancient author made a living from the public sales of his literary work. If he was not a prominent noble like Lucan, Persius, Tacitus, or Pliny, he was obliged, in order to live or at least in order to live well, to find himself a patron. The concern of the ancients for the welfare of poets and writers never went beyond the institution of patronage. The *bibliopola*, to whom the writer turned over his manuscript for reproduction and "publication," [16] seems to have paid him nothing for it.[17] And I know of no instance of a writer complaining about this state of affairs. Juvenal and Martial complain about the dearth of patrons or about their stinginess; [18] Martial had an elegant, indirect way of advertising or begging; [19] sometimes he even poked fun at friends who wished to borrow his manuscript in order to save the price of a copy; he finds the price asked by Tryphon the bookseller for his book too high.[20] But though he deplored with a shrug that he derived no material profit from the celebrity and popularity of his books,[21] neither he nor any other writer, as far as we know, ever criticized the system or suggested a remedy. All this seemed perfectly natural to authors and public alike, because the notion of literary property was unheard of and there was consequently no copyright law. The right to an author's work resided solely in possession of the manuscript (*solo cedit superficies:* the building goes with the ground). And as soon as the first copies produced by the *bibliopola* were in the hands of the public, his competitors or indeed anyone with competent scribes at his disposal could turn out as many additional copies as

16. Pliny uses the terms *edere, emittere, publicare, in manus hominum dare.*
17. The only passage mentioning the sale of a manuscript is Juvenal 7.82–90, in which it is related that Statius, in spite of the success of his *Thebaid,* would have gone hungry if the famous actor Paris had not bought, obviously in order to stage it, the manuscript of his tragic pantomime *Agave.*
18. Juvenal, particularly in the seventh satire; Martial 11.3 and 11.108.
19. E.g., 6.82, where he narrates how a stranger looked at him for a long time and then said: "What! You are the famous Martial? Then why do you have such an ugly cloak?"
20. By present standards, books were very expensive. Cf. H. L. Pinner, *The World of Books in Classical Antiquity,* pp. 37f.
21. Cf. the first quotation in n. 15 above.

he pleased. Under these circumstances the publishing business was far too unpredictable to permit of author participation in the receipts. Still, one wonders whether a well-known author may not have been able to sell his unpublished manuscript to the bookseller offering the highest price.[22] We cannot be sure; all we know is that there is no mention of any such thing.[23] In any case no large sums of money can have been involved. If an author wished to be published by one *bibliopola* rather than another, it was largely no doubt because the publisher of his choice was known for his faithful copies and attractive presentation, requirements which in Rome seem first to have been fully met by Atticus. In general the situation is explained by the ancient conception of the dignity of intellectual labor and the prevailing acceptance of patronage. It seems to have been perfectly respectable for a poor author to live at the expense of his rich friends, but not from the sale of his works.

The production of copies came to be very important as a means of disseminating literary works and of establishing texts. Nevertheless, this mode of publication was not really in keeping with the character of ancient and in particular Roman society, which looked upon literary life as a way in which cultivated men of the upper classes, whose serious occupation was politics, might spend their hours of leisure together, and upon literature as something not to be read in silence but to be listened to. Thus by far the greatest number of literary works were first launched not through manuscript copies but through readings. In principle, at least, these were held in private informal gatherings of the author's friends. Authors who could afford it, such as Horace or Pliny the Younger, were able to maintain this custom; they read their works only to their friends, that is, a group of the social and intellectual elite. Here and there in his poems we gain an intimation of the envy this brought upon the lowborn Horace and of his

22. Martial 1.2 and 1.117 makes it clear that the same book, in different presentation, could be bought from two different *bibliopolae*.
23. For these questions, cf. Milkau-Leyh, *Handbuch der Bibliothekswissenschaft* (2nd edn.), I, 863, with further bibliographical references.

appealing though mildly snobbish reluctance to be "published."[24] But with increasing literary production the readings soon took on enormous proportions. They were held in the *triclinia* and *auditoria* of the great houses and in all manner of public places, where they were often improvised. From the reign of Hadrian on, there were public buildings devoted exclusively to this purpose.[25] The satirists poked fun at this frenzy for public readings;[26] from Pliny, who was a devoted listener (he himself made extreme demands on his friends' patience), we learn that even in the circles he frequented, the reader did not always receive the undivided attention of his audience.[27]

It was only natural that these readings should assume such proportions. In a society where literary activity was regarded as the only suitable recreation of the elite, almost everyone wrote, either because he belonged or because he wished to belong to that elite; and reading aloud was the simplest and most effective way of making one's works known. In such readings the author directly addressed those whom he wished to please; and moreover, a "publisher"[28] was not likely to invest money in a manuscript that had not yet gained a reputation by being read in the circles that counted. Thus it was public readings that decided the fate of a work. An unknown work was usually read aloud by the author himself; if he thought himself unfit for the task, a reader took his place.[29] If he enjoyed a social position, he invited only a

---

24. Horace, *Sat.* 1.4.71–78; *Epist.* 1.19.32ff., and 1.20. For Pliny, see 7.17 and 2.19. Concerning his friend Octavius' dislike of the public reading, 2.10.
25. Carcopino, *Vie quotidienne*, pp. 226–234 (Amer. edn., pp. 193–201).
26. Horace (in the passage cited above, *Sat.* 1.4.74–76) refers to the reading in the baths where the resonance is so splendid. The beginning of Juvenal's first satire and 7.39–52 is significant. Most entertaining is Martial's description of the frantic poet, eager to recite his poems on every possible occasion, 3.44f.: *currenti legis et legis cacanti* (you read to me when I am running and you read to me when I am defecating).
27. *Epist.* 1.13; 6.15 and 17; 8.12.
28. The *bibliopola* was at once publisher and bookseller.
29. Suetonius, *Claudius* 41; Pliny, *Epist.* 9.34.—When a work seemed likely to be successful, a bookseller might have been expected to publish an edition on the basis of copies made in secret; a good system of stenography was available. But nothing of the sort is reported. The case of Quintilian (cf. his *Prooemium ad Marcellum*) is different, for here a professor's lecture and students are involved. Cf. Pinner, *World of Books*, pp. 39ff.

few highly cultivated friends to his first reading. From them he expected not only an opinion about the work as a whole but detailed suggestions for improvement. Pliny worked out a whole system of successive readings as a means of polishing his works.[30] Apart from the novel, the only literary genre not read aloud or at least intended to be was the prose letter, as initiated by Cicero's correspondence. And even this genre fell in with what, despite the large number of persons involved, remained the ideal of literary life under the empire, namely, a mode of personal association among highly educated individuals belonging to the same social class. With the novel, particularly in its later development, the case may have been different; but this was more important for the eastern than for the western part of the empire.

Despite the absence of political freedom Roman society during the first two centuries of the empire was rich and colorful, diversified in its currents, and uncommonly liberal in its forms. It was not until the third century that the sclerosis set in which gradually led to its death. Soon this society spread from Rome to other cities of Italy and the provinces, especially Gaul, but as long as it really flourished, Rome remained its center.[31] For writers without large fortunes life in Rome was far from simple or comfortable, and in Rome, moreover, everyone suffered from the chicanery and humiliations resulting from the patronage system. Only the emperor was entirely immune to them. But all these difficulties were outweighed by the social warmth, the stimulating atmosphere, the rich intellectual life of the capital. Rome fostered a sense of well-being which

---

30. *Epist.* 7.17; 8.21, and passim.
31. Even in later times Rome continued to be praised as the hub of the world. Sidonius Apollinaris 1.6 calls it *domicilium legum, gymnasium litterarum, curiam dignitatum, verticem mundi, patriam libertatis, in qua unica totius orbis civitate soli barbari et servi peregrinantur* (the home of laws, the school of letters, the meeting place of dignitaries, the head of the world, the fatherland of liberty, the only city in the whole world where only slaves and barbarians are not citizens). And in Cassiodorus, *Variae* 4.6.3, we may read: *Nulli sit ingrata Roma, quae dici non potest aliena, illa eloquentiae fecunda mater, illa virtutum omnium latissimum templum* (Rome, of which no one can say that she is foreign, should not be unpleasant to anyone. She is the fruitful mother of eloquence, the richest shrine of all the virtues).

encouraged intellectual activity, so that it was not felt to be work. In the melancholy preface to the twelfth book of his epigrams, written on his return to his Spanish Bilbilis, Martial tells how he missed what his Roman public (*auditor*) had given him: [32] *illam iudiciorum subtilitatem, illud materiarum ingenium, bibliothecas, theatra, convictus, in quibus studere se voluptates non sentiunt* . . . (elegance of critical judgment and spontaneity of talent, libraries, theaters, banquets, where pleasures come without being sought after).[33]

The predominance of oral reading suggests certain reflections about the structure of the public and about Roman literary life in general. Of course ancient literature had always been largely intended to be spoken or sung. But now the literary theater and political oratory underwent an almost simultaneous decline, while the predominantly rhetorical education, which inspired literary interests and activity in the educated classes, remained unchanged —or rather, its rhetorical character grew more pronounced than ever. Thus all types of literature became material to be read aloud, and the setting for these readings was provided by more or less intimate, more or less fashionable social gatherings. Tragedies and comedies were written that were intended solely to be read aloud; Seneca's tragedies are of this kind, and Pliny also speaks of such plays in his correspondence (e.g., 6.21). From Pliny we also learn that forensic and ceremonial addresses which had first been delivered publicly, in the Senate for example, were read again in circles of friends, where they were discussed, improved upon, and put into their final literary form. Literary pieces of every genre were composed as a kind of exercise, and again the group of friends to whom they were read served as a forum. A group of friends: when we think of other epochs in the history of literature, this sounds like youth, struggle, and passion. But these friends were not young, not at least in mind and spirit; they were cultivated men of the world. Under the circumstances, literature as a whole

32. This is reminiscent of Jean de La Bruyère: *Je rends au public ce qu'il m'a prêté.*
33. Martial, *Epigr.* 12 praef.

took on a social character; the accent shifted from grand impassioned movement to elegance and novelty of expression, to ornament and impressive sound effects; more and more, rhetorical declamation was taken as a substitute for passion. Gradually literature lost its function. Ultimately social satire, with its direct grip on life, was abandoned, and the other forms of literature became pompously rhetorical. The literary public lost its contact with the lower classes, ceased to be embedded in the greater community of the people, from which it is always distinct, but with which it must maintain constant communication if it is to survive. At the end of the first and the beginning of the second century, only the first intimations of this development are discernible. Tacitus was still alive, and men like Juvenal and Martial were still writing. But the political and social conditions foreshadowing the future isolation and sclerosis of literary life were already present. It is curious to come across a premonition of this in Pliny the Younger, who all in all was not exactly fitted, either by inclination or talent, to understand himself or the problems of his time. To a friend who had begged him for longer and more frequent letters, he wrote:

> . . . neque enim eadem nostra condicio quae M. Tulli, ad cuius exemplum nos vocas. Illi enim et copiosissimum ingenium et par ingenio qua varietas rerum qua magnitudo largissime suppetebat; nos quam angustis terminis claudamur, etiam tacente me perspicis, nisi forte volumus scholasticas tibi atque, ut ita dicam, umbraticas litteras mittere.[34]

> . . . but my situation is quite different from that of Cicero, to whose example you refer me. He had a very fertile mind, and the variety and grandeur of his themes were in accord with it. I have no need to tell you what narrow limits are imposed on me; and I will not write you any letters that are mere exercises in declamation.

What Pliny is alluding to is the concentration of power in the hands of the *princeps* and the resultant political paralysis of the

34. *Epist.* 9.2.2f.

ruling classes. He and his kind were virtually obliged to live in comfortable retirement. They still held high positions and performed prescribed administrative duties. But the great game of public life, the struggle for power, in which the personality unfolds before the eyes of all and men stake their lives—this game was no longer played.

In the period of decline, on the other hand, the practice of reading aloud in gatherings and the concomitant isolation of the educated classes helped to preserve culture. Literary life was split up into many little groups. Rome was still its center, and some of the larger provincial cities played a similar role. But the groups were not wholly dependent on the cities or, in general, on the functioning of any political organization. The spirit of ancient culture remained alive for a long time despite the decline of the empire and the cities. It survived the anarchy of the third century; it even survived for a time, in a few islands, the terrible shocks of the fifth. The insularity of intellectual life in the early Middle Ages is prefigured in the last years of the Western empire.

The "spirit" or "culture" of the Roman public under the empire is something elusive and difficult to describe; at best we may speak of a continually changing yet fundamentally stable body of traditions, knowledge, tastes, and inclinations. But it was based on a perfectly concrete common factor which *can* be described, namely, a common language, the language of the educated classes, the literary language, or *Hochsprache*. The existence of such a language, which can take form only gradually, is the constituent prerequisite for the formation of the social class that we have called the public and, it goes without saying, for the creation of a literature that requires such a public. Now, from its very beginnings the educated Roman public possessed not one but two literary languages—Greek and Latin. Until late in the empire educated Romans were bilingual; they knew Greek literature, interspersed their conversation and letters with Greek quotations and phrases, and in many cases wrote Greek poems.[35] When Vespa-

35. Cf. Pliny, *Epist.* 3.1; 4.3; 7.25; 8.4.

sian established the first state professorships in Rome, he set up
one for Latin and another for Greek rhetoric.[36] This was no
unique or fortuitous phenomenon; an educated public almost always possesses more than one language and often takes a particular foreign literary language as a model for the development of
its own. But here we are dealing with the later destinies of the
Latin literary language, to which Greek had ceased to make a
creative contribution.

A literary language is distinguished from the general language
of daily life by its selectivity, homogeneity, and conservatism. I
should state at this point that by literary language I understand
not only the written language but also the spoken, everyday language of the educated classes; that is why I have employed the
term *Hochsprache*, coined by German philologists. As for the
word "selectivity," it should be taken not only in a negative sense
but also in the positive sense of gathering and assimilating: a literary language becomes an artificial or technical language as soon
as it ceases to take in material from the spoken tongue. Nor is it
necessarily true, even of the ancient civilizations, that the literary
language is exclusively an ennobled or fashionable form of the
general spoken tongue. Even in antiquity uneducated speech was
used in literature, though of course in a calculated and stylized
form: the best-known examples are Plautus and Petronius. In antiquity as in modern times the everyday language of the educated
classes was light, idiomatic, and elegantly informal, and certain
types of literature were written in this light style—Cicero's letters,
for example. A literary language can be lofty but need not be.
In other words, there is room for various gradations or levels of
style. Such distinctions were far more strictly and consciously observed in antiquity than in modern times. There was a lofty and
sublime, a middle and pleasing, and a practical or comic "low"
style; in principle each of the many literary genres had its own
traditional style level. Toward the end of the empire this wealth
of distinctions began to be lost, not by any means in theory but

36. Suetonius, *Vespasianus* 18.

in practice, for all the literary genres then in use came to be per-
meated with rhetorical mannerism. But this was a symptom of decay, and it should be clearly borne in mind that the homogeneity
of literary languages, which we shall discuss in the following,
takes in a wide variety of style levels.

The homogeneity of the literary language, or one might say
the language of the literary public, resides in the fact that it is the
same throughout the given language zone. In this sense it contrasts
with the various dialects and with the specialized languages of the
various occupations; these are sometimes used deliberately in imi-
tative literature but otherwise are excluded both from literature
and from educated conversation. In modern times this is strictly
true only of the written and printed language and not of conversation, since most educated people show a slight local coloration
in their spoken German, English, French, etc., and often go so
far as to cultivate it. Whether in late Roman antiquity the language of the educated classes was colored by local dialect, I do
not know. The Roman knight in the anecdote related at the beginning of this chapter could not tell whether his neighbor at the
games was an Italian or a provincial. This of course is insufficient
evidence. But the existence of marked local variations in the language of the educated people does not seem likely because there
were not many cultural centers, as in a modern nation, but only
one, namely, Rome. Moreover, in the late period of the empire
a deliberate effort was needed to maintain the literary language.
Spelling and grammar had been standardized only relatively late,
toward the end of the republic. For a long time there was no central authority to regulate linguistic usage. In modern times the
automatic centralization of languages has made such enormous
strides, thanks to printing, unified administration, compulsory education, the daily press, and more recently the cinema, the radio,
mass shifts of population, and wholesale travel, that in spite of na-
tionalist propaganda not only the dialects but also the weaker languages (including that of the cultivated classes) are in danger of

disappearing. In antiquity virtually none of these forces were at work. In all the western regions Latin was a superimposition, introduced in its most popular form, in permanent conflict with the native languages and under the influence of their vocabulary and habits of pronunciation. Inevitably very divergent dialects arose. The impulses toward a common popular language, encouraged by commercial relations and the religious movements pouring in from the East, were for the most part Greek and for a long time, in any case, seem to have had no connection with culture or literature. In the third century, when the central administration was compelled to take more energetic measures against political and economic disintegration and the bureaucracy became larger and more effective, we hear of an extension of elementary education. A passage in a *Digest* (Ulpian) mentions village schoolteachers.[37] But this did not impede the development of the Vulgar Latin dialects in the last centuries of the empire.

This brings us to the third characteristic of the literary language, its conservatism. The everyday language changes constantly; in a few centuries it is radically transformed. In late antiquity Vulgar Latin became Romance. By comparison the literary language remained relatively stable; once established, it changed only very slowly. The works regarded as models of style were handed down in their original form and imitated; throughout the empire Ennius and Plautus were regarded as archaic, while the masters of the Ciceronian and Augustan periods were looked upon as classical models. Even under the empire there were frequent fashions in style, but for the most part they were historical if not archaistic. In any event they were limited to style; they did not affect the fundamental character of the traditional Latin language; there was little change in vocabulary and none at all in phonetics and morphology. Conservatism is a universal trait of literary languages, but it was particularly marked in the later days of the empire, because few new models were created and productive

---

37. *Dig.* 50.5.2.8, cited by M. Rostovtzeff, *Gesellschaft und Wirtschaft im röm. Kaiserreich*, II, 136 and 346, n. 46 [Engl. edn., p. 707, n. 48].

contact with the masses was gradually lost. Of course we can say this with certainty only of the written language; we do not know to what extent the pronunciation of the educated classes was affected by the popular development. Our only evidence is the spelling of the time, which may be misleading and is in any case subject to different interpretations. We know from modern languages, French and English for example, how much more conservative spelling is than the pronunciation even of the highly educated classes. But from the pedantry, cultural arrogance, and mannerism of the last cultivated classes of the empire, and from the purism revealed by certain statements of the grammarians, we may gather that even in their pronunciation the educated public did not make many concessions to the historical development of the language. We have the impression (it is no more than an impression) that in the fifth century the senatorial aristocracy and related circles spoke a homogeneous "High Latin" and that the common man had difficulty in understanding it—especially in view of the fact that the vulgar dialects, already highly differentiated in the various provinces, were now in many places exposed to Germanic influence. Toward the end of the fifth and the beginning of the sixth century the last remnants of the well-to-do groups with a Roman education died out or were swallowed up by other groups. This was the end of the ancient literary public.

But the Latin which had been the organ of these educated classes lived on in the form of a purely written language. It was bound to survive because there was no other written language and because it had long served, with the same homogeneity and the same conservatism but with a somewhat different principle of selection, as the specialized language of the various branches of public life. Written Latin lived on as the language of jurisprudence, of government chancelleries, and above all of the Church. It was taught in the schools and so transmitted. We have already said that in the last centuries of the Western Roman Empire the imperial administration took a more systematic interest than before in the school system.[38] The number of schools maintained by the municipalities, often under supervision of the imperial government, seems to have grown considerably; evidently far more officials were needed for the increasingly centralized administration, and the rhetorical curriculum still seemed suitable and adequate as a preparation for the administrative career. Thus numerous young educated men of middle-class origin (including Christians, such as the young Augustine) were educated with a view to a career in the civil service.

But the Roman school system in the Western provinces was gradually disrupted by the barbarian invasions. For a while private teachers were maintained in the houses of certain great lords and for a longer time probably in some of the cities. A few barbarian princes also made an effort to maintain schools for their chancelleries. In Italy Theodoric tried to preserve Roman civilization and the rhetoric that went with it; his efforts were abandoned only after his death. But most important, the Church, which for a surprisingly long time had contented itself with the Roman school system and its pagan, rhetorical spirit, began after the collapse of that system to build up schools of its own. Chief among these in this early period were the monastery schools; but the episcopal and even the presbytery schools can also be traced back to the sixth century.[39] Soon almost all education was in the hands of the Church,[40] and outside the Church there was neither learning nor culture. All educational institutions of this period (sixth to eighth centuries) were designed for practical purposes, and most of them were very modest in their aims and demands. From ancient culture these schools took over a predominantly rhetori-

38. On what follows, cf. H.-I. Marrou, *Histoire de l'éducation dans l'antiquité*, pp. 398–461 [Amer. edn., pp. 299–350].
39. Cf. Marrou, pp. 439–443 [Amer. edn., pp. 333–336].
40. There is no agreement among specialists as to whether there were any secular schools under the Merovingians; I do not believe that they can have had any importance. Cf. Marrou, p. 569, n. 9 [Amer. edn., pp. 448f.], and the essay, to which he refers, by H. Pirenne in the *Revue Bénédictine*, XLVI (1934). In some Italian towns the system of private tutors seems never to have died out completely.

cal conception of education, especially of the first steps, and they also, it goes without saying, took over its homogeneous written language. But they were far removed from the liberal, aristocratic spirit of cultivated ancient society; and where not altogether forgotten, the old social forms were imitated in such a way as to lose their original meaning. The survival of the homogeneous literary language was at times seriously threatened, especially in the Romance countries. There were few schools, their teaching was largely superficial; and on the other hand, the clergy was faced with the task of presenting the written teachings of Christianity in an intelligible form. Since in the Romance countries the vernaculars were still closely related to Latin, it was inevitable that many vernacular forms should make their way into written documents and into the liturgy. We have many examples of this from earlier periods, but the trend became really pronounced in the sixth century; certain of the texts that have come down to us from these first centuries of the Middle Ages show extensive, more or less deliberate compromises with the Romance vernaculars. The Carolingian educational reform put an end to this tendency, in principle at least. The consequence was an irrevocable cleavage between written Latin and the popular tongues. Latin lived on as an international organ of cultural life, as a language without any corresponding popular idiom from which to draw new life.

And so the literary or educated public had disappeared, and its idiom had become a specialized language: the language of the liturgy, of the chancelleries, and of a few scholars who learned it as a foreign tongue, though usually at an early age. Even in ancient times the literary public had constituted a minority of the population, but in many places a large minority. In varying degrees it maintained contact with the people, which, at least in part, understood and took an interest in certain literary productions and even—with its living language—exerted an influence on literature. Now the participants in intellectual life were few; they lived in schools dispersed throughout Europe, communicating only irregularly with one another. Even later, when they became more numerous, they remained an isolated social group consisting solely of teachers and students. The purpose of their activity was knowledge and doctrine far more than enjoyment; there was no longer a group or class capable of deriving cultivated pleasure from literature. Here we come to the core of the present discussion: a time had dawned and would long endure when the leading classes of society possessed neither education nor books nor even a language in which they could have expressed a culture rooted in their actual living conditions. There was a learned language, and there were spoken languages that could not be written; there was no language of general culture. Greatly as the successive periods of the Middle Ages differed from one another, they had one thing in common: the absence of a cultivated public. Such a public began to take form only in the last, transitional period. Recently attempts have been made to discredit the concept of a Renaissance which took its first steps in Italy in the fourteenth century and flowered throughout Western Europe in the sixteenth, by proving that a number of ancient works, ideas, and forms had previously been well known and influential in certain learned circles and that there were individuals and groups in the Middle Ages who understood ancient culture and thought it worth imitating. This is true, and it was assuredly of the highest significance for the preservation and development of the tradition. But it does not diminish the essential structural difference between the Middle Ages and the Renaissance. A civilization that can meaningfully be compared with that of antiquity requires a sizable minority of educated persons, and such a minority could form a social class only when the mother tongue had once again become the true vehicle of culture.

The latest description known to us of a Roman public occurs in the letters of Sidonius Apollinaris, written in the second half of the fifth century. Sidonius came of a Gallo-Roman family of big landowners with senatorial rank. Avitus, one of the last Western Roman emperors, was his father-in-law. In 468 Sidonius became Prefect of Rome (under Anthemius) and *patricius*. But he died some twenty years later as bishop of Clermont, the subject of a Visigothic king.

As reflected in most of his letters the aristocratic, literary life of Gallo-Roman society seems relatively intact. Not only Sidonius but many of his friends and fellow aristocrats were men of refined taste, extremely well read, and themselves engaged in literary pursuits. Their judgment was purely esthetic, rhetorical, and often pedantic; but thanks to its rhetorical and esthetic character, it was also thoroughly liberal. In describing the library of a friend, for example, Sidonius expresses his regret that the older pagan authors should be placed separately from the Christian authors (the Christians near the ladies' seats, the pagans near those of the gentlemen); for despite the difference in subject matter, Augustine, he says, ought to be classified with Varro and Prudentius with Horace (*Epist.* 2.9.4). Sidonius' style and taste are rhetorical and manneristic, as might be expected in view of the whole trend in literature under the empire. And still it is surprising when we consider the situation in which he wrote these letters. For there can be no doubt that the ground was trembling beneath the feet of these thoroughly Romanized and highly cultivated aristocrats.[41] A large and steadily increasing part of their country was already in the hands of the Burgundians and Visigoths. And worse, the intellectual domain in which they lived was shrinking. Barbaric forms were invading the language (2.10; 4.17); even in the leading classes there were not only traitors who sided with the invaders [42] but uneducated persons who were hardly better than barbarians.[43] But these and other indications of doom are

41. Sometimes it looks as if the Celtic aristocracy were so enthusiastic about Romanization only when confronted by the Germanic peril. Cf. Sidonius, *Epist.* 3.3.2f.

42. Cf., for example, *Epist.* 5.7 and also 5.17, which describes a joyous gathering and says (in § 5): *praeterea, quod beatissimum, nulla mentio de potestatibus aut de tributis, nullus sermo qui proderetur, nulla persona quae proderet* (above all, the greatest blessing, namely, no talk about rulers or taxes, no conversation by which to be betrayed, no betrayer).

43. *Epist.* 7.14 reveals that a large gathering of *summates viri* (men in office) included many *rustici* (countryfolk), *idiotae* (ignorant), and *imperiti* (inexperienced men).

communicated to the reader in playful rhetorical figures,[44] which, it must be admitted, are often expressive—but how vapidly pedantic! Sidonius compliments Count Arbogast in Trier on his excellent Latin style (4.17), which he has preserved in the midst of barbarians (*sic barbarorum familiaris, quod tamen nescius barbarismorum:* thus you are the companion of barbarians, yet you are free from barbarisms), and continues:

> quocirca sermonis pompa Romani, si qua adhuc uspiam est, Belgicis olim sive Rhenanis abolita terris in te resedit, quo vel incolumi vel perorante, etsi apud limitem ipsum Latina iura ceciderunt, verba non titubant.

> The luster of Roman speech has long since vanished from Belgica and the Rhenish regions, but in you it still survives; Latin dominion in those borderlands has fallen, but as long as you live and speak, the Latin language will not falter.

This is at once horrifying and grotesque. Another example: while Sidonius as bishop was trying to organize the defense of Clermont against the Visigoths, he wrote to Calminius, a friend of senatorial rank, whom the Visigoths had compelled to take part in the attack on the city, though it was his native place and he would much rather have defended it against them. The letter conveys the misery and gloom of the situation, and we feel how much is left unsaid. Nevertheless the text is full of ornaments like the following: *ubi ipse in hoc solum captivus adduceris, ut pharetras sagittis vacuare, lacrimis oculos implere cogaris* (where you are led a captive against your own land, forced to empty your quivers of arrows and to fill your eyes with tears).[45] Under the circumstances there is something spooky about such playfulness. It is true that mannerism had become second nature to Sidonius, and perhaps he was unaware of its incongruity. In any event it is certain that a public which expresses itself in such a way or takes pleasure in

44. The most recent work on the subject is André Loyen, *Sidoine Apollinaire et l'esprit précieux.*
45. Sidonius 5.12.

such expression when its very existence is threatened has become hopelessly cut off from reality. Such a style could surely have had no appeal even for an elite among the Germanic barbarians, and it was just as surely inaccessible to the average member of the Gallo-Roman population. Sidonius wrote with great skill. His art resembles a difficult game which consists in capturing the truth and even the concrete reality of things in a mesh of rhetorical figures; amazingly often it is successful, and his style was highly esteemed and much imitated in the schools of the Middle Ages. But it is a game for the initiate; only a small clique could appreciate without effort his incessant parallel figures, his unduly rich and select vocabulary, and his tricky sentence structure. In the period of the Germanic invasions, at all events, this way of life strangled itself. Its last highly aristocratic representatives became bishops.[46] But as early as the next century, the sixth, we hear a very different language in the Gallic bishoprics.[47]

From the sixth century on, as we have said, there ceased to be an educated public. This is the extreme limit. No one has ever stated an explicitly different view, but recent studies dealing with the perpetuation of ancient culture in the new Germanic kingdoms contain certain statements that may lead to misunderstandings.

In Italy a good deal of the ancient tradition survived into the Ostrogothic period. In the city of Rome there was still a highly educated aristocracy, as is attested by Boethius and his friend, the poet Maximianus,[48] and also by the editions of classical and post-classical authors that were issued in these circles down to the first

46. Cf. the description of the style of his fellow bishop, Remigius of Reims, in *Epist.* 9.7.2f., a fine piece of writing; unfortunately, the sermons to which it refers have not been preserved. Remigius (St. Rémy) was also of the higher Gallic aristocracy; he became bishop at the age of twenty-one. It was he who, on the occasion of the baptism of Clovis in 496, used a rhetorical figure (*commutatio*) which became famous: *adora quod incendisti, incende quod adorasti* (honor what you have burned, burn what you have honored).
47. See above, pp. 87ff., on Caesarius of Arles.
48. F. J. E. Raby, *A History of Secular Latin Poetry in the Middle Ages*, I, 124f.

third of the sixth century.[49] Undoubtedly this was still an "educated society," although Boethius' lament at the beginning of his *Consolatio philosophiae* makes no mention of any such society, in which supposedly he had once lived; he speaks only of his lonely study and of his political friends and enemies. Moreover, the character of his writing is already learned rather than cultivated; it is marked by the mixture of rhetoric, allegory, and philosophy which late antiquity bequeathed to the Middle Ages. After Boethius, in any event, in the struggles and crises of the sixth century, the Roman senatorial aristocracy vanished forever.

To me it seems impossible to regard Theodoric's court as a center of Roman culture. It is difficult to form a precise idea of Theodoric's mentality; in any case it is not permissible to judge by Cassiodorus' collection of letters, the *Variae*. Cassiodorus played an important political role only for a brief period during Theodoric's lifetime; and even if the king understood Cassiodorus' Latin (he probably knew very little Latin), what Cassiodorus has to say is assuredly no expression of Theodoric's personality. On political grounds he tried to encourage Roman culture, but outside of his family he met with little understanding for this policy among the Goths. He himself was a Gothic military and political leader; anyone who wished to speak with him and be properly understood had to speak Gothic. The *Variae* are significant documents; but their manneristic, self-satisfied, unctuously didactic character is entirely that of Cassiodorus and not of a Germanic prince who is reliably reported to have been unable to write. Cassiodorus' style in the *Variae* no longer presupposes the existence of any literary public, Italo-Roman or otherwise; it is a rhetorical chancellery style, a remote ancestor of the *Artes dictandi* of the Trecento. Especially the supposedly personal letters which Cassiodorus wrote for Theodoric, such as 1.45 to Boethius or 5.41 to the Roman senate about Cyprianus (accuser of

49. A. van de Vyver, "Cassiodore et son œuvre," 280f. and 281, n. 1; also E. Norden, "Römische Literatur" in Gercke-Norden, *Einleitung in die Altertumswissenschaft* (3rd edn.), 1: 4, 96.

Albinus and enemy of Boethius, who is known to have spoken Gothic with the king), are so learned and contrived that the king cannot have known any more about them than the gist, which he himself had dictated. There was no other chancellery style than the rhetorical, and Theodoric wished to carry on the Roman tradition.[50]

Thanks to the Amaling policy, which was pro-Roman and friendly to culture, a few schools and literary groups in the Roman tradition survived in Italy longer than elsewhere. To the entourage of the Amalings belonged Ennodius, court poet and bishop of Pavia, and the somewhat younger and in his way more important Arator, who later as a subdeacon in Rome won considerable fame with his poem *De actibus apostolorum*, which was at once typological and rhetorical in the ancient sense. Soon after the death of Theodoric the only surviving representatives of the ancient rhetorical tradition were to be found in the Church. But rhetorical mannerism was not the only current in Church Latin; meanwhile a simpler style, closer to spoken Latin in sentence structure at least, had developed in hymns and sermons.

Venantius Fortunatus, who in 565 went to Gaul, where he acquired a strange and unique position in the society of the Merovingian kingdom, was a product of the Ravenna school of the post-Gothic Byzantine period. His prestige can no doubt be explained by the fact that on the one hand the wellsprings of literary culture had run dry since the days of Sidonius, so that there were no longer any elegant writers, and on the other hand that Roman rhetoric was still held in high esteem. Thus Fortunatus,

50. On all this, see L. Schmidt, "Cassiodor und Theoderich," and the study by A. van de Vyver referred to in n. 49. These studies are also cited by R. R. Bezzola, *Les Origines et la formation de la littérature courtoise*, I, 17, n. 1. But they do not seem to have convinced him, although he himself (p. 18, n. 5) wonders to what extent the king understood the style of Ennodius.—The sentence to the effect that Roman rulers were superior because of their education (*eloquentia*), from *Variae* 9.21.4 (Bezzola, p. 15 and n. 1), is already written in the name of the grandson Athalaric and has the character of a highly political *topos;* the passages in the correspondence with other Germanic rulers, which allude to the superiority of the Roman outlook, are also political in signifiance. Cf. van de Vyver, pp. 245f.

gifted, affable, and apparently endowed with great personal charm, was virtually the only, or in any event by far the best purveyor of a commodity that was in great demand. His clientele comprised kings and bishops, great lords (including Franks) and well-to-do merchants; for them he wrote epithalamia, panegyrics, epitaphs, and in general all types of occasional verse, both ecclesiastical and profane. Undoubtedly some of his friends and customers still understood his writing, which is not always rhetorical and manneristic; in addition to thoroughly manneristic pieces, such as the *Praefatio* addressed to Gregory of Tours or numerous passages from the *Vita Martini*, we have such simple compositions as the *Hymnus de Leontio episcopo*,[51] the popular simplicity of which has been noticed by Ebert. Fortunatus had at his command the plainest forms of Christian *sermo humilis* as well as the mannerism of late antiquity. His admirers included Gregory of Tours, who by express statements as well as his own far more significant but also far less cultivated writing shows how isolated and inaccessible the stylistic tradition that survived in Fortunatus had become. He seems also to have been admired by a few Frankish nobles, which is only natural in view of the enormous prestige enjoyed by Roman civilization. But all this does not add up to a literary public in the ancient or modern sense. Such a public has definite tastes, characteristic of the times, and literary needs exceeding mere occasional verse. Fortunatus' finest poems, by the way, are a few of his Christian hymns. He found a niche for himself in Poitiers with the widow of Chlotar I, the Thuringian princess Radegundis, who had founded a convent there. He died as bishop of Poitiers.

In any event the society of Gaul in Fortunatus' day, at the end of the sixth century, was the last in connection with which the question of a literary public can even arise. Later on, no such social group existed anywhere in Europe. The only literature that remained was of an erudite and ceremonial character, in a lan-

---

51. *Carm.* 1.16 in *Venanti . . . Fortunati . . . Opera poetica,* ed. F. Leo (pp. 19–21).

guage understood by only a very few persons of exceptional education. Under such circumstances any real development or creativeness was unthinkable. It is true that with the coming of the Lombards the study of ancient culture did not entirely cease in the monasteries and other schools of Italy, but any possible basis for a cultivated society was destroyed. In Visigothic Spain all cultural activity seems to have been clerical and erudite from the start. In Gaul the last remnants of Roman culture collapsed, and with the new schools founded by Irish and Scottish monks cultural life entered upon the long period of monastic isolation that was to set in somewhat later in England and western Germany. In the seventh and early eighth century, the Arabs conquered North Africa and Spain, and the Romanized Merovingians were ousted by the Austrasian Carolingians; Latin culture sank very low on the European continent and was even in danger of being submerged entirely by the Romance vernacular languages. When it was saved and renewed by Charlemagne, who gathered round him the foremost Latin scholars of Italy and England, it had definitely become an artificial language, so different from the spoken Romance dialects that the people could no longer understand it. The only link between the two, a very important one to be sure, was the liturgy, whose most important words and most frequently repeated formulas became engraved on the popular mind. In French, which generally speaking moved farthest away from Latin of all the Romance languages, many ecclesiastical terms were taken over almost unchanged.

The period during which there was in Europe no cultivated society as we understand it, was very long, extending from 600 at the latest to 1100 at the earliest, and even then the process of reconstruction was very slow. The ruling classes were uneducated for at least five hundred years. During this period certain courts, about which R. R. Bezzola has written an excellent book,[52] were centers of culture. But in spite of Bezzola's efforts there remain certain incontrovertible facts, which I shall here briefly outline,

52. Cf. above, n. 50.

leaving exceptions and reservations for later: there was virtually no possibility of obtaining even an elementary education except in the Church schools; only in rare and exceptional cases did these schools accept students who were not destined for an ecclesiastical career; [53] the education there administered had as its instrument a foreign language which was nowhere in use as the language of daily life; the mother tongues had no culture, it was not even possible to write them. By far the greater number of the small and medium landholders and, indeed, most of the great lords could neither read nor write; laymen who could do so with ease were very rare until far into the twelfth century.

Exceptions were the reigning families. Most of the kings and emperors enjoyed some education; some were highly educated and were among the leading minds of their day. Yet, as Marc Bloch has observed, there is a characteristic exception to this general rule: [54] when a new dynasty took power, the first king was still poorly educated, even though (as must always have been the case) he came of the high nobility; this state of affairs changed only with the second, or even the third, generation. This observation applies to the first Carolingians (even in the case of Charlemagne one still has the impression that he obtained his education only as an adult); it applies to the Frankish Emperor Conrad I, to the first Ludolfings Henry I and Otto I, and likewise to Hugh Capet. From this it seems to follow that not even an elementary education was customary in the families of dukes and other high feudal nobles. Still, we must not oversimplify. The culture of the early Middle Ages is very uneven; local tradition, wealth, inclination and talent, the availability of an able educator, and later, interest in political and intellectual questions played a considerable part; moreover, the accounts of the education of individual princes are so meager and often so schematic that it is hard to form a reliable judgment. Certain feudal lords of southern France seem at an

53. Cf. E. Lesne, *Histoire de la propriété ecclésiastique en France,* v, 430ff.; see below, p. 282 and n. 86.
54. *La Société féodale,* i, 128 [Engl. edn., p. 79].

early date to have been better educated than the princes of the north, and Wipo, chaplain of Conrad II and author of the *Victimae paschali* sequence, expresses the belief in the 1140's (i.e., somewhat later than the period of which we have been speaking) that the Italian nobility were better educated than their German peers.[55] This passage is often cited, but it is couched in very general terms and is hard to verify. Moreover, it should not be forgotten that many members of the high clergy came of leading feudal families, that when chosen for the ecclesiastical career, they were given an appropriate education, and that some of them, such as Bruno of Cologne and certain Lorraine prelates of the tenth century, were learned and cultivated. A few women of these circles were also carefully educated and learned to have opinions of their own in intellectual matters. From all this it may be inferred that even during these centuries education and culture were fairly widespread in the ruling families, though in varying degree. Nevertheless one cannot speak of a lay culture and much less of a "cultivated society." From the most elementary beginnings this culture was Latin;[56] it was dispensed by ecclesiastics, and its very schematic content derived from the ecclesiastical and erudite tradition of late antiquity. Few laymen partook of it; thus all cultural life was in the hands of a small ecclesiastical elite. The vast majority of the well-to-do nobles were dependent for their entertainment on the arts of the *mimi* and *histriones,* or, especially in the Germanic countries, on the *scops,* or singers in the vernacular, who were long to play a considerable role. The two groups gradually merged. As soon as they tried to commit their vernacular repertory to writing, they were subjected, if only on technical grounds, to clerical influence. Or perhaps it would be more accurate to say that as soon as the members of the clergy

55. In his *Tetralogus,* addressed to Henry III. Cf. M. Manitius, *Gesch. d. lat. Lit. d. Mittelalters,* II, 321f. For the much debated question of secular schools in northern Italy in the eleventh century and earlier, see the survey by H. Wieruszowski, "Arezzo as a Center of Learning . . . ," especially pp. 328f. and n. 28.
56. For Anglo-Saxon, see below.

began to take an interest in vernacular literature, it came to be recorded occasionally in writing, and that this would have been impossible without their help.

Two of the courts that were cultural centers require special treatment even in this brief survey. First, of course, the Carolingian court in the ninth century. I should like the reader to bear in mind that the criteria according to which medieval cultural centers have hitherto been judged, though perfectly sound in themselves, are not conclusive in the present context. The study of the Latin tradition by a small circle does not imply the existence of a literary public, and the restoration of correct Latin in the liturgy and administration is significant for us largely because, especially in the Gallo-Roman regions, it definitively cut the already feeble ties of intelligibility between Latin and the vernacular languages, thus preparing the way for an independent development of the Romance literary languages. The Carolingian renaissance played an important part in preserving the European tradition; but essentially it was not so much a rebirth as an endeavor to preserve and transmit certain elements of ancient culture. The efforts of Charlemagne and his first successors to disseminate education more widely do not seem to have been successful. In the long run they were unable to raise the cultural level of the lower clergy or to create a class of educated laymen. Charlemagne's learned entourage included a few laymen such as Einhard the chronicler, Angilbert,[57] and his son Neithard; some of the Frankish nobles seem to have objected to all this learning at Charlemagne's court; others must have taken a keen interest in it, otherwise such books as De institutione laicali, which Bishop Jonas of Orléans dedicated to a great lord of his diocese (perhaps Count Matfrid of Orléans) in the reign of Louis the Pious, could not have been written.[58] But this book, like much of Carolingian literature, is a clerical compilation. The culture of the Carolingian

57. Angilbert later became abbot of Saint-Riquier.
58. Cf. M. L. W. Laistner, *Thought and Letters in Western Europe* A.D. *500 to 900*, p. 256.

court remained entirely within the clerical tradition of late antiquity, which Charlemagne merely adapted to new political aims
arising from new conditions. This puts him at the beginning of
the political Middle Ages. But he and his followers were still isolated; we sense no movement from below that might have sustained the Carolingian renaissance. The intellectual activity had
its source in Charlemagne, in a few of his learned friends, and in
a few of his successors in the next two generations; and it does
not seem to have gone beyond this narrow circle. Everyone else
seems to have remained inert, learning little and expressing nothing.

Einhard tells us (29) that Charlemagne had the barbarous old
songs (*barbara et antiquissima carmina*) celebrating the wars and
deeds of the old kings committed to writing,[59] and even that he
ordered (*inchoavit*) a grammar of his mother tongue, namely, the
Frankish of the Rhineland. In addition, wishing the laity to understand the laws, he decreed that they should be translated into
all the vernacular languages and read aloud.[60] The fragment of a
ninth-century translation of the *lex Salica*, found on the cover of
an incunabulum in Trier, is probably a monument to this decree.[61]
It seems to have been his desire, if only for practical reasons, to
make written languages of the vernacular tongues and above all
of his own Frankish. But this effort brought little lasting results.

Under his successors, Louis the Pious and Louis the German,
adaptations of the Gospels were written in the Germanic tongues.
Some of these have been preserved complete in manuscripts spe-
cially devoted to them; one such work is the rather popular Old
Saxon *Heliand*, and another is the more learned gospel book of
Otfried of Weissenburg. Otfried, who was clearly aware of the

59. Compare the well-known letter from Alcuin to Bishop Higbald of Lindis-
farne (*MGH Epist. sel.*, IV, 181–184), in which Alcuin protests against
the pleasure taken in "pagan" heroic songs. Charlemagne appears to have
been more broad-minded and more farsighted in this matter.
60. A. Boretius (ed.), *Capitularia regum Francorum*, I, 234f., no. 116, cap. II.
Cf. G. Ehrismann, *Gesch. d. deutschen Lit. bis zum Ausgang d. Mittelalters*
(2nd edn.), I, 353.
61. Ehrismann, ibid., I, 352f.

literary problems involved in his task, speaks of the pains he went to with his spelling, and there is no doubt that for a long time to come anyone attempting to render the sounds of the vernaculars in Latin signs was embarking on an arduous adventure. But apart from the *Heliand* and Otfried's gospel book, the only vestiges of German literature we possess from the Carolingian period (we shall later make the same observation in connection with the early Romance literatures) were recorded on unused pages or in margins of Latin manuscripts. The most important of these are the *Wessobrunn Prayer*, the *Muspilli*, the Old Saxon *Genesis*, the magic spells, and above all the only surviving example of the *barbara et antiquissima carmina* mentioned by Einhard, namely, the *Hildebrandslied*, which has come down to us in a theological manuscript from Cassel, where it was recorded incompletely, as space permitted, on the first and last pages. The *Hildebrandslied* was committed to writing (unless this version is already a copy) by two Saxon or perhaps even Anglo-Saxon monks. It is safe to say that all the vernacular texts recorded in the Carolingian period and, indeed, until the twelfth century were written down by scribes trained in clerical schools, for nowhere else could one learn to write. The people to whom these poems were addressed and most of the minstrels who sang them were illiterate.

In the Romance countries the Carolingian period witnessed only the barest beginnings of vernacular literature, but in England there was already a literary culture in the language of the people. This brings us to the second center of courtly culture of which I have to speak, the court of Alfred the Great in Wessex. The Anglo-Saxons were not converted to Christianity by foreign conquerors, nor were they, like the Franks in Gaul or the Lombards in Italy, a minority whose national character was absorbed by the older stratum of population. Their conversion did not in nearly equal degree impair their language and tradition. Far more of the old Germanic epic poetry dating back to the days of the migrations was preserved in England than on the continent, and the first Christian poetry in the vernacular made its appearance in the

Anglo-Saxon world—an event which Bede records with all its legendary significance in his famous account of Caedmon the bard. All this happened in the seventh or early eighth century; Boniface, the Anglo-Saxon founder of the mission in Germany, lived in the same period. Anglo-Saxon influence is discernible in almost all old German Christian poetry. No doubt we should possess far more of the Anglo-Saxon literature of that time if the libraries and in general the culture of Northumbria had not been destroyed by the Danish raids. In any event the foundations of Anglo-Saxon literature were so firmly established that far more account was taken of the vernacular tongue in the West Saxon educational reform introduced by Alfred in the ninth century than in the comparable Carolingian reform by which Alfred was influenced. Even as a child Alfred seems to have read Anglo-Saxon poems and learned them by heart. Later he himself wrote in this language; he translated the Latin works most important for his learned and educational purposes or had them translated by the scholars of his entourage. He also took measures to ensure the elementary education of young nobles and, it would seem, of many commoners as well, and this educational activity was carried on largely in Anglo-Saxon.[62] All this presupposed a standardization of spelling and grammar, at least in the West Saxon tongue, something that was not achieved until much later on the continent. This achievement was probably due to Alfred himself, who in this respect was more successful than Charlemagne and certainly had abler helpers.[63] The ninth and tenth centuries were marked by vigorous literary activity which continued down to the Norman Conquest and did not entirely cease even then. To this period belong the manuscripts in which the Anglo-Saxon monuments of the seventh and eighth centuries have come down to us, the Beo-

62. The most important sources, cited and discussed in all relevant studies, are chapters 75 and 102 of the biography of Alfred by Asser (ed. W. H. Stevenson), together with Alfred's own preface to the translation of Gregory the Great, *Regula pastoralis* (ed. and tr. H. Sweet). Aelfric's Latin grammar in the Anglo-Saxon language dates from about 1000.
63. In Germany there is nothing comparable until much later, at the beginning of the eleventh century, at Saint Gall, under Notker Labeo.

wulf manuscript of the British Museum, the Archbishop Usher manuscript of early Christian poetry at Oxford, the *Book of Exeter*, and the Vercelli manuscript. In spite of all this no "cultivated society" or "literary public" in our use of the terms developed in England under Alfred the Great and his successors. The writing of the period is clerical, erudite, and didactic, and there is no sign of the liberal-mindedness characteristic of a true literary movement. Nevertheless the nobility did participate in this literary activity. Quite possibly their example may have contributed to the significant development of Old French and Anglo-Norman literature, brought about by the conquerors in the twelfth century; for it is among the high Norman nobility that we discern the first indications that a new literary public was beginning to take form. Bezzola believes [64] that the conquerors developed their own vernacular literature in competition with that of the native nobility. This view is not entirely unfounded. But between the Norman Conquest and the independent and characteristic development of courtly literature in the West French and Anglo-Norman sphere, at least eighty years elapsed, and the character of this literature is fundamentally different from that of Anglo-Saxon literature. A new world had come into being.

Latin, which in this whole period down to the twelfth century was virtually the sole vehicle of intellectual life and written communication, and which even afterward lost this position of predominance only very gradually, was a foreign language that had to be learned; in the Germanic and Celtic countries this had always been the case, and in the Romance regions it had been true since the early Carolingian period at the latest. Latin was cut off from the spoken language and scarcely affected by its development. Still, it would not be correct to call it a dead language; even before 1100 this was not the case, and afterward still less so. Medieval Latin was extremely varied from the first, and from the eleventh century on it produced an abundance of new and living forms. The language was not static except for the spelling and

64. *Origines,* I, 238f.

morphology, and these only relatively so. The vocabulary, syntax, style level, and versification were so richly varied that one can speak of many different worlds of medieval Latin. Consequently no specialist in the subject has ever attempted to characterize it as a whole, much less write its inner history.

The period before 1100, that is, before the flood of polemical works inspired by the investiture conflict, was relatively dead and stagnant. The prose works of the time were theological (exegetic, polemical, homiletic) or didactic in the broadest sense. There were also chronicles, biographies, collections of letters, laws, and documents. The poetry was extremely varied, for side by side with the learned verse in ancient meters, cultivated for example at the Carolingian court, there were liturgical poems in accentual meters, in which rhyme was beginning to develop. Because of their official function, because of the music that accompanied them, and because parts of them at least could be understood by the audience as a whole, these were perhaps the most influential element of the Latin literature of the time. The same period witnessed the first sequences—a momentous development—and the beginnings of the liturgical drama. But this is not all. From the very earliest years there had been accentual poems both of a manneristic and of a semipopular character; in the latter we seem to catch an occasional echo of the vernacular poetry. In prose as in poetry the style levels are extremely varied. We find turns of phrase which almost suggest the vernacular and at times possess a rough dignity. There are almost perfect imitations of classical symmetry, and most of the theological and philosophical works reveal a certain classical tradition based chiefly on Augustine and Gregory the Great. At the same time, sometimes even in clumsy writers, we find the most immoderate mannerism, exceeding that of late antiquity in extravagance and absurdity; in those days very few writers were entirely free from a taste for complicated trifling with words. The variety of this literature becomes even more evident when we compare concrete examples. Side by side with the comparatively simple prose of Bede or Paulus Diaconus or such

almost classical stylists as Lupus of Ferrières or Gerbert of Aurillac, we find such expressive mannerists as Rather of Verona or
Bruno of Querfurt. And what a gulf there is in poetry between
the elegance of Walafrid or the genius of Gottschalk and the
awkward and manneristic Abbo of Saint-Germain. But in addition
there is Notker's sequence; there are pieces, such as the Benevento
poem on Ludwig or the *Carmen de Fontaneto*, in which the construction comes close to the vernacular. And finally let us not forget Hrotswith of Gandersheim. Other scholars would give a different selection of names and works; it is somewhat a matter of
individual taste or the direction one's studies have taken. In any
event a comparatively small production reveals a whole diversity
of style. This resulted in part from the fragmentation of the
literary milieu, which before and after the unification under
Charlemagne was dispersed among a number of isolated schools
with widely divergent standards and traditions. But it also had to
do with the many different functions performed by the written
language at a time when there was no social class possessed of a
literary taste that might have produced a regulative effect. Latin
was the language of the administration, of the liturgy, of learning,
of historiography, of epideictic court poetry; it was all this in
one, and in addition it was the only instrument by which the experience and feeling of the individual or the community could be
expressed in writing. It may well be that in those centuries experience and feeling had developed little maturity of form and articulation, and that Latin with its almost overarticulated structure
was not the most suitable instrument for the direct expression of
the experience and feeling of the early Middle Ages. But here the
Christian, Augustinian element, the *sermo humilis*, sometimes func-
tioned as a mediator, enabling certain authors even in the early
Middle Ages—Gottschalk and especially Rather of Verona, for example—to express themselves fully in Latin.

In the eleventh century a change set in. An inner movement,
probably stimulated by the monastic reforms of the tenth century,
made itself felt in European society. At first the movement was

local and limited in its aims, but it gradually spread, giving rise to conflicts, ideas, controversies, and new movements, which released new ideas, conflicts, and undertakings. The movement against the feudalization and corruption of the Church, against simony, led to the investiture conflict and the related crises, which in turn provoked the beginnings of political thought in post-Roman Europe. All this agitation was reflected in the great heresies, the idea of a holy war, and the Crusades, which did so much to broaden the cultural and economic horizon. A European art was born, first Romanesque, then Gothic; a new and characteristic scientific method was developed in philosophy and jurisprudence. Gradually more and more people became involved in these movements and awakened to intellectual self-awareness. In maturing, thought and sensibility molded appropriate instruments of expression. Ultimately this development transformed the vernacular tongues into independent literary languages. But at first they were quite unprepared for such a task. Latin had an enormous head start, it enjoyed enormous prestige as a literary language and, as would soon become apparent, still possessed enormous powers of adaptation. Only gradually could the vernaculars begin to compete with it; only with Dante did they seriously take up the struggle with Latin; and not until the sixteenth century, with its vernacular humanism and the related classicism of the academies, was the struggle finally decided in their favor.

In any event it is almost miraculous how Latin, which for so long had been virtually a dead language, began in the eleventh century to take on new life and to put forth the most variegated flowers. First came the new development of the hymns and sequences, which, though most strikingly exemplified by Adam of Saint-Victor, began as early as the eleventh century (*Verbum bonum et suave*). The special flavor of this liturgical poetry derives from the ingenious combination of varied phonetic effects with equally varied typological metaphors.[65] Later, under the

65. Cf. my essay "Dante's Prayer to the Virgin (*Paradiso*, xxxiii) and Earlier Eulogies."

influence of the Dominicans and Franciscans, a new change set in; hymns richer in dogmatic content or feeling (*Adoro te* and *Stabat Mater*) were composed. An entirely different but equally new variety of Latin poetry was that of the itinerant students, or goliards. Between the eleventh and the thirteenth centuries the number of those who taught and learned Latin must have increased enormously—in the cities, where gradually independent universities developed, the students became a conspicuous and sometimes turbulent section of the population; scholars also became far more numerous than before at courts both large and small. This entire group was the source of the famous Latin poetry of the goliards, for the most part erotic or satirical, occasionally religious in content, and often coming close to the vernacular languages in syntax. Some of the Cambridge *carmina* show that here again the tradition extends back at least to the eleventh century; but the great period, that of Hugh Primas of Orléans and the Archpoet, was the mid-twelfth century. Still another, entirely different trend in the Latin of this time was rhetorical mannerism. Going back directly in an unbroken chain to late antiquity, it achieved triumphs in philosophico-allegorical poetry in the twelfth century (Alan of Lille) and in the thirteenth attained a new flowering in the *ars dictaminis* that dominated the prose of the Italian chancelleries. Its methods—rhythmical movement of clauses, rhymed prose, sound patterns and figures of speech, unusual vocabulary, complex and pompous sentence structure—stem from the ancient tradition, but now they are used more freely, richly, and organically. The conception of sublime style underlying this mannerism still exerted a powerful influence on Dante's generation and on Dante himself.

Be that as it may, the Latin literature of the high Middle Ages reveals two main trends, significant in their own time and for the future as well; one was pre-humanist and rhetorical, the other scholastic and dialectical. Much has been written about the humanism of the twelfth century. There had long been occasional proficient imitators of the classical Latin authors; with the end of the eleventh century they became numerous, and though this imitation of antiquity did not give rise to a view of the world and of history such as later made its appearance in humanism proper, many of these writers developed a distinctly classical sense of style. This was true not only of such celebrated writers as Hildebert of Lavardin or John of Salisbury, or such authors of classical epics as Walter of Châtillon and Joseph of Exeter, but also of many mystico-typological authors who are not ordinarily considered in this connection, such as Hugh of Saint-Victor or Bernard of Clairvaux. At least from the standpoint of style it is a misunderstanding to call Bernard of Clairvaux an antihumanist. Antischolastic, yes, but he was one of the great masters of Christian rhetoric. His style derives from Cicero by way of Augustine; among those employing the theological *sermo humilis* of the Middle Ages, it is he who came closest to the classical tradition.

The dialectical, scientific Latin of scholasticism developed in a direction contrary to humanistic rhetoric. Scholasticism exerted a revolutionary effect on the language, for, breaking drastically with the tradition of literary Latin, which had hitherto been essentially rhetorical and even manneristic, it concentrated for the first time on scientific accuracy. For scientific purposes the isolation of medieval Latin from everyday usage proved to be a significant advantage. This circumstance—the freedom of words from current associations—made it relatively easy for theology and philosophy (as well as jurisprudence, which, to be sure, had a tradition to refer back to) to create a clear and precise language in which to express their specialized concepts. This of course required the use of neologisms which sounded barbarous to the classically trained ear and the abandonment of the harmonious sentence structure of classical rhetoric. But the great achievements of scholastic logic, its combination and creation of ideas, would not have been possible without such an instrument; and such an instrument could have developed at that time only on the basis of a pre-existing written language distinct from the spoken tongue.

Scholastic Latin emerged with the generation of Abelard; in the thirteenth century, thanks to the controversy over Arabic

Aristotelianism and the influence of the mendicant orders, it attained the peak of its development and achieved wide currency. Somewhat larger circles were initiated into the vital philosophical questions of the day, such as: Was the world created, or is it eternal? Is the individual soul or only a world soul, the *intellectus agens*, immortal? During the thirteenth century scholastic dialectic almost entirely crowded out the rhetorical humanistic tendencies, and it was not until Petrarch's generation that humanism reawakened. The struggle between these two forms of the learned language was something new. In late antiquity, especially in Rome, where science had never achieved any autonomy, specialization ranked low, and what knowledge was to be recognized as worth knowing had to be expressed in a generally intelligible, rhetorical form. Now, an urgent demand for exact, specialized knowledge gave rise to an antirhetorical tendency, which laid claim to intellectual leadership. Humanistic reactions, both classical and Christian in inspiration, soon made themselves felt; the humanists vaunted the man of universal culture, expressing himself in well-chosen but generally intelligible terms as opposed to the mere specialist and his jargon. This conflict persisted for centuries in innumerable forms, varying with the needs and conditions of each particular period. From the beginning there was an inner contradiction within the humanistic trend: on the one hand it espoused the ideal of an elegant mode of expression, readily intelligible to an elite of many-sided culture, in opposition to the barbarous learned language of the scholastics; on the other it fought for the model on which this style was based, classical Latin, which had to be learned in the schools. This problem became urgent and ripe for solution when a high society expressing itself in the vernacular, a "public," began to make its appearance, and the solution was the vernacular humanism in which the literary languages of antiquity served no longer as means of expression but only as models and prototypes for literary expression in the vernacular.

If we survey the Latin of the period we have been discussing, and in particular of the twelfth century, we are amazed and often delighted to note how much more richness and originality of thought, how much more intensity and directness of feeling it expresses than the Latin of the earlier Middle Ages. In every domain of thought the vernacular literature lagged far behind; intellectual matters were beyond its scope. It was only in the thirteenth century, and then very slowly and spottily, that all this began to change. But richness of feeling and expression made its appearance almost simultaneously in Provençal lyric poetry and in Latin, in the poetry of the wandering scholars and in typological hymns in the manner of Adam of Saint-Victor. French soon followed, and most of the other vernacular languages somewhat later, toward 1200. Latin had behind it a long classical and Christian tradition; both its forms and its stock of ready-made themes gave it an advantage over the vernaculars; and furthermore clerics schooled in Latin possessed a monopoly on writing. But this development in Latin letters took place in the late eleventh and in the twelfth century; if after long stagnation the power of Latin writers to express themselves revived so forcefully at the very moment when the vernacular languages were also beginning to awaken, we must conclude that both movements sprang from a common source. True, there are demonstrable economic factors, greater prosperity, more freedom of travel and commerce, increasing population, more social life in the cities. As a result of all this more people participated directly or indirectly in intellectual and artistic movements, and this made for a greater likelihood that talents would be discovered and developed. But all in all, the spontaneous force which at a given moment gives rise to such movements and enables them to unfold is no more subject to analysis than the force which gives rise to individual talents.

In the twelfth century Latin performed a unique function. Those who really mastered it, though far more numerous than before, were still a small minority composed entirely of learned clerics. And yet the life of the times began to find expression in Latin: in hymns, in the satirical and polemical poems of the itinerant scholars, in chronicles and historico-mystical speculations, and sometimes even in didactic allegories. Despite the strong scholastic tinge of this literature, it discloses more universal trends and moods. The situation was unusual and not an easy one to analyze or describe. There existed a very ancient learned language, accessible only to a body of specially trained readers, and yet this language began to put forth new shoots, bearing witness to the rise of new ideas and new modes of feeling. At the same time the popular tongues were gradually attaining self-awareness, though at first literary expression in the vernaculars was limited to lyric poetry and to narrative. In many respects the vernacular still required Latin tutelage, but sustained by other, broader sections of the population, they followed their own inherent motivations. Little by little they rose to maturity and in the end fashioned a literary public of their own.

We must now deal with this rise of the vernacular languages. It began in Gallo-Roman territory, then in other Romance countries. What we have said of the first written records of Old High German (pp. 265 ff.) is also true of the first Romance writings. A few have come down to us from as early as the ninth century. But manuscripts in any appreciable number are preserved only from the thirteenth century on. We have few from the twelfth century, and from earlier centuries we possess not a single manuscript devoted exclusively or even principally to a Romance text.[66] The Strasbourg Oaths of 843 appear in the midst of Neithard's Latin text. The Eulalia sequence, from the end of the ninth century, is written on an unused sheet of a patristic text copied at the monastery of Saint-Amand sur l'Elnon; it is followed by the Old High German *Ludwigslied*, written at about the same time and, rather surprisingly, in the same hand. (Thus there were those whose recording activities included the Rhenish-Frankish language as well as Gallo-Romanic.) The *Passion du Christ* and the *Vie de Saint Léger* were written in the unused space of a Latin glossary compiled during the tenth or early eleventh century in Clermont-

---

66. An excellent treatment of the subject is provided by so early a writer as Paul Meyer in "Anciennes Poésies religieuses en langue d'oc."

Ferrand. The still uninterpreted but impressive Provençal refrain of a Latin *alba*, or dawn song (*L'Alba par umet mar* . . .) [67] was inscribed beside a column of Latin *notae juris* in the free space of a manuscript from Fleury-sur-Loire, now in the Vatican (probably tenth or early eleventh century). The earliest document of any length in Provençal is, to my knowledge, a fragment of the Song of Boethius; it occupies the last seven pages (further pages are missing) of a tenth-century manuscript, also from Fleury-sur-Loire and now in Orléans; the preceding 268 pages are taken up with Latin sermons and parts of the Bible.[68] Among early Italian texts we might mention the riddle in verse *Boves se pareba*, in the margin of a liturgical manuscript (*Orazionale mozarabico*) in the Biblioteca Capitolare in Verona, written as early as the early ninth century; the formulas for legal testimony in the region of Montecassino, written about 960, in the Latin text of the protocol; [69] and perhaps the inscription on a mural painting in the lower church of San Clemente in Rome,[70] which must be assigned to the late eleventh century. Even then, in the eleventh and early twelfth centuries, manuscripts entirely in the vernacular are very rare, though fragments of all sorts are comparatively frequent. The sixteen sheets of the Leiden manuscript of the Provençal *Sancta Fides* might in a pinch be termed an independent manuscript because they were devoted chiefly to the poem; but Ernest Hoepffner has proved that the Leiden fragment was removed from a far larger Latin manuscript (again from Fleury-sur-Loire).[71] The oldest manuscript of the *Vie de Saint Alexis*, in Hildesheim, dates from the twelfth century, likewise the famous Oxford manuscript of the *Chanson de Roland;* and the London manuscript of the

67. *MGH Poet.*, 111, 702, n. 6; the text has frequently been reprinted, for example, in Förster-Koschwitz, *Altfranzösisches Übungsbuch* (6th edn.), pp. 265ff (with a survey of the attempts at interpretation), and in K. Vossler, *Die Dichtungsformen der Romanen*, pp. 153f.
68. Cf. P. Meyer in *Romania*, 1 (1872), 227.
69. F. A. Ugolini (ed.), *Testi antichi italiani*, pp. 1 and 129; Walther von Wartburg, *Raccolta di testi antichi italiani*, p. 7.
70. Ugolini, p. 134; cf. also E. Monaci, *Crestomazia italiana dei primi secoli* (new edn. by F. Arese), pp. 7f.
71. E. Hoepffner and P. Alfaric (eds.), *La Chanson de Sainte-Foy*, 1, 3-19.

Chanson de Guillaume, from the thirteenth. In all three cases the works themselves seem to have originated several decades or even a whole century earlier.[72] If, with this in mind, we look through Gröber's *Liedersammlungen der Troubadours*[73] or the list of manuscripts of the Provençal troubadours in Pillet-Carstens,[74] it becomes clear that not only the original *breus de pergamina* (Jaufre Rudel), the song sheets, have gone astray, but also the twelfth-century collections whose existence is postulated by Gröber[75] and some of which at least must have been in the hands of the *joglars;* Pillet-Carstens does not list a single manuscript from the twelfth century. Jeanroy's *Bibliographie sommaire des chansonniers français* suggests the same conclusion;[76] the great French song collections begin with the thirteenth century. However, we do find a number of vernacular fragments and remnants from the twelfth century. Examples are the *Sponsus*[77] or the paraphrase of the Song of Songs in Latin manuscripts of the Bibliothèque Nationale; the Franco-Provençal *Alexander* fragment in a Latin manuscript of the Laurenziana in Florence; the *Ritmo Cassinese* in Montecassino; and many more may be found in the anthologies. Among Spanish documents I might mention the *Auto de los tres reyes*, which is written in the unused space of a twelfth-century Latin manuscript devoted to exegetical writings. To the same class

72. The oldest MSS of the Chansons de geste are listed by L. Gautier, *Les Épopées françaises* (2nd edn.), I, 224–228. These are the so-called jongleur manuscripts; they are small in size, carelessly executed, and badly worn. Thus it seems very likely that they were part of the jongleurs' repertory. Cf. also Laborde's *La Chanson de Roland*, which contains (pp. 1–50) C. Samaran, "Étude historique et paléographique." See especially pp. 36–41.

73. *Romanische Studien*, II (1877).

74. *Bibliographie der Troubadours*, pp. x–xliv. Cf. also the chronological table in C. Brunel, *Bibliographie des manuscrits littéraires en ancien provençal*, pp. 111f.

75. Loc. cit., pp. 356f.—The existence of the *breus de pergamina* and of early collections in general is denied for good reasons (though they do not apply to every individual case) but without sufficient chronological discrimination by F. Gennrich, "Die Repertoire-Theorie."

76. Les Classiques français du Moyen Age: Manuels.

77. The very interesting manuscript (*1139 fonds latin*) comes from Saint-Martial at Limoges and is described in the *Catalogue général des manuscrits latins (Bibliothèque Nationale)*, ed. P. Lauer, I, 415f.

belong no doubt the recently deciphered and now well-known *cancioncillas de amigo*, preserved as the conclusions (*jarcha*) of Hebrew (and Arabic) poems in an Arabic poetic form (*muwas-saha*);[78] some of these strophes assuredly date back far into the eleventh century, and they may be much older. The manuscripts are indeed from a later period, but the method of recording must have been the same from the first. Finally I wish to mention the only document of the Rhaeto-Romanic literature of the Middle Ages to have come down to us, namely, an interlinear translation of a Latin homily, inscribed probably at the beginning of the twelfth century in a much older Latin manuscript (in Einsiedeln).[79]

Even if there should be a few gaps and inaccuracies in this compilation (the dating of certain manuscripts is controversial), it gives a picture of the situation: we possess written documentation in the vernacular languages from the ninth, tenth, and eleventh centuries, but they are still fragmentary, and even in the twelfth century fully recorded works and manuscripts of any length are very rare. This confirms what may be presumed from other evidence: that there were no readers of the vernacular languages and that the rare persons who did read read the literary language, which in Christian Europe was Latin. Nevertheless there were persons at a very early date who ventured to commit vernacular composition to writing.[80] Let us attempt on the basis of the available

78. Of the extensive literature, I list what I myself have read: D. Alonso in *Revista de filologia española*, XXXIII (1949), 297ff.; L. Spitzer in *Comparative Literature*, IV (1952), 1–22; P. Le Gentil, *Le Virelai et le villancico*.
79. Cf. T. Gartner, *Handbuch der rätoromanischen Sprache und Literatur*, pp. 274–278.
80. Cf. What has been said above, in connection with Otfried von Weissenburg, pp. 266f. The two extremes between which the recorders of Romance texts moved are Latinism and a phonetic reproduction of the native dialect. Cf. C. Beaulieux, *Histoire de l'orthographe française*, I, 30–34. But the method is often arbitrary and haphazard. Ferdinand Lot adduced good reasons for the view that it is pointless to try to establish the dialect of the Oaths of Strasbourg (*Romania*, LXV, 145ff.). Complicated situations arise in Old German as well when the scribe copied a document composed in some idiom other than his own. The only vulgar tongue to have developed a written koine by late Carolingian times is probably Anglo-Saxon, see pp. 267ff., above. On the attempts to create an Old High German written language, see Brigitta Schreyer in Braune, Paul, and Sievers, *Beiträge zur Gesch. der deutschen Sprache und Literatur* (1951).

material to determine on what occasions and for what purposes this was done.

First of all there were juridical or political statements, the exact wording of which it was important to record. The most important document of this kind is the Strasbourg Oaths, but the Montecassino declarations of witnesses and a few similar fragments belong to the same class. It should be added that there are documents dating from shortly after the year 1000, the earlier of which are written partially and others wholly in the vernacular.[81] But the Strasbourg Oaths in themselves show what would be self-evident in any case, that not only the testimony of witnesses in legal proceedings but also declarations of great political importance were couched in the vernacular; such documents required carefully prepared texts, to be preserved in the archives. The meeting in Strasbourg was not the only event of this kind.[82] Even in a much later day the kings, princes, and barons with rare exceptions (cf. above, pp. 262ff.) knew little or no Latin. These lords spoke to one another in the vernacular, and even when the document in which the results of their negotiations were recorded was in Latin, the notes taken by the *clerici* in the course of the discussions were often in the vernacular. Moreover, even bishops and other high ecclesiastics did not always carry on their business together in Latin; many would have been unable to; even at synods the proceedings do not seem to have usually been conducted in Latin.[83]

Most frequently, the vernacular writings were religious and, particularly, hagiographic. There was a widespread need for such

81. See H. Bresslau, *Handbuch der Urkundenlehre* (2nd edn.), II: 1, 381ff.; M. Raynouard, *Choix des poésies originales des Troubadours*, II, 48–72; A. Giry, *Manuel de diplomatique*, pp. 464–476. The Provençal texts are reproduced by C. Brunel, *Les Plus Anciennes Chartes en langue provençale* and in the *Supplément* published in 1952.

82. Another similar oath, which survives only in a Latin version, was sworn by Carolingian rulers at Koblenz in 860 (A. Boretius [ed.], *Capitularia regum Francorum*, II, 152–158).—The phrasing is formulaic and, as the controversy between A. Ewert ("The Strasburg Oaths") and M. Roques ("Les Serments de Strasbourg") has shown, is frequently similar to Latin formulations used in other protocols of agreement made by the three brothers.

83. Cf. Richer, *Historiarum* 4.100, on the Synod of Mouzon in 995.

literature, which was indispensable as a means of exerting direct influence on the laity. The Latin liturgy was only half intelligible to the great mass of the faithful and even to some of the clergymen who took an active part in it. In principle the sermon was the only part of the service couched in the vernacular, but it alone did not suffice for the instruction and guidance of the congregations. Furthermore, it seems likely that over a period of centuries few sermons were delivered in most of the churches and that those were very poor. Caesarius of Arles had already complained that his bishops did not wish to preach and claimed to be unable to.[84] It is hard to say how deep and lasting an effect was produced by the decisions, perhaps suggested by Caesarius, of the second Council of Vaison in 529, calling on the priests to train their successors (presbyterial schools).[85] The attempts of Charlemagne to provide for the education of the lower clergy seem to have been a total failure.[86] In the councils of the ninth century, where the problem of sermons in the vernacular was discussed for the first time, the translation of patristic homilies was recommended and collections of Latin models were compiled (that of Paulus Diaconus dates from the end of the eighth century). From the late eighth century we also have the recommendation *qui scripturas nescit saltem notissimum dicat*,[87] and from the second half of the

84. See above, pp. 89ff.
85. Marrou, *Hist. de l'éduc.*, pp. 442f. [Amer. edn., p. 336].
86. Cf. E. Lesne, *Hist. de la propriété ecclés. en France*, v: 15ff.; 414ff., and passim; also P. Mandonnet, "La Crise scolaire au début du XIIIe siècle . . ."; and, finally, some material in P. Delhaye, "L'Organisation scolaire au XIIe siècle."
87. *Hortamur vos paratos esse ad docendas plebes. Qui scripturas scit, praedicet scripturas: qui vero nescit, saltem hoc quod notissimum est plebibus dicat. . . . Nullus ergo se excusare poterit, quod non habeat linguam, unde possit aliquem aedificare* (We exhort you to be ready to teach the people. He who knows the Scriptures, let him preach the Scriptures; but he who does not know them, let him at least tell the people what he knows best. . . . Then no one will be able to shirk his duty on the pretext that he has no tongue to edify someone). From the *Capitulare ad parochiae suae sacerdotes* of Bishop Theodulf of Orléans, 797; text in Hardouin's *Acta conciliorum*, iv, col. 918.—At the beginning of the ninth century the councils (Tours and Mainz, 813) recommend the use of the vulgar tongue in preaching in order that all may understand more easily what is said (*quo facilius cuncti possint intelligere quae dicuntur*).

tenth century a few sentences from the *Synodica* of Rather of Verona (*Ad presbyteros* . . . 12) that are worth citing here: [88]

> De ministerio etiam vobis commisso vos admonere curamus, ut unusquisque vestrum, *si fieri potest*, expositionem symboli et orationis Dominicae juxta traditionem orthodoxorum penes se scriptam habeat, et eam pleniter intelligat, et inde, *si novit*, praedicando populum sibi commissum sedulo instruat. . . . Orationes missarum et canonem bene intelligat; et si non, saltem memoriter ac distincte proferre valeat.

> Furthermore, in connection with the ministry that has been entrusted to you, we urgently recommend that if possible each one of you have in his possession an explanation of the Creed and the Lord's Prayer according to the orthodox tradition, learn to understand it fully, and then, *if he is able*, conscientiously instruct his flock in sermons. . . . Let him fully understand the prayers and Canon of the Mass, or if he cannot do that, at least learn them properly by heart and say them plainly and clearly.

Throughout the Middle Ages pictorial representation played an important role in the religious education of the people. In a passage that is significant for a number of reasons,[89] Gregory the Great had already declared that painting fulfilled the same function for the ignorant as writing for those able to read; and recent investigations and discoveries seem to indicate that mural paintings, which were relatively inexpensive, were common even in the smaller churches at a much earlier date than was formerly supposed.[90] But all this was no adequate substitute for instruction and indoctrination in the mother tongue; there was the most urgent need for a popular Christian literature in the vernacular. In connection with the word "popular," I wish to repeat that in

---

88. *PL*, cxxxvi, 563f. The italics, naturally, are mine.
89. *PL*, lxxvii, 1128.
90. Cf., for instance, H. Focillon, *Peintures romanes des églises de France*. Fine reproductions are to be found in Paul H. Michel, *Romanesque Wall Paintings in France*. Most of this painting is post-Carolingian, but some is much older. Early medieval wall paintings are preserved in Lorsch, Auxerre, Saint-Denis, Müstair (Grisons), in the Reichenau, probably at Castelseprio near Milan, and elsewhere. See also E. W. Anthony, *Romanesque Frescoes*.

this context the "people" may be taken to include all those who did not read and understand Latin without difficulty, that is, nearly the whole nobility and a considerable part of the clergy; and in reference to the word "literature," that these works were intended to be heard and not read, in other words, to be sung or read aloud. None of what was written down in a vernacular language before the end of the twelfth century was addressed to readers, and even in the second half of the twelfth century readers in the vernacular were very rare; those who were sufficiently educated to read with ease read Latin. It would also be a mistake to interpret my word "popular" to mean "free from learned influences"; "popularity" of this kind did not exist in the European Middle Ages, since clerical or clerically educated scribes presided over everything that found its way into writing. Even the most profoundly popular poetry that has come down to us from the early Middle Ages includes forms of classical origin. Nevertheless the word "popular," as applied by Romantic philologists to the beginnings of medieval literature in the vernacular languages, is quite justified; since there was no class educated in the vernacular to impose its taste, the most deep-seated preoccupations of the people found expression in this literature.[91]

Thus the early Christian literature in the vernaculars, of which the surviving texts form only a small part, was intended to be read aloud to the faithful, though it is not always entirely clear by whom and on what occasions. It seems that on certain holidays, at certain services, more on a regional than on a general basis, the vulgar tongue was occasionally used in the liturgy itself; in any event vernacular compositions were read in close connection with it [92] in the church or outside it or in cloisters, by clerics and also

91. Of course, this did not prevent great lords, who were at the same time princes of the Church and able to read Latin, from taking an interest in literature written in the vulgar tongue. We know from the letters of the cathedral schoolteacher Meinhard written about 1060 (C. Erdmann and N. Fickermann, *Briefsammlungen der Zeit Heinrichs IV.*, particularly letter 73, p. 121) that this was true of Bishop Gunther of Bamberg.

92. This is attested for the so-called *Epîtres farcies*, the best known example of which is the *Epître de Stéphan* (Förster-Koschwitz, *Altfranz. Übungs-*

by jongleurs. Although most ecclesiastical pronouncements on the subject express undiminished disapproval of *mimi et ioculatores*,[93] a collaboration seems to have developed in many places between the clergy and the jongleurs[94] by the eleventh century, so much

buch [6th edn.], cols. 167–172; a Provençal text is reproduced by C. Appel, *Provenzalische Chrestomathie* [4th edn.], No. 104, pp. 145–147). See E. Martène, *De antiquis ecclesiae ritibus* (ed. novissima), I, 102; III, 35 and 39. It is also attested for songs used during the vigils; on this, see P. Alfaric, historical commentary on the *Chanson de Sainte Foy d'Agen*, II, 68ff., which is based on a passage of the *Liber miraculorum Sancte Fidis* 2.12, ed. A. Bouillet, pp. 120–122; but I am not convinced that all his conclusions are tenable. Cf. E. Martène, III, 18 (lib. IV, cap. VII, X). Alfaric also mentions a Provençal strophe which would require a precise liturgical commentary; it is found in the MS from Saint-Martial, which also contains the *Sponsus*, and which is reproduced, among others, by P. Meyer, "Anciennes Poésies religieuses," 492, where see particularly n. 3. To the same category belong the insertions in the vulgar tongue found in liturgical plays, some of which go back to the eleventh century; the most celebrated example is the *Sponsus*, written in Latin mixed with French; also the early paraliturgical plays entirely in the vulgar tongue, for example, the *Repraesentatio Adae* from Tours and the Spanish *Misterio de los reyes magos*. These texts have survived by chance, each in a single copy, and do not give the impression of being the first and earliest of their kind.—For the use of the vulgar tongue in Jewish religious services, cf. H. Peri (Pflaum), "Prayer in the Vernacular during the Middle Ages," and "Old French Poems from the Mahzor."

93. They also serve to show that certain relations had existed for a long time previously; time and again the clergy were expressly forbidden to take excessive interest in the recitations and tricks of the mimes, or, for that matter, themselves to take part in such performances.

94. Of the very extensive literature on these questions, I shall mention the two well-known books by E. Faral, *Les Jongleurs . . .* , and R. Menéndez Pidal, *Poesía juglaresca y juglares*. Pidal uses the term *clérigo ajuglarado*. Much interesting material is to be found in A. E. Schönbach in *SitzBer. Wien*, CXLII: 7 (1900), 56–89; in V. de Bartholomaeis, "Giullari Farfensi"; in A. Viscardi, *Le origini*, pp. 466ff. For the position and growth of the clergy, see P. Delhaye, "L'Organisation scolaire," particularly the first few pages and notes.—E. Faral (op. cit., p. 50), following G. Paris, believes that the oldest French form of the *Vie d'Alexis* was intended for reading in church. In any event it is attested, for a very early date, that jongleurs recited lives of saints independently of the divine service. In a *Vita sancti Ayberti*, who died in 1140 (E. Faral, op. cit., p. 277), it is related that in his youth the saint heard an actor singing about the life and conversion of St. Theobald and the harshness of his life (*audivit mimum cantando referentem vitam et conversionem sancti Theobaldi et asperitatem vitae ejus*). A similar story is that of Peter Waldo's religious awakening (circa 1173) thanks to a jongleur who one Sunday recited the *Vie d'Alexis* in public (M. Bouquet, *Recueil des historiens*, XIII, 680, *ex chronico anonymi canonici ut videtur Laudunensis*). A very old testimony is also to be found in E. du Méril, *Mélanges archéologiques et littéraires*, p. 300.—Further testimonies and opinions concerning the liturgical or paraliturgical use of the

so that the two functions were sometimes combined in one person. The reasons for this are obvious. Clerics composed hagiographic legends in the vernacular,[95] and they needed jongleurs to recite them; or sometimes they themselves recited their works and tried to learn from the jongleurs the methods by which they held the interest of their audience.[96] And soon the clergy discovered how important it was to gain an influence over the profane popular epic. Conversely, it was to the interest of the jongleurs to maintain good relations with ecclesiastical circles; literary and musical training of a type somewhat superior to their own was obtainable from no other source; Church festivals were the chief occasions for their activity, and bands of pilgrims provided an appreciative audience. In the twelfth century, with its increasing prosperity and higher cultural demands, the courtly clerics made their appearance. These curialists,[97] as they were called, performed no ecclesiastical function. We shall have more to say of them in a little while.

Only a very few of the early documents deal with profane subjects. To my knowledge, no manuscript dating from earlier than 1100 contains even fragments of any epic work in a Romance language, and the only example of lyric poetry is the presumably

---

vulgar tongue and the appearance of jongleurs in the divine service will be found in H. von Schubert, *Gesch. d. christl. Kirche im Frühmittelalter,* p. 654; R. Menéndez Pidal, p. 17 and passim; P. Browe, *Die Pflichtkommunion im Mittelalter,* pp. 93ff.; J. H. Jungmann, *Missarum sollemnia* (3rd edn.), I, 159f. and 503, n. 26 [Amer. edn., I, 143ff.; 487, n. 28].

95. For example, Tedbald of Vernon.—Wace begins his *Vie de Saint Nicolas* (ed. E. Ronsjö, p. 113) as follows:

> *A ces qui n'unt aprises*
> *Ne lur ententes n'i ont mises,*
> *Deivent li clerc mustrer la lei,*
> *Parler des seinz, dire pur chei*
> *Chescone feste est controvee.*

(To those who have not learned letters or put their mind to them, clerics should expound the law, speak of saints, and say why holidays have been established.) This may recall the etiological tradition, Ovid's *Fasti,* etc.

96. The jongleur's touch is clearly apparent in the *Chanson de Sainte Foy d'Agen* (cited above, n. 71).

97. Cf. P. Delhaye, *L'Organisation scolaire,* p. 212.

Provençal refrain of the Latin *alba* from Fleury-sur-Loire (cf. p. 278). The Hebrew manuscripts in which the above-mentioned (pp. 279–80) Mozarabic-Andalusian strophes occur are considerably later than that containing the Provençal refrain, but from the start such pieces owed their preservation to the fact that they were used within poems written in a literary language; if they were written down, it was only because they occurred in this context. These vernacular texts (or at least the types to which they belonged) must have been very old, for only traditional poetry could have been used in this way. Dámaso Alonso is right in saying: *El canto, es decir la lírica, es una inalienable necesidad del ser humano* (song, that is, lyric poetry, is an inalienable need of man).[98] I myself should go further and include epic poetry.

But why was virtually no profane poetry in the vernacular committed to writing before 1100, very little before 1150, and not so very much even in the second half of the century—although we know how many significant works were created in that period? Various answers are possible. First of all, it may be presumed that the transmission of these works remained largely oral because the poets and performers were unable to write, and it is certain that even in the twelfth century and later a good deal of poetry was composed and sung that was never written down; assuredly many of the jongleurs were still illiterate,[99] and it is unlikely that the

---

98. D. Alonso, "Cancioncillas 'de amigo' mozárabes," p. 343.—L. Spitzer in *Comparative Literature* (1952) overinterprets a few words of mine which I wrote in *Romance Philology*, IV (1950–1951), pp. 65–67. I have always been a partisan of the romantic theory of the national spirit and it seems to me that there too I said so clearly enough. Nevertheless, I believe that the theory is in need of reformulation. Cf. pp. 19ff. above.

99. In *Ioannis Cottonis Musica*, of the first half of the twelfth century, we may read (in M. Gerbert, *Scriptores ecclesiastici de musica sacra*, II, 232, col. 2, *sub finem*): *Musica una est ex septem artibus, quas liberales appellant, naturalis quidem quemadmodum et aliae; unde et ioculatores et histriones, qui prorsus sunt illiterati, dulcisonas aliquando videmus contexere cantilenas* (Music is one of the seven so-called liberal arts; like the others, it is grounded in nature; thus it comes about that we sometimes see jugglers and players who are wholly without letters compose sweet-sounding songs). But this does not necessarily mean that all the jongleurs, without exception, were illiterate. Cf. also *Musica Aribonis scholastici*, of the eleventh century, in Gerbert, II, 225.

scholae mimorum of which Léon Gautier speaks[100] existed at so
early a date. But we know from many sources, from the autobiography of Guibert of Nogent[101] for example, that educational
opportunities had considerably increased since the second half of
the eleventh century, and at roughly the same time (as Bédier
conclusively showed) the clergy must have developed an interest
in the profane epic themes. Gröber already established the likelihood that the Provençal troubadours committed their poems to
writing.[102] The *chansons de geste* contain formulas of a type characteristic for oral transmission, but by the twelfth century such
formulas had already become traditional archaisms and the genre
preserved this formulaic character to the very end. This bears
witness to the great age of the *chansons de geste* but does not imply
that they continued to be transmitted exclusively or even predominantly by word of mouth. Thus I believe that from the
beginning of the twelfth century some of the vernacular literature
that has come down to us, and from the middle of the century
a good deal of it, was committed to writing immediately but
that few copies of the texts were prepared, and these carelessly.
For they were still not intended for readers and collectors but
only for performers; some of these "stage scripts" are extant[103]
(and a few from a somewhat later period), but most of them were
destroyed by wear and tear. Moreover, the change in handwriting
from the Carolingian to the Gothic script that took place in the
second half of the twelfth century may have helped to make
these old manuscripts seem ugly and worthless to the men of later
days. And indeed, relatively few of the early scholastic manuscripts which passed from hand to hand among the teachers and
students of the twelfth century[104] have survived. But the main

100. *Les Épopées françaises* (2nd edn.), II, 173–177.
101. *PL*, CLVI, 837–962, especially 844.
102. "Die Liedersammlungen der Troubadours"; see above, p. 279 and n. 75,
    where the divergent view of F. Gennrich is also mentioned. Cf., too, for
    instance, R. Menéndez Pidal, pp. 433ff.
103. Cf. above, n. 72.
104. Cf. J. W. Thompson, *The Medieval Library*, p. 130; or K. Christ in
    Milkau-Leyh, *Handbuch der Bibliothekswissenschaft* (2nd edn.), III: 1,
    427–429.

reason is that up to 1150 very few princes or other patrons commissioned expensive and durable manuscripts of works in the vernacular languages. Such a class of patrons developed very slowly. There was still no market for manuscripts in the vernacular.

On the other hand, a market for Latin manuscripts was beginning to develop.[105] In the twelfth century the rise of scholastic and legal studies led to the organized production of manuscripts, first in such great academic centers as Paris and Bologna. The trade in manuscripts took on considerable proportions, and perhaps most important of all, lending libraries were opened. The *stationarii*, who made their appearance toward the end of the century, maintained a stock of the most important textbooks and lent them to students at fixed fees controlled by the academic authorities. These textbooks were of course in Latin. Nothing of the sort existed for vernacular literature; the number of readers was still too limited.

However, from the beginning of the twelfth century on, we hear of French and Provençal princes and other great lords who commissioned not copies of manuscripts but poems in the vernacular, or at least allowed such poems to be dedicated to them. Bishop Eustorgius of Limoges (1106–1137) commissioned a Provençal poem about the First Crusade, written by a knight from the Limousin.[106] The *Voyage de Saint Brandan* was written for

---

105. On the following, cf. G. Battelli, *Lezioni di paleografia* (2nd edn.), pp. 200ff., and E. Lesne, *Hist. de la propriété ecclés.*, v. 564; above all, H. J. Chaytor, *From Script to Print*, who stresses the great part played by oral delivery even in the later Middle Ages.—Some information also in A. Kirchhoff, *Die Handschriftenhändler des Mittelalters* (2nd edn.), e.g., pp. 61ff.

106. This occurs in the Chronicle of Geoffroy de Vigeois (*Chronica Gaufredi . . . prioris Vosiensis coenobii*), printed in P. Labbé, *Nova bibliotheca manuscriptorum librorum*, II, 279–342. Here is the text, ch. 30 (p. 296), which is interesting for many reasons: *Gregorius, cognomento Bechada de castro de Turribus, professione miles, subtilissimi ingenij vir, aliquantulum imbutus litteris, horum gesta preliorum materna, ut ita dixerim, lingua ritmo vulgari, ut populus pleniter intelligeret, ingens volumen decenter composuit; et ut vera et faceta verba proferret, duodecim annorum spacio super hoc opus operam dedit. Ne vero vilesceret propter verbum vulgare, non sine precepto episcopi Eustorgij et consilio Gauberti Normanni hoc opus agressus est* (Gregory, surnamed Bechada of Castrum de Turribus, by profession a soldier, a man of the keenest mind, endowed

one of the wives of Henry I Beauclerc, perhaps his first, Mahalt; Philippe de Thaun wrote his bestiary for the second, Aaliz de Louvain. In this period most of the patrons of vernacular poetry seem to have been ladies of the Anglo-Norman nobility. The widowed Aaliz de Louvain commissioned a long poem, now lost, on the life of King Henry from an otherwise unknown poet by the name of David; this we learn from the epilogue of the *Estoire des Engles,* written by Gaimar about 1140 for another lady of the Anglo-Norman nobility, Constance Fitz Gilbert of Lincolnshire.[107] This work, which unfortunately has come down to us in rather poor condition, contains an interesting account of how Gaimar, with the help of his patroness, procured the manuscript sources (Anglo-Saxon, French, and Latin) on which his work is based. Constance, so Gaimar tells us, had one manuscript, namely, the above-mentioned poem on the life of Henry I, copied for one mark of silver (apparently a high price) and "often reads it in her room." This is an important passage. It introduces us to Constance Fitz Gilbert, a lady who commissioned vernacular manuscripts and also read them "in her room"—as far as I know, she is the first person concerning whom such a statement is made.

Somewhat later, the Anjou-Plantagenets of England were great patrons of vernacular, that is, French literature. Wace,[108] Benoît

with a little knowledge of letters, fittingly composed a huge book of the accounts of these battles, in the commonplace rhythms of his mother tongue, as it were, in order that the people might fully understand; and with a view to publishing his story in true and elegant language, he devoted twelve years of effort to this work. And lest anyone deprecate his use of the common tongue, let it be known that this work was undertaken at the bidding of Bishop Eustorgius and on the advice of Gaubertus the Norman).—A fragment of the poem is extant. It was published by P. Meyer, in *Archives de l'Orient latin,* II (1884), *Documents,* 467–509. A sample in C. Appel, *Provenz. Chrestomathie* (4th edn.), pp. 33ff. It is composed in the style of the *chansons de geste.* Cf. G. Paris, in *Romania,* XXII (1893), 358–361.

107. Maistre Geffrei Gaimar (tr.), *Lestorie des Engles* . . . (ed. and tr. Hardy and Martin), lines 6436–6498. Cf. A. Bell, "Maistre Geffrei Gaimar."—P. A. Becker, in his masterly study of the octosyllabic couplet ("Der gepaarte Achtsilber . . ."), expresses the view that David's poem may have been a Latin work. In view of Gaimar's description, this seems to me altogether unlikely.

108. In the *Roman de Rou* (ed. H. Andresen), II: 3, 164f., Wace declares that he writes for those who have income and money, because for them books are made: *Ki unt les rentes e le argent, / Kar pur eus sunt li liure fait . . .*

de Sainte-Maure, and others whose names have been lost worked for Henry II and his wife Eleanor of Aquitaine, granddaughter of William of Poitou, whose example was followed by the French princes of the second half of the century; this is known of Eleanor's two daughters by her first marriage, Marie de Champagne and Aalis de Blois, of Philip of Flanders, and many other feudal lords and ladies in northern and southern France. They commissioned poems and rewarded and protected the poets. Whether they also commissioned manuscripts of works that were not dedicated to them, and whether any systematic provision was made for the circulation of manuscripts, it is hard to determine. To my knowledge, there is only one piece of evidence; I shall speak of it later. In all likelihood few persons at this time felt the need to own manuscripts; the court epic was intended chiefly to be read aloud, though the number of persons capable of doing so had greatly increased. There were far more courtly clerics than before; many of them wrote poems in the vernacular, and many (Chrétien de Troyes, for example) show no sign of ecclesiastical ties despite their clerical education. And there were many more educated persons than before among the feudal nobility; of this there are many indications, but I shall cite only a few. In the *Yvain* (line 5366) of Chrétien de Troyes there is a sixteen-year-old girl, the daughter of a knight, who reads a *roman* to her parents in the garden. Bernard de Ventadour and Marie de France ("Yonec") also mention women capable of reading. In *Floire et Blancheflor* there is a description of the education of highborn children, who also read Latin: *Livres lisoient paienors, u ooient parler d'amors* (They read books of the pagans in which they heard speak of love).[109] It should be borne in mind that at that time reading and writing were still usually learned in Latin. On the other hand, it should not be supposed that at the end of the twelfth century there was already a large educated society in

109. The text of MS A, ed. W. Wirtz, lines 231f. The MS B, ed. M. Pelan, mentions Ovid.—Cf. also the description of Thomas à Becket's education as a young man in Guernes de Pont-Sainte-Maxence (ed. E. Walberg), pp. 201ff.

which ability to read and write was taken for granted. On the contrary, there are numerous indications that, though such skills were more common than before, they were still regarded as unusual among the laity, even the nobles.[110] There are many intermediate stages between total illiteracy and real proficiency at reading and writing, and there is a great difference between persons who have vaguely learned their letters, who are able to write their names and jot down a few numbers, but have little occasion or desire to make further use of these skills, and those who read fluently and do so for their pleasure and instruction.

At the end of the twelfth and the beginning of the thirteenth century written records came into wide use in commercial transactions. As late as 1910 Werner Sombart was still teaching that down to the late Middle Ages commercial activity was carried on almost exclusively by word of mouth. Since then Henri Pirenne and other scholars, Italians for the most part, have proved that this applies only to the tenth and eleventh centuries and that even then there were many exceptions.[111] In the twelfth century, not to mention the thirteenth, when a highly developed bill-of-exchange and clearinghouse system had developed in the markets

110. In the *chansons de geste* the ability of laymen to read is often mentioned as something unusual. In *Anseÿs de Mes* (ed. H. J. Green), lines 714ff., a king hands a letter to his cleric to read. Further examples in H. J. Chaytor, *From Script to Print*, pp. 108–112. See also the quotation from Philippe de Harvengt, *De institutione clericorum* 110, in P. Delhaye, *L'Organisation scolaire*, p. 211, n. 2, which gives an idea of the actual state of affairs. Cf. also Hartmann von Aue in the opening lines of *Der arme Heinrich*:

> Ein ritter sô gelêret was
> daz er an den buochen las
> swaz er dar an geschriben vant

(Once there was a knight so learned that he could read what he found written in books).

111. No doubt the most important contribution to the whole problem is H. Pirenne, "L'Instruction des marchands au moyen âge." See also the studies by Sapori, Fanfani, and R. S. Lopez. A Venetian text, half Latin, half vernacular, from the middle of the twelfth century, cited in *Speculum*, xxxi (1956), 177f., by R. S. Lopez, who calls it "by far the oldest holograph commercial paper that has come down to us from the Middle Ages," was first published by Morozzo della Rocca in the *Giornale Economico della Camera di Commercio, Industria ed Agricultura di Venezia*, March, 1954.

of Flanders and Champagne, for example, this would hardly have been conceivable. Our first report of an independent municipal school intended primarily to meet the needs of the business community is from Ghent some time after 1179. The establishment of such schools led at first to conflicts and protests, but by the middle of the thirteenth century they had become a permanent institution in many localities. In Italy business transactions were probably recorded in the vulgar tongue still earlier than in the north; thirteenth-century fragments of the business records of Florentine bankers seem to suggest a long-established practice.[112]

Between 1172 and 1174 Garnier de Pont-Sainte-Maxence wrote his French poem on the life of St. Thomas of Canterbury. In it he tells how a first draft containing errors had been stolen from him and distributed, and that to his regret many wealthy persons had bought copies. These lines (141–160) are to my knowledge the oldest reference to the book trade and the market for manuscripts in the vernacular languages, for the story about Constance Fitz Gilbert gives the impression of referring to an isolated and relatively rare occurrence. It is perhaps no accident that this first indication of a manuscript trade on a relatively large scale refers to a work dealing with Thomas à Becket and his death, one of the most impressive figures and one of the most exciting events of the time.

Roughly in 1200, works began to appear which show by their form or content or both that they were intended for distribution in the form of manuscripts, for reading in small circles or even individually. In France narrative prose developed with the accounts of the Fourth Crusade by Villehardouin and Robert de Clari and with the cyclical prose versions of the Celtic *romans*. In the course of the thirteenth century there was also a marked development of didactic and allegorical literature in the vernacular. The courtly public expanded: lyrical and dramatic poetry (in forms that continued to develop up to the sixteenth century) was

112. The most recent edition of the text in E. Monaci, *Crestomazia*, pp. 36–45. Cf. also the comments (pp. 36f.) of P. Santini, the first editor of this text.

demanded for entertainment in a musical setting. Thus we might speak of several stages in the development of the courtly style, comparable to the phases of Gothic architecture. Especially in the cities of northern France and Flanders the prosperous bourgeoisie began to read, and though here too the literature of courtly entertainment was welcome, a realistic satirical literature, more bourgeois in character, also made its appearance. Such sociological distinctions, however, should be applied with caution; we must examine each of these compositions carefully to make sure that it is not more in the nature of the traditional clerical satire of the schools. At an early date the bourgeoisie participated in literary life, but in the north it was relatively late to achieve social self-awareness. In any case, the number of extant vernacular manuscripts increases appreciably when we come to the thirteenth century; a circle of wealthy connoisseurs who commissioned and collected manuscripts had gradually developed.[113]

In the thirteenth century the rise of vernacular literature was not limited to France and Provence. Similar trends may be noted throughout Romance Europe and in Germany as well. The Gallo-Roman court style exerted an important influence everywhere, but the social structure varied from region to region, and it was only in Germany that literature retained a strictly feudal, aristocratic character. In a moment we shall speak briefly of the special conditions prevailing on the Iberian peninsula and in England. The development is most striking in Italy—in Bologna and the cities of Tuscany—and it is here that we can best observe the beginnings of a modern public.

For in Italy far earlier than elsewhere political and social life was carried on in independent urban communities, and far more people were involved. The feudal aristocracy (and the courtly clerics who formed a part of it) were without cultural significance in northern and central Italy. But in Bologna, Florence, Arezzo,

113. On this, see H. J. Chaytor, *From Script to Print*, 107f., and the works (to which he refers) by M. Deanesly and L. H. Loomis, which, however, deal only with England.

and Siena, for example, there was a relatively numerous class of urban patricians, constantly changing in composition, which took a leading part in public life and were in need of education. This led to the establishment of a kind of municipal school system, which turned out a comparatively large group of educated laymen; and though ecclesiastical institutions and clerics may have played a considerable part in it, this school system was far more practical and worldly in character than in the north. If we omit medicine in the present context, the aim of this instruction, which, it goes without saying, was still carried on largely in Latin, was to prepare men to take part in public affairs, in other words, to produce lawyers and notaries, and this purpose was served by a rhetorical propaedeutics termed *ars dictaminis*, which we have mentioned above (p. 273).

Strangely enough, in view of the practical ends pursued, this Latin was excessively rich in rhetorical figures, pompous and sometimes obscure. In Italy the ornate, majestic tradition of the chancelleries of late antiquity, renewed in the Sicilian epistolary style of Frederick II and of his chancellor Pier della Vigna, had lived on and now provided a welcome medium in which to express the political ambition of the towns and parties and their sense of independence. This style exerted a great influence on the nascent vernacular literature.[114] Another influence tending in the same direction was supplied by the obscure and difficult poetic art of the Provençal poets of the *trobar clus*, which was also inspired by manneristic rhetoric. Moreover, it is among the Provençal poets that we find the first examples of political polemics in a vernacular language. Other currents at work in this early Italian poetry were the realism and mordant wit of the Italian urban population, the religious poetry of the *laude*—strongly popular in character, though

114. There are excellent investigations of this influence, the central work being that of A. Schiaffini, *Tradizione e poesia*. . . . As a summary and example of the most recent research, I have found the study by H. Wieruszowski, "Arezzo as a Center of Learning and Letters in the Thirteenth Century," very useful.

derived in part from the Biblical typological tradition—and scholasticism, with its conceptualism and technique of disputation.

Toward the end of the thirteenth century popular, manneristic, philosophical, and political influences combined to impose a new character on the courtly themes, and a new group made its appearance among those to whom literature was addressed. Although we have no very clear idea of the education practiced in the patrician families of the cities at this time—we know next to nothing even of Dante's education except for what he tells us in *Convivio* 2.13 about his studies as an adult—it is certain that many more people of this group than of any other participated in education and culture and that at a very early date they began to use the vernacular language with a new independence, seriousness, and dignity. As early as the first half of the thirteenth century we find a group of poets who were neither nobles nor ecclesiastics and who wrote in the vernacular although what they had to say was in no sense popular. More concretely than Jean de Meun, for example, these men opposed nobility of heart to nobility of birth, and, though actively engaged in political affairs, give the impression of a secret society of initiates. In their poems love mysticism and philosophical and political elements form a unity that is often hard to account for. They appear to have striven more clearly and consciously than the poets of any other country to create a sublime style in their native language.

Who made up the public for which these poets wrote? It would be difficult to answer this question directly. But we do know very well how the poets of the *dolce stil nuovo*, as Dante, the youngest among them, termed the new literary manner, pictured their prospective readers. From the very first these poets addressed an elite, the elite of the *cor gentile*, and from the very outset it was their endeavor to create a conscious elite by summoning a few and rejecting the rest. Such an attitude is already discernible in Guido Guinizelli, and in Cavalcanti it is perfectly clear. It is explicit in Dante's *Vita nuova* and in the *canzoni;* it is also formulated in the *Convivio*, where Dante takes the part of those cultivated in the vulgar tongue against the Latin scholars (1.9). This is the most significant evidence we have of a public educated in the vernacular in the early fourteenth century, and though it is very well known, I shall quote it here.

> Chè la bontà de l'animo, la quale questo servigio [the allegorical and philosophical explanation of his *canzoni*, an extremely difficult topic, which is contained in the *Convivio*] attende, è in coloro che per malvagia disusanza del mondo hanno lasciata la litteratura [Latin literature] a coloro che l'hanno fatta di donna meretrice; e questi nobili sono principi, baroni, cavalieri, e molt' altra nobile gente, non solamente maschi ma femmine, che sono molti e molte in questa lingua, volgari, e non letterati.

> For goodness of mind, which awaits this service, is to be found in them who, by the grievous disuse of the world, have abandoned literature to such as have made her a harlot instead of a lady; which noble ones are princes, barons and knights, and many other noble folk, not only men but women, of which men and women alike there are many of this tongue who command the vernacular but are not lettered. (Tr. Wicksteed.)

In Dante's other great Italian work, the *Divine Comedy*, this attitude toward the public, implicit in the *stil nuovo*, attains its full development. It is most evident in the many apostrophes to the reader that occur throughout the poem.[115] Such appeals to the reader are to be found in ancient literature in Ovid and Martial, for example. The tradition runs through the Latin literature of the Middle Ages. In the vernacular literature, as one might expect, such appeals are addressed to the listener rather than the reader. In every case the purpose is to gain the sympathy of the audience: the author wishes to command attention, to gain favor, approval, and

---

115. There are several recent studies of Dante's addresses to the reader in the *Divine Comedy:* by H. Gmelin in the *Deutsches Dante-Jahrbuch*, xxix/ xxx (1951), 130–140; by myself in *Romance Philology*, vii (1953–1954), 268–278; and by L. Spitzer in *Italica*, xxxii (1955), 143–165. Spitzer, who displays his customary mastery in his analyses, takes issue with some of my observations. But he does not seem to have entirely grasped my purpose; I hope I have succeeded this time in expressing myself more clearly.

prestige; or he may plead for indulgence or thank the audience for its benevolence. Such invocations are seldom couched in the sublime style, and they occur only rarely in works of the sublime genres. But in the Christian era a new relationship had developed between the speaker or writer and his audience: the author no longer curried favor, but admonished, preached, and instructed. This form of address to the reader has two special characteristics: in principle the author directed his criticism not at any specific vice or section of society but at the corruption of fallen man as such; and the second characteristic, which follows from the first but requires special mention, is that the writer or speaker identified himself with those he was addressing.[116] The consequence is an interweaving of accusation and self-accusation, earnestness and humility, the superiority of the teacher and brotherly love. The dialectical and Augustinian urgency in the relationship between author and audience (which is an element in what we have described as *sermo humilis*) is infrequent and nowhere highly developed in vernacular writing before Dante. There are few direct appeals to the audience in the religious documents that have come down to us, and moreover, the vernacular languages had not yet developed a truly lofty style, which is after all one component of the tone we have in mind.

After these preliminary remarks, let us examine more closely a few of Dante's invocations to the reader. We shall begin with one of the least impassioned. In the tenth canto of the *Paradiso* Dante and Beatrice are about to leave the third heaven, that of Venus, and ascend to that of the sun. The passage is introduced as follows:

> *Guardando nel suo Figlio con l'Amore*
> *che l'uno e l'altro etternalmente spira,*
> *lo primo ed ineffabile Valore,*   3
> *quanto per mente e per loco si gira,*
> *con tant' ordine fè, ch' esser non puote*
> *sanza gustar di lui chi ciò rimira.*   6

116. As so often Baudelaire at once echoes and caricatures a Christian theme: *Hypocrite lecteur, mon semblable, mon frère* . . .

Leva dunque, lettore, a l'alte rote
meco la vista, dritto a quella parte
dove l'un moto e l'altro si percuote;   9
e lì comincia a vagheggiar ne l'arte
di quel maestro che dentro a sè l'ama,
tanto che mai da lei l'occhio non parte.   12
Vedi come da indi si dirama
l'oblico cerchio che i pianeti porta,
per sodisfare al mondo che li chiama.   15
E se la strada lor non fosse torta,
molta virtù nel ciel sarebbe in vano,
e quasi ogni potenza qua giù morta;   18
e se dal dritto più o men lontano
fosse il partire, assai sarebbe manco
e giù e su de l'ordine mondano.   21
Or ti riman, lettor, sovra 'l tuo banco,
dietro pensando a ciò che si preliba,
s'esser vuoi lieto assai prima che stanco.   24
Messo t' ho innanzi: omai per te ti ciba;
chè a sè torce tutta la mia cura
quella materia ond' io son fatto scriba.   27

Gazing upon the Son with the love that both breathe forth eternally, the primal and ineffable worth made all things that circle through mind or space with so great order that no one can behold them without gaining some taste of Him.

Here, it can be seen, we are offered instruction in astronomy. God, says Dante approximately, so arranged all spiritual and spatial movement that whoever surveys this ordering inevitably partakes of something of the divine essence. He goes on:

Raise, then, reader, your eyes to the lofty spheres, to the exact spot where the one movement (the celestial equator) intersects the other (the zodiac); and there begin to look lovingly upon the art of that master who so loves the art within Him (creation) that he never averts his eyes from it. See how from there the oblique circle branches off, which bears the planets to satisfy the world that needs them. If there were not that angle between their paths, or if it were larger or smaller than it is, there would be no life on earth, and the order of the world would be imperfect. And now, reader, remain seated on your bench and meditate on what is here

foreshadowed if you wish to taste the joy of knowledge, which
is greater than all the effort you expend upon it. I have started
you on the way; now seek nourishment for yourself. For all my
strength is required by the theme whose scribe I have become.

Instruction in astronomy and the other sciences is frequent both
in ancient and medieval poetry. Here, however, it is not presented
as part of a general system of astronomy but as an isolated lesson
suggested by the point the poet happens to have reached on his
journey (lines 28–36). The lines do not impart astronomical theory
for its own sake but describe a moment in Dante's journey, a part
of the world order as experienced by the poet. Through the
invocation—*leva dunque, lettore*—the reader is drawn into the
scene, one might even say into the journey, and with Dante he
looks upon a significant part of Creation, which enables those who
contemplate it with love to gain some understanding of the divine
order of the world. Like a teacher or big brother Dante seems
to take the reader by the hand and point out the sights: Look up
as I do, there, that is the place, and begin to contemplate—see how
things are ordered, and reflect on what would happen if they
were ordered otherwise. And then, interrupting with authority,
sending his erstwhile companion in contemplation back to his
place as a reader: You stay here on your bench; I must go on;
it is up to you to derive further benefit from my teaching; I have
shown you the way.

What strikes us here is first the almost dramatic situation which
transforms a lesson, a fragment of cut-and-dried knowledge, into
an event, and then the mixture, unique in its kind, of brotherliness
and authority in Dante's attitude toward his reader. The reader is
summoned, adjured, and finally commanded to continue on in the
direction indicated. This, as we have said, is a relatively gentle
passage, although it too has a directness, a way of pulling the
reader out of the poem,[117] that probably has no parallel in earlier
literature. Moreover, for the reader thus addressed this passage

117. Cf., for example, the sudden (*Inf.* 22.118): *O tu che leggi* (O you, who
read).

is a comparatively easy one, for Dante has clearly shown him the direction his thoughts should take.

In other passages the contrast between brotherly affection and didactic authority (which taken together produce an effect of urgency) is still more incisive, the urgency still more dramatic, and the command, throwing the reader back upon his own resources, harder to follow. There are two closely related passages —*Inferno* 9.61 (*O voi ch' avete li 'ntelletti sani* . . . : O ye of sound understanding) and *Purgatorio* 8.19 (*Aguzza qui, lettor, ben li occhi al vero:* Here, reader, sharpen well thine eyes to the truth)—where Dante in an impressive situation summons the reader to right understanding. In both passages the immediate action is of great dramatic power, whereas the task imposed by Dante, namely, to understand these strange lines or to penetrate the thin veil, is by no means as simple as Dante purports to believe. In any case the critics over a period of six centuries have come to no agreement as to how the lines should be interpreted. As in all revelations of a transcendent order there remains an inexplicable, mysterious element that holds the reader in suspense. Of course he is free to feel that what is not said is ineffable and that the true mystery is incommunicable, but he is nevertheless goaded into trying to track it down and penetrate Dante's meaning.

The apostrophes to the reader are almost all couched in the imperative; none contains a plea for favor or indulgence, and nowhere does Dante speak like an author who looks upon his readers as customers. When Dante expresses his hope of favor and fame, he seems to be addressing posterity; and when he confesses his insufficiency, he is not pleading for indulgence but only explaining the superhuman dimensions of his task. From the very start he leaves no doubt as to his confidence in accomplishing as much as the powers of human expression permit; as early as the fourth canto the great poets of antiquity accept him as their peer (*Inf.* 4.102): *sesto tra cotanto senno* (the sixth amid such intellects).

But this imperative that steps out of the poem to confront the reader has its own way of enlisting sympathy; by summoning and adjuring the reader it makes him into a participant in Dante's experience, challenges him, and holds him in suspense. A claim is made upon his whole being. In the second canto of the *Paradiso* (2.1–18) there is a celebrated apostrophe which is not, as usual, addressed to the reader but metaphorically to those who desire to follow Dante's ship in a small boat over an untraveled sea. Most are rejected, only a very few may follow—those few who at the right time stretched out their necks for the bread of the angels. Of course no one who has reached this point in the *Divine Comedy* has ever allowed these words to discourage him from going on, and Dante knew it. He knew that anyone who relished the food he had to offer would not be likely to leave the table before the meal was ended.[118] What then is the purpose of this apostrophe? First, no doubt, it was a way of solemnly marking off the action of the third canto from what had gone before (similar to the address to the reader at the entrance to Purgatory: *Lettor tu vedi ben*, Reader, well thou seest, etc.; *Purg.* 9.70–72). But at the same time it really calls upon the reader to be prepared; it compels him to participate intensely; it binds Dante's followers more firmly to one another and to him, Dante, the poet, and his poem. By rejecting, Dante lures, demands, and binds; by always seeming to promise more than he says or can be said (if only the reader stretches out his neck for the bread of the angels), he binds him to his unfathomable theme.

This brings us to Dante's theme; for it is obviously his theme that justifies him in addressing the reader so authoritatively and directly. His theme is the divine order of the world, not as a theoretical system but as his immediate vision, which he communicates to others who have not had it. This lends him, the narrator, enormous authority and arouses in his readers or hearers an extreme interest in what he has to relate, especially since this vision of the divine order of the world includes in the most concrete

118. *Pensa, lettor, se quel che qui s' inizia / non procedesse* (Reflect, reader, if what is here begun were not to proceed). *Par.* 5.109f.

possible form God's judgment concerning the forms of human society and the conduct of individual human beings. The reader is not merely informed that certain sins are punished, certain vices atoned for, and certain virtues rewarded; instead, he encounters an individual, historically known man in the drama of his concrete earthly situation, which provokes fear and sympathy; he is shown concretely how this particular man is judged by divine justice; and sometimes in clear words, sometimes in intimations and prophecies, a definite social order is proclaimed as the system willed by God. The sum of political ideas, passions, and symbols that had accumulated since the investiture conflict are here digested, synthesized, and identified with a definite cause which is championed by heaven itself. Even in the Empyrean, Beatrice, Divine Wisdom, the *typos* and mirror of Christ, closer to the contemplative than to the active life, proves to be a Ghibelline.

We shall speak further on of certain of the individuals who, in the *Divine Comedy*, are subjected to divine judgment, each in his historical situation. But we shall start by discussing a somewhat older text which provides a suitable introduction. It is by Peter of Blois (Petrus Blesensis), an elegant Latinist living in the second half of the twelfth century, a cleric of high rank and an experienced, widely traveled man, thoroughly familiar with courtly culture.[119] In a short treatise on confession [120] he discusses the value of tears in true repentance and in this connection has the following to say of the courtly epic:

> Vera siquidem poenitentia non in lacrymis momentaneis, aut horaria compunctione consistit. Nulla etiam affectio pia meritoria est ad salutem, nisi ex Christi dilectione procedat. Saepe in tragoediis et aliis carminibus poetarum, in joculatorum cantilenis describitur aliquis vir prudens, decorus, fortis, amabilis et per omnia gratiosus. Recitantur

119. For a time he was secretary to King Henry II Plantagenet and, on his demise, to his widow Eleanor. See J. de Ghellinck, *L'Essor de la littérature latine au XIIe siècle*, I, 132–135.
120. *Liber de confessione sacramentali*, PL, ccvii, 1088f.

etiam pressurae vel injuriae eidem crudeliter irrogatae, sicut de Arturo et Gangano [121] et Tristanno fabulosa quaedam referunt histriones, quorum auditu concutiuntur ad compassionem audientium corda, et usque ad lacrymas compunguntur. Qui ergo de fabulae recitatione ad misericordiam commoveris, si de Domino aliquid pium legi audias, quod extorqueat tibi lacrymas, nunquid propter hoc de Dei dilectione potes dictare sententiam? [122] Qui compateris Deo, compateris et Arturo. Ideoque utrasque lacrymas pariter perdis, si non diligis Deum, si de fontibus Salvatoris,[123] spe scilicet fide et charitate, devotionis et poenitentiae lacrymas non effundis.

But true repentance does not consist in the tears of the moment or the compunction which lasts for an hour, for no pious disposition contributes to salvation unless it issues from the love of Christ. Often in tragedies and other compositions of the poets or in the songs of the jongleurs you will find descriptions of a man prudent, worthy, strong, amiable, and agreeable in all things. You will find also the account of the trials and injuries cruelly inflicted on him, just as actors repeat certain tales about Arthur and Gangano [? Gawain] and Tristan, at which the hearts of the audience are stirred with compassion and pierced to the point of tears. You therefore who are moved to pity by the recitation of romances, if tears are drawn from you by something pious that is read to you about the Lord, does that mean that you are able to make pronouncements about the love of God? You who lament over God lament also over Arthur. Therefore you are wasting your tears on both counts if you do not love God, if you do not shed tears of devotion and repentance from the fountain of the Saviour; from the fountain, namely, of faith, hope, and charity.

This is one of the few extant passages in which the reference of a learned ecclesiastic of the twelfth century to the profane

121. Very probably this refers to Gauvain [Gawain]. L. Spitzer writes to me: "Gaugain > Galgano (common name in thirteenth-century Italy) > Gangano. Gangano may be also a misreading for Gaugano."

122. The sentence in the second person is clearly addressed to the public of courtly Romans, and to a listening public at that. I am not altogether sure what *dictare sententiam* means here. Perhaps quite generally: "Do you think that on this account you are also able to have your say about the love directed to God, to have an opinion about it?"

123. An allusion to Isa. 12:3.

courtly epic is not merely conventional.[124] What older clerical statements about profane poetry have come down to us treat the subject in a purely traditional way and for the most part lump vernacular poetry together with crude buffoonery. But such an appraisal had long ceased to reflect the true situation (if it had ever done so), and we often encounter attempts on the part of the clergy to make martyrs and saints out of the heroes of the vernacular epic. In the case of the courtly epic these efforts were not very successful. Peter of Blois is one of the first, perhaps the first, who, obviously disturbed by the effect of courtly poetry on a public of developing sensibility, saw the problem of earthly tragedy (one might almost say the problem of the pleasure afforded by tragic themes) and its importance for the unity of Christian feeling. He does not refer to works that might have been regarded as base or immoral in the usual sense; in speaking of Tristan he does not even mention the immoral aspect of an adulterous love. With great acuteness and a clear eye for the essential he realizes that this is not the crux of the matter. He speaks of the sufferings and conflicts of the noble and lovable hero, which move the listener to tears. Peter of Blois condemns these tears. Tragic compassion with persons involved in earthly tragedies is not compatible with religion, which has concentrated all tragedy in the cardinal point of history, the divine sacrifice of Christ. This event has absorbed all the grief of the world; worldly grief has lost its independent value and has no further claim to tragedy in its own right. Peter of Blois does not even mention the fact—because it is obvious—that saints and martyrs as imitators of Christ are entitled to our tears. He speaks of purely earthly tragedy, which for him was unjustified. The tears shed over such tragedy are worthless, so much so that the tears shed over Christ

124. Polemic statements to the effect that more interest is taken in secular themes (Roland and Olivier are most frequently named) than in the story of Christ are fairly common from the beginning of the thirteenth century on. Examples are the prologue of the so-called *Passion des jongleurs*, cited by G. Frank, *The Medieval French Drama*, p. 125, and a quotation from a sermon in B. Hauréau, *Notices et extraits*, IV, 24f.

by those who weep for King Arthur or Tristan lose their value. *Qui compateris Deo, compateris et Arturo.*

Rather more than a hundred years later Dante wrote the *Divine Comedy*, a vision of the divine order of the universe, and into that transcendent order he gathered the entire living reality of his time, the here and now of Florence and Italy in 1300, with all its passions and tragic involvements. In so doing he carried the problem discussed by Peter of Blois to its extreme limits and did not solve it, for it is insoluble. Since the eleventh century increasing numbers of people had become keenly and deeply aware of the political conflicts of their time and their connection with religious and ecclesiastical conflicts; the idea of divine justice, more than any other, had aroused the fervor of men, and at the same time the personal passions, which previously had been little more than instinctual drives, had risen to a position of prestige and dignity. In his three realms Dante brings all these motifs together. The *Inferno* contains the most important examples: the story of Francesca and her love or of Ulysses the intrepid discoverer lose none of their dramatic power, because we know that Dante approves of their condemnation. Dante's tears and his tone, which not only expresses compassion, admiration, respect, and the fire of earthly passion but also communicates them to the reader, are not invalidated by this knowledge. Throughout the *Inferno* we encounter an earthly nobility, the just but tragic condemnation of which arouses "fear and compassion"; nowhere is earthly passion stifled by death which extinguishes all things, or even deprived of its earthly existence by an unfeeling justice which punishes sinners solely in accordance with the categories to which they belong. Quite on the contrary, men stand before us in all their historical involvements; many tears are shed for others than Christ; the poet expresses much admiration (even for Brutus in the jaws of Lucifer) and veneration—both at variance with God's judgment. Dante and Virgil and the reader are not always in agreement with the line from the *Inferno* (20.28): *Qui vive la pietà quand' è ben morta* (Here pity lives when it is quite dead).

But this does not apply to the *Inferno* alone. Wherever it is possible, Dante brings out the earthly drama: the eternal, irrevocable judgment helps him to develop earthly tensions in all their existential power. Many of those atoning for their sins in Purgatory—one need only think of Oderisi of Gubbio or Pia de' Tolomei—move the reader because of their lot on earth; Sordello's greeting of Virgil, the recognition scene between Dante and Forese Donati, and many other passages in the *Purgatorio* are charged with human emotion, and their situation in the divinely ordered world makes them all the more moving. Virgil too is tragic, we may weep for him too,[125] although God has condemned him justly. Even in many of the blessed, the earthly drama is still discernible; Dante's political partisanship is expressed more forcefully than ever in the higher regions extending from the earthly paradise (end of *Purg.*) to the *primum mobile* (*Par.* 27–30). Here, to be sure, it is represented as partisanship for God's cause; but does God's cause require such militant, insatiable,[126] vituperative partisanship in the very spheres of heaven? Is such *buon zelo* compatible with the peace and beatitude of the *visio Dei?* Is it compatible with the unity of Christian thought to represent an infringement on the prerogatives of the empire as a second Fall (*Purg.* 33.55–57) or to compare the darkening of the heavens during Peter's lamentations over the corruption of the papacy with the eclipse of the sun when Christ was crucified (*Par.* 27.35–36)? Even in Dante's paradise the passions are alive; it is a world of men, unfinished and mirroring the dramatic conflicts of an unfinished earthly history.

But this direct association of historical existence with the kingdom of God is also a Christian heritage: from the outset Christianity was never a mere doctrine or myth but was deeply involved in historical existence. This is a significant, if not the most

---

125. Not only in the same sense as when Dante weeps over him, when Virgil leaves him and Beatrice addresses him by name. The main passage for the tragic situation of Virgil is *Purg.* 3, particularly line 45: *e più non disse, e rimase turbato* (and he said no more and remained troubled).

126. Cf. especially *Par.* 27.55–60.

significant, aspect of its specific character. On the one hand Christ became flesh in a definite historical situation, an earthly here and now, in which he participated by his acts and his suffering—while on the other hand, by thus atoning for Adam's guilt, he restored man's share in the kingdom of God, which Adam had lost. Adam in paradise can hardly be regarded as historical man; rather, history was a consequence of the Fall. But Christ, the second Adam, did not redeem men from history, or at least he has not yet done so; the process has not been as swift as the first generations of believers expected. In terms of the human life-span the time was not short, as Paul (I Cor. 7:29ff.) had predicted, and ultimately Christians found themselves unable to use this world "as though they used it not." Christian society had to adjust itself to a historical, unfinished, provisional world; even now there was no other. But it was no longer so easy to look upon earthly concerns with the indifference that had been so dear to the philosophers of late antiquity, or even to strive for their equanimity.

The world, *saeculum*, was regarded as evil or as a testing ground, or in any case as a place of suffering and struggle (for even contemplation was always a contemplation of the Incarnation and the Passion, hence of tragic earthly events). This view of the world gave deeper urgency to all earthly happenings, conflicts, and passions, and gave rise to a contradiction which it became increasingly difficult to bridge. The longer the Second Coming was delayed, the more urgent it became to act in behalf of God's cause on earth. Increasing ethical and political awareness brought forth men and movements who were neither able nor willing to reconcile themselves with the historical world as it was because it presented too glaring a contrast to Christian teachings and the kingdom of God. They planned utopian, chiliastic reforms on a religious and ethical foundation, such as the ancients —in Europe, at least—could never have dreamed of; they demanded a realm of peace and justice on earth, the new and perfect millennium, which alone could usher in the Second Coming of Christ.

But God's will on earth was not revealed; God did not tell His militants how to participate in or direct earthly affairs. Once the law was replaced by divine grace, by virtue of the Incarnation, He merely made it clear that during the brief interval preceding Christ's return, the faithful should submit to the powers that govern this world. The kingdom of God on earth, seen as a just earthly order, became an object of human conflict, increasing in intensity as the participants become more and more convinced of the truth of their own interpretation of God's will. The contestants made use of Biblical exegesis in order to represent their own convictions as the will of God.

From the standpoint of unity and power of expression, Dante's passionate will and genius made him the summit and turning point in this dialectical process. There had already been plenty of controversy, especially since the eleventh century, and we have shown how this conflict gave rise to the first ideas since antiquity about sovereignty and the division of power. Many had endeavored in the course of this debate to represent their own ideas as the will of God by citing the authority of ambiguous authors. But Dante was the first and last to undertake on the basis of his own historical existence a total view of the universe with the political life of man on earth as its arena and center. In the process he was led—he could not have done otherwise—to project his own experience and his own will into the kingdom of God, and to represent his own will as God's will. When I say "his own will," I am aware of course that Dante derived most of his political beliefs from tradition and the discussions of his own time. But the remainder—namely, his choice and combination and treatment of his themes, the direction and purpose he pursued in his elaboration of them, and his individual view of the relative value of human actions—was original with him and crucial. All this was molded by his own experience and his powerful personality. The *parte per se stesso*, taken not only in the limited political sense but as the over-all view of human actions that he had acquired in his own here and now, is represented as the party of God; the most radical subjectivity, rooted in the conviction that it is inspired by God's special grace and in an incomparable power of expression, is represented as the law of the world.

It is strange, perhaps, and yet quite in keeping with the dialectic according to which each new development springs from a conflict of opposites, that this triumph of autonomous humanity and of a specifically human will should in all sincerity have represented itself as a vision of the divine order of the world, and that the man who stepped forward as judge and prophet of the earthly world (very learned, though a layman, Villani says of him) should have introduced himself as a profoundly humble sinner who had escaped eternal damnation only by a special act of grace: in short, that this extreme subjectivity, or at least a subjectivity hitherto unequaled in its vast range and sharpness of expression, had sprung from a devoted Imitation of Christ and an endeavor to record faithfully what is enacted (not only decided, but actually carried out) in the kingdom of God. Many Christian visionaries have proclaimed God's will, but they have neither given so comprehensive a view of it, taking in the whole universe, nor given so concrete a version of divine judgment, applied so closely to concrete historical happenings. They contented themselves with much more general statements and so left God much greater freedom of action. The only freedom of action that Dante leaves God on earth applies to particulars of the political future. Dante, to be sure, claims to have learned these too, but here his expression is purposely enigmatic and opaque. However, the general trend of the future (of the earthly future, that is) is laid down as imperial and chiliastic.

These remarks about his theme, it seems to me, show the urgency of Dante's need for expression and explain why he was so intent on influencing the reader and drawing him into the magic circle of his vision. This preoccupation is expressed in the appeals to the reader, but not in them alone; we have chosen the apostrophes as examples of immediacy, urgency, and dramatic force because they can be conveniently singled out. The essential is the theme itself and the fact that Dante treated it as he did. For Dante does not relate the destinies of figures out of the remote past, like Roland or Tristan in the epic, who, touching and interesting as they may be, are far removed from the reader or listener and leave him uninvolved. His theme is the quintessence of the concrete, earthly here and now, as it appears to the eye of God. It concerns every single man just as it concerns Dante. And in this connection it becomes clear why a work such as the *Divine Comedy* could not be written in Latin. Here we might repeat a certain amount of what Dante says in the passage from the *Convivio*, a part of which we have quoted above (1.9.2): for example, *non avrebbe lo latino così servito a molti* (there are many for whom Latin would not have served); far more numerous were those whom he could address in Italian, and he could speak with far greater directness in Italian to those who understood Latin a little, or who understood it quite well after a moment's reflection, but who did not understand it immediately, completely, and without difficulty. But his essential motivation was *lo naturale amore de la propria loquela* (the natural love of my own tongue; *Conv.* 1.10.5); for assuredly this *pronta liberalità* (zealous liberality) stemmed also from his knowledge, born of experience, that for his purposes he could say much more in his *volgare* than in Latin —or rather, in one of the various Latins at his disposal, which differed from one another in vocabulary, syntax, rhetorical style, and prosody. Dante needed all these forms, the *artes dictandi* of the chancelleries, the erudite figures of the allegorists, the sharp conceptual structure of the philosophical schools, the satire of the strolling scholars, the charming rhymes of the typological hymns, and the pious rhetoric of Franciscan and Cistercian mysticism. But he needed them all together, fused into one. Certain of these elements had penetrated the vernacular even before the *Divine Comedy*. The *volgare* also offered possibilities of its own, the *laude*, the realistic anecdotes, and the beginning of a lofty tone in the *stil nuovo:* this was an area of unrealized potentiality; it was possible to pour in and fuse elements which in Latin were separated

it proved to be one spirit. For its innermost essence and unique, most cherished possession was the profoundly human story of the Incarnation and Passion of Christ; and this story was framed in by many other stories, some of which prefigured it, while others imitated and confirmed it. By virtue of these stories, which expressed a single view of cosmic and human happening, Christianity had become in Europe a common possession; this process had taken place in the popular consciousness and ultimately in the popular tongues. Through the living fabric of the vernacular languages, to which so many had contributed down through the ages, this Christian, European spirit had gained a new immediacy and warmth, and in many cases it had even succeeded in drawing the non-Christian traditions of the vernacular languages, the heroic legends and other folk elements, into its sphere. But through the gradual rise of the vernacular languages other spiritual currents, more difficult to assimilate or alarming once assimilated, became ripe for expression. There were political currents which for the most part made their appearance in the form of Christian heresies, and there was also a tendency to free the human emotions from the religious frame, to consider the human tragedy as an absolute, independent of Christ's Passion. This latter tendency cropped up in the courtly culture which, beginning at the end of the twelfth century, spread among the upper classes in Europe. There were indeed attempts at compromise, attempts to interpret chivalric love and the ahistorical quest for adventures in a Christian light; but even so, we encounter a hitherto unknown subjectivism, a tendency to endow the human passions with an unprecedented dignity and freedom. However, the vernacular culture of the courts was very limited in scope; even in the thirteenth century it lived, as it were, on the fringe of European life. It was remote from living reality, it had no discernible ties with the schools or with political movements. Its lyric poetry was shackled by conventional themes and a playful rhetoric based on rhymes and empty concepts, so that the great and tragic were immersed in obscure artifice and could not take on concrete form;

with its fairy-tale settings and the ahistorical unreality of its episodes, the courtly epic declined responsibility for the human implications of its themes.

In the *Divine Comedy* Dante found a place in the divine order
for the historical here and now of human destinies and passions;
his vision was at once timely and all-encompassing. In his Italian
poem, which merged all the forms of the Latin heritage, he imposed order upon the world but at the same time breathed life
into it. In so doing, he made Italian (not as such but as one of
the vernacular languages) into the language of the European spirit.
And by letting earthly destinies and earthly passions, with all their
tragic conflicts, live on within the divine order, he focused attention on man in a new way. Thus he inaugurated modern European literature (or perhaps it would be more accurate to say the
modern self-portrayal of man) and began to build up a public
that would be receptive to this literature.

A further example may serve to clarify my meaning. In the
eighth heaven, the heaven of fixed stars (*Par.* 24), Dante is exam-
ined by the Apostle Peter on the subject of Faith, and he replies
to the Apostle's satisfaction. The light in which Peter's soul appears circles three times round Dante's head, blessing him and, as
it were, crowning him. In the ensuing twenty-fifth canto Dante
is tested on Hope by the Apostle James. Between the two passages the following lines are intercalated. They form the beginning of the twenty-fifth canto:

> Se mai continga che 'l poema sacro
> al quale ha posto mano e cielo e terra,
> sì che m' ha fatto per più anni macro,   3
> vinca la crudeltà che fuor mi serra
> del bello ovile ov' io dormi' agnello,
> nimico ai lupi che li danno guerra;   6
> con altra voce omai, con altro vello
> ritornerò poeta; et in sul fonte
> del mio battesmo prenderò 'l cappello;   9
> però che ne la fede, che fa conte
> l'anime a Dio, quivi intra' io, e poi
> Pietro per lei sì mi girò la fronte.

If it should ever happen that the sacred poem to which both
heaven and earth have so set hand that it has made me lean for
many years, should overcome the cruelty which bars me from
the fair sheepfold, where a lamb I slept, foe to the wolves that
give it war, then with other voice, with other fleece, a Poet will
I return, and at the font of my baptism will I take the crown;
because there I entered into the Faith which makes the souls
known to God; and afterward Peter, for its sake, thus encircled
my brow.

This is not an address to the reader, but it too is an impassioned
interruption of the action, in which the author steps out of his
poem. In the midst of the Elysian fields, not far from the vision
of God, Dante's earthly destiny, his human existence, stands out
in its concrete actuality; even here he does not hesitate to represent it as meaningful, and it cannot be denied that the tragic tension of his existence takes on, by virtue of the place where it is
expressed, a depth and dignity which no other place would be
likely to confer on it. And what is expressed? The yearning of
the exile, condemned to eat the bread of strangers, to return home
with honor, thanks to his poem. This work, which, like an exercise in ascetic penance, has made him lean for many years, is a
sacro poema, a sacred poem, and yet he hopes it will bring him
fame both among his contemporaries and among the men of a
later day, overcome the cruelty of the wolves, his political enemies, and enable him to return and to receive the poet's crown
in the place where he was baptized, *mio bel San Giovanni;* there
he was received into the faith, for the sake of which Peter "encircled" his brow. No ancient poet could have tied the tragic fate
of a hero living here and now so closely to the divine order, for
the godhead of the ancients had not, like Christ, become flesh in
the midst of men's historical existence. On the other hand, no
Christian poet before Dante had so concretely represented the
existence of an individual man (except for the saints who followed in Christ's footsteps) as tragic and worthy of interest within
the divine order.

Here it must be asked: can Dante's participation in the political
struggles of his day, his hate-love for the Florentines, his hope of

the poet's crown (even for a *sacro poema*), be identified with the Imitation of Christ? Can the tears shed for Dante (or for others of his characters) in the poem be equated, in the sense spoken of by Peter of Blois, with tears shed for God? I raise the question but I do not answer it. Neither yes nor no would be a satisfactory answer, and both would lead to misunderstandings. There is no need to answer; it suffices to know that the question can be asked. Through the triumph of Christianity interest in the acts and sufferings of men had come to be concentrated upon the acts and sufferings of one man, who was God incarnate. Nothing seemed worthy of extreme interest except these acts and sufferings and the happenings which prefigured them or the deeds of those who imitated them. Thanks to the concrete character of this story, every particular of which stands for the whole and which carries meaning for every single human being, it had aroused deeper and more universal concern than any purely human story could have done. In intention this concern was "religious" and not literary or in any sense artistic, but here such a distinction has no relevance. Beyond a doubt the story of Christ, with all its implications, had been for Europeans a school of human sympathy and spontaneous feeling, portrayal, and expression, and this development becomes more marked with the emergence of the vernacular languages as literary instruments. At the same time there arose an upper class, which began to achieve self-awareness. The members of this class now took an interest in human destinies and passions not exactly connected with the life of Christ and tried to express them in the vernacular tongues. Thanks to the great movement that had gripped Europe since the days of Cluny and the investiture conflict, political thinking had begun to revive and achieve a certain autonomy, at least to the extent that political thinkers now concerned themselves more intensely and consciously than before with a satisfactory or eschatologically ideal order of earthly existence. Dante incorporated all these earthly realities and strivings for earthly autonomy into his picture of the Christian universe, and he endowed them not only with fervor and tragic depth but above all with the central position implied by their integration into the Christian cosmos. By so doing, he wrote the first and, for a long time to come, the only work of lofty style in a vernacular language, treating of important and tragic human affairs. He organized his poem according to the scholastic scheme, which strikes us as specifically medieval; the whole world, for all its superabundant color and richness, is neatly divided into numerous compartments; everything is in its proper place, and every particular is considered in terms of the whole. Through this total world there journeys a penitent pilgrim whose destiny encompasses the destinies of all others, a man of the here and now who at the same time stands for all men but who has nevertheless built up this world, which is a poem, in accordance with his own will.

If Dante is regarded as a "link in a chain of development," the chain breaks off with him. It can indeed be shown how all the previous currents and voices that had emerged in Christian literature since the eleventh century converged and culminated in him. But no one carried on his work as a whole. No one was able to continue or to extend his total cosmic and historical edifice, for it collapsed; Dante's view of history lost its actuality even sooner than did his cosmology. Nothing similar took the place of Dante's world order, and for this reason no poet of the earthly world has been able to address the reader with like authority as one who has attained knowledge by divine grace. More than two centuries passed before anyone took the individual earthly man as seriously and as tragically as Dante had done—and then, of course, the divine judgment which, by giving this tragedy its place in the cosmos, made it real and eternal, was lacking; later, the individual man was alone, his tragedy ended with his life.

But the elements of Dante's work, his manner of handling language and of dealing with things in language, exerted an influence, first in Italy and gradually, through the Italian literature of the fourteenth century, elsewhere as well.

With Dante Italy registered an enormous advance from the

brittle, thin, occasionally didactic style, not yet sure of its subject matter and therefore obscure, which characterized the later
Provençal poets and the *stil nuovo*, and developed a full-bodied
literary art in firm command of its themes and expressing them
forcefully. But for the present, this development was limited to
Italy. The Italians learned to control the devices of rhetoric and
gradually to rid them of their coldness and obtrusive pedantry.
In this respect Petrarch's Italian poetry is markedly superior even
to Dante's, for a feeling for the limits of expressibility had become second nature to Petrarch and accounts in good part for his
formal clarity, while Dante had to struggle for these acquisitions
and had far greater difficulty in maintaining them in the face of
his far greater and more profound undertaking. With Petrarch
lyrical subjectivism achieved perfection for the first time since
antiquity, not impaired but, quite on the contrary, enriched by
the motif of Christian anguish that always accompanies it. For it
was this motif that gave lyrical subjectivism its dialectical character and the poignancy of its emotional appeal.

Through Dante's influence Italian and Latin moved closer together, and this rapprochement between Latin and the vernacular
was also at first a purely Italian development. It seems to me that
the word *rapprochement* provides the best means of summing up
the complicated relations between the two languages in Italy during the two centuries after Dante's death: both languages strove
to become the organ of "culture," or of humanism. Through
Dante's influence Italian had risen above the level of a second-
rank literary language, useful only for entertainment and vulgari-
zation. Dante had first addressed himself to a public which, although not mastering Latin, was very much in need of and receptive to solid spiritual food, the στερεὰ τροφή of the Epistle to
the Hebrews—in short, a "cultivated" elite. Through his influence,
though only after him, a clear dividing line was drawn between
erudition and cultivation. This, it seems to me, was the central
achievement of Italian humanism and the essence of its influence
on the rest of Europe. Thanks to early humanism and especially

to Petrarch, Latin ceased on the one hand to be a specialized language of the schools. Though still restricted to a minority of the elite, it tended toward the far more universal scope which the classical literary languages had enjoyed in their prime. It became an organ of human self-cultivation, of a well-rounded individual culture, the organ of those who possessed the intelligence and leisure for such self-cultivation. Accordingly, there is every justification for regarding this period, the *quattrocento*, as the beginning of humanism, for it was then that Ciceronian classicism became a way of life. With Petrarch and Boccaccio, on the other hand, something very similar was achieved for the Italian language; pedantry and academic rhetoric, still present in Dante's Italian, disappeared, making way for a cultivated Italian rich in shadings. The conflict between Latin and Italian finally gave rise to the compromise of vernacular humanism, first prefigured by Dante. The idea of vernacular humanism, that is, the idea of using the ancient languages as models and so making the vernacular languages into worthy vehicles for literature and culture, finally gained acceptance outside of Italy, first of all in France. Out of it grew the academic classicism of the Renaissance, the movement through which the literary languages of the various European peoples finally shook off Latin and became standardized. This idea of vernacular humanism also gave rise to cultivated society, the modern public. Beyond a doubt far more children learned Latin from the early sixteenth century on than in Dante's time, and there was no need to write Italian for them on the ground that they did not know Latin. Yet the overwhelming majority of these children became in later life *volgari e non letterati*—which I shall translate here, for my own purposes, as "cultivated but not learned." They studied Latin not for erudite (scholastic or even philological) ends but as the foundation for self-cultivation or culture in the sense of an imitation of antiquity, and they expressed their culture in their mother tongue; Montaigne, who had learned Latin before he learned French, was an extreme—because relatively early—example, but his case is quite characteristic. But we have got ahead of ourselves and must go back to the fourteenth century.

As we have said, the advance from courtly poetry to the lofty style in the early fourteenth century was a peculiarly Italian development; it was made possible by Dante's concern with the life of his time and his incorporation of it into the temporal-atemporal Christian structure of history. But in the course of the fourteenth century men in other countries as well were discovering the living world, beginning to take an interest in the daily life around them, and to write of these matters without schematic didacticism. For it was in the realm of contemporary reality that the vernacular most readily achieved independence of Latin. In this domain its vocabulary was superior; its material was at hand, and all that was needed was sufficient self-confidence to make use of this material for literary purposes. France had made a beginning as early as the twelfth century, especially in the versified farces; but the richest and most significant fruits of this "realism" made their appearance in the fourteenth century in those languages which had hitherto, each for a different reason, been rather on the fringe of the development.

From the very start the Iberian peninsula was in a special situation, for there the Romance popular idioms had to contend not with the unchallenged domination of Latin but with several languages which served both for spoken and written expression and had developed in a variety of ways. In Andalusia, with its elegant and colorful popular culture, Mozarabic Spanish came into contact with other languages; the Arabs and Jews adopted it, employing it, for purposes of entertainment, in the poetic forms of their own languages, and it seems likely that Romance poetry was nowhere committed to writing so soon as here, within the frame of the Arabic and Hebrew *muwassahas*. In the Spanish Middle Ages Latin was not the uncontested written language; the Carolingian renaissance left only feeble traces, and despite the great importance of Spain for the transmission of Aristotelianism, a Latin scholasticism was late to develop. With the increase of

French political influence in the course of the Reconquest, Latin began indeed to play a more influential role, but at the same time French and Provençal poetic forms made their way into various parts of the peninsula. Here they had to adapt themselves to different social circumstances. There was no courtly culture after the French and Provençal pattern, because the high feudal nobility had scarcely come into existence. The *chanson de geste* underwent the radical transformation known to us from the *Cantar de mio Cid*. Here there is no legendary transfiguration or clownish burlesque of a nebulous figure from the remote past; the narrative is much less stylized. The subject is a hero who had died only recently, and he is shown in an almost contemporary world. Spanish began to emerge as an independent literary language in the fourteenth century, and the most significant work in this period of development is *El Libro de buen amor* by Juan Ruiz, archpriest of Hita, which seems to have been written somewhat later than the *Divine Comedy*.

This archpriest was a leisurely narrator, rich in perception and irony, a master of word and rhyme, which lend themselves freely to his ironic attitude. His main concern is the human passions, particularly his own. (Whether they are the passions of the archpriest himself or of the person who says "I" in the poem is of no importance; he fails to make this clear, and that is the poet's privilege.) Though deploring the passions, for after all he is a moralist and a priest, he lives in them and with them. He invents little, borrowing the main themes of his love stories as well as his moralistic fables from the Latin and French traditions. He also uses the technique of amplification (i.e., variations on a theme) frequent with the clerical satirists of the Middle Ages. But the situation he describes and the richness of his observation are strikingly original. The central figure is a priest whose passions drive him continually to women; women are his whole life; they involve him in many adventures, most of them rather grotesque and seldom turning out as he wished. Following famous literary models, but in his own way, he makes use of a procuress. The main narrative is written in the so-called *cuaderna via* or mono-rhymed quatrain (*copla*) of long lines with a marked caesura. At several climaxes, lively, grotesquely sensual popular songs (*serranillas*) are introduced; there are also religious songs. On the whole the archpriest is a mixture, such as can be found much earlier in the Middle Ages, of the cleric and the jongleur. Typical of this mixture are his Christian themes, his moralizing, his sensuality, and his verve. Moreover, like Rather of Verona the archpriest is something of a clown. This mixture of the cleric and the jongleur seems perfectly natural, for both were engaged in literary activity and it was their common trade to speak to the hearts of men. And yet between the two components there is a tension which can often take on a tragic quality. But in a country characterized by all manner of mixtures, a country where he, a priest, could say that he had written many songs for Jews and Moors, many love songs, and more of the same nature (copla 1513), Juan Ruiz expresses the irony inherent in such a mixture far more than the tragedy and the tension. What I have in mind is not so much a conscious irony of the poet, though that too is plentiful, as a kind of objective irony implicit in the candid, untroubled coexistence of the most incompatible things. Let us consider, for example, the invective against death brought on by the sudden loss (1520) of Trotaconventos, the procuress. The passage begins (1520–43) with a collection of moralistic commonplaces about the bitterness of death: it carries away all alike, it is inexorable, it comes unheralded, it is hated by all, the dying and dead are forsaken, they no longer have any friends, the rich man no longer has any profit from his wealth—therefore do good today, tomorrow it may be too late (traditional association with the *cras* of the raven who feeds on corpses); it is vain to heap up riches; when you are dying or dead, your heirs care nothing for you, all they want is your money (1541, *Ellos lievan el algo, el alma leyva Satán:* They make off with the goods, Satan makes off with the soul). After this first part, devoted entirely to moralistic generalities, there is a transition in which death is equated with sin (1544–

64): death is all-powerful, it destroys all things (here there are four coplas consisting of antithetical isocola),[127] it belongs in hell, which was made for it; if men lived eternally (without sin), they would not fear it. "Death, you have depopulated the earth and even heaven (by the revolt of the angels). You have even slain the Lord who created you. But that was your undoing. You saw only his human nature, which led you astray, not His divine nature, which vanquished you." This too is a traditional theme and it is treated in a traditional way: Christ's descent into hell, the liberation of the righteous of the Old Covenant, and all the rhetorical figures that have always been used in this connection (e.g., 1559, *Diónos vyda moriendo al que tú muerte diste:* He to whom you gave death gave us life by dying).

And yet this second part, Christ's victory over death (here perhaps for the first time expressed in Spanish) is very moving and powerful. And surprising as it may be to the unprepared modern reader, the ensuing third part (1565–78) is also moving and powerful. It begins with a transition: Christ has freed the righteous, but all the rest have been engulfed by death and hell. "God, shield us from dread death, I commend myself to thee, there is no other salvation; death, what do you want of me? Where is my good old woman? You have killed her. Christ redeemed her with his sacred blood, and for its sake he forgave her. Ah, my faithful Trotaconventos, where have they taken you? No one can say for sure. Those who have taken your path bring back no news. Surely you are with the martyrs in paradise." And in the following coplas he praises the loyalty and cleverness of the old procuress (1571, *que más leal trotera nunca fué en memoria:* a more loyal bawd there never was within memory of man; 1573 and 1574 are still more shocking) and laments his grievous loss. The whole ends with an epitaph which the archpriest has composed for her.

It seems to me that this passage has often been overinterpreted

127. For instance, strophe 1549: *Despreçias loçanía, el oro escureçes, / Desfases la fechura, alegría entristeçes . . .* (If you despise the glamor of youth, you miss the gold. / If you destroy what is made, you sadden joy . . .).

in one way or another. Actually there is nothing to interpret, it must merely be taken for what it is. It is certainly a mistake to regard the lament for Trotaconventos as a conscious blasphemy, a mockery of Christianity. To regard it as a satirical attack on a corrupt priest and a procuress strikes me as equally unjustified. This would imply that the third part of our passage had been written in a different spirit from the first two parts, a supposition not borne out by the text itself, which shows perfect unity of movement. Moreover there is nothing the least bit blasphemous about hoping that God will forgive a sinner, particularly one who has sinned out of covetousness and not out of malice and rebellion. What this passage expresses is the irony implicit in things themselves. The archpriest is sincerely afraid of death, he sincerely hopes for redemption through Christ, he is sincerely shaken by the sudden death of the poor old woman, who was loyally devoted and, what with his intense lusts, indispensable to him. He is really stricken with grief and perfectly sincere both in his admiration for her skill and in his hope that God will have mercy on her soul.

The need to dominate life and to impose an order upon it, which had led Dante to his sublime style,[128] is not to be found in the archpriest of Hita, but his language is vibrant with reality and reacts with precision to innumerable shadings of experience and feeling; correspondingly, his public may be pictured not as humanistic and cultured but as socially heterogeneous, sharp-witted, and intelligent.

A comparable alertness and racy wit are to be found in the fourteenth century in the literature of another country on the fringe of Europe, namely, England; and here too they permit inferences as to the character and composition of the public. The early development of Anglo-Saxon culture (see pp. 267 ff.) had been interrupted by the superimposition of a new ruling class. But soon

128. Cf. Dante's sonnet "Tanto gentile" (*Vita nuova*, fifteenth sonnet) and similar poems in the new style with the figure of Doña Endrina in the *Libro de Buen Amor*, strophes 653f.

it became clear that the language of the thin Norman upper crust would not in the long run be the literary language of the country. In the course of the fourteenth century Anglo-Saxon, whose literary tradition had never entirely died out and which had meanwhile developed into Middle English, attained a great literary flowering and with it the beginnings of standardization. And despite the medieval heritage common to all western Europe, despite the ancient, Christian, and French influences reflected in its themes, ideas, and forms of expression, a strong individuality and popular character are apparent from the first, owing perhaps to the fact that English had to assert itself not so much against Latin as against the French of the courts. Another factor is the political, religious, and economic awakening of the masses, which, if it did not occur earlier than elsewhere, was more thoroughgoing. Nowhere else during the Middle Ages are profound and varied social currents described with so much concrete truth, so much sympathy and humor as in fourteenth-century England. I am thinking of course of Chaucer's *Canterbury Tales*, which equal the *Decameron* in color and are superior to the Italian work as a living picture of the times. The essential difference may be gathered from a comparison of the frames: Chaucer's narrators are pilgrims from all walks of life; they are sharply characterized, and the relations between them are vividly set forth. Thus the frame alone supplies a lively picture of the social scene in England. Boccaccio's narrators are a group of fashionable and cultivated young people who have fled to a country villa from the plague; they all belong to the same upper class of society and are only dimly characterized. Thus the *Decameron* conveys the atmosphere of a homogeneous culture, and its vulgar elements are absorbed into this cultivated medium. Medieval object lessons and compilations are almost entirely absent, and there is never any awkwardness or rupture of style. Chaucer, on the other hand, does not hesitate to employ as narrators persons such as Boccaccio uses only as characters *in* his stories. In thus representing much lower social classes as endowed with awareness and judgment,

That laborers and lowe folke · taketh of her maistres
It is no manere Mede · but a mesurable hire ·
In marchandise is no mede · I may it wel a-vowe;
It is a permutacioun apertly · a penyworth for an othre ·
Ac reddestow neuere Regum · *þow recrayed Mede,*
Whi þe veniaunce fel · on Saul and on his children? . . .

Priests and parsons who desire pleasure; who take mede (which here means illicit profit) and money for the masses they sing, they took their mede here, as Matthew teaches us: Amen, amen, they have their reward (Matt. 6). What workmen and humble folk take from their masters (i.e., probably, employers) is no mede but a measurable wage; in commercial dealings there is no mede, I assure you of that; it is clearly a giving and taking, one pennyworth for another. Have you never read in the Book of Kings (O accursed mede) why retribution fell upon Saul and his children? . . .[129]

The practical concreteness of these social preachings is as characteristic as their invocation of the Bible. The alliteration which survived down to the fourteenth century, or which, rather, was revived in that century, is also significant. The Germanic element with its strong Biblical imprint (it should be recalled that Aldhelm and Bede were the first to recommend the Bible as a model of style) provided a foundation for and counterweight to Italian and vernacular humanist currents.

Turning finally to the German-speaking countries, we encounter a confusing spectacle. Nowhere had the possibility, as well as the difficulty, of creating a native literary language been recognized so early as in Germany (by Otfried of Weissenburg), and in the Hohenstaufen period chivalric culture had molded a poetic language (High German in the main, though no one dialect had achieved unquestioned dominance). But this brief flowering was followed by a general collapse. There was no political and intellectual rallying point, exerting a natural attraction, where the national literary language might quickly have developed into a living reality. There was nothing comparable to Florence, Castile,

129. There follows the tale of Saul and Agag the king of the Amalekites, I Sam. 15.

the Ile de France, or London. From the flowering of the *Minnesang* during the first half of the thirteenth century to the second half of the eighteenth century there was no nationally recognized literary language and no German public homogeneous in its social composition, tastes, and forms of expression. By far the strongest impulse experienced by the German public at large during this long lapse of time was the Reformation, especially Luther in his early period and the first parts of his Bible translation. The impact on the German mind and language was enormous, but because of the confessional schism provoked by Luther, the unifying power of his German made itself felt only slowly and indirectly. German literature had no late Middle Ages, no Renaissance, and no Baroque. In each of these periods there were impressive literary figures but no writers of wide scope, capable of representing the whole nation: there was nothing comparable to the Italian development from Dante to Tasso, to Spanish literature from the archpriest of Hita to Cervantes, Gracián, and Calderón, to French literature from the *Roman de la Rose* to Rabelais, Montaigne, and Racine, or to English literature from the sixteenth to the eighteenth century.

Konrad Burdach has tried to represent the court of Charles V in Prague as the starting point of a Petrarchan humanistic development of High German and *Der Ackermann von Böhmen* as the great German humanistic work of the late Middle Ages: a grandiose effort but a failure, for Burdach's conception has been largely refuted by linguistic geography and the study of the archives of the period. It seemed likely from the outset that Burdach and his collaborators had overestimated the importance of their discoveries. For in modern European history great intellectual centers and literary works capable of molding a national language cannot very well be so thoroughly forgotten that they have to be rediscovered by so late a scholar; their full significance would have been recognized at the very latest by nineteenth-century historicism; and it is perfectly evident that the great humanistic rhetoric of *Der Ackermann* was not taken up by the German literature of a later day.

The unusual precision and thoroughness with which German linguistic geography (which accurately reflects the political history of the German-speaking territories) has been investigated, has given us a fairly accurate idea of the events which gradually led to the formation of the universal German *Hochsprache*. It did not develop in any of the old cultural centers of the west or south, but in Upper Saxony (the region surrounding Meissen), a newly colonized area east of the Saale that had been reconquered from the Slavs. Here settlers from southern Germany, Thuringia, and Low Germany converged, and their dialects mingled. The mixture produced an Upper Saxon language. Supported by the chancellery in Wettin and the intellectual influence of the *studium generale* in Erfurt, and favored by subsequent economic and political developments, this language gradually spread and provided the essential foundation of the German koine, which slowly crystallized. So early a writer as Luther says in a famous passage that he spoke in the manner of the "Saxon chancellery, which is followed by all the princes and kings in Germany. . . . And for that reason it is the most universal German language." Here, of course, he is referring only to phonetics and morphology, for his style and vocabulary are derived from the tradition of the *sermo humilis*, which his genius incorporated into the German language. But even so, the role played by this Upper Saxon tongue, which further increased its prestige in the seventeenth and eighteenth centuries, is remarkable enough. Nowhere else has a border region, settled at a late date, contributed more than the old cultural centers to the development of the national *Hochsprache*. The part played by Castile in the growth of the Spanish literary language is not comparable; the territory regained in the Reconquest was not a cultural wilderness like the Slavic regions to the east of the Saale, and the northern Spanish regions that were the starting point of national reunification had no cultural centers equivalent to those of the Rhineland, Upper Franconia, Bavaria, and Austria.

In all these German cultural centers, as elsewhere in Europe, the use of the mother tongue made significant progress toward the end of the Middle Ages in commercial and legal matters and in literature. The first important printing establishments (which, to be sure, long continued to print chiefly Latin works) were founded in the central and upper Rhineland. But particularism was so strong that a number of literary (and printed) dialects arose, none of which became definitely predominant.[130]

Nevertheless, toward 1300, the period of Dante, Germany witnessed a highly characteristic phenomenon which was without counterpart in any other country of western Europe and seems to have foreshadowed the future. This was the mysticism of the Dominican friar Eckhart, who wrote and preached in German. In the preceding century a mystical literature in the vernacular, originating for the most part with noble ladies, had made its appearance in the Netherlands and in Thuringia. But it was through Meister Eckhart that this mysticism achieved maturity of thought and expression, for with him for the first time the substructure of Dominican rationalism was carried to the extreme and transcended—and all this is voiced in the German language. His style is characterized by a combination of elements which would at first sight seem irreconcilable. The content seems in the highest degree idealistic and disembodied, a striving away from the concrete, created world. Even within the realm of abstract thought Eckhart seems to strive for still greater purity of thought. Yet he expresses himself in a personal, familiar, one might almost say neighborly language, emphasizing experience in the here and now by his use of "you and I" and "mark my words" and "only today, as I was walking down the street" and his simple similes and examples. This, it seems to me, is more important than the humanistic rhetoric of the *Ackermann* for the future of the German language, for it is certain that in none of the literary languages of western

---

130. For all this, see Arno Schirokauer, "Frühneuhochdeutsch." The quotation from Luther given according to T. Frings, *Die Grundlagen des Meissnischen Deutsch*, p. 23.

Europe was the influence of vernacular humanism so indirect, impure, dispersed, and all in all so feeble as in German. In German literature there is nothing comparable to the influence of Dürer in art; in German, Goethe and Hölderlin were the first to revive the spirit of antiquity, and they did so under conditions that were entirely different from those attending the original humanism. German literary classicism was free from Romance influence, and even the intellectual vocabulary has scarcely been affected by it. The incomparable power and originality that this gave the German language are especially evident to one who is obliged to express his ideas in several European languages.

Eckhart too was an "orator." Apart from the much-praised eloquence of the words and meanings he created, there is a great deal of subtle artistry in the word order and cadence of his sentences: there are similarly constructed, antithetical cola; there are series rising in intensity, and throughout, in question and answer, in the formulation and solution of problems, in his repeated addresses to the reader, the liveliest rhythmic movement. His adjurations are less dramatic and for the most part less powerful than Dante's, if only because they are so frequent, as is natural in sermons. But with him, too, the device can convey extreme urgency, as when he introduces something new that he has never said before. On the whole his sentences are lively, clear, penetrating and harmonious; they make his thought seem transparent even when we are not sure we understand it. It is not easy to say in a few words what forces molded his rhetoric. In his way he was doubtless a Latin scholar; he himself wrote a good deal in that language, although his models were the Latin Church fathers rather than the classics. There is no opposition between the echoes of Augustine and the reminiscences of dialectical scholasticism in his German style. Since in the German of that time a philosophical language had in any case to employ native neologisms, which did not strike the audience as barbarous or forbiddingly technical but seemed at once familar and mysterious (for they were merely new combinations and new ways of utilizing old friends), the antithesis between rhetoric and dialectic was smoothed away. Eckhart's style is a variant of the *sermo humilis*, and this, like everything connected with him, is somewhat paradoxical, for the ultimate foundation of the *sermo humilis*, the historicity of Jesus, was alien to him, and he refused to have anything to do with it.[131] And yet the mixture of daring, upward-striving, almost ethereal ideas and of words addressed in friendship to his neighbor is in the tradition of the *sermo humilis*, and coming from that source Eckhart founded the German language of the intellect. Still other significant types of German *sermo humilis* or Christian German date back to the thirteenth and fourteenth centuries. The popular preachers and early translators of the Bible were preparing the groundwork of the language that attained perfection with Luther.

We have come to the point at which the national tongues began to shake off their dependence on Latin and to develop forms of their own. Each had its work to do, varying with the local situation, but these parallel tasks were part of a common European effort. All over Europe, first in Italy, then in the Iberian peninsula, France, and England, an educated public with a *Hochsprache* of its own now made its appearance, still a small group compared to the population at large but steadily increasing in numbers. The rise of printing greatly accelerated this growth. The period of French classicism in the seventeenth century provides the best basis for a social definition of the "public" over against the uneducated common people on the one hand and the learned specialists on the

131. Cf., for instance: *Her umbe sprichet daz wörtelin, daz ich für geleit hân "got hât gesant sînen einbornen sun in die welt," daz sunt ir niht verstân für die ûzwendigen welt; als er mit uns az unde tranc: ir sünt ez verstân für die inren welt.* (Therefore the word that I have put before you says: "God sent his only begotten Son into the world." You should not understand this with reference to the exterior world, when he ate and drank with us; you must understand it as concerning the inner world.) I am quoting from Pfeiffer's edition, where this is sermon 13 (p. 65, 36–38). In Quint's edition it is sermon 6 (pp. 83ff.). Quint's translation is on p. 178 of his *Meister Eckehart: Deutsche Predigten und Traktate* (with a very good introduction).

other. It was then that the public first came to be known as *la cour
et la ville*, a phrase which makes possible a sociological analysis
of the public of that time. I undertook such an analysis in an earlier
essay; [132] but today I wonder whether, though my findings still
strike me as correct in themselves, I may not have interpreted them
too one-sidedly. My aim at the time was to show that the absence
of function, common to the aristocracy that had been stripped of
its feudal character and to the wealthy bourgeoisie which had begun
to turn away from gainful occupations toward *otium cum dignitate*,
fused these two groups into a single class, namely, *la cour et la ville*.
This was a political and cultural situation conceivable only in a
period of absolutism and classicism. It was then that the ideal of the
honnête homme, very similar to that of the "gentleman," took
form. Even then it was clear to me that no social class can maintain a position of dominance on the sole basis of functionlessness
and that even in its prime this class was obliged to replenish itself
from below. But I did not sufficiently stress the fact. Certainly in
the eighteenth century the class I have termed *la cour et la ville*
was everywhere, and assuredly in France, an expanding class that
was rapidly renewing its membership. Soon the "public" came,
throughout Europe, to be dominated by *la ville*, the bourgeoisie.
Even the most oppressed bourgeoisie, the German, awoke at that
time from the depths of its national amorphousness and, precisely
because Germany was not a nation, was able to create a genuine
universality, the European internationalism of national diversity and
historical perspectivism. From the eighteenth century on, it was
the educated bourgeoisie which determined the character of literature and the literary language throughout Europe; from its ranks
came also the rebels who were to combat it in the nineteenth century. Today the domination of the bourgeoisie seems gradually
to be drawing to an end, but only because it has so expanded,
thanks to its own activity, as to embrace a large percentage of the

132. First published as "Das französische Publikum des 17. Jahrhunderts"; reprinted under the title "La Cour et la ville" in my *Vier Untersuchungen
zur Geschichte der französischen Bildung.*

population. It has ceased to be a minority and an elite. Its adversaries, the proletariat, whose leadership it has provided, are beginning, both in their private and public lives, to resemble it like two peas in a pod. This bit of history is only an aspect of the long economic and political domination of the bourgeoisie, a class which has always owed its memberships to a natural and continuous selection from among the common people. All this seems rather obvious; I mention it here only to stress the contrast with late antiquity. Today the existence of this elite minority, the "public," is threatened by expansion; then, it shrank into nothingness.

The ancient public died of shrinkage. After Hellenistic-Roman culture in the three centuries from the fall of Carthage to the last of the Antonines had conquered the whole western Mediterranean world and the literary public seemed solidly implanted both in Rome and in many smaller centers throughout the Western part of the empire, it slowly began to die of old age. After a long transitional period marked by rhetorical sterility, the language lost its richness and flexibility, the free play of thought and sensibility died out, and what shortly before had been a highly refined *Hochsprache* succumbed to sclerosis and surrendered to the inarticulate stammerings of barbaric peoples. The cultivated public of antiquity does not seem to have been destroyed by the power or superior numbers of the barbarians. It had always been a small minority; but in its prime it had possessed prestige and authority, it had exerted an influence on the masses and remained in contact with them through a variety of intermediate groups. During the late republic and the first century of the empire, it had no doubt expanded considerably, and this growth may even have continued during the happy period of the Antonines. But even then, at the end of the second century, before the catastrophes set in, Latin literature seems to have lost its creative energies. The disease from which the literary public suffered can scarcely have been anything other than its isolation, a loss of contact with the urban middle class from which it had been able to draw new blood with relative ease as long as political and literary life had derived their nourishment from the same source, namely, the schools of philosophy and rhetoric. The political and cultural life of antiquity was grounded in the old city-state, with its institutions and its mentality. Shaken by the inauguration of the empire, these institutions were gradually destroyed. Political and cultural life moved apart. An education based on rhetoric and philosophy proved to be unsuited to the military, administrative, technical, and economic needs of the new imperial government. It is true that great jurists participated in the government to the very end, but otherwise, from the third century on, the overgrown, increasingly centralized state took its leaders where it found them, largely from the army and seldom if ever from the social and cultural elite, which became isolated. The urban bourgeoisie, from which the elite might have derived a homogeneous new membership, was ruined by the anarchy of the third century and the confiscatory taxes of the fourth. We cannot but be impressed by the persistence of a venerable tradition when we observe that as late as the sixth century the senatorial aristocracy, so often murdered off and replaced by new men (who were *homines novi* in a far more radical sense than Cicero or Agrippa in their time), still represented some vestige of what they formerly had been.

When finally, at a time when this disintegration was already far advanced, Christianity was able to spread freely and, as was only natural, made use of the rhetorically molded Latin it found available, it filled this language with new content and gave it a special style which we have termed *sermo humilis*. But the Christians, even the most cultivated among them, had no desire to adopt this decaying culture. They made use of it, but they did not concern themselves with it or take care of it. They enlisted rhetorical education into the service of the Church, but only in so far as it seemed practically utilizable for sermons, apologetics, and polemics. Any further preoccupation with the language aroused criticism, which was sometimes self-criticism. The Church adapted ancient rhetoric to its needs, or rather it took people as it found them; it abandoned the rhetorical arts without regret as soon they ceased to seem necessary, and it did not—not yet, that is—feel responsible for the cultivation of literary expression. Only very late, when the pagan school system had broken down, was the Church obliged for practical reasons to set up schools of its own, and so became, against its will, the custodian of the shards of ancient culture. But by then ancient culture had long since lost all spontaneity. Cultural activity consisted only in learned conversation, compilation, and exegesis; by then no one understood the older literature spontaneously, in its own spirit.

But then almost involuntarily and by the mere force of events the attitude of the Church toward ancient culture underwent a change. Formerly the Church had lived in ancient culture, had been a part of it, had drawn on its energies as the need arose. Now it had become the custodian and administrator, one might say the owner, of the old culture—or at least of so much of it as could be preserved and owned. The entire heritage became a single corpus, the property of the Church, and as such began to have its effect. At times the rigorists denounced the pagan authors, but this did not mean the same thing as in the past, when Jerome in self-accusation had called himself a Ciceronian. For it was not possible to denounce Jerome himself, or Augustine, Ambrose, Gregory, Isidore, Prudentius, and Fortunatus; and yet they too had become a "heritage from antiquity"; antiquity lived in them because they had lived in antiquity. Some of them had even preserved what the great pagan authors had possessed, namely, a free, varied, disciplined yet not strained articulation of ideas and a free flow of rich and varied sensibility attuned to their subject matter and sustained without effort by the language.

At the same time, however, the Church became involved in political and economic life. The Roman Empire had recognized it and made it into a state institution, but the Church had no share in the roots and structure of a political edifice that was so incomparably older, that had so long been hostile to it, and that had grown up on such very different foundations. In the West the Church now inherited the universality of Rome and in many places participated in the founding of new kingdoms; ecclesiastics drew up laws and administered, they were active as educators and arbiters. Through its possessions, through its activities, in short, by the very force of events the Church was drawn into the new feudal economy of the Middle Ages. It involved itself and its members in the affairs of earthly life and took a leading part in them, often overtly; and it participated in its corruption, so making the scandal all the more blatant.

All this points to the strange moral dialectic of Christianity. God's realm is not of this world; but how can living men remain aloof from the earthly? And are they justified in doing so, since Christ himself entered into earthly affairs? Their duty as Christians is not a stoical aloofness from earthly concerns but submission to suffering. And is it tolerable that the Church itself, the Pope, the bishops, and the monasteries should sink into the depths of earthly corruption, so that souls are led astray and fall victims to eternal damnation? And if not, how can it be averted if not by energetic counteractivity in the world, where on the other hand the activity of mortal man can never be anything but earthly?

Originally and essentially Christianity as a religion of salvation stood aloof from all political strivings, which held no meaning for men convinced that the end of the world was at hand. But no sooner did it enter into the earthly world and, as was inevitable, become involved in it than it became—far more than other, more rational religions, taking a friendlier view of life or at least adapting themselves more readily to practical common sense—a never-resting force for ethical action in politics. In conformity with its origin and essence Christianity carried the demands of an absolute, extrahistorical realm into earthly life, so provoking restless activity. Because in the life story of Christ and the typological interpretation of history based on it Christianity possessed a universally appealing view of earthly events, in which human destinies are dramatized, it succeeded in imbuing men with its substance and in becoming, through them, a constant source of political, intellectual, and individual agitation. From the investiture conflict to the Reformation the upheavals which set so deep an ethical and revolutionary imprint on the history of Europe and finally gave Europe its exemplary position in the world of men were caused by Christian unrest. And even the later, modern movements, which were no longer called forth by Christian concerns, have preserved in their aims and propaganda an element of Christian eschatological unrest. But political action is only one aspect of Christian influence. Both lyrical and dramatic poetry derived their first forms from the liturgy. By lending the feelings of men a new depth the Christian dialectic of suffering and passion laid the groundwork for what is most significant and characteristic in the poetry of modern times; and the confrontation between ancient thought and the paradoxes of the Christian faith was the school that made European philosophy what it is.

The disintegration of the Western Roman empire and the long period during which the various countries grew to maturity under varying conditions produced many European cultures. When once again a society came into being that possessed cultural self-awareness and a will to cultivate its humanity, it was not one but many, each possessing its forms and its language. Nevertheless we may venture to speak of *a* European society and even of a European *Hochsprache*. What unites them is their common root in antiquity and Christianity. For this combination contains the dialectical force which—even if Europe, like Rome before it, should now lose its power and even cease to exist as such—has prefigured the forms of a common social and cultural life on our planet.

ABBREVIATIONS

LIST OF WORKS CITED

ABBREVIATIONS

Used in the footnotes and in the List of Works Cited.

ALMA   *Archivum latinitatis medii aevi* (*Bulletin Du Cange*)

CCSL   *Corpus Christianorum, series latina*

CSEL   *Corpus scriptorum ecclesiasticorum latinorum*

DACL   *Dictionnaire d'archéologie chrétienne et de liturgie*

MGH   *Monumenta Germaniae historica*

        AA   *Auctores antiquissimi*

        Briefe   *Die Briefe der deutschen Kaiserzeit*

        Epist.   *Epistolae*

        Epist. sel.   *Epistolae selectae*

        Leg.   *Legum sectio* . . .

        Poet.   *Poetarum latinorum medii aevi* . . .

        Scr.   *Scriptorum* . . .

        Scr. rer.   *Scriptores rerum Germanicarum* . . .
          Germ.

        Scr. rer.   *Scriptores rerum Langobardicarum et Itali-*
          Lang.   *carum saec. VI–IX* . . .

        Scr. rer.   *Scriptores rerum Merovingicarum* . . .
          Mer.

PL   Migne. *Patrologiae cursus completus: series latina*

PMLA   *Publications of the Modern Language Association of America*

SitzBer.   *Sitzungsberichte der preussischen Akademie der Wissen-*
Berlin   *schaften zu Berlin, Philosophisch-historische Klasse*

LIST OF WORKS CITED

Ackermann von [aus] Böhmen, Der. See JOHANN, OF SAAZ.

Acta Sanctorum. See BOLLANDUS.

ADAM, AUGUST. *Arbeit und Besitz nach Ratherius von Verona.* (Freiburger Theologische Studien, 31.) Freiburg im Breisgau, 1927.

ADAM DE LA HALLE. See LE BOSSU.

ADAM OF SAINT-VICTOR. *Œuvres poétiques* . . . précédées d'un essai sur sa vie et ses ouvrages. Ed. L. Gautier. 2 vols. Paris, 1858–59; 3rd edn., 1894.

[AELFRIC.] *Aelfrics Grammatik und Glossar.* Ed. Julius Zupitza. (Sammlung englischer Denkmäler in kritischen Ausgaben, 1.) Berlin, 1880.

AGNELLUS. *Liber pontificalis ecclesiae Ravennatis.* In: *MGH Scr. rer. Lang.,* ed. O. Holder-Egger, pp. 265–391. Hanover, 1878.

[ALAN OF LILLE (ALANUS DE INSULIS).] *Alain de Lille.* Ed. Robert Bossuat. (Textes philosophiques du moyen âge, 1.) Paris, 1955.

ALCUIN. *Epistulae.* In: *MGH Epist.,* IV: *Epistolae Karolini Aevi,* II. Ed. Ernestus Duemmler. Berlin, 1895.

———. *Beati Flacci Albini seu Alcuini Grammatica* = PL, CI, 849–902.

ALFARIC. See HOEPFFNER.

ALFRED. *King Alfred's West-Saxon Version of Gregory's Pastoral Care.* Ed. and tr. Henry Sweet. (Early English Text Society, 45, 50.) London, 1871.

ALONSO, DÁMASO. "Cancioncillas 'de amigo' mozárabes (Primavera temprana de la lírica europea)," *Revista de filología española,* XXXIII (1949), 297–349.

AMBROSE. *De bono mortis* = PL, XIV, 539–568; *De Noe et arca* = PL, XIV, 361–416; *De officiis ministrorum libri tres* = PL, XVI, 23–184;

343

Epistolae = *PL*, xvi, 875–1286; *Expositionis Evangelii secundum Lucam libri X* = *PL*, xv, 1527–1850.

AMMIANUS MARCELLINUS. *Rerum gestarum libri qui supersunt.* Ed. Carolus U. Clark, L. Traube, and G. Heraeo. 2 vols. Berlin, 1910–15.

Ansëys de Mes According to Ms. N (Bibl. de l'Arsenal 3143): Text, Published for the First Time in Its Entirety, with an introduction by Herman J. Green. Columbia University Ph.D. diss. Paris, 1939.

ANTHONY, EDGAR WATERMAN. *Romanesque Frescoes.* Princeton, 1951.

APPEL, CARL. *Provenzalische Chrestomathie.* 4th edn., Leipzig, 1912.

ARATOR SUBDIACONUS. *De actibus apostolorum.* Ed. Arthur Patch McKinlay. (*CSEL*, LXXII.) Vienna, 1951. / = *PL*, LXVIII, 81–246.

[ARIBO.] *Musica Aribonis scholastici.* In: GERBERT, M. *Scriptores ecclesiastici de musica sacra* (q.v.), II, 197–230.

ARNOBIUS. *Adversus nationes libri VII.* Ed. August Reifferscheid. (*CSEL*, IV.) Vienna, 1875.

[ASSER.] *Asser's Life of King Alfred together with the Annals of Saint Neots.* . . . Ed. William H. Stevenson. Oxford, 1904.

Aucassin et Nicolete. Chantefable. . . . Ed. Mario Roques. (Classiques français du moyen âge, 41.) Paris, 1925.

AUERBACH, ERICH. *Dante als Dichter der irdischen Welt.* Berlin and Leipzig, 1929. / = *Dante: Poet of the Secular World.* Tr. Ralph Manheim. Chicago and London, 1961.

———. "Dante's Addresses to the Reader," *Romance Philology,* VII (1953–54), 268–278.

———. "Dante's Prayer to the Virgin (*Paradiso*, XXXIII) and Earlier Eulogies," *Romance Philology,* III (1949–50), 1–26.

———. "Figura," *Archivum Romanicum,* XXII (1938), 436–489; repr. in his *Neue Dantestudien* (q.v.), pp. 11–71.

———. "La Cour et la ville." In: *Vier Untersuchungen zur Geschichte der französischen Bildung,* pp. 12–50. Bern, 1951. [First published as "Das französische Publikum des 17. Jahrhunderts," *Münchener romanistische Arbeiten,* 1933.]

AUERBACH, ERICH. "Lateinische Prosa des 9. und 10. Jahrhunderts (Sermo humilis II)," *Romanische Forschungen*, LXVI (1955), 1–64.

———. *Mimesis: Dargestellte Wirklichkeit in der abendländischen Literatur*. Bern, 1946. / = *Mimesis: The Representation of Reality in Western Literature*. Tr. Willard R. Trask. Princeton, 1953.

———. *Neue Dantestudien*. (Istanbuler Schriften, 5.) Istanbul, 1944.

———. "Passio als Leidenschaft," *PMLA*, LVI (1941), 1179–1196.

———. "St. Francis of Assisi in Dante's *Commedia*," *Italica: Quarterly Bulletin of the American Association of Teachers of Italian*, XXII (1945), 166–179.

———. "Sermo humilis," *Romanische Forschungen*, LXIV (1952), 304–364.

———. "Typological Symbolism in Medieval Literature," *Yale French Studies*, 9 (1952), 3–10.

———. *Typologische Motive in der mittelalterlichen Literatur*. In: *Schriften und Vorträge des Petrarca-Instituts in Köln*, fasc. 2. Krefeld, 1953.

———. Review of T. Frings's *Minnesinger und Troubadours*, in *Romance Philology*, IV (1950–1951), 65–67.

AUGUSTINE. *Confessionum libri tredecim*. Ed. Pius Knöll. (*CSEL*, XXXIII.) Prague, Vienna, Leipzig, 1896. / = *The Confessions of Saint Augustine*. Tr. Francis J. Sheed. New York and London, 1951.

———. *De civitate Dei*. Ed. Bernard Dombart. 3rd edn. (ed. Alphonsus Kalb), Leipzig, 1928. / = *CCSL*, 47, 48. 2 vols. Turnhout, 1955.

———. *De doctrina christiana libri IV* = *PL*, XXXIV, 15–122. / Ed. H. J. Vogels. (Florilegium Patristicum, 24.) Bonn, 1930.

———. *De nuptiis et concupiscentia*. Ed. C. F. Urba and J. Zycha. In: *CSEL*, XLII, 207–319. n.p., 1902.

———. *De Trinitate libri XV* = *PL*, XLII, 819–1098.

———. *Epistulae*. Ed. A. Goldbacher. (*CSEL*, XLIV.) Vienna, Leipzig, 1904.

———. *Enarrationes in Psalmos* = *PL*, XXXVI–XXXVII. / Ed. D. Eligius Dekkers and Iohannes Fraipont. (*CCSL*, 38, 39.) Turnhout, 1956.

AUGUSTINE. *In Joannis Evangelium tractatus CXXIV* = *PL*, xxxv, 1379–1976. / Ed. D. Radbodus Willems. (*CCSL*, 36.) Turnhout, 1954.

——. *Quaestionum in Heptateuchum libri VII.* Ed. Iosephus Zycha. (*CSEL*, xxviii.) Prague, Vienna, Leipzig, 1895.

——. *Sermones* = *PL*, xxxviii.

BAEHRENS, EMIL (ed.). *Poetae latini minores*, iii. Leipzig, 1881.

BARTHOLOMAEIS, VINCENZO DE. "Giullari Farfensi," *Studi Medievali*, N.S. I (1928), 37–47.

BARTSCH, KARL. *Chrestomathie provençale* (*Xᵉ–XVᵉ siècles*). 6th edn. (ed. Eduard Koschwitz), Marburg, 1904.

BATTELLI, GIULIO. *Lezioni di paleografia.* 2nd edn., Vatican City, 1939.

B[AXTER], J. H. "Colloquialisms in St. Augustine," *ALMA*, iii (1927), 32–33.

BEAULIEUX, CHARLES. *Histoire de l'orthographe française.* 2 vols. Paris, 1927.

BECK, HENRY G. J. *The Pastoral Care of Souls in South-East France During the Sixth Century.* (Analecta Gregoriana, 51.) Rome, 1950.

BECKER, PHILIP AUGUST. "Der gepaarte Achtsilber in der französischen Dichtung," *Abhandlungen der sächsischen Akademie der Wissenschaften* (Leipzig), *Phil.-hist. Klasse*, xliii (1934): 1. 1934.

BEDE. *Historia[m] ecclesiastica[m] gentis Anglorum. . . .* Ed. Charles Plummer. 2 vols. Oxford, 1896.

——. *In Cantica Canticorum allegorica expositio* = *PL*, xci, 1065–1236.

BÉDIER, JOSEPH (ed.). *Les Deux Poèmes de La Folie Tristan.* (Société des anciens textes français.) Paris, 1907.

BEEK, CORNELIUS J. M. J. VAN (ed.). *Passio Sanctarum Perpetuae et Felicitatis.* Nijmegen, 1936. Also in: Florilegium Patristicum, 43. Bonn, 1938.

BELL, ALEXANDER. "Maistre Geffrei Gaimar," *Medium Aevum*, vii (1938), 184–198.

BENEEIT (BENOIT) DE SAINTE-MAURE. *Le Roman de Troie.* Ed. Léopold Constans. (Société des anciens textes français.) 6 vols. Paris, 1904–1912.

BENVENUTO DE RAMBALDIS DE IMOLA. *Comentum super Dantis Aldigherij Comoediam.* . . . I: *Infernus* I–XVII. Ed. Jacobus Philippus Lacaita. Florence, 1887.

BERNARD OF CLAIRVAUX. *De diligendo Deo* = PL, CLXXXII, 973–1000; *De gradibus humilitatis et superbiae tractatus* = PL, ibid., 941–972; *Epistolae* = PL, ibid., 67–716; *In Feria IV Hebdomadae Sanctae sermo* = PL, CLXXXIII, 263–270; *Sermones de diversis* = PL, ibid., 537–748; *Sermones in Cantica Canticorum* = PL, ibid., 785–1198.

BEZZOLA, RETO R. *Les Origines et la formation de la littérature courtoise en Occident* (*500–1200*), I: *La Tradition impériale de la fin de l'antiquité au XIᵉ siècle.* (Bibliothèque de l'École des Hautes Études, 286.) Paris, 1944.

BLAISE, ALBERT. *Manuel du latin chrétien.* Strasbourg, 1955.

BLOCH, MARC. *La Société féodale: La Formation des liens de dépendance.* (L'Évolution de l'humanité: Synthèse collective, 34.) Paris, 1939. / = *Feudal Society.* Tr. L. A. Manyon. London, 1961.

BOETHIUS, ANICIUS MANLIUS SEVERINUS. *Philosophiae consolationis libri V.* Ed. Wilhelm Weinberger. (*CSEL*, LXVII.) Vienna, Leipzig, 1934.

BOLLANDUS, JOANNES, et al. (ed.). *Acta Sanctorum . . . Martii tomus primus.* Paris, Rome, 1865.

BONAVENTURE (Bonaventura). *Breviloquium* = *Opera omnia*, V (Ad Claras Aquas [= Quaracchi], 1891); *De perfectione vitae ad sorores* = Ibid., VIII, 107–127 (1898); *Itinerarium mentis in Deum* = Ibid., V (1891); *Lignum vitae* = Ibid., VIII, 68–86 (1898).

PSEUDO-BONAVENTURA. *Diaeta salutis.* Venice, 1518.

PSEUDO-BONAVENTURA. *Meditationes vitae Christi* = *Opera omnia . . . ,* ed. A. C. Peltier, XII, 509–630 (Paris, 1868); *Stimulis amoris* = Ibid., XII, 631–703.

BONIFACE. *Die Briefe des heiligen Bonifatius und Lullus.* Ed. Michael Tangl. (*MGH Epist. sel.*, I.) Berlin, 1916.

BONNET, MAX. *Le Latin de Grégoire de Tours.* Paris, 1890.

BORETIUS, ALFRED (ed.). *Capitularia regum Francorum.* (*MGH Leg.*, II.) 2 vols. Hanover, 1883 and 1897.

BOUILLET, AUGUSTE (ed.). *Liber miraculorum Sancte Fidis publié d'après le manuscrit de la Bibliothèque de Schlestadt avec une introduction et des notes.* . . . Paris, 1897.

BOUQUET, MARTIN. *Recueil des historiens des Gaules et de la France.* New edn. by Léopold Delisle, XIII. Paris, 1869.

BOWEN, LEE. "The Tropology of Mediaeval Dedication Rites," *Speculum,* XVI (1941), 469–479.

BOWRA, MAURICE. "Dante and Arnaut Daniel," *Speculum,* XXVII (1952), 459–474.

BRESSLAU, HARRY. *Handbuch der Urkundenlehre für Deutschland und Italien,* II: 1. 2nd edn., Berlin, Leipzig, 1931. 3rd edn., Berlin, 1958.

BRINKMANN, HENNIG. *Zu Wesen und Form mittelalterlicher Dichtung.* Halle, 1928.

BROWE, PETER. *Die Pflichtkommunion im Mittelalter.* Münster in Westphalia, 1940.

BRUNEL, CLOVIS. *Bibliographie des manuscrits littéraires en ancien provençal.* (Société de publications romanes et françaises, 13.) Paris, 1935.

———. *Les Plus Anciennes Chartes en langue provençale: Recueil des pièces originales antérieures au XIIIᵉ siècle.* Paris, 1926. Supplément: Paris, 1952.

BRUNO OF QUERFURT. *S. Adalberti vita secunda.* Ed. G. H. Pertz. (*MGH Scr.,* IV, 596–612.) Hanover, 1841; repr. Leipzig, 1925.

———. *Vita quinque fratrum.* Ed. Reinhard Kade. (*MGH Scr.,* XV: 2, 709–738.) Hanover, 1888.

BRUYNE, EDGAR DE. "De Boèce à Jean Scot Erigène," in *Études d'esthétique médiévale.* (Rijksuniversiteit te Gent: Werken uitgegeven door de Faculteit van de Wijsbegeerte en Letteren, 97.) Bruges, 1946.

CAESARIUS. *Opera omnia*, I: *Sermones seu Admonitiones;* II: *Opera varia.* Comp. Germain Morin. 2 vols. Maredsous, 1937, 1942.

———. *Sermones.* Ed. Germain Morin. (*CCSL*, 103, 104.) 2nd edn., Turnhout, 1953.

CAPELLA, MARTIANUS. See MARTIANUS CAPELLA.

CARCOPINO, JÉRÔME. *La Vie quotidienne à Rome à l'apogée de l'Empire.* Paris, 1939. / = *Daily Life in Ancient Rome: The People and the City at the Height of the Empire.* Tr. E. O. Lorimer. New Haven, 1940; London, 1941.

———. *Les Secrets de la correspondance de Cicéron.* 2 vols. Paris, 1947. / = *Cicero: The Secrets of His Correspondence.* Tr. E. O. Lorimer. 2 vols. New Haven and London, 1951.

CASSIAN (JOANNES CASSIANUS). *Collationes* = *PL*, XLIX, 477–1328. / Ed. Michael Petschenig. (*CSEL*, XIII.) Vienna, 1886.

———. *De institutis coenobiorum et octo principalium remediis libri XII* = *PL*, XLIX, 53–476. / = Ed. Michael Petschenig. (*CSEL*, XVII.) Vienna, Prague, Leipzig, 1888.

CASSIODORUS, MAGNUS AURELIUS. *In Psalterium expositio* = *PL*, LXX, 9–1056.

———. *Institutiones.* Ed. Roger A. B. Mynors. Oxford, 1937.

———. *Variae.* Ed. Theodor Mommsen. (*MGH AA*, XII.) Berlin, 1894.

CHARLES, PIERRE. "L'Élément populaire dans les sermons de saint-Augustin," *Nouvelle Revue Théologique*, LXIX (1947), 619–650.

La Chastelaine de Vergi. Ed. Gaston Reynaud. 3rd edn., revised by Lucien Foulat. Paris, 1921.

CHAYTOR, H. J. *From Script to Print: An Introduction to Medieval Vernacular Literature.* Cambridge, England, 1945.

CHODERLOS DE LACLOS, PIERRE. See LACLOS.

CHRÉTIEN DE TROYES. *Der Percevalroman* (*Li contes del Graal*). Ed. Alfons Hilka. In: *Christian von Troyes: Sämtliche erhaltene Werke*, ed. Wendelin Foerster, v. Halle, 1932.

———. *Philomena: conte raconté d'après Ovide par Chrétien de Troyes.* Ed. C. de Boer. Paris, 1909.

CHRIST, KARL (suppl. by ANTON KERN). "Das Mittelalter." In: MILKAU, *Handbuch der Bibliothekswissenschaft* (q.v.), III: 1, 243–498.

Chronicon anonymi canonici ut videtur Laudunensis. In: BOUQUET, *Recueil* . . . (q.v.), XIII, 677–683.

CROSLAND, JESSIE. " 'Eneas' and the 'Aeneid,' " *Modern Language Review*, XXIX (1934), 282–290.

CURTIUS, ERNST ROBERT. *Europäische Literatur und lateinisches Mittelalter.* Bern, 1948. / = *European Literature and the Latin Middle Ages.* Tr. Willard R. Trask. New York (Bollingen Series, XXXVI) and London, 1953.

DANTE ALIGHIERI. *The Convivio.* Tr. Philip H. Wicksteed. (Temple Classics.) London, 1903.

———. *De vulgari eloquentia.* Ed. Aristide Marigo. Florence, 1938.

———. (*The Divine Comedy.*) *Inferno; Purgatoria; Paradiso.* With tr. by Philip H. Wicksteed. (Temple Classics.) 3 vols. London, 1899–1900.

———. *Rime.* Ed. Gianfranco Contini. Turin, 1939.

———. *Über das Dichten in der Muttersprache: De vulgari eloquentia.* Tr. and explained by Franz Dornseiff and Joseph Balogh. Darmstadt, 1925.

DEANESLY, M. "Vernacular Books in England in the Fourteenth and Fifteenth Centuries," *Modern Language Review*, XV (1920), 349–358.

DEFENSOR. *Scintillarum liber = PL*, LXXXVIII, 597–718.

DELEHAYE, HIPPOLYTE. *Les Passions des martyrs et les genres littéraires.* Brussels, 1921.

DELHAYE, PHILIPPE. "L'Organisation scolaire au XIIe siècle," *Traditio*, V (1947), 211–268.

DÖLGER, FRANZ JOSEPH. *Antike und Christentum: Kultur- und Religionsgeschichtliche Studien*, II. Münster in Westphalia, 1930.

DRESEMIUS, SAMUEL. See under JOSEPH OF EXETER.

DU CANGE, CHARLES. *Glossarium mediae et infimae latinitatis.* New edn. by L. Favre. Paris, 1938.

Du Méril, Édélestand. *Mélanges archéologiques et littéraires*. Paris, 1850.

Eckhar[d]t. *Meister Eckharts Predigten*. Ed. Josef Quint. In: *Die deutschen Werke (Die deutschen und lateinischen Werke)*, I. Im Auftrage der Deutschen Forschungsgemeinschaft.) Stuttgart, Berlin, 1936.

———. *Meister Eckehart: Deutsche Predigten und Traktate*. Ed. and tr. Josef Quint. Munich, 1955.

———. *Meister Eckhart*. Ed. Franz Pfeiffer. 4th edn. photomechanical reprint of the 1857 edn., unchanged. Göttingen, 1924.

Éginhard. See Einhard.

Ehrismann, Gustav. *Geschichte der deutschen Literatur bis zum Ausgang des Mittelalters*, I: *Die althochdeutsche Literatur*. (Handbuch des deutschen Unterrichts an höheren Schulen, VI: 1.) 2nd edn., Munich, 1932; repr. 1954.

Einhard (Eginhard). *Vie de Charlemagne*. Ed. and tr. Louis Halphen. (Les Classiques de l'histoire de France au moyen âge, 1.) Paris, 1923.

Enéas: Roman du XIIe siècle. Ed. J.-J. Salverda de Grave. (Les Classiques français du moyen âge.) 2 vols. Paris, 1925, 1929.

Ennodius, Magnus Felix. *Opera omnia*. Ed. G. Hartel. (*CSEL*, VI.) Vienna, 1882.

Erdmann, Carl. "Das Ottonische Reich als Imperium Romanum," *Deutsches Archiv für Geschichte des Mittelalters*, VI (1943), 412–441.

———, and Norbert Fickermann (eds.). *Briefsammlungen der Zeit Heinrichs IV*. (*MGH Briefe*, v.) Weimar, 1950.

Ewert, A. "The Strasburg Oaths," *Transactions of the Philological Society*, 1935, pp. 16–35.

Faral, Edmond. *Les Arts poétiques du XIIe et du XIIIe siècle: Recherches et documents sur la technique littéraire du Moyen Age*. (Bibliothèque de l'École des Hautes Études, 238.) Paris, 1924.

———. *Les Jongleurs en France au moyen âge*. (Bibliothèque de l'École des Hautes Études, 187.) Paris, 1910.

FARAL, EDMOND. *Recherches sur les sources latines des contes et romans courtois du moyen âge.* Paris, 1913.

———. "Sidoine Apollinaire et la technique littéraire du Moyen Age," *Miscellanea Giovanni Mercati,* II, 567–580. (= *Studi e Testi,* CXXII.) Vatican City, 1946.

Floire et Blancheflor. Ed. Margaret Pelan, with commentary. (Publications de la Faculté des Lettres de l'Université de Strasbourg: Textes d'étude, 7.) Paris, 1937.

Flore et Blancheflor nach der Pariser Handschrift 375 (A). Ed. Wilhelmine Wirtz, with Glossary. (Frankfurter Quellen und Forschungen zur germanischen und romanischen Philologie, 15.) Frankfurt am Main, 1937.

FOCILLON, HENRI. *L'An mil.* (Collection Henri Focillon, 2.) Paris, 1952.

———. *Peintures romanes des églises de France.* With 130 photographs by Pierre Devinoy. Paris, 1938.

FOERSTER, WENDELIN (ed.). *Li Dialoge Gregoire lo Pape: Altfranzösische Übersetzung des XII. Jahrhunderts der Dialoge des Papst Gregor, mit dem lateinischen Original.* Halle, Paris, 1876.

———, and E. KOSCHWITZ. *Altfranzösisches Übungsbuch: Die ältesten Sprachdenkmäler, mit einem Anhang.* 6th edn. (ed. by Alfons Hilka), Leipzig, 1921.

FOLCUIN. *Gesta abbatum Lobiensium.* Ed. Georgius H. Pertz. (*MGH Scr.* IV, 52–74.) Hanover, 1841; repr. Leipzig, 1925.

La Folie Tristan. See BÉDIER, JOSEPH (ed.).

FORTUNATIANUS, C. CHIRIUS. *Artis rhetoricae Libri III.* In: CARL F. HALM. *Rhetores latini minores,* q.v. (81–134).

FORTUNATUS. See VENANTIUS.

FRANK, GRACE. *The Medieval French Drama.* Oxford, 1954.

FRINGS, THEODOR. *Die Grundlagen des Meissnischen Deutsch: Ein Beitrag zur Enstehungsgeschichte der deutschen Hochsprache.* Halle, 1936.

[FULGENTIUS PLANCIADES.] *Fabii Planciadis Fulgentii V.C. Opera. Accedunt Fabii Claudii Gordiani Fulgentii V.C. De aetatibus mundi et hominis.* Ed. Rudolf Helm. Leipzig, 1898.

GAIMAR, MAISTRE GEFFREI (tr.). *Lestorie des Engles solum la Transla-cion Maistre Geffrei Gaimar.* Ed. and trans. (into English) Thomas Duffy Hardy and Charles Trice Martin. (Rerum Britannicarum Medii Aevi Scriptores, 91.) 2 vols. London, 1888 (text) and 1889 (translation).

GANSHOF, FRANÇOIS-L. "Charlemagne et l'usage de l'écrit en matière administrative," *Le Moyen Age,* LVII (1951), 1–25.

[GARNIER DE PONT-SAINTE-MAXENCE.] *La Vie de saint Thomas le Martyr par Guernes de Pont-Sainte-Maxence: Poème historique du XIIᵉ siècle (1172–1174).* Ed. E(mmanuel) Walberg. (Acta Reg. Societatis Humaniorum Litterarum Lundensis, 5.) Lund, 1922.

GARTNER, THEODOR. *Handbuch der rätoromanischen Sprache und Literatur.* (Sammlung kurzer Lehrbücher der romanischen Sprachen und Literaturen, 5.) Halle, 1910.

GAUTIER, LÉON. *Les Epopées françaises: Étude sur les origines et l'histoire de la littérature nationale.* 2 vols. 2nd edn., Paris, 1878, 1892.

GEBHARDT, OSKAR LEOPOLD VON (ed.). *Acta martyrum selecta: Ausge-wählte Märtyreracten und andere Urkunden aus der Verfolgungs-zeit der Christlichen Kirche.* Berlin, 1902.

GENNRICH, FRIEDRICH. "Die Repertoire-Theorie," *Zeitschrift für fran-zösische Sprache und Literatur,* LXVI (1956), 81–108.

GEOFFREY OF MONMOUTH. *Historiae Regum Britanniae.* With contribu-tions to the study of its place in early British history by Acton Griscon. New York, 1929.

GEOFFROY DE VIGEOIS. *Chronica Gaufredi coenobitae monasterii sancti Martialis Lemovicensis, ac Prioris Vosiensis. . . .* In: PHILIPPE LABBÉ. *Nova bibliotheca MSS. librorum sive specimen antiquarum lectionum Latinarum et Graecarum.* 3 parts. Paris, 1653 [1652].

GERBERT OF AURILLAC (Silvester II). *Lettres de Gerbert (983–997).* Ed. Julien Havet. (Collection de textes, 6.) Paris, 1889.

GERBERT, MARTIN (comp.). *Scriptores ecclesiastici de musica sacra potissimum ex variis Italiae, Galliae et Germaniae codicibus manu-scriptis,* II. n.p., 1784.

GHELLINCK, JOSEPH DE. *L'Essor de la littérature latine au XIIe siècle.* (Museum Lessianum, Sect. hist., 4.) 2 vols. Brussels, Paris, 1946.

———. *Littérature latine au moyen âge.* (Bibliothèque catholique des sciences religieuses, 85, 86.) 2 vols. Paris, 1939.

GILBERT OF HOYLAND. *Sermones in Canticum Salomonis* . . . = PL, CLXXXIV, 11–252.

GIRY, A. *Manuel de Diplomatique.* Paris, 1894. New edn., 1925.

GMELIN, HERMANN. "Die Anrede an den Leser in Dantes Göttlicher Komödie," *Deutsches Dante-Jahrbuch,* XXIX/XXX (1951), 130–140.

GOTTSCHALK (GOTTESCHALCUS). *Opera quae supersunt.* Ed. with a biography and an introduction by G. L. Perugi. Rome, 1911. / = PL, CXXI, 347–372.

GREGORY I THE GREAT. *Dialogorum libri IV, de vita et miraculis Patrum Italicorum, et de aeternitate animarum* = PL, LXXVII, 149–430. / = *Dialogi. Libri IV.* Ed. Umberto Moricca. (Istituto storico italiano: Fonti per la storia d'Italia, Scrittori, Secolo VI, 57.) Rome, 1924. / See also ALFRED; FOERSTER.

———. *Moralia in Job* = PL, LXXV, 509–LXXVI, 782.

———. *Registrum epistolarum.* Ed. P. Ewald and L. M. Hartmann. (*MGH Epist.,* I.) Berlin, 1891.

GREGORY VII. *Das Register Gregors VII.* Ed. Erich Caspar. (*MGH Epist. sel.,* II.) 2 vols. Berlin, 1920, 1923.

GREGORY OF TOURS. *Opera omnia* = PL, LXXI.

———. *De gloria beatorum confessorum* and *De virtutibus beati Martini episcopi.* (*MGH Scr. rer. Mer.,* I: 2: *Gregorii Turonensis Miracula et opera minora.*) Ed. W. Arndt and Bruno Krusch. Hanover, 1885.

———. *Libri Historiarum X.* Ed. W. Arndt and Bruno Krusch. (*MGH Scr. rer. Mer.,* I: 1.) Hanover, 1884. 2nd edn. (ed. Bruno Krusch and Wilhelm Levison), Hanover, 1951.

———. *Grégoire de Tours: Histoire des Francs. Texte de manuscrits de Corbie et de Bruxelles.* Ed. Henri Omont and Gaston Collon. (Collection de textes, 47.) New edn. (ed. René Poupardin), Paris, 1913.

GREGORY OF TOURS. *Zehn Bücher Fränkischer Geschichte von Bischof Gregorius von Tours.* Tr. Wilhelm von Giesebrecht. (Die Geschichtschreiber der deutschen Vorzeit, Zweite Gesamtausgabe, 8, 9.) 2 vols. 4th edn. (ed. Siegmund Hellmann), n.p., 1911 and 1913.

GRÖBER, GUSTAV. "Die Liedersammlungen der Troubadours," *Romanische Studien,* II (1877), 337–670.

GUALAZZINI, UGO. *Ricerche sulle scuole preuniversitarie del medioevo: Contributo di indagini sul sorgere delle università.* (R. Università di Parma: Monografie sulla storia dell'Ateneo.) Milan, 1943.

GUERNES DE PONT-SAINTE-MAXENCE. See GARNIER DE PONT-SAINTE-MAXENCE.

GUIBERT OF NOGENT. *De vita sua sive monodiarum libri tres* = PL, CLVI, 837–962.

HALLINGER, KASSIUS. *Gorze-Kluny: Studien zu den monastischen Lebensformen und Gegensätzen im Hochmittelalter.* (Studia Anselmiana, 22, 25.) 2 vols. Rome, 1950, 1951.

HALM, CARL F. *Rhetores latini minores.* Leipzig, 1863.

HALPHEN, LOUIS. *Études critiques sur l'histoire de Charlemagne.* Paris, 1921.

HARDOUIN, JEAN. *Acta Conciliorum et Epistolae decretales ac Constitutiones summorum pontificum,* IV: *Ab anno DCCLXXXVII ad annum DCCCXLVII.* Paris, 1714.

HARTMANN VON AUE. *Der arme Heinrich.* Ed. Hermann Paul. 11th edn. (ed. Ludwig Wolff; Altdeutsche Textbibliothek, 3), Tübingen, 1958.

HAUCK, ALBERT. *Kirchengeschichte Deutschlands,* III. 8th edn., Berlin, 1954.

HAURÉAU, BARTHÉLEMY. *Notices et extraits de quelques manuscrits de la Bibliothèque Nationale.* 6 vols. Paris, 1890–93.

HAUVETTE, HENRI. "L'Antiquité dans l'œuvre de Dante," *Revue des Cours et Conférences,* 2nd ser. 36 (1934–35), I, 481–497, 580–594, 695–707; II, 322–341, 417–432.

HEIRICUS. *Carmina.* In: *MGH Poet.,* III: *Poetae Latini aevi Carolini,* ed. Ludwig Traube, 421–517. Berlin, 1896.

Heliand. Ed. O. Behaghel. (Altdeutsche Textbibliothek, 4.) Halle, 1882.

HIERONYMUS. See JEROME.

HILARY (HILARIUS). *In Evangelium Matthaei commentarius* = *PL*, IX, 917–1078.

Hildebrandslied, Das. Eine geschichtliche Einleitung . . . mit . . . alt- und neuhochdeutschen Texten. Ed. Georg Baesecke. Halle, 1945.

HOEPFFNER, ERNST, and P. ALFARIC (eds.). *La Chanson de Sainte-Foy.* (Publications de la Faculté des Lettres de l'Université de Strasbourg, 32.) 2 vols. Paris, 1926.

Ioannis Cottonis Musica. In: GERBERT, *Scriptores ecclesiastici de musica sacra* (q.v.), II, 230–265.

ISIDORE OF SEVILLE. *Etymologiarum sive Originum libri XX.* Ed. W. M. Lindsay. Oxford, 1911.

———. *Sententiarum libri tres.* Ed. Faustino Arevalo = *PL*, LXXXIII, 537–738.

JACOPONE DA TODI. *Le laude.* Ed. Giovanni Ferri. 2nd edn. (ed. Santino Caramella; Scrittori d'Italia), Bari, 1930.

———. *Le poesie spirituali del B. Jacopone da Todi . . .* con le scolie et annotationi del Fra Francesco Tresatti. Venice, 1617.

———. A selection from the Spiritual Songs, translated by Mrs. Theodore Beck. In: EVELYN UNDERHILL. *Jacopone da Todi . . . A Spiritual Biography.* New York and London, 1919.

JANTZEN, HANS. *Ottonische Kunst.* Munich, 1947.

JEANROY, ALFRED. *Bibliographie sommaire des chansonniers français (manuscrits et editions).* (Les Classiques français du moyen âge: Manuels.) Paris, 1918.

JENSEN, CHRISTIAN. "Herakleides von Pontos bei Philodem und Horaz," *SitzBer. Berlin,* fasc. 23 (1936), 292–320.

JEROME. *Commentariorum in Epistolam* [*Sancti Pauli*] *ad Galatas libri tres* = *PL*, XXVI, 307–438.

———. *Epistolae.* Ed. Isidor Hilberg. (*CSEL*, LIV.) Vienna, Leipzig, 1910. / = *PL*, XXII, 325–1224. / See also *Select Letters.* Tr. F. A. Wright. (Loeb Classical Library.) London and New York, 1933.

JEROME. *In Psalterium Praefatio* / = *PL*, XXVIII, 1123–1128.

JOHANN, OF SAAZ. *Der Ackermann aus Böhmen.* Ed. Alois Bernt. Heidelberg, 1929.

JOHANNES, ABBOT OF ST. ARNULF. *Vita Iohannis Abbatis Gorziensis.* In: *MGH Scr.*, ed. G. H. Pertz, IV, 335–377. Hanover, 1841; repr. Leipzig, 1925.

JORGA, NICULAE. "Cărţi representative în viaţa omenirii, Seria A II-a: Ratherius, Richerius, Liutprand," *Revista istorică*, XIII (1927), 329–361. (Reviewed by R. Ortiz in *Studi Medievali*, N.S. 1 (1928), 602–604.)

JOSEPH OF EXETER. *De bello Troiano.* In: SAMUEL DRESEMIUS (ed.). *Dictys Cretensis et Dares Phrygius: De bello Trojano: Accedunt Josephi Iscanii De bello Trojano libri sex*, II, 364–576. London, 1825.

JULIANUS POMERIUS. *De vita contemplativa libri tres* = *PL*, LIX, 415–520.

JUNGMANN, JOSEF ANDREAS. *Missarum sollemnia: Eine genetische Erklärung der römischen Messe.* 2 vols. 3rd edn., Vienna, 1952. / = *The Mass of the Roman Rite: Its Origins and Development.* Tr. Francis A. Brunner. 2 vols. New York, 1951, 1955.

KIRCHHOFF, ALBRECHT. *Die Handschriftenhändler des Mittelalters.* 2nd edn., Leipzig, 1853.

KLAUSER, THEODOR. "Der Übergang der römischen Kirche von der griechischen zur lateinischen Liturgiesprache," *Miscellanea Giovanni Mercati*, I, 467–482. (= *Studi e Testi*, CXXI.) Vatican City, 1946.

KNOPF, RUDOLF, and GUSTAV KRÜGER (ed.). *Ausgewählte Märtyrerakten.* (Sammlung ausgewählter Kirchen- und Dogmengeschichtlicher Quellen-Schriften, N.S. 3.) 3rd edn., Tübingen, 1929.

LABORDE, COMTE ALEXANDRE DE (ed.). *La Chanson de Roland: Reproduction phototypique du MS Digby 23 de la Bodleian Library d'Oxford.* (Société des Anciens Textes Français.) Paris, 1933.

LACLOS, PIERRE CHODERLOS DE. *Les Liaisons dangereuses.* Amsterdam and Paris, 1782 / = *Dangerous Acquaintances.* Tr. Richard Aldington. (Broadway Translations.) London and New York, 1924.

LAISTNER, MAX L. W. *Thought and Letters in Western Europe* A.D. *500 to 900.* Ithaca, N. Y., 1931; new edn., 1957.

[*Lancelot.*] *The Vulgate Version of the Arthurian Romances.* Ed. H. Oscar Sommer. Vols. 3–5: *Le Livre de Lancelot del Lac.* (Carnegie Institute of Washington, publication no. 74.) 1910–1911.

LANGLAND, WILLIAM. *The Vision of William concerning Piers the Plowman, together with Vita de Dowel, Dobet, et Dobest, secundum Wit and Resonn,* pt. II: *The 'Crowley' Text; or Text B.* Ed. Walter W. Skeat. (Early English Text Society, 38.) London, 1869.

LANGLOIS, ERNEST. "Chronologie des romans de *Thèbes,* d'*Eneas* et de *Troie,*" *Bibliothèque de l'Ecole des Chartes,* LXVI (1905), 107–120.

LAPESA, RAFAEL. *Historia de la lengua española.* 2nd edn., Madrid, 1950.

LAUER, P. *Catalogue général des manuscrits latins (Bibliothèque Nationale),* I. Paris, 1939.

[LE BOSSU, ADAM (DE LA HALLE).] *Adam Le Bossu, trouvère artésien du XIIIᵉ siècle: Le Jeu de la Feuillée.* Ed. Ernest Langlois. (Les Classiques français du moyen âge.) 2nd edn., Paris, 1951.

LECLERCQ, HENRI. "Perpétue et Félicité (Saintes)," *DACL,* XIV, 1, cols. 393–444. Paris, 1939.

LE GENTIL, PIERRE. *Le Virelai et le villancico: Le problème des origines arabes.* (Collection Portugaise, 9.) Paris, 1954.

LEHMANN, PAUL. "Das literarische Bild Karls des Grossen vornehmlich im lateinischen Schrifttum des Mittelalters," *Sitzungsberichte der bayerischen Akademie der Wissenschaften* (Munich), *Phil.-hist. Abt.,* Heft 9 (1934), pp. 13–18.

LERCH, EUGEN. " 'Passion' und 'Gefühl,' " *Archivum Romanicum,* XXII (1938), 320–349.

LESNE, ÉMILE. *Histoire de la propriété ecclésiastique en France,* v: *Les Écoles de la fin du VIIIᵉ siècle à la fin du XIIᵉ.* (Mémoires et travaux des Facultés Catholiques de Lille, 50.) Lille, 1940.

LEVISON, WILHELM, and HEINZ LÖWE. "Die Karolinger: Vom Anfang des 8. Jahrhunderts bis zum Tode Karls des Grossen." In: Wattenbach-Levison's *Deutschlands Geschichtsquellen im Mittelalter: Vorzeit und Karolinger.* Weimar, 1953.

Liber miraculorum Sancte Fidis. See BOUILLET.

LIUDPRAND. *Opera (Antapodosis libri VI; Historia Ottonis; Relatio de legatione Constantinopolitana).* In: *MGH Scr.,* ed. G. H. Pertz, III, 264–363. Hanover, 1839; repr. Leipzig, 1925.

———. *Die Werke Liudprands von Cremona.* Ed. Joseph Becker. (Scriptores Rerum Germanicarum in usum scholarum ex *MGH* separatim editi.) 3rd edn., Hanover and Leipzig, 1915.

———. *Aus Liudprands Werken.* Tr. K. von der Osten-Sacken. (Die Geschichtschreiber der deutschen Vorzeit, 29: Zehntes Jahrhundert, 2.) 2nd edn. (ed. W. Wattenbach), Leipzig, 1890.

[LONGINUS.] *On the Sublime [Peri hypsous].* Ed. and tr. W. Rhys Roberts. 2nd edn., Cambridge, Eng., 1907; repr., 1935.

LOOMIS, LAURA ALANDIS. *Medieval Romance in England. A Study of the sources and analogues of the non-cyclic metrical romances.* New York, 1924.

LOPEZ, ROBERT SABATINO. Review of various Venetian notarial documents edited by L. Lafranchi, A. Lombardo, et al., in: *Speculum,* XXXI (1956), 177f.

LORRIS, GUILLAUME DE, and JEAN DE MEUN. *Le Roman de la Rose.* Ed. and comm. M. Gorce. (Collection des textes rares ou inédits.) Paris, 1933.

LOT, FERDINAND. *Etudes sur le règne de Hugues Capet et la fin du Xe siècle.* (Bibliothèque de l'École des Hautes Études, 147.) Paris, 1903.

———. "Le Dialecte roman des Serments de Strasbourg," *Romania,* LXV (1939), 145–163.

———. *Les Derniers Carolingiens: Lothaire—Louis V—Charles de Lorraine (954–991).* (Bibl. de l'École des Hautes Études, 87.) Paris, 1891.

LÖWE, H. See LEVISON, WILHELM.

LOYEN, ANDRÉ. *Sidoine Apollinaire et l'esprit précieux en Gaule aux derniers jours de l'Empire.* (Collection d'Études Latines, Série scient. 20.) Paris, 1943.

LUCILIUS. *C. Lucilii Carminum reliquiae.* Ed. Fridericus Marx. 2 vols. Leipzig, 1904, 1905.

[LUPUS OF FERRIÈRES.] *Loup de Ferrières: Correspondance.* Ed. and tr. Léon Levillain. (Les Classiques de l'histoire de France au moyen âge, 10, 16.) 2 vols. Paris, 1927, 1935.

MABILLON, JEAN (ed.). *Acta Sanctorum Ordinis S. Benedicti in saeculorum classes distributa,* v: *Saeculum* v. Paris, 1685.

MALNORY, A. *Saint Césaire évêque d'Arles 503–543.* (Bibl. de l'École des Hautes Études, 103.) Paris, 1894.

MANDONNET, P. "La Crise scolaire au début du XIIIe siècle et la fondation de l'ordre des Frères-Prêcheurs," *Revue d'histoire ecclésiastique,* XV (1914), 34–49.

MANITIUS, MAX. *Geschichte der lateinischen Literatur des Mittelalters,* II. (Handbuch der Altertumswissenschaft, Bd. IX: Abt. 2, Teil 2.) Munich, 1923.

MARIE DE FRANCE. *Die Lais.* Ed. Karl Warnke. (Bibliotheca normannica, 3.) 3rd improved edn., Halle, 1925.

MARROU, HENRI-IRÉNÉE. *Histoire de l'éducation dans l'antiquité.* Paris, 1948. / = *A History of Education in Antiquity.* Tr. George Lamb. New York, 1956.

MARTÈNE, EDMOND. *De antiquis ecclesiae ritibus libri tres.* Editio novissima. 4 vols. Bassano, 1788.

MARTIANUS CAPELLA. *De nuptiis Philologiae et Mercurii libri VIII.* Ed. Adolf Dick. Leipzig, 1925.

MARTIN OF BRAGA (MARTINUS BRACARENSIS). *Opera omnia.* Ed. Claude W. Barlow. (Papers and Monographs of the American Academy in Rome, 12.) New Haven, 1950.

MATHILDE. See *Vita Mathildis.*

MENÉNDEZ PIDAL, RAMÓN. *Poesía juglaresca y juglares: Aspectos de la historia literaria y cultural de España.* Buenos Aires, Mexico, etc., 1942.

MEYER, PAUL. "Anciennes Poésies religieuses en langue d'oc," *Bibliothèque de l'École des Chartes,* ser. V, vol. 1 (1860), 481–497.

MEYER, PAUL. "Fragment d'une Chanson d'Antioche en provençal," *Archives de l'Orient latin*, II (1884): *Documents*, 467–509.

———. "Le Poème de Boèce revu sur le manuscrit," *Romania*, I (1872), 226–234.

MICHEL, PAUL HENRI. *Romanesque Wall Paintings in France*. Tr. Joan Evans. London, 1950.

MILKAU, FRITZ (ed.). *Handbuch der Bibliothekswissenschaft*, I, III. 2nd edn. (ed. Georg Leyh), Wiesbaden, 1952, 1955.

MOHRMANN, CHRISTINE. "Le Latin commun et le Latin des Chrétiens," *Vigiliae Christianae: A Review of Early Christian Life and Language*, I (1947), 1–12.

MONACI, ERNESTO. *Crestomazia italiana dei primi secoli con prospetto grammaticale e glossario*. New edn. (ed. Felice Arese), Rome, 1955.

MONTICELLI, GIUSEPPE. *Raterio vescovo di Verona (890–974)*. Milan, 1938.

MULLER, HENRY FRANÇOIS. *L'Époque mérovingienne: Essai de synthèse de philologie et d'histoire*. New York, 1945.

NORBERG, DAG. "Syntaktische Forschungen auf dem Gebiete des Spätlateins und des frühen Mittellateins," *Uppsala Universitets Årsskrift*, 1943, fasc. 9.

NORDEN, EDUARD. *Die antike Kunstprosa vom VI. Jahrhundert v. Chr. bis in die Zeit der Renaissance*. 2 vols. Leipzig, 1915; repr. 1923.

———. "Die römische Literatur." In: ALFRED GERCKE and EDUARD NORDEN. *Einleitung in die Altertumswissenschaft*, I: 4. 3rd edn., Leipzig, Berlin, 1927. (Published separately: 5th edn., Leipzig, 1954.)

On the Sublime. See LONGINUS.

ORTIZ, R. See under JORGA.

[OTFRIED OF WEISSENBURG.] *Otfrids Evangelienbuch*. Ed. Oskar Erdmann. 2d edn. rev. by Edward Schröder. Halle, Berlin, 1934.

Ottimo Commento della Divina Commedia: Testo inedito d'un contemporaneo di Dante. 3 vols. Pisa, 1827–1829.

OWEN, E. C. E. *Some Authentic Acts of the Early Martyrs*. Translated with notes and introductions. . . . Oxford, 1927.

PARIS, GASTON. "La Chanson d'Antioche provençale et la Gran Conquista de Ultramar," *Romania*, XVII (1888), 513–541; XVIII (1890), 562–591; XXII (1893), 345–363.

Passio Martyrum Scillitanorum. In: *Analecta Bollandiana*, VIII (1889), 6–8.

Passio Sanctarum Perpetuae et Felicitatis. See BEEK.

PAULUS DIACONUS. *Historia Langobardorum*. Ed. L. Bethmann and G. Waitz. In: *MGH Scr. rer. Lang*. Hanover, 1878.

PAUPHILET, ALBERT. "Eneas et Enée," *Romania*, LV (1929), 195–213.

PAVANI, GIUSEPPE. *Un vescovo belga in Italia nel secolo decimo: Studio storico-critico su Raterio di Verona*. Turin, 1920.

PELAN, M. See *Floire et Blancheflor*.

PERI, H. (Hiram Pflaum). "Old French Poems from the Mahzor," *Tarbiz: A Quarterly for Jewish Studies*, XXV (1955–1956), 154–182; English summary, pp. ii–iii.

———. "Prayer in the Vernacular during the Middle Ages," *Tarbiz*, XXIV (1954–1955), 426–440; English summary, pp. iv–v.

Peri hypsous. See LONGINUS.

PETRUS BLESENSIS (PETER OF BLOIS). *Liber de confessione sacramentali* = *PL*, CCVII, 1077–1092.

PHILIPPE DE HARVENG(T). *De institutione clericorum tractatus sex* = *PL*, CCIII, 665–1206.

PHILIPPE DE THAUN. See THAUN.

Piers the Plowman. See LANGLAND, WILLIAM.

PILLET, ALFRED. *Bibliographie der Troubadours*. (Schriften der Königsberger Gelehrten Gesellschaft, Sonderreihe, 3.) Rev. edn. (ed. Henry Carstens), Halle, 1933.

PINNER, H. L. *The World of Books in Classical Antiquity*. Leiden, 1948.

PIRENNE, HENRI. "De l'état de l'instruction des laïques a l'époque mérovingienne," *Revue Bénédictine*, XLVI (1934), 165–177.

PIRENNE, HENRI. "L'Instruction des marchands au moyen âge," *Annales d'histoire économique et sociale*, 1 (1929), 13–28.

PIVEC, KARL. "Die Briefsammlung Gerberts von Aurillac," *Mitteilungen des österreichischen Instituts für Geschichtsforschung*, XLIX (1935), 15–74.

PORPHYRIO, POMPONIUS. *Commentarii in Q. Horatium Flaccum*. Ed. Wilhelm Meyer. Leipzig, 1874.

RABY, F. J. E. *A History of Secular Latin Poetry in the Middle Ages*. 2 vols. Oxford, 1934. (Vol. I in 2nd edn., 1957.)

RATHER OF VERONA. *Opera omnia*. Ed. Pietro and Geronimo Ballerini. Verona, 1765. / = *PL*, CXXXVI. (*De contemptu canonum; Discordia; Excerptum ex dialogo confessionali; Phrenesis; Praeloquia; Qualitatis coniectura cuiusdam; Synodica ad presbyteros* . . . ; *Vita Sancti Ursmari*.)

———. *Die Briefe des Bischofs Rather von Verona*. Ed. Fritz Weigle. (*MGH Briefe*, I.) Weimar, 1949.

RAYNOUARD, M. *Choix des poésies originales des Troubadours*, II. Paris, 1817.

RICHER. *Historiarum libri IIII*. Ed. Georg H. Pertz. (*MGH Scr.*, III.) Hanover, 1839; repr. Leipzig, 1925.

———. *Historiarum libri IIII*. (Scriptores Rerum Germanicarum in usum scholarum ex *MGH* recusi.) 2nd edn. (ed. Georg Waitz), Hanover, 1877.

———. *Richers vier Bücher Geschichten*. Tr. Karl von der Osten-Sacken. (Die Geschichtschreiber der deutschen Vorzeit, 37: Zehntes Jahrhundert, 10.) 2nd edn. (ed. W. Wattenbach), Leipzig, 1891.

RIESE, ALEX, and F. BUECHELER (eds.). *Anthologia latina sive Poesis Latinae supplementum*. Leipzig, 1906.

ROCCA, MOROZZO DELLA. [A Venetian text of the mid-twelfth century.] In: *Giornale Economico della Camera di Commercio, Industria ed Agricultura di Venezia*, March, 1954.

Le Roman de la Rose. See LORRIS, G. DE.

Le Roman de Thèbes. Ed. Léopold Constans. (Société des anciens textes français.) 2 vols. Paris, 1890.

Le Roman de Troie. See BENEEIT (BENOIT) DE SAINTE-MAURE.

ROQUES, MARIO. "Les Serments de Strasbourg," *Medium Aevum,* v (1936), 157–172.

ROSTOVTZEFF, MICHAEL. *Gesellschaft und Wirtschaft im römischen Kaiserreich.* Tr. Lothar Wickert. 2 vols. Leipzig, 1929. / = *The Social and Economic History of the Roman Empire.* 2nd edn., revised by P. M. Fraser. 2 vols. Oxford, 1957 (1st edn., 1926).

RUIZ, JUAN. *Libro de buen amor.* (Clásicos Castellanos.) 2 vols. 4th edn. (ed. Julio Cejador y Frauca), Madrid, 1937.

RUOTGER. *Vita Brunonis.* Ed. Georg H. Pertz. In: *MGH Scr.,* IV, 252–275. Hanover, 1841; repr. Leipzig, 1925.

——. *Lebensbeschreibung des Erzbischofs Bruno von Köln.* Ed. Irene Ott. In: *MGH Scr. rer. Germ.,* N.S. x. Weimar, 1951.

——. *Lebensbeschreibung des heiligen Erzbischofs Bruno von Köln.* Tr. Irene Schmale-Ott. (Die Geschichtschreiber der deutschen Vorzeit, xxx.) Münster, Cologne, 1954.

RUPPRECHT, ERNST. "Bemerkungen zur Passio SS. Perpetuae et Felicitatis," *Rheinisches Museum für Philologie,* N.F. 90 (1941), 177–192.

Saint-Alexis. See *Vie de Saint-Alexis.*

SAMARAN, C. "Étude historique et paléographique." In: A. DE LABORDE, *La Chanson de Roland . . .* (q.v.), pp. 1–50.

SCHIAFFINI, ALFREDO. *Tradizione e poesia nella prosa d'arte italiana dalla latinità medievale a G. Boccaccio.* Genoa, 1934; 2nd rev. edn., Rome, 1943.

SCHIROKAUER, ARNO. "Frühneuhochdeutsch." In: WOLFGANG STAMMLER, *Deutsche Philologie im Aufriss,* cols. 1013–1076. Berlin, 1952. 2nd edn., reworked by Stammler, cols. 855–930; Berlin, 1957.

SCHMIDT, LUDWIG. "Cassiodor und Theoderich," *Historisches Jahrbuch im Auftrage der Görres-Gesellschaft,* XLVII (1927), 727–729.

SCHÖNBACH, ANTON E. "Studien zur Geschichte der altdeutschen Zeugnisse Bertholds von Regensburg zur Volkskunde," *Sitzungs-*

berichte der Phil.-hist. Classe der Kaiserlichen Akademie der Wissenschaften zu Wien, CXLII: 7 (1900), 56–89.

SCHRAMM, PERCY ERNST. *Kaiser, Rom und Renovatio: Studien und Texte zur Geschichte des römischen Erneuerungsgedankens vom Ende des Karolingischen Reiches bis zum Investiturstreit.* (Studien der Bibliothek Warburg, 17.) 2 vols. Leipzig, Berlin, 1929.

SCHREYER, BRIGITTA. "Eine althochdeutsche Schriftsprache." In: WILHELM BRAUNE, HERMANN PAUL, EDUARD SIEVERS. *Beiträge zur Geschichte der deutschen Sprache und Literatur*, ed. T. Frings, LXXIII: 3, 351–386. Halle, 1951.

SCHRIJNEN, JOSEF. *Charakteristik des Altchristlichen Latein.* (Latinitas Christianorum Primaeva: Studia ad sermonem Latinum Christianum pertinentia, 1.) Nijmegen, 1932.

SCHUBERT, HANS VON. *Geschichte der Christlichen Kirche im Frühmittelalter.* Tübingen, 1921.

SCHUCHTER, EDITH. "Zum Predigtstil des hl. Augustinus," *Wiener Studien*, LII (1934), 115–138.

SCHWARK, BRUNO. *Bischof Rather von Verona als Theologe.* (Bonn Univ. Ph.D. diss.) Königsberg, 1915.

SENECA, LUCIUS ANNAEUS. *Ad Lucilium Epistularum Moralium quae supersunt.* Ed. Otto Hense. Leipzig, 1898; 2nd edn., 1914.

[SERVIUS.] *Servii grammatici qui feruntur in Vergilii Carmina commentarii, 1: Aeneidos librorum I-V commentarii.* Ed. Georg Thilo. Leipzig, Berlin, 1881.

SEVERUS, EMMANUEL VON. *Lupus von Ferrières: Gestalt und Werk eines Vermittlers antiken Geistesgutes an das Mittelalter im 9. Jahrhundert.* (Beiträge zur Geschichte des alten Mönchtums und des Benediktinerordens, 21.) Münster in Westphalia, 1940.

SEVERUS, SULPICIUS. *Libri qui supersunt.* Ed. C. Halm. (*CSEL*, 1.) Vienna, 1866.

SIDONIUS APOLLINARIS. *Epistulae et Carmina.* Ed. Christian Luetjohann. (*MGH AA*, VIII.) Berlin, 1887.

SILVESTRE, H. "Comment on rédigeait une lettre au Xe siècle: L'épître d'Éracle de Liège à Rathier de Vérone." *Le Moyen Age*, LVIII (1952), 1–30.

SNIJDERS, CHERUBINE. *Het Latijn der brieven van Lupus van Ferrières, Middeleeuws humanist.* (Thesis.) Amsterdam, 1943.

SPITZER, LEO. "The Addresses to the Reader in the 'Commedia,'" *Italica*, XXXII (1955), 143–165.

———. "The Mozarabic Lyric and Theodor Frings' Theories," *Comparative Literature*, IV (1952), 1–22.

———. Review of Erich Auerbach's "Remarques sur le mot 'passion'," *Neuphilologische Mitteilungen*, XXXVIII (1937), 218–224, in *Romania*, LXV (1939), 123f.

Suetonius. Tr. J. C. Rolfe. (Loeb Classical Library.) Cambridge, Mass., and London, 1951.

SULPICIUS SEVERUS. *See* SEVERUS.

SUSO, HENRY. *Horologium sapientiae.* Ed. Joseph Strange. New edn., Cologne, 1861.

SÜSS, WILHELM. "Das Problem der lateinischen Bibelsprache," *Historische Vierteljahrschrift*, XXVII (1932), 1–39.

———. *Studien zur lateinischen Bibel, I: Augustins Locutiones und das Problem der lateinischen Bibelsprache.* (Acta et Commentationes Universitatis Tartuensis [Dorpatensis], [Ser.] B: Humaniora, XXIX, fasc. 4.) [Tartu, 1932.]

TERTULLIAN. *Adversus Marcionem libri quinque* = PL, II, 243–524. / = *CSEL*, XLVII (ed. Emil Kroymann, 1906), 290–650.

———. *De spectaculis.* Ed. E. Dekkers. (*CCSL*, I, 225–253.) Turnhout, 1954.

THAUN, PHILIPPE DE. *Li Livre des Creatures. The Bestiary of Philippe de Thaun.* Ed. T. Wright. London, 1841.

Thesaurus linguae latinae. Editus auctoritate et consilio Academiarum quinque Germanicarum Berolinensis Gottingensis Lipsiensis Monacensis Vindobonensis. Leipzig, 1900ff. (in progress).

THOMPSON, JAMES WESTFALL. *The Medieval Library.* (The University of Chicago Studies in Library Science.) Chicago, 1939; repr., with a supplement by Blanche B. Boyer, New York, 1957.

UGOLINI, FRANCESCO A. (ed.). *Testi antichi italiani.* Turin, 1942.

VACCARI, A. "Volgarismi notevoli nel latino di S. Cesario di Arles (†543)," *ALMA*, XVII (1943), 135–148.

VENANTIUS FORTUNATUS. *Opera poetica*. Ed. Fridericus Leo. (*MGH AA*, IV: 1.) Berlin, 1881.

———. *Opera pedestria*. Ed. Bruno Krusch. (*MGH AA*, IV: 2.) Berlin, 1885.

———. *Vita sanctae Radegundis*. Ibid.

VICO, GIAMBATTISTA. *La Scienza Nuova giusta l'edizione del 1744 con le varianti*. . . . Ed. Fausto Nicolini. Bari, 1928. / = *The New Science of Giambattista Vico*. Tr. from the 3rd edn. (1744) by Thomas Goddard Bergin and Max Harold Fisch. Ithaca, N. Y., 1948.

La Vie de Saint-Alexis. Ed. M[ario] R[oques]. (Classiques français du moyen âge.) Paris, 1911.

VIRGIL (PUBLIUS VERGILIUS MARO). *The Aeneid*. Tr. C. Day-Lewis. New York and London, 1952.

VISCARDI, ANTONIO et al. (ed.). *Le origini: Testi latini, italiani, provenzali e franco-italiani*. (La letteratura italiana: Storia e testi, 1.) Milan, Naples, n.d. (1939?).

[*Vita Mathildis*.] *Vita Mahthildis reginae*. Ed. Georg H. Pertz. In: *MGH Scr.*, IV, 282–302. Hanover, 1841; repr. Leipzig, 1925.

———. *Das Leben der Königin Mathilde*. Tr. P. Jaffé. (Die Geschichtschreiber der deutschen Vorzeit, 31: Zehntes Jahrhundert, 4.) 2nd edn. (ed. W. Wattenbach), Leipzig, 1891.

VOGEL, ALBRECHT. *Ratherius von Verona und das zehnte Jahrhundert*. 2 parts. Jena, 1854.

VOSSLER, KARL. *Die Dichtungsformen der Romanen*. Ed. Andreas Bauer. Stuttgart, 1951.

[*Voyage de Saint Brandan*.] *Die altfranzösische Prosaübersetzung von Brendans Meerfahrt nach der Pariser Hdschr. Nat. Bibl. fr. 1553*. . . . Ed. Carl Wahlund. (Skrifter utgifna af K. Humanistika Vetenskaps-samfundet i Upsala, vol. 4, pt. 3.) Upsala, 1900.

VYVER, A. VAN DE. "Cassiodore et son œuvre," *Speculum*, VI (1931), 244–292.

[WACE.] *La Vie de Saint Nicolas par Wace: Poème religieux du XIIe siècle.* Ed. Einar Ronsjö. (Études Romanes de Lund, 5.) Lund, Copenhagen, 1942.

———. *Maistre Wace's Roman de Rou et des ducs de Normandie, nach den Handschriften.* Ed. Hugo Andresen. 2 vols. Heilbronn, 1877, 1879.

WALTER OF CHÂTILLON (WALTER OF LILLE). *Alexandreis.* In: W. MÜLDENER. *Die zehn Gedichte des Walter von Lille.* Hanover, 1859. / = *PL,* CCIX, 463–572.

WALTHER VON WARTBURG. *Raccolta di testi antichi italiani.* (Bibliotheca Romanica, Series altera: Scripta Romanica Selecta, 1.) Bern, 1946.

WATTENBACH-LEVISON. See LEVISON.

WEHRLI, FRITZ. "Der erhabene und der schlichte Stil in der poetisch-rhetorischen Theorie der Antike." In: *Phyllobolia für Peter von der Mühll zum 60. Geburtstag am 1. August 1945 von Olof Gigon et alii,* pp. 9–34. Basel, 1946.

WEIGLE, FRITZ. "Die Briefe Rathers von Verona," *Deutsches Archiv für Geschichte des Mittelalters,* 1 (1937), 147–194.

———. "Ratherius von Verona im Kampf um das Kirchengut 961–968," *Quellen und Forschungen aus italienischen Archiven und Bibliotheken,* XXVIII (1937–38), 1–35.

———. "Urkunden und Akten zur Geschichte Rathers in Verona," ibid., XXIX (1938–39), 1–40.

———. "Zur Geschichte des Bischofs Rather von Verona: Analekten zur Ausgabe seiner Briefe," *Deutsches Archiv für Geschichte des Mittelalters,* V (1942), 347–386.

WELTER, J.-T. *L'Exemplum dans la littérature religieuse et didactique du Moyen Age.* (University of Paris Ph.D. diss.) Paris, Toulouse, 1927.

WENDLAND, PAUL. *Die hellenistisch-römische Kultur in ihren Beziehungen zu Judentum und Christentum.* Tübingen, 1907. 2nd and 3rd edn. in: *Handbuch zum Neuen Testament,* I: 2. Tübingen, 1912.

WIERUSZOWSKI, HELENE. "Arezzo as a Center of Learning and Letters in the Thirteenth Century," *Traditio*, IX (1953), 321–391.

WILAMOWITZ-MOELLENDORFF, ULRICH VON. "Der kynische Prediger Teles." In: *Philologische Untersuchungen*, IV, 292–319. Berlin, 1881.

WILMART, A. "Allocutions de Saint Augustine pour la Vigile Pascale et compléments des sermons sur l'Alleluia," *Revue Bénédictine*, XLII (1930), 136–142.

[WIPO.] *Die Werke Wipos*. (Scriptores Rerum Germanicarum in usum scholarum ex *MGH* separatim editi.) 3rd edn. (ed. Harry Bresslau), Hanover, Leipzig, 1915.

WIRTZ, W. See *Flore et Blancheflor*.

YOUNG, KARL. *The Drama of the Medieval Church*. 2 vols. Oxford, 1933.

ZOEPF, LUDWIG. *Das Heiligenleben im 10. Jahrhundert*. (Beiträge zur Kulturgeschichte des Mittelalters und der Renaissance, 1.) Leipzig, Berlin, 1908.

ZONTA, GIUSEPPE (ed.). "Il Raverta: Dialogo di Messer Giuseppe Betussi nel quale si ragiona d'Amore e degli effetti suoi," *Trattati d'amore del Cinquecento*. (Scrittori d'Italia.) Bari, 1912.

INDEXES

GENERAL INDEX

Entries preceded by * indicate a quotation. For an index of Latin words, see p. 389.

INDEX OF LATIN WORDS DISCUSSED OR
COMMENTED ON

BIBLIOGRAPHY OF THE WRITINGS

OF ERICH AUERBACH

ArR   *Archivum Romanicum*. Florence.

      Die Argonauten. Heidelberg.

CL   *Comparative Literature*. Eugene, Oregon.

      Convivium. Turin.

      Cultura italiana e tedesca. Berlin.

DL   *Deutsche Literaturzeitung*. Berlin.

DVLG *Deutsche Vierteljahrsschrift für Literaturwissenschaft und Geistesgeschichte*. Halle.

      Felsefe Arkivi. Istanbul.

GRM *Germanisch-romanische Monatsschrift*. Heidelberg.

      Gnomon. Berlin.

      Göttingische gelehrte Anzeigen. Berlin.

      Historiche Zeitschrift. Munich.

      The Hopkins Review. Baltimore.

      Hudson Review. New York.

      Das humanistische Gymnasium. Leipzig.

      Inventario. Florence.

      Italica. Menasha, Wisconsin.

      Journal of Aesthetics and Art Criticism. New York.

      Kenyon Review. Gambier, Ohio.

LGRP *Literaturblatt für germanische und romanische Philologie*. Leipzig.

MLN *Modern Language Notes*. Baltimore.

      Münchner romanistische Arbeiten. Munich.

393

Neue Jahrbücher für Wissenschaft und Jugendbildung. Leipzig and Berlin.

Der neue Merkur. Munich.

NS *Die neueren Sprachen.* Marburg.

NRS *Neue Rundschau.* Berlin.

NM *Neuphilologische Mitteilungen.* Helsinki.

Partisan Review. New York.

PMLA *Publications of the Modern Language Association of America.* New York.

Romanic Review. New York.

RF *Romanische Forschungen.* Frankfurt a. M.

RPh *Romance Philology.* Berkeley, California.

Speculum. Cambridge, Massachusetts.

Studi francesi. Turin.

Yale French Studies. New Haven.

Zeitschrift für romanische Philologie. Halle.

[Rev.] At beginning of entry, indicates a review by Erich Auerbach of the work cited.

[Tr.] At beginning of entry, indicates a translation by Erich Auerbach.

NOTE: The arrangement is alphabetical within years. When no translator is named, there was no mention of one in the publication.

1913

Die Teilnahme in den Vorarbeiten zu einem neuen Strafgesetzbuch. Heidelberg University, doctoral dissertation in law. Berlin: Juristische Verlagsbuchhandlung.

1921

a. [Tr.]   Dante: *La Vita nuova,* Sonetto XV. Petrarch: Sonetti LXX, CI, CCXLI. In *Die Argonauten,* No. 10/12.

b. "Zur Dante-Feier," *NRs,* XXXII (Sept.).

c. *Zur Technik der Frührenaissancenovelle in Italien und Frankreich.* Greifswald University, doctoral dissertation in romance philology. Heidelberg: Carl Winter.

1922

a. "Giambattista Vico," *Der neue Merkur,* VI (July).

b. "La Fontaine und Pierre Mille," *NRS,* XXXIII (April).

1924

a. [Tr.]   Petrarch: Sonetti LXXX, CII. In *Cultura italiana e tedesca,* II (April–May).

b. "Stefan Georges Danteübertragung," *Cultura italiana e tedesca,* II (Jan.).

c. [Tr.]   Giambattista Vico: *Die neue Wissenschaft über die gemeinschaftliche Natur der Völker* [*La Scienza nuova,* 1744 edn.]. Munich: Allgemeine Verlagsanstalt. (1929, publication taken over by Walter de Gruyter, Berlin.)

1926

a. "Paul-Louis Courier," *DVLG,* IV, No. 3. (= 1951g, 3.)

b. "Racine und die Leidenschaften," *GRM,* XIV, No. 9/10.

1927

a. [Tr., with Theodor Lücke.] Benedetto Croce: *Die Philosophie Giambattista Vicos* [*La Filosofia di Giambattista Vico*]. Tübingen: J. C. B. Mohr.

b. "Marcel Proust: Der Roman von der verlorenen Zeit," *NS*, XXXV (Jan.–Feb.).

c. "Über das Persönliche in der Wirkung des heiligen Franz von Assisi," *DVLG*, V, No. 1.

1928

a. "Die Randglossen des Cod. Hamilton 203 zum ersten und zweiten Gesang der göttlichen Komödie." In *Von Büchern und Bibliotheken*. (Ernst Kuhnert Festschrift.) Berlin: Struppe und Winckler.

b. [Rev.] Luigi Valli: *Il Linguaggio segreto di Dante e dei "fedeli d'Amore"* (Rome: Casa Optima, 1928). In *DL*, No. 28.

1929

a. *Dante als Dichter der irdischen Welt*. Berlin and Leipzig: Walter de Gruyter. (Tr. = 1961a, 1963, 1.)

b. [Rev.] *Deutsches Dante-Jahrbuch X* (Weimar: Böhlau, 1928). In *DL*, No. 11.

c. "Entdeckung Dantes in der Romantik," *DVLG*, VII, No. 4.

d. [Rev.] Richard Peters: *Der Aufbau der Weltgeschichte bei Giambattista Vico* (Berlin: J. G. Cotta, 1929). In *DL*, No. 8.

e. "Vico," *Vossische Zeitung* (Berlin), June 5.

1930

a. [Rev.] Franz Dornseiff and Joseph Balogh (trs.): Dante, *Über das Dichten in der Muttersprache* [*De Vulgari Eloquentia*] (Darmstadt: Reichl, 1925). In *Gnomon*, VI (Sept.).

b. [Rev.] *Deutsches Dante-Jahrbuch XI* (Weimar: Böhlaus Nach-
folger, 1929). In *DL*, No. 4.

c. [Rev.] Theodor Ostermann: *Dante in Deutschland*. Heidelberg:
Carl Winter, 1929. In *LGRP*, IX–X.

1931

a. "Dante und Virgil," *Das humanistische Gymnasium*, IV–V.

b. "Das italienische Buch in Deutschland." In *Atti del primo congresso
mondiale delle biblioteche e di bibliografia Roma–Venezia 15–30
giugno 1929*, Vol. III. Rome: Istituto Poligrafico dello Stato.

c. [Rev.] Giambattista Vico: *La Scienza nuova*, Vols. I and II, ed.
Fausto Nicolini (Bari: Giuseppe Laterza, 1928). In *DL*, No. 26.

1932

a. [Rev.] Gustave Cohen: *Le Théâtre en France au moyen âge*, Vol.
II (Paris: Rieder, 1931). In *DL*, No. 5.

b. "Der Schriftsteller Montaigne," *GRM*, XX (Jan.–Feb.).

c. [Rev.] Leo Spitzer: *Romanische Stil- und Literaturstudien* (Marburg: Elwert, 1931). In *DL*, No. 8.

d. "Über den historischen Ort Rousseaus," *NS*, XL (Feb.).

e. "Vico und Herder," *DVLG*, X.

1933

a. [Rev.] Dante: *Il Convivio* (Vatican: Biblioteca Apostolica Vati-
cana, 1932). In *DL*, No. 4.

b. "Das französische Publikum des 17. Jahrhunderts," *Münchener romanistische Arbeiten*, III.

c. [Rev.] Leonardo Olschki: *Die romanischen Literaturen des Mittelalters* (Potsdam: Akademische Verlagsgesellschaft Athenaion, 1928).
In *Göttingische gelehrte Anzeigen*, No. 9.

d. "Romantik und Realismus," *Neue Jahrbücher für Wissenschaft und
Jugendbildung*, IX, No. 2.

1934

a. [Rev.] *Die Handschriften des Briefes an Can Grande della Scala,* ed. Friedrich Schneider (Zwickau: F. Ullmann, 1933). In *Historische Zeitschrift, CL,* No. 3.

b. [Rev.] Hans Rabow: *Die "asolanischen Gespräche" des Pietro Bembo* (Leipzig: Paul Haupt, 1933). In *DL,* No. 51.

1936

"Giambattista Vico und die Idee der Philologie." In *Homenatge a Antoni Rubió i Lluch.* (Miscel·lània d'Estudis Literaris Historics i Lingüistics, I.) Barcelona: Institut d'Estudis Catalans. (Tr. = 1956a.)

1937

a. [Rev.] Paul Binswanger: *Die ästhetische Problematik Flauberts* (Frankfurt a. M.: Klostermann, 1934). In *LGRP,* III–IV.

b. "Remarques sur le mot 'passion,'" *NM,* XXXVIII.

c. "Sprachliche Beiträge zur Erklärung der Scienza Nuova von G. B. Vico," *ArR,* XXI, No. 2/3.

d. *Über die ernste Nachahmung des Alltäglichen.* (Istanbul Üniversitesi Edebiyat Fakültesi Yayinlari II.) Istanbul: Devlet Basimevi.

1938

a. "Figura," *ArR,* XXII (Oct.–Dec.). (= 1939 [offprint], 1944a, 2; tr. = 1959b, 1, 1963, 3.)

b. [Rev.] Fritz Schalk: *Einleitung in die Enzyklopädie der französischen Aufklärung* (Munich: Hueber, 1936). In *LGRP,* III–IV.

1939

Figura. Florence: Leo S. Olschki. (Offprint of 1938a; = 1944a, 2; tr. = 1959b, 1, 1963, 3.)

1941

a. "Passio als Leidenschaft," *PMLA*, LVI (Dec.).

b. "Sacrae scripturae sermo humilis," *NM*, III–IV. (= 1944a, 1, 1952d; tr. = 1947b, 1963, 2.)

1944

a. *Neue Dantestudien.* (Istanbuler Schriften, 5.) Istanbul: I. Horoz.
   (1) "Sacrae scripturae sermo humilis." (= 1941b, 1952d; tr. = 1947b, 1963, 2.)
   (2) "Figura." (= 1938a, 1939; tr. = 1959b, 1, 1963, 3.)
   (3) "Franz von Assisi in der Komödie." (Tr. = 1945; 1959b, 2, 1963, 4.)
b. *Roman Filolojisine Giriş.* (Tr. of 1949c, Suheyla Bayrav.) Istanbul: I. Horoz.

1945

"St. Francis of Assisi in Dante's *Commedia*" (tr. of 1944a, 3, Catherine Garvin), *Italica*, XXII (Dec.).

1946

a. "Figurative Texts Illustrating Certain Passages of Dante's *Commedia*," *Speculum*, XXI (Oct.). (Tr. = 1963, 5.)

b. *Mimesis. Dargestellte Wirklichkeit in der abendländischen Literatur.* Bern: A. Francke. (= 1959a; tr. = 1951c, 1953b, 1956b, 1957a, 1957b.)

c. "Der Triumph des Bösen, Versuch über Pascals politische Theorie," *Felsefe Arkivi*, I, No. 2/3. (Tr. = 1951e; revision = 1951g, 2; tr. of revision = 1957c, 1959b, 3.)

1947

a. "Önsöz." In *Garp Filolojileri Dergisi.* (Istanbul Üniverstesi [*sic*] Edebiyat Fakültesi Yayinlarindan No. 361.) Istanbul: Üçler Basimevi.

b. "Sacrae scripturae sermo humilis." In *Garp Filolojileri Dergisi*. (Istanbul Üniverstesi [*sic*] Edebiyat Fakültesi Yayinlarindan No. 361.) Istanbul: Üçler Basimevi. (Tr. of 1941a.)

c. "Voltaire ve Burjua zihniyeti." In *Garp Filolojileri Dergisi*. (Istanbul Üniverstesi [*sic*] Edebiyat Fakültesi Yayinlarindan No. 361.) Istanbul: Üçler Basimevi.

1948

[Rev.] Leo Spitzer: *Essays in Historical Semantics* (New York: S. F. Vanni, 1948) and his *Linguistics and Literary History* (Princeton: Princeton University Press, 1948). In *RF*, LXI, No. 2/3.

1949

a. [Rev.] Thomas Bergin and Max Fisch (trs.): [Giambattista Vico], *The New Science of Giambattista Vico* [*La Scienza nuova*] (Ithaca, New York: Cornell University Press, 1948). In *MLN*, LXIV (March).

b. "Dante's Prayer to the Virgin (*Paradiso*, XXXIII) and Earlier Eulogies," *RPh*, III (Aug.). (Tr. = 1963, 7.)

c. *Introduction aux études de philologie romane*. Frankfurt a. M.: Vittorio Klostermann. (Tr. = 1944b, 1961b.)

d. "Rising to Christ on the Cross (*Paradiso*, XI, 70–72)," *MLN*, LXIV (March).

e. "Saul's Pride (*Purg.*, XII, 40–42)," *MLN*, LXIV (April). (Tr. = 1963, 6.)

f. [Rev.] Leo Spitzer: *Linguistics and Literary History* (Princeton: Princeton University Press, 1948). In *CL*, I (winter).

g. "Vico and Aesthetic Historism," *Journal of Aesthetics and Art Criticism*, VIII, No. 2. (= 1959b, 5.)

1950

a. [Rev.] Ernst Robert Curtius: *Europäische Literatur und lateinisches Mittelalter* (Bern: A. Francke, 1948). In *MLN*, LXV (May).

b. [Rev.]   Ibid. In *RF*, LXII, No. 2/3.

c. "La Dignità estetica delle 'Fleurs du Mal,' " *Inventario*, III (summer). (Tr. of 1951g, 4.)

d. "The Esthetic Dignity of the *Fleurs du Mal*," *The Hopkins Review*, IV (fall). (Tr. of 1951g, 4.)

e. [Rev.]   Theodor Frings: *Minnesinger und Troubadours* (Berlin: Akademie-Verlag, 1949). In *RPh*, IV (Aug.).

f. "The Scar of Ulysses" (tr. Willard R. Trask), *Partisan Review* (May–June). (Coll. in *Mimesis*, 1953b; = 1953c.)

g. [Rev.]   Charles S. Singleton: *An Essay on the Vita Nuova* (Cambridge: Harvard University Press, 1949). In *CL*, II.

h. "The World in Pantagruel's Mouth" (tr. Willard R. Trask), *Partisan Review* (Sept.–Oct.). (Coll. in *Mimesis*, 1953b.)

1951

a. [Rev.]   Hugo Friedrich: *Montaigne* (Bern: A. Francke, 1949). In *MLN*, LXVI (Dec.).

b. "In the Hotel de la Mole" (tr. Willard R. Trask), *Partisan Review* (May–June). (Coll. in *Mimesis*, 1953b.)

c. *Mimesis*. (Spanish tr. of 1946b, I. Villanueva and E. Imaz.) Mexico: Fondo de Cultura Económica.

d. "Nathan und Johannes Chrysostomus (Dante, *Par.* XII, 136–37)," *Zeitschrift für romanische Philologie*, LXVII, No. 1/3.

e. "The Triumph of Evil in Pascal," *Hudson Review*, IV (spring). (Tr. of 1946c.)

f. "Die verzauberte Dulcinea," *DVLG*, XXV. (Coll. in *Mimesis*, 1959a.)

g. *Vier Untersuchungen zur Geschichte der französischen Bildung*. Bern: A. Francke.
   (1) "La Cour et la Ville." (Tr. = 1959b, 4.)
   (2) "Über Pascals politische Theorie." Rev. and enl. from "Der Triumph des Bösen," 1946c. (Tr. = 1957c, 1959b, 3.)
   (3) "Paul-Louis Courier." (= 1926a.)
   (4) "Baudelaires Fleurs du Mal und das Erhabene." (Tr. = 1950c, 1950d, 1959b, 6.)

1952

a. "Farinata and Cavalcante" (tr. Willard R. Trask), *Kenyon Review*, XIV (spring). (Coll. in *Mimesis*, 1953b.)

b. [Rev.] Antoinette Fierz-Monnier: *Initiation und Wandlung. Zur Geschichte des altfranzösischen Romans im zwölften Jahrhundert von Chrétien de Troyes zu Renaut de Beaujeu* (Bern: A. Francke, 1951). In *Romanic Review*, XLIII (Oct.).

c. "Philologie der Weltliteratur." In *Weltliteratur, Festgabe für Fritz Strich*. Bern: A. Francke.

d. "Sermo humilis," *RF*, LXIV, No. 3/4. (= 1941b, 1944a, 1; tr. = 1947b, 1963, 2.)

e. "Typological Symbolism in Medieval Literature," *Yale French Studies*, No. 9.

f. [Rev.] Karl Vossler: *Die Dichtungsformen der Romanen* (Stuttgart: K. F. Koehler, 1951). In *MLN*, LXVII (Feb.).

1953

a. "Epilegomena zu Mimesis," *RF*, LXV, No. 1/2.

b. *Mimesis*. (Tr. of 1946b, Willard R. Trask.) Princeton: Princeton University Press.

c. "The Scar of Ulysses" (tr. Willard R. Trask). In *New Partisan Reader*. New York: Harcourt, Brace. (Coll. in *Mimesis*, 1953b; = 1950f.)

d. *Typologische Motive in der mittelalterlichen Literatur.* Cologne: Petrarca-Institut.

1954

a. [Rev.] John Paul Bowden: *An Analysis of Pietro Alighieri's Commentary on the Divine Comedy* (New York: Columbia University Press, 1951). In *RPh*, VIII (Nov.).

b. "Dante's Addresses to the Reader," *RPh*, VII (May). (Tr. = 1963, 8.)

c. [Rev.] Paul Renucci: *L'Aventure de l'humanisme européen au moyen-âge* (Paris: Société d'Édition Les Belles Lettres, 1953). In *CL*, VI (spring).

1955

a. [Rev.] Francis Fergusson: *Dante's Drama of the Mind* (Princeton: Princeton University Press, 1953). In *RPh*, VIII (Feb.).

b. "Lateinische Prosa des 9. und 10. Jahrhunderts," *RF*, LXVI, No. 1/2.

c. "Vico und der Volksgeist." In *Wirtschaft und Kultursystem*. (Festschrift für Alexander Rüstow.) Zurich and Stuttgart: Eugen Rentsch. (= 1956c.)

1956

a. "Giovambattista Vico e l'idea della filologia," *Convivium*, IV. (Tr. of 1936.)

b. *Mimesis*. (Italian tr. of 1946b, Alberto Romagnoli and Hans Hinterhaüser.) Turin: Giulio Einaudi.

c. "Vico und der Volksgeist." In *Studia Romanica*. (Gedenkschrift für Eugen Lerch.) Stuttgart: Port, 1955. (= 1955c.)

d. [Rev.] René Wellek: *A History of Modern Criticism* (New Haven: Yale University Press, 1955). In *RF*, LXVII.

1957

a. *Mimesis*. (Tr. of 1946b, Willard R. Trask.) New York: Doubleday Anchor Books. (Paperback reprint = 1953b.)

b. *Mimesis*. (Hebrew tr. of 1946b, Baruch Karu.) Jerusalem, Israel: Bialik Institute.

c. "La Teoria politica di Pascal," *Studi francesi*, I (Jan.–April). (Tr. of 1951g, 2.)

d. "Über das altfranzösische Leodegarlied." In *Syntactica und Stilistica*. (Festschrift für Ernst Gamillscheg.) Tübingen: Max Niemeyer.

1958

a. *Literatursprache und Publikum in der lateinischen Spätantike und im Mittelalter.* Bern: A. Francke. (Tr. = 1960, 1965.)

b. "Vico's Contribution to Literary Criticism." In *Studia philologica et litteraria in honorem L. Spitzer.* Bern: A. Francke.

1959

a. *Mimesis.* 2d rev. and enl. edn., Bern: A. Francke. (= 1946b.)

b. *Scenes from the Drama of European Literature.* New York: Meridian Books.
   - (1) "Figura." (Tr. of 1938a, Ralph Manheim.)
   - (2) "St. Francis of Assisi in Dante's 'Commedia.'" (Tr. of 1944a, 3, Catherine Garvin.)
   - (3) "On the Political Theory of Pascal." (Tr. of 1951g, 2, Ralph Manheim.)
   - (4) "La Cour et la Ville." (Tr. of 1951g, 1, Ralph Manheim.)
   - (5) "Vico and Aesthetic Historism." (= 1949g.)
   - (6) "The Aesthetic Dignity of the 'Fleurs du Mal.'" (Tr. of 1951g, 4, Ralph Manheim.)

1960

Lingua letteraria e pubblico nella tarda antichità latina e nel medioevo. (Tr. of 1958a, Fausto Codino.) Milan: Feltrinelli.

1961

a. *Dante, Poet of the Secular World.* (Tr. of 1929a, Ralph Manheim.) Chicago and London: University of Chicago Press.

b. *Introduction to Romance Languages and Literature.* (Tr. of 1949c, Guy Daniels.) New York: Capricorn Books.

1963

Studi su Dante. Milan: Feltrinelli.

(1) "Dante, poeta del mondo terreno." (Tr. of 1929a, Maria Luisa De Pieri Bonino.)

(2) "Sacrae scripturae sermo humilis." (Tr. of 1941b, Maria Luisa De Pieri Bonino.)

(3) "Figura." (Tr. of 1938a, Maria Luisa De Pieri Bonino.)

(4) "Francesco d'Assisi nella 'Commedia.'" (Tr. of 1944a, 3, Maria Luisa De Pieri Bonino).

(5) "Passi della 'Commedia' dantesca illustrati da testi figurali. (Tr. of 1946a, Dante Della Terza.)

(6) "L'Orgoglio di Saul (*Purg.*, XII, vv. 40–42)." (Tr. of 1949e, Dante Della Terza.)

(7) "La Preghiera di Dante alla Vergine (*Par.*, XXXIII) ed antecedenti elogi." (Tr. of 1949b, Dante Della Terza.)

(8) "Gli Appelli di Dante al lettore." (Tr. of 1954b, Dante Della Terza.)

1965

Literary Language and Its Public in Late Latin Antiquity and the Middle Ages. (Tr. of 1958a, Ralph Manheim.) New York: Bollingen Foundation (Bollingen Series LXXIV); London: Routledge and Kegan Paul.

ERICH AUERBACH

Erich Auerbach was born in Berlin on November 9, 1892. Before and after the first World War he studied law, the history of art, and philology at the University of Berlin and other German universities. He earned a doctorate in law in 1913 and a Ph.D. degree in Romance philology in 1921. After working as librarian in the Preussische Staatsbibliothek in Berlin, he was professor at the University of Marburg from 1929 until 1935, when he was dismissed by order of the Nazi regime. He left Germany in 1936 and settled in Istanbul, where he was professor of Romance languages at the Turkish State University. It was there that he wrote, between May 1942 and April 1945, his greatest book, *Mimesis: The Representation of Reality in Western Literature*. This study of the changing conceptions of reality throughout twenty centuries is a classic of humanistic studies; it has been called the most important book of our time in the field of aesthetics and the history of literature. In 1947 he came to the United States. He spent over a year on the faculty of Pennsylvania State University and one at the Institute for Advanced Study in Princeton, and joined the faculty of Yale University in 1950. He was appointed Sterling Professor of Romance Philology at Yale in 1956. Erich Auerbach died on October 13, 1957, in New Haven, Conn.

His books and papers on Italian, French, and medieval Latin literature, on Christian symbolism and its literary influence, and on methods of historical criticism established him as one of this century's great scholars and one of its most influential teachers.